MULTINATIONAL STRATEGIC ALLIANCES

Refik Culpan, PhD
Editor

SOME ADVANCE REVIEWS

"This book is an important edition to the literature on international strategic alliances. It contains an excellent collection of fourteen papers which will appeal to both experts and non-specialists interested in the nature and consequences of the explosive growth in strategic alliances."

Bernard M. Wolf, PhD
Professor of Economics and International Business
Director of the International Business Program
Faculty of Administrative Studies
York University
Ontario, Canada

"By pulling together the latest thinking and research, this book provides powerful insights into why global alliances are rapidly becoming the strategy of choice."

Len Korot, PhD
Professor
School of Business and Management
Pepperdine University

"The entire text addresses crucial, leading issues on global strategic alliances. The varied backgrounds of the contributors enrich the text by providing specific insights on the alliance formation process."

Kofi Afriyie, MBA, PhD
Assistant Professor
International Business Graduate School of Management
Rutgers University

Multinational Strategic Alliances

INTERNATIONAL BUSINESS PRESS
Erdener Kaynak, PhD
Executive Editor

New, Recent, and Forthcoming Titles:

International Business Handbook edited by V. H. (Manek) Kirpalani

Sociopolitical Aspects of International Marketing edited by Erdener Kaynak

How to Manage for International Competitiveness edited by Abbas J. Ali

International Business Expansion Into Less-Developed Countries: How to Use the International Finance Corporation Mechanism by James C. Baker

Product-Country Images: Impact and Role in International Marketing edited by Nicolas Papadopoulos and Louise A. Heslop

The Global Business: Four Key Marketing Strategies edited by Erdener Kaynak

Multinational Strategic Alliances edited by Refik Culpan

Market Evolution in Developing Countries: The Unfolding of the Indian Market by Subhash C. Jain

Multinational Strategic Alliances

Refik Culpan, PhD
Editor

International Business Press
An Imprint of The Haworth Press, Inc.
New York • London • Norwood (Australia)

Published by

International Business Press, an imprint of The Haworth Press, Inc., 10 Alice Street, Binghamton, NY 13904-1580

Library of Congress Cataloging-in-Publication Data

Multinational strategic alliances / Refik Culpan, editor.
     p. cm.
    Includes bibliographical references and index.
    ISBN 1-56024-322-8 (acid free paper).
    1. Strategic alliances (Business) 2. International business enterprises. I. Culpan, Refik.
HD69.S8M84   1993
658'.049–dc20
                                              92-20709
                                                CIP

To My Parents

CONTENTS

List of Tables and Figures   xiii

About the Editor   xv

Contributors   xvii

Editor's Comments   xxiii

Foreword   xxvii
William F. Christ

Preface   xxix
B. Nino Kumar

Introduction   1

I. CONCEPTUAL FOUNDATIONS OF MULTINATIONAL STRATEGIC ALLIANCES

Chapter 1. Multinational Competition and Cooperation: Theory and Practice   13
Refik Culpan

Theoretical Considerations   15
A Model for Cooperative Strategies   18
Implications and Conclusions   27

Chapter 2. Hybrid Arrangements as Strategic Alliances: Theoretical Issues in Organizational Combinations   33
Bryan Borys
David B. Jemison

The Nature of Hybrids   34
Hybrids as Theoretical Orphans   35
A Theory of Hybrids   39

Generating Insights into Hybrid Management   49
Conclusion   54

**Chapter 3. Forms of Interorganizational Governance
for Multinational Alliances   59**
    Richard N. Osborn
    C. Christopher Baughn

Governance Forms and Transaction Costs   60
Optimizing Relations Among Transaction, Technology,
    and Structure   62
Alliances, Measures, and Statistical Analyses   67
Results   71
Discussion   73

**Chapter 4. A Process Model on the Formation
of Multinational Strategic Alliances   81**
    Gregory E. Osland
    Attila Yaprak

Introduction   81
Forms of Strategic Alliances   82
A Process Model to Explain Strategic Alliance Formation   84
Conclusion   95

**II. THE FUNCTIONAL DIMENSION OF GLOBAL
  BUSINESS ALLIANCES**

**Chapter 5. Cross-National Corporate Partnerships:
Trends in Alliance Formation   103**
    Refik Culpan
    Eugene A. Kostelac Jr.

Introduction   103
Trends and Patterns in Cross-National Alliances   104
An Empirical Investigation   108
Results   109
An Evaluation of Strategic Alliances   114
Conclusion   120

Chapter 6. Technology-Based Cross-Border Alliances   **123**
Philippe Gugler
John H. Dunning

Introduction   123
The Analytical Framework of the Determinants of Strategic
    Alliances and Some Empirical Evidence   128
Managing Strategic Alliances   140
The Mechanisms of R&D Alliances: A Network Approach   145
Some Reflections on the Efficiency of R&D Alliances   154
Conclusions   158

**Chapter 7. Protection of Competitive Advantage
in U.S./Asia-Pacific Joint Ventures
from High-Technology Industries**   **167**
John D. Daniels
Sharon Magill

Introduction   167
Methodology   168
Low Incidence of Joint Ventures   171
Rationale and Advantages of Ownership Sharing   174
Control   175
Protection of Technology   178
Conclusions   181

**Chapter 8. Building Partnerships with Japanese
Corporate Groups**   **183**
Douglas N. Ross

Context: The Network of Relations of the Partner Firm   183
Strategic Alliances   184
The Nature of Corporate Groupings   185
Experiences with International Strategic Alliances   190
Guidelines for a Japanese Partnership   194
Conclusions   198

Chapter 9. Ownership and Control in East-West Joint Ventures   **203**
J. Michael Geringer

The Importance of Control in East-West Joint Ventures   206
The Ownership-Control Dilemma in East-West Joint
  Ventures   207
Exercising Effective Control Over East-West Joint Ventures 209
Achieving and Maintaining a Control "Fit" in East-West
  Joint Ventures   216
Conclusions   218

Chapter 10. Strategic Alliances in the Global Container Transport Industry   **221**
Mary R. Brooks
Robert G. Blunden
Cheryl I. Bidgood

Introduction   221
Common Forms of Strategic Alliances in Ocean Transport   222
Conceptual Bases   225
Case Studies   237
Discussion   245

III. THE BEHAVIORAL AND HUMAN RESOURCES MANAGEMENT DIMENSIONS OF INTERNATIONAL JOINT VENTURES

Chapter 11. Planning International Joint Ventures: The Role of Human Resource Management   **251**
Deepak K. Datta
Abdul M. A. Rasheed

Introduction   251
The IJV Planning Framework   253
Conclusions   268

Chapter 12. Ethnocentrism and Group Cohesiveness: Implications for International Joint Ventures   273
       Hoon Park
       Pamela S. Lewis
       Patricia M. Fandt

Background   275
A Model of the Determinants of Group Cohesiveness   277
Managerial Implications   287

Chapter 13. Self-Management Training for General Managers of International Joint Ventures   293
       Colette A. Frayne
       J. Michael Geringer

The Role of the IJVGM   295
The Self-Management Approach   300
Application of Self-Management to IJVGMs   303
Training Benefits   308
Measuring the Effectiveness of IJVGM Training Programs   309
Conclusions   311
Appendix 13.1: Details of Pilot Study Examining IJVGMs
     and Their Roles   313

IV. THE FUTURE OF GLOBAL BUSINESS ALLIANCES

Chapter 14. Global Dependence and Corporate Linkages   321
       Refik Culpan

Changes in Global Market and Future Trends   322
Future Corporate Linkages   330
Conclusions   340

Index   347

List of Tables and Figures

Tables

2.1. Research Propositions Regarding Hybrid Organizational
Arrangements   41

3.1. Characteristics of the Multinational Alliances Studied   69

3.2. Characteristics of Variables and Intercorrelations   70

3.3. Results of Discriminant Analysis   72

5.1. Industry Listing of Corporate Partnerships   111

6.1. Evolution of Cooperative Agreements Established Annually
(1974-1989)   125

6.2. Distribution Per Sectors of U.S. International Joint Ventures
Created in 1980 and in 1987 (Percent)   126

6.3. Distribution Per Sectors of JVs in the EC (1984-1989)   127

6.4. Major Types of Agreements Formed by 750 U.S. Electronics
Firms in 1990 and Expected for 1990-1995 (Percentage
of Total Respondents)   148

8.1. Context for Japanese Corporate Groupings   187

8.2. Guidelines for Partnering with a Corporate Group Firm   195

10.1. Cost Comparison Between Two Trans-Atlantic Service
Alternatives   234

11.1. Summary of Key HRM Questions in the Planning
of International Joint Ventures   269

14.1. U.S.-Japanese Joint Ventures in the U.S. Steel Industry   327

14.2. Comparison of Strategic Choices   333

14.3. Forging Closer Ties in the U.S. Automobile Industry   334

Figures

1.1. A Conceptual Framework for Cooperative Strategies   19

4.1. A Process Model of Strategic Alliance Formation   85

5.1. Alliance Trends   110

5.2. Form of Alliance   112

5.3. Alliance Purpose   113

5.4. Country Origin of U.S. Partner   114

6.1. The Value of Strategic Alliances   135

6.2. Alliances Networks in the Semiconductor Industry (1990)   151

6.3. Interfirms Clusters and Networks in the Telecommunication Industry   152

8.1. Toshiba's Global Strategic Alliances   191

10.1. Range of Strategic Alliances in the Container Transport Industry I   226

10.2. Range of Strategic Alliances in the Container Transport Industry II   227

10.3. A Model of Strategic Behavior in the Container Transport Industry   229

10.4. Strategies of Selected Container Carriers   236

11.1. IJV Planning Framework   254

11.2. Developing IJV HR Strategies   265

12.1. Group Cohesiveness Determinants Affected by Ethnocentrism   278

ABOUT THE EDITOR

Refik Culpan, PhD, is Associate Professor of Management and International Business at the School of Business Administration, Pennsylvania State University at Harrisburg, where he has served as Management Program Chair for five years. An active researcher, he has published numerous articles in the areas of strategic management, international business, and multinational firms. His research interest and areas of consultation include international corporate strategy, comparative and cross-cultural management, organization development and design, and management of strategic change. Dr. Culpan belongs to the Academy of International Business and the Academy of Management, Division of Business Policy and International Management.

CONTRIBUTORS

C. Christopher Baughn is an instructor in the School of Business Administration, Wayne State University, and a doctoral candidate in industrial/organizational psychology at the university. His research interests include studies of international corporate alliances, technology management, and international human resource management.

Robert G. Blunden is an associate professor of business policy and entrepreneurship at the School of Business Administration, Dalhousie University, Halifax, Canada. He holds business degrees from Dalhousie University and Northwestern University and is currently a doctoral candidate at the University of Western Ontario. His research focuses on the strategic issues of organizations, especially on the application of strategic management to entrepreneurial contexts.

Cheryl I. Bidgood is a graduate of Mount Allison University, Sackville, New Brunswick, and of Dalhousie University, Halifax, Nova Scotia. She received her MBA from Dalhousie University in May 1991, with a concentration in marketing and transportation. Prior to receiving her degree, she spent six years working in the publishing industry.

Bryan Borys is a doctoral candidate in Organizational Behavior at the Graduate School of Business, Stanford University.

Mary R. Brooks holds a BOT (McGill University), an MBA in finance and international business (Dalhousie University), and a PhD in marine transportation/marketing strategy (University of Wales). She is currently an associate professor of marketing at Dalhousie University. Dr. Brooks is an internationally recognized researcher in export and transportation. She has conducted exporting studies in Canada and Latin America and has also consulted widely in the transportation industry, completing assignments for industry and government in Canada, the Caribbean, and Southeast Asia. She is a co-author of *Excellence in Exporting,* has published a number of monographs on various marine transportation topics, and has developed exporting computer software and case studies.

Refik Culpan (PhD, New York University) is an associate professor of management and international business at the School of Business Administration, Pennsylvania State University at Harrisburg. In addition to his long teaching career, he has executive experience in business. He has many publications in the areas of countertrade, export management, cross-cultural management, and multinational corporations. His work has appeared in such journals as: *Journal of Business Research; Journal of Management Issues; Journal of Business Strategies; Business; Management Decision; Journal of Applied Business Research; Journal of Teaching in International Business; Journal of International Marketing and Marketing Research;* and *Annals of Tourism Research; Management International Review.* He also authored a chapter for *Advances in International Comparative Management Volume 6.* His recent research interests include global corporate strategies, strategic alliances, and cross-cultural management.

John D. Daniels is a professor of international business at Indiana University. He is the past president of the Academy of International Business and is a member of that organization's Fellows. He is also past chairman of the International Division of the Academy of Management. He has served on the editorial boards of the *Academy of Management Journal; Essays in International Business; Journal of Business Research; Advances in International Marketing; Multinational Management Review;* and the *Journal of International Business Studies.* His co-authored text *International Business: Environments and Operations* is now in its sixth edition.

Deepak K. Datta is an associate professor of management at the School of Business, University of Kansas. He holds a PhD in strategic planning and policy from the University of Pittsburgh, an MBA from the Indian Institute of Management, Calcutta, and a B. Tech in Mechanical Engineering from the Indian Institute of Technology. Prior to receiving his PhD, he worked as a manager in multinational corporations in India. Professor Datta has published in the *Strategic Management Journal; Journal of Management; Journal of Management Studies; Long-Range Planning;* and *Journal of General Management.* He has also presented a number of papers at various international and national meetings. His current research interests are in the areas of mergers and acquisitions, joint ventures, and strategic planning systems.

John H. Dunning has been researching into the economics of international direct investment and the multinational enterprise since the 1950s. He has authored, co-authored, or edited 32 books on this subject and on industrial and regional economics; he is currently writing a major monograph on *Multinational Enterprise and the Global Economy.* He has a dual appointment as an Imperial Chemical Industries (ICI) research professor in international business studies at the University of Reading, U.K., and as State of New Jersey Professor of International Business at Rutgers University, New Jersey. He is also Senior Economic Adviser to the Executive Director of the U.N. Center on Transnational Corporations (UNCTC) in New York as well as Chairman and Director of the London-based Economic Advisory Group, a consulting firm that specializes in research on international and regional economic and business issues.

Patricia M. Fandt is an associate professor of management at the University of Central Florida, where she teaches courses in organizational behavior, organizational theory, and managerial skills. In 1986, she received her PhD in organizational behavior from Texas A&M University. Her research interests include accountability, decision making, and team development. She has published articles in a number of management and organizational behavior journals.

Colette A. Frayne (PhD, University of Washington) is a professor of organizational behavior and international human-resource management at California Polytechnic State University. Her consulting and research interests include a variety of international and domestic human-resource management issues, including training and development, self-management, and executive compensation. In addition to a book on self-management techniques, Dr. Frayne's work has been published in a variety of journals, such as *Journal of Applied Psychology; Business Quarterly; International Human Resource Management; Personnel Journal; Supervisory Management;* and *Management International Review.*

J. Michael Geringer (PhD, University of Washington) is a professor of business policy and international business at California Polytechnic State University. In addition to three books, Dr. Geringer has published over two dozen articles on the formation and management of joint ventures and multinational enterprises. His work has appeared in such journals as *Columbia Journal of World Business; Journal of International Business Studies; Management International Review;* and *Strategic Management Journal.*

Philippe Gugler studied international production and Transnational Corporation strategies at the Graduate School of Management, Rutgers University, under the supervision of Professor John Dunning. His doctoral dissertation deals with transnational strategic alliances, and he has done research on Japanese transnational corporations for the Economic Commission for Europe/UNCTC Joint Unit on Transnational Corporations in Geneva. He also conducted some consultancy studies for the Economic Advisory Group (U.K.) and has worked at the Centre de researches en economie de l'espace, Fribourg University (Switzerland) on the effect of Europe 1992. Presently, he is employed by the Federal Office of External Economics Affairs (Switzerland).

David B. Jemison (PhD, University of Washington) is an associate professor of management and Joseph Paschal Dreibelbis Fellow at the Graduate School of Business, University of Texas at Austin, where he teaches in the strategic management area. Jemison's research focuses on the strategic management process in diversified firms. His work has appeared in a variety of journals, including *Strategic Management Journal; Academy of Management Review; Management Science; Harvard Business Review;* and *Sloan Management Review.* He is coauthor of *Management Acquisitions: Creating Value Through Corporate Renewal* with Philippe Haspeslagh of INSEAD.

Eugene A. Kostelac Jr. is manager of international accounting/administration for AMP, Inc. He has an MBA from Pennsylvania State University and is a CPA in Pennsylvania. Mr. Kostelac has eight years of experience dealing with financial and administrative issues associated with a large multinational manufacturing company that has facilities in 28 countries.

Pamela S. Lewis is an assistant professor of management at the University of Central Florida, where she teaches business policy and strategy and international management. She completed her PhD at the University of Tennessee in the area of strategic planning/international business. Dr. Lewis' research interests are in international strategy and management. She is the co-author of a forthcoming book entitled *International Management* and has published several articles about international strategy.

Sharon L. Magill is an assistant professor at the University of Louisville. She has published articles in *Journal of High Technology Management Research, Mid-American Journal of Business, and Business Horizons.* Her research interests include organizational adaptation, top management teams, and international alliances.

Richard N. Osborn (DBA, Kent State University) is a professor of management and organizational sciences in the School of Business Administration, Wayne State University. His current research interests focus on the interplay among environmental conditions, strategy, and performance, particularly for multinational firms using advanced technologies.

Gregory E. Osland is a doctoral candidate at Michigan State University, majoring in marketing. He previously worked in a cooperative alliance in China, teaching marketing and doing consulting for Chinese factories. He has published research on such topics as doing business in China, the product life cycle, and organizational learning in alliances.

Hoon Park is an assistant professor of international business and finance at the University of Central Florida, where he teaches in the area of international business. Prior to pursuing his doctorate at Georgia State University, he worked for several international joint ventures. Dr. Park's research and publications have been primarily in the areas of international joint-venture management and cross-cultural behavior.

Abdul M. A. Rasheed is currently an assistant professor in the management department at the University of Texas at Arlington. He holds a PhD in strategic planning and policy from the University of Pittsburgh, an MBA from the Indian Institute of Management, Calcutta, and a BS in physics from Kerala University. His primary research interests are environment-organization interactions, problem structuring and diagnosis, diversification and performance, and international corporate strategy. Prior to receiving his PhD, Professor Rasheed held several executive positions in the banking industry in India and the Middle East.

Douglas N. Ross (DBA, University of Colorado) is an assistant professor of management at the School of Business and Economics, Towson State University (University of Maryland system). His current research interests include comparative international industrial organization and management, and comparative ethical systems.

Attila Yaprak (PhD, Georgia State University) is an associate professor of marketing at the School of Business Administration, Wayne State University. His research interests are in global marketing strategy, cross-national consumer behavior, international strategic alliances, and global business policy. He was the associate editor for international business at the *Journal of Business Research* and is a member of the editorial boards of *International Marketing Review* and *Journal of International Consumer Marketing*. His research has been published in the *Journal of International Business Studies; Journal of Advertising; International Marketing Review; Advances in International Marketing; Management International Review;* and *Management Decision.* Chapters authored by Yaprak have appeared in *International Marketing Management, World Food Marketing Systems,* and *Product and Country Images: Research and Strategy.*

Editor's Comments

The inspiration for the preparation of this anthology of readings emanated from the recent increased importance of multinational interfirm cooperative ventures in the global marketplace. As a result, both popular business and academic publications started carrying articles about various interfirm linkages involving multinational companies (MNCs). This recent development has caught my attention and inspired me to raise questions concerning interfirm partnerships: For instance, why do companies get involved in strategic partnership? What causes an international firm to establish a linkage with its competitor(s)? What are the common forms of interfirm cooperations? Are some of these forms of cooperation more popular than others? Do strategic alliances take place between firms that are located in certain nations? What kinds of international companies are most involved in these cooperative ventures? What types of cooperative ventures have proven successful? What factors account for success? What does the future hold for international strategic alliances? Do these alliances offer management a viable strategic alternative, or do they merely present a new fad? This book is designed to answer all of these important questions.

A recent burst of activities in the theoretical and conceptual treatment of cooperative ventures has generated some confusion. This confusion about strategic alliances stems from several factors. First, the phrase "strategic alliance" means different things to different people. For instance, it may include joint ventures (JVs), equity participation, licensing agreements, research and development (R&D) partnerships, marketing agreements, supplier agreements, buyer agreements, consortiums, and even mergers and acquisitions. In particular, the question of whether the last two forms (mergers and acquisitions) are representative of a typical interfirm cooperative venture has been debated extensively. For example, only one firm exists after merger, or an acquisition transaction;

whereas via a collaborative transaction, at least two distinct firms survive. Some experts (Borys and Jemison, Chapter 2 of this book; Nevaer and Deck, 1990) hold that mergers and acquisitions are forms of interfirm collaboration. They maintain this idea on the basis that the cooperative intentions and efforts of parties involved gain consideration both before and during the merger and acquisition and not after such transactions. For other experts, strategic alliance refers only to nonequity agreements made by firms. Herein, strategic alliance is defined as an interfirm collaboration requiring resource commitment by each party for operational efficiency, for market power, or for risk sharing in the short- or long-term.

Second, the different forms of strategic alliances may cause confusion. In the past, conventional alliances were primarily joint ventures and licensing types and, to some extent, equity investments. A variety of other forms of alliances have emerged among firms. That is, international linkages such as R&D agreements, marketing agreements, equity swaps, supplier agreements, customer agreements, and consortiums are used more frequently today than they have been in the past. Most of the joint-venture and licensing deals that had occurred earlier were between a firm in an industrialized country and a firm, usually a state-owned enterprise, in a developing country. Such agreements mostly involved one-way transfer of a technology from a Western firm to a firm in a Third World country. Today, however, such traditional forms of cooperation are undertaken in conjunction with a new philosophy of business strategy that emphasizes learning and benefitting from one's business associates, including its competitor(s).

Third and final, the formation of strategic alliances presents a paradox in terms of interfirm competition. Cooperation had been considered earlier as a concept that is contradictory to gaining competitive advantage. It was also believed that cooperative ventures tended to fail; therefore, they were held in low esteem as a fundamental business strategy. Despite this skepticism, why, then, have cooperative ventures proliferated in recent years? Changing economic conditions, competitive climate, and technological advances have increased interfirm dependency and, to some extent, they have also changed the perception of business executives regarding interfirm collaboration (which is now seen in a positive light).

Until recently, most of our understanding of business firms has come from our focus on competition among firms. Corporate behavior and strategy have been explained by theories and models developed on the concept of competition only. The problem with these explanations was their one-dimensional character: no consideration was given to the possibility that competing firms could also cooperate. Researchers, and managers too, have tended to assume that nothing but competition determines the strategy of a firm.

Today, we no longer have the luxury of reducing multinational corporate strategy to the level of one-dimensional interfirm rivalry. As Porter's industry model (1980) aptly demonstrates, the competitive posture of a firm is determined by various forces in the business environment, in addition to interfirm rivalry. Despite the sophistication of theories of competition, the current literature of corporate strategy still needs to address the interfirm cooperations already operating in the global marketplace. In light of these recent developments, this volume will attempt to highlight the issues that are of vital importance for the formation and management of multinational strategic alliances.

During the preparation of this volume, I have received help and encouragement from many individuals. First, I thank the contributors of this volume, who made it all possible, and Erdener Kaynak, the executive editor of The Haworth Press' International Business Press, who made invaluable suggestions throughout my editing. I also thank the following individuals who have kindly reviewed the chapters for this volume: C. Christopher Baughn, Wayne State University; Nakiye Boyacigiller, San Jose State University; Oya Culpan, Pennsylvania State University at Harrisburg; J. Michael Geringer, California Polytechnic State University; David Morand, Pennsylvania State University at Harrisburg; Richard N. Osborn, Wayne State University; Arvind Phatak, Temple University; Abdul Rasheed, University of Texas at Arlington; Vern Terpstra, University of Michigan; and Attila Yaprak, Wayne State University. Furthermore, I must acknowledge invaluable critiques of professors Bernard M. Wolf and Len Korot from York University and Pepperdine University respectively, and William F. Christ, Hershey International. Additionally, I appreciate Burcu Culpan's conscientious efforts in organizing the indices.

Finally, my special thanks go to my wife, Oya, and to our children, Burcu and Alpay, for their support and understanding throughout the completion of this project.

Refik Culpan
Hershey, Pennsylvania

REFERENCES

Nevear, L. E. V. & Deck, S. A. (1990). *Strategic corporate alliances: A study of the present, a model for the future*. New York: Quorum Books.

Porter, M. E. (1980). *Competitive Strategy*. New York: The Free Press.

Foreword

Multinational Strategic Alliances is an outstanding compendium of research on the theoretical and practical aspects of the various forms of strategic alliances presently being utilized throughout the world in successful and unsuccessful interfirm partnerships. A thorough analysis of the types of strategic alliances and the reasons for them, along with a comprehensive investigation into the internal, competitive, and cooperative benefits of these corporations, is provided in this work. The advantages and disadvantages, pitfalls, and rewards of strategic alliances are also presented. It is a good source for further understanding the reasons for successes and failures of various types of interfirm partnerships. I consider it excellent reading prior to setting or establishing a firm's strategic growth and alliance goals and their means of achievement. As a reference tool, the reader can choose the relevant chapters that may address present concerns.

I highly recommend Part I of the book which deals with the conceptual foundations and provides a thorough review of the various forms. In Part II, building partnerships with Japanese corporate groups is extremely important. In today's highly competitive environment with Japanese firms, this section provides an outstanding framework for understanding the Japanese corporate groups and their forms of strategic alliances. In Part III, the role of human resource management should be required reading for anyone considering the various forms of strategic alliances prior to the actual assignment of personnel. Probably the greatest reason for success or failure of a strategic alliance is the human resource element. A deeper and more informed understanding of these elements would most certainly lead to a higher success rate in strategic alliances.

William F. Christ
President, Hershey International
A Division of Hershey Foods Corporation

Preface

This volume, edited by Professor Refik Culpan, deals with the significant topic of international cooperative ventures which have become an integrated part of the strategy repertoire of many international firms within the last decade. For several reasons, a single company faces limitations in managing global markets by itself. Some of the imposing constraints are:

- globalization and regionalization of markets, e.g., "Europe 1992,"
- technological innovation and shorter product life cycles, and
- higher entry barriers in markets due to rising costs of technology and marketing.

Alliances have been instrumental in enhancing the proactive strategic posture of companies in several ways. They can help:

- widen the product–market mission,
- increase the geographic scope,
- extend the value chain,
- secure resources, and
- broaden core competencies.

While collaborations help to widen and strengthen the global scope of firms, they can, on the other hand, pose serious problems in terms of their management. Basically limitations incur due to increased requirements on management capacity, as well as because of conflicting interests, views and behavior between the parties. International business literature abounds with examples of corporate alliances which began with great expectations, but resulted in failures due to managerial inability to cope with organizational complexity and partner strife. There was a pressing need for a comprehensive treatment of multinational strategic alliance.

Merit goes to Professor Culpan for successfully putting together a fine set of articles covering the broad range of topics on interfirm collaborations. Although recent literature has addressed some of the problems of international business alliances and cooperations in a piecemeal manner, this volume stands out by offering the integrated and clear concept of the subject and illustrative examples. The four parts, which are self-contained, are well knitted together to form a consistent framework, but the variety and diversity of thoughts and views which are so important for a reader are not neglected.

Although Part I is basically theoretical, it has a lot to offer practitioners as well. One of the unsolved problems in international business is determining the right choice of alliance out of various alternatives. Part I provides salient information in understanding the influencing factors on the formation of cooperative ventures.

Part II and III offer a substantial amount of insight into the management of alliances which hitherto has been neglected. There is no doubt that cooperative ventures in international business will gain importance in the future, especially in transitional economies in many parts of the world, as East European and Third World countries increasingly seek assistance in development.

Part IV successfully reviews the prospects in interfirm cooperations in the light of economic, political, and technological changes around the world and demonstrates future corporate linkages skillfully.

Overall, the volume offers great opportunity for practitioners and academicians alike to understand various aspects of cooperative ventures drawn from conceptual models and empirical findings. This book is presented at a time of rapid transformation in economic and political systems as insight emerges that isolation is dysfunctional and cooperation can be fruitful. I consider this book to be a significant contribution to the international business literature.

Professor B. Nino Kumar
Universitat der Bundeswehr Hamburg
Germany

Introduction

To gain or sustain competitive advantages, strategic alliances among firms have recently become a very popular international business approach. For instance, a growing number of companies from various countries have adopted collaborative strategies despite the low rate of success of these ventures in the past. At the same time, writings about collaborative strategies have spurred others, adding to the rich body of literature being created. Nevertheless, there is still a void in the literature regarding a systematic treatment of interfirm collaboration.

The purpose of this volume is to clarify the conceptual, the theoretical, and the practical dimensions involved in understanding and managing cooperative ventures. Strategic alliance poses an enormously challenging problem to theoreticians and to practitioners alike. Hence, the motives, the structures, and the processes of strategic alliances need to be understood by all parties. At the same time, collaborative ventures frequently require changes in business strategy, in organizational structure, and in many other aspects of operations of multinational businesses. Careful attention to the timing, execution, and control of such decisions may be considerably rewarding.

The present volume offers a balanced view of prominent theories, concepts, and practices. It consists of a selection of readings "blind-reviewed" by at least two experts in international business. All of the chapters are authored by scholars and practitioners, who explicitly deal with differing yet related aspects of strategic alliances. They present a variety of analyses, syntheses, business implications, and they also predict probable future trends in interfirm partnership. The author of each chapter provides unique insights into the breadth and direction of strategic alliances. One admires the value of different viewpoints only after hearing from various experts whose views explain the same phenomenon from different perspectives.

The book consists of four parts and fourteen chapters. Part I, "Conceptual Foundations of Multinational Strategic Alliances," describes the ways in which interfirm partnership emerges and how such cooperation affects corporate strategy and management. Its main thrust is the development of an understanding of the ideas underpinning the concept of business cooperation. Thus, conceptual frameworks explain the nature of, and the reasons for, the forms of cooperative ventures and the dynamics found in such undertakings. Part II, "The Functional Dimension of Global Business Alliances," deals with the operational aspects of interfirm partnerships. It provides general insights into various cooperative practices, as well as detailing such practices in specific countries and in selected industries. In particular, Part II includes: the trends in alliance formation; alliances with Japanese firms; protection of competitive advantage in U.S./Asia-Pacific joint ventures from high-technology industries; technology-based cross-border alliances; the control issues in East-West joint ventures; and global partnerships in the container industry. Part III, "The Behavioral and Human Resources Management Dimensions of International Joint Ventures," explores an important but often neglected dimension in the study of strategic alliances. That is, managerial behavior and effective management of human resources as key elements leading to the success of such cooperation. Here, three notable chapters address the role of human resource management in international joint ventures; how to overcome managerial ethnocentrism by building group cohesiveness; and presentation of an alternative training technique (self-management training) for managers of international joint ventures. Part IV, "The Future of Global Business Alliances," discusses prospects for strategic alliances in light of global market trends.

The focus of this book is on the international business linkages of multinational companies (MNCs), which are named differently in the business literature. Some experts call these companies Multinational Enterprises (MNEs), while others call them Transnational Corporations (TNCs). Since all these terms are accepted in the literature, they are used interchangeably in this volume. They simply refer to large-scale international business firms that conduct their operations across nations and generate a substantial portion of their revenues from such overseas activities. The book covers cooperative relations among MNCs as well as between MNCs and small- and medium-sized domestic firms.

As strategic alliances grow in number and importance, more debate will emerge in relation to theory and practices of collaborative ventures. This book should contribute to an expansion of present knowledge by providing information that adds to an understanding of the formation of strategic alliances in a variety of different settings. It also offers useful, practical guidelines for managers of international firms interested in cooperative ventures. To accomplish its objective, this book contains both essential information and a thorough examination of strategic alliances. Its contents can be summarized as follows.

Chapter 1, "Multinational Competition and Cooperation: Theory and Practice," studies cooperative ventures between MNCs and offers a conceptual framework for analysis of such interfirm collaborations. Theoretical foundations backed by cases of cooperative relationships between MNCs are provided. Furthermore, it examines a conceptual model made up of: environmental forces; motives of the collaborating parties; their cooperative strategies; modes of cooperation; forms of agreements; and expected outcome. Environmental forces leading to interfirm cooperation are discussed in relation to intense international competition, technological advancement, and globalization of business strategies. Motives of the participating parties are combined into two major categories: resource pooling and risk/cost sharing. Cooperative strategies encompass market development and expansion, R&D partnership, production sharing, and countertrade alliance. Modes of cooperation may take three principal forms: (1) first cooperate, then compete, (2) cooperate while competing, and (3) cooperate among themselves and compete with non-partners. Forms of agreement consist of equity investments (e.g., international joint venture (IJV) and equity participation) and nonequity involvements (e.g., licensing, joint marketing, supplier agreement, and switch agreement). The final component of this model is "expected outcomes," which refers to the benefits to be gained from such ventures.

In discussing the implications of alliance developments, potential drawbacks are outlined, as well as the strategic requirements of cooperative ventures. It is recommended that MNCs view interfirm partnership as a viable strategic alternative and begin preparations for implementing such arrangements.

Chapter 2, "Hybrid Arrangements as Strategic Alliances: Theoretical Issues in Organizational Combinations," moves into a discussion of the realm of organizational patterns used in cooperative arrangements. It examines hybrid organizational arrangements that use resources and/or governance structures of more than one organization. Based on a review of previous research, the authors identify four key issues–breadth of purpose, boundary determination, value creation, and stability mechanism–that form the core of a theory of hybrid arrangements. Furthermore, they extend this theory to (1) generate researchable propositions that explore differences among types of hybrids and (2) offer insights for managers of hybrid organizations.

Chapter 3, "Forms of Organizational Governance for Multinational Alliances," focuses on technological factors, building upon previous research in transaction cost economics, international strategy, and organization theory. The authors report their empirical findings regarding governance forms for multinational alliances. The analysis of 153 strategic alliances announced between U.S. and Japanese industrial firms between 1984 and 1986 suggested that the selection of contractual agreements (nonequity involvements) or a joint venture as form of governance was influenced by the intent to conduct R&D, the technological intensity of the alliance product area alone, and the interactive combination with the parent firms. The authors conclude that "technological factors are important for examining multinational strategic alliances but not necessarily in the manner much current transaction cost theorizing has suggested."

Chapter 4, "A Process Model on the Formation of Multinational Strategic Alliances," explains the formation of multinational alliances from a behavioral standpoint and describes various forms of strategic alliances on a continuum of dependence. Such forms include minority equity alliances, joint venture, contractual collaborations, and informal agreements. Then, the authors present a process model explaining the formation of international alliances. This model is based on the assumption that firms experiencing a strategic gap try to fill this gap by forming strategic alliances. By doing so, according to the authors, firms perceive the fulfillment of three needs or dependencies. These are greater market power, increased efficiency, and improved competencies. The impact of each of these needs is demonstrated via practical examples. According to this process model, such a strategic gap motivates a search for closure, which, in turn, leads to communication between firms. Communication helps to build interfirm trust. The authors emphasize that "a consequence of trust is cooperation, evidenced by the formation of strategic alliance" and also that interfirm cooperation results in performance sentiment, producing either satisfaction or dissatisfaction with outcomes of cooperation.

Chapter 5, "Cross-National Corporate Partnerships: Trends in Alliance Formation," first reviews the literature of strategic alliance literature in the following dimensions: trends, industry settings, forms of alliances, purposes, and country of origin of participating firms. Next, it reports the findings of an empirical investigation of the four-year period (1986-1989) with the same dimensions as theoretical landscape. The findings show that an explosion in alliance formations had occurred in 1988, although an overall increase was evident throughout the period studied. A large portion of alliances occurred in such industries as electronics involving substantial operating risks, high entry costs, and rapidly changing technology. Joint ventures predominated over other forms of cooperation. Most of these cooperative ventures were formed to engage in joint manufacturing and production activities. An increasing trend was observed in U.S. partnerships with Western Europe and East Europe. Additionally, cross-national partnerships are evaluated in terms of their advantages and disadvantages. Managers are encouraged to weigh the benefits and costs of an alliance against those of "going it alone."

Chapter 6, "Technology-Based Cross-Border Alliances," provides a broad view of major developments in research and development (R&D) alliances across national borders, with special attention given to high-technology industries. It also indicates the probable impact of technological agreements from a private and social point of view. The chapter shows that the world's leading high-technology companies are operating through a large web of cooperative agreements. The authors examine the determinants of R&D alliances by providing an analytical framework and some empirical evidence.

They elaborate on managing strategic alliances by pointing out the risks involved in cooperative agreements and by describing protective devices against such risks. In explaining the mechanism of R&D cooperative agreements, the authors classify R&D alliances, describe the dynamics of corporate networks, and illustrate the role of transnational alliance networks in technological innovation. Finally, they present examples of the successes and failures of R&D alliances and examine the efficiency of such alliances by discussing their economic and social costs.

Chapter 7, "Protection of Competitive Advantage in U.S./Asia-Pacific Joint Ventures from High-Technology Industries," introduces the findings of a survey on nine U.S. high-technology firms regarding 11 of their international joint ventures (IJVs) with Asia-Pacific companies. The authors explore the rationale for these ventures, the control of key resources, and the success of high-tech IJVs.

Although the rationale for these alliances varied from one case to another, the general reasons were gaining access to the market and achieving distribution-scale economies (for only drug and research firms). The control of key resources was accomplished by holding key resources outside the operation, owning an equal or majority of voting shares, dispersing other voting shares when holding a minority, making frequent contacts, standardizing reports, building of corporate culture, staffing key positions with one's own personnel, and assuring sufficient representation within the board of directors. To protect their technology, the American firms used various control mechanisms, including conducting R&D at the parent company, choosing asymmetrical partners, developing trust, restricting to non-high-tech (no leading-edge) activities, building interdependence, and making separate licensing agreements.

Based on their preliminary study, the authors conclude that such alliances, if established with trustworthy partners, can be successful while requiring only minimal transaction costs and minimal control efforts.

Chapter 8, "Building Partnerships with Japanese Corporate Groups," explores the strategic importance of a possible partner firm's set of interrelationships with reference to the Japanese industrial context and corporate networking practices. It presents cases and suggests guidelines for managers interested in establishing linkages with Japanese corporate groups (*keiretsu*). The chapter deals with the role, structure, and intra-alliances of *keiretsu*, and then it moves on to a discussion of the global links Toshiba (a giant Japanese electronics firm) has with other firms. Furthermore, it inquires into U.S.-Japanese collaborations in the commercial aircraft and automobile industries.

The author underscores the peculiar nature of collaborations within a *keiretsu* environment. Japanese corporate groups called G-form organizations present multiple hierarchies consisting of upper-echelon relationships (i.e., with intra-alliance cooperations and intra-company cooperations) and lower-echelon relationships (i.e., with suppliers and subcontractors in the marketplace). The contextual analysis offered in this chapter includes collective strategy development and the process of cooperation; the prospective collaborator's understanding and positioning of itself relevant to the Japanese multi-hierarchy groups; international technology transfers; and authority relationships in joint ventures.

In conclusion, the author suggests that a contextual analysis is extremely important for a foreign firm seeking collaborative relationships within a corporate grouping that would be influential on a competitive industry structure.

Chapter 9, "Ownership and Control in East-West Joint Ventures," shows that management control is a critical determinant of joint-venture (JV) performance and the attainment of parent company objectives. The author claims that control is particularly important for East-West JVs, given the challenging economic and political environment in which they operate. He examines the importance of JV control, including the relationship with division of ownership. In attempting to design an effective control system, this chapter identifies three underlying dimensions of JV control: focus, extent, and mechanism. Focus refers to the scope of activities over which a parent company seeks to preside, or to *not* exercise control. Extent of control means the degree of control exercised by a parent company over individual JV activities. Finally, control "mechanism" represents the positive and negative means by which parent companies exercise control over a JV. Moreover, as this chapter shows, "there is a 'fit' between the parents' strategies and the JV's control structure when the benefits outweigh the costs of control, and this 'fit' is best when the margin between benefits and costs is optimized." By addressing strategic control in East-West JVs, this chapter deals with a critical issue influencing JV direction and performance and provides a perspective for better understanding and management of these ventures.

Chapter 10, "Strategic Alliances in the Global Container Transport Industry," identifies the driving forces behind and the types of strategic alliances in the container transport industry. It outlines such major alliance forms as conferences, slot charters, coordinated services, equipment- /chassis-sharing agreements, and consortia. Although the cooperative arrangements covered in this chapter are unique to the container transport industry, the cooperative behavior of firms in this industry displays some common characteristic for interfirm partnerships in general. Furthermore, these alliances are presented in two conceptual frameworks. Additionally, a model is offered for delineating environmental forces shaping the industry, which influences a carrier's performance. A cooperative arrangement in the global container transport industry is deemed one of the chief strategic responses by a carrier to changes in industry structure. In this respect, five interesting cases are introduced: Sea-Land Service Inc., Maersk Line, Happag-Lloyd, Compagnie General Maritime, and Atlantic Container Line (ACL). The authors conclude that strategic alliances will play an ever-increasing role in the global container transport industry.

Chapter 11, "Planning International Joint Ventures: The Role of Human Resource Management," delineates that many management problems in IJVs–as well as the failure of such ventures–can be attributed to human resource management (HRM) issues. Yet HRM issues constitute one of the most neglected aspects in the planning of IJVs. Thus, this chapter presents a framework that identifies the various steps associated with such planning. This framework is then used to identify and discuss the importance of HRM issues affecting each step of the planning process. The chapter notes that even after the completion of the initial planning phase of an IJV, several HRM issues still require attention. The authors outline cultural, personal, and administrative problems as HRM issues that have a potential for derailing an IJV, and they propose solutions to such problems from an HRM perspective.

Chapter 12, "Ethnocentrism and Group Cohesiveness: Implications for International Joint Ventures," analyzes some of the dysfunctional behaviors hindering the managing of an IJV from a viewpoint of organizational behavior. The authors point out that managerial problems of IJVs can be attributed to subtle ethnocentric attitudes of venture managers. Ethnocentric attitudes, reflection of different value systems, and cultural orientations among managers may prevent the achievement of common group goals and the development of group cohesiveness, which can be detrimental to the performance of the firm. The authors then offer a conceptual framework in which the determinants of group cohesiveness can be presented to remedy the dysfunctional effect of ethnocentrism. According to their model, group cohesiveness is influenced by the achievement of goal congruence, development of an organizational system consisting of a communication structure, a reward system and an orientation (corporate culture), and the existence of effective leadership. To increase cohesiveness in IJVs, the authors suggest fostering the forces leading to it by providing individual managers with cross-cultural cognitive and experiential training, to reduce the ethnocentric attitudes and to expand the ability to adapt to cultural differences.

Chapter 13, "Self-Management Training for General Managers of International Joint Ventures," turns the reader's attention to the role of an International Joint Venture General Manager (IJVGM) and offers an alternative human resources training technique. Based on a pilot study, this chapter shows that the majority of parent companies usually fail to provide clear guidelines for the role of an IJVGM, which often requires managerial initiative; therefore, the self-management approach is viewed as an appropriate alternative for an IJVGM. The authors identify six essential components for a comprehensive IJVGM self-training program: (1) self-assessment; (2) goal-setting; (3) self-monitoring; (4) self-evaluation; (5) written contracts to help one to set goals and to take necessary actions; and (6) maintenance, which involves training IJVGMs to recognize common problems and pitfalls in applying self-management training techniques and to develop strategies for overcoming these pitfalls.

After listing the benefits to be obtained from implementing training in self-management, the authors propose a means for the measurement of effectiveness of a training program according to four criteria: (1) reaction of IJVGM to the program; (2) learning, meaning an assessment of the knowledge and the skills acquired by the trainee; (3) cognitive self-reports, or querying one's perceived self-efficacy and outcome expectancies; and (4) behavioral criteria concerned with the performance of the trainee in the IJV work setting. Overall, the authors conclude that self-management training for IJVGMs provides a comprehensive approach for managers to monitor their own behavior, and to obtain feedback about their performance and the degree of control exercised over their environment.

Chapter 14, "Global Dependence and Corporate Linkages," evaluates recent changes in the global market and predicts developments in strategic alliances. Moreover, it attempts to integrate the fundamentals of the previous chapters. Changes in the global market are discussed in relation to: (1) the emergence of regional trading blocks consisting of a single market of Europe, North America, and Japan, (2) the evolution of new markets, including Eastern Europe, the former U.S.S.R., and Newly Industrialized Countries (NICs), and (3) the dispersion of technology leading to international corporate linkages.

Future corporate linkages are examined in the forms of equity participation, international joint ventures, international subcontracting, supplier and channel agreements, and other linkages that include R&D partnership, joint marketing, production sharing, and service accords.

The author claims that within a foreseeable future, companies will engage in a variety of equity or nonequity forms of strategic relationships. Strategic alliances will proliferate in particular in industries undergoing structural change or escalating competition. For practitioners, the author lists the features of, and the prospects for, the formation of strategic alliances.

This volume comprises twelve original essays and two reprints (Chapters 2 and 3). All in all, it conveys the message that strategic alliances are now becoming more instrumental than ever before in shaping corporate strategies and performances for the future. An understanding of strategic alliances will allow managers to bring about successful cooperative ventures for their firms.

I. CONCEPTUAL FOUNDATIONS OF MULTINATIONAL STRATEGIC ALLIANCES

Chapter 1

Multinational Competition and Cooperation: Theory and Practice

Refik Culpan

In the last decade, while international business competition intensified, cooperation among rival multinational companies has increased. At first glance, these two developments seem to contradict each other. A closer examination, however, reveals that multinational corporations (MNCs) engaged in such cooperative ventures have sought competitive advantage from such arrangements. Nevertheless, some important questions can be raised about strategic alliances. How realistic are their expectations? Will multinational cooperation become a common practice in the foreseeable future? Does this trend mean new strategic requirements for MNCs? All of these questions imply that multinational cooperation adds a new dimension for study in the field of strategic management.

Because of the recent popularity of such cooperative ventures, many scholars and practitioners have studied this phenomenon. Contractor and Lorange (1988) introduced a model for cooperative ventures; Borys and Jemison (Chapter 2) have developed research propositions in regard to hybrid structures of strategic alliances; and Osborn and Baughn (Chapter 3) have examined forms of inter-organizational governance. Ohmae (1989) has pointed out the necessity for strategic alliances.

The purposes of this chapter are threefold. First, to discuss theoretical foundations of strategic alliances. Second, to introduce a

The author wishes to thank David Morand for his helpful comments on an earlier draft of this chapter.

conceptual framework within which the recent proliferation of multinational alliances can be examined. (The conceptual framework contains a variety of elements for examination: environmental forces leading to multinational cooperation, motives of the parties, major cooperative strategies, modes of cooperations, forms of agreements, and expected outcome.) Third, to discuss implications of cooperative ventures for multinational strategy formulation and implementation.

In this chapter, cooperative ventures are defined as a host of joint collaborative arrangements between multinational firms to pursue a common goal (Morris and Hergert, 1987). They include such forms of alliances as licensing, joint venture, research and development (R&D) partnership, joint marketing, consortium, and countertrade agreements.

Even though cooperation among MNCs is not new, the recent advent of multinational cooperative arrangements goes beyond the conventional partnership scheme between two firms. For example, Contractor and Lorange (1987) claim that "instead of the traditional pattern of a large 'foreign' firm trying to access a market by associating itself with a 'local' partner, many recent partnerships involve joint activities in several stages of the value-added chain, such as production, sourcing and R&D" (p.83). At present, strategic partnerships basically manifest a variety of linkages between the parties. Perlmutter and Heenan (1986) assert that "increasingly, to be globally competitive, multinational corporations must be globally cooperative. This necessity is reflected in the acceleration of global strategic partnerships among companies large and small" (p. 136). Porter (1986) also recognizes the significance of these cooperative ventures, calling the process "coalition" among multinationals. He considers such arrangements part of the changing pattern of international competition. On the other hand, Auster (1990) believes that an inter-organizational network "offers a means to diversify costs and risks and co-opt or block competition while gaining access to new technologies, customers, products, distribution channels, and resources." In a similar fashion, Neilsen (1986, 1987) emphasizes the role of less popular cooperative strategies for mutual gains, versus traditional strict competition.

Given the extent to which multinational alliances go beyond conventional forms of cooperation, and establish their presence on a truly global scale never before witnessed, it is important to heighten and to clarify our understanding of how and why such forms of cooperation take shape. To this end, then, consider the following views.

THEORETICAL CONSIDERATIONS

Most literature about the subject deals with joint ventures rather than other forms of alliances. However, the underlying theories explaining joint ventures can be extended to interpret other forms of interfirm partnerships. The three principal theories used to explain joint ventures are transaction cost economics, organization theory, and business strategy (Kogut, 1988a).

Transaction cost economics was developed by Williamson (1975), who suggested that firms choose alternative arrangements that minimize the sum of production and transaction costs. Production costs consist of a variety of costs incurred during the transformation of various inputs (materials, components, labor, information, etc.) into products or services. "Transaction costs refer to the expenses incurred for writing and enforcing contracts, for haggling over terms and contingent claims, for deviating from optimal kinds of investments in order to increase dependence on party or stabilize a relationship, and for administering a transaction" (Kogut, 1988a, p. 320).

Transaction cost theory predicts that strategic alliances are designed to achieve such a minimum cost arrangement. For example, about two decades ago Hymer (1968) predicted that "[a] firm can agree with others to divide the market into spheres of influence . . . , or it can establish tighter cooperative links and share with others the risk of certain operation . . . " (p. 973). Transaction cost theory assumes that firms only pursue reactive strategies; therefore, the creation of a new market cannot be explained by this approach. Firms, however, may take a proactive stand as well, as Horaguchi and Toyne (1990) claim:

> Heterogeneity and asymmetrical distribution of managerial resources among firms *evolve over time* and create unique ad-

vantages for each firm. Thus, firms as combinations of managerial resources can create new markets. Moreover, additional managerial resources are accumulated during the process of innovation and contingency toward the new market which also contribute further to its advantage. That is, a firm is not just reactive (cost reducing internalization markets), it is also proactive in that it creates new products, new markets, new organizations, new management techniques, and new technology. As a result of proactive action, a firm enhances both its product lines and the spatial domain of activities . . . (p. 491)

Thus, when transaction costs are high, firms tend to collaborate to minimize those costs and to gain a proactive posture through partnership. This view especially explains international R&D partnerships for undertaking large-scale or innovative projects. Kogut and Singh (1988) articulate this phenomenon as follows: ". . . in growing industries where R&D investment is important, foreign entrants may create joint ventures with larger firms in order to acquire technology from incumbents for use in their home markets or gain marketing arms for their innovations" (p. 241). For example, GE Aircraft Engine and United Technologies' Pratt & Whitney recently agreed to a joint study of the possibility of developing new types of commercial supersonic engines. The agreement occurred because both companies acknowledged formidable technical challenges in meeting current emissions and noise standards with a new generation of such engines.

The second theory of strategic alliance is associated with organization theory; specifically, the resource dependence approach suggesting that organizations depend on other organizations within their environment to acquire needed resources. Pfeffer and Salancik (1978) describe "how organizations cope with the uncertainty created by interdependence by managing interdependence through interorganizational coordinations" (p. 282). Pfeffer and Nowak (1976) believe that the formation of joint ventures is a means for stabilizing the flow of resources that a company needs and also reduces the uncertainty confronted by it.

Examples of inter-organizational interdependence are abundant in practice. To transform itself from a stodgy home-appliance maker into a leading, fully integrated technology company, Matsushita has recently developed a broad licensing agreement with Sun Microsystems. Matsushita, eager to bolster its minuscule computer business, plans to develop a new line of "high performance" machines using the basic design of Sun Microsystems, the leading U.S. maker of engineering workstations (*The Wall Street Journal,* 1990). The Japanese company will also use Sun's Sparc microprocessor in its consumer electronics products. This agreement is significant for Sun, as it searches for allies interested in becoming the de facto standard in the growing market for the powerful desktop machines.

The third approach to strategic alliance deals with competitive strategies of firms. Porter (1980, 1985) has developed profound theories of competitive advantage. Porter's approach (1980) is based on the analysis of five competitive forces in a given industry. These forces include the threat of new entrants, the bargaining power of suppliers, the bargaining power of buyers, the threat of substitute products, and rivalry among other firms. Within the context of Porter's framework, an analysis of these five factors should shape the development of a business strategy. To deal with these five forces and outperform other firms in the industry, Porter (1985) suggests three generic strategies: low-cost leadership, product differentiation, and focus.

A strategic alliance may provide these competitive advantages; namely, relative cost advantages deriving from economies of scale, differentiated products because of superior technology or product quality, or segmenting markets and appealing to only a limited group of consumers or industrial buyers. For example, Daimler-Benz and Mitsubishi are currently exploring a global alliance for about a dozen products ranging from cross-country vehicles to semiconductors. These two companies have also established a joint venture along with Yanase, a Japanese distributor of imported cars, to expand Mercedes-Benz's sales network in Japan. The agreement also includes an arrangement for some Mitsubishi dealers to sell Mercedes, a differentiated product of the German company.

Furthermore, Porter and Fuller (1986) view strategic alliances ("coalitions" in their terms) in the context of a firm's international strategy. Then,

. . . two key dimensions of international strategy are the international configuration of a firm's activities (where and how many places they are located) and the extent to which activities located in different countries are coordinated (how do they relate). Coalitions are a means of performing one or more activities in combination with another firm instead of autonomously–they are thus a means of configuration. The choice of a coalition implies that it is perceived as a less costly or more effective way to configure than the alternatives of, on the one hand, developing the skills to perform the activity in-house or, on the other hand, of merger to gain the capability to perform the activity or to buy products or skills in arm's length transaction. (p. 321)

The expectations from strategic alliances in both configuration and coordination can become clear by relating coalitions to the activities on the value chain, which disaggregates a firm into the discrete activities performed in developing, producing, marketing, selling, and servicing after sale of a product or service (Porter and Fuller, 1986). In technology development, for example, Toshiba (Japan) has established a cooperative relationship with Siemens (Germany) in the semiconductor field. This tie-in began with the transfer to Siemens of Toshiba's dynamic random-access-memory technology. This step has been followed by joint development work on application-specific integration circuits, including standard cells.

Although these general theories at present provide insight into the nature of strategic alliances, they are inadequate for illustrating completely the details and dynamics of such partnerships in various forms. We need mid-range theories and models to demonstrate the peculiarities and complexities of interfirm collaborations. Moreover, the multinational cooperative movement mentioned above compels us to create a conceptual model to study comprehensively how and why such enterprises emerge. Thus, a model for cooperative strategies is constructed to analyze and better understand the motives and behavior of MNCs in cooperation.

A MODEL FOR COOPERATIVE STRATEGIES

As illustrated in Figure 1.1, the proposed conceptual model consists of several components: (1) environmental forces, (2) motives

FIGURE 1.1. A Conceptual Framework for Cooperative Strategies

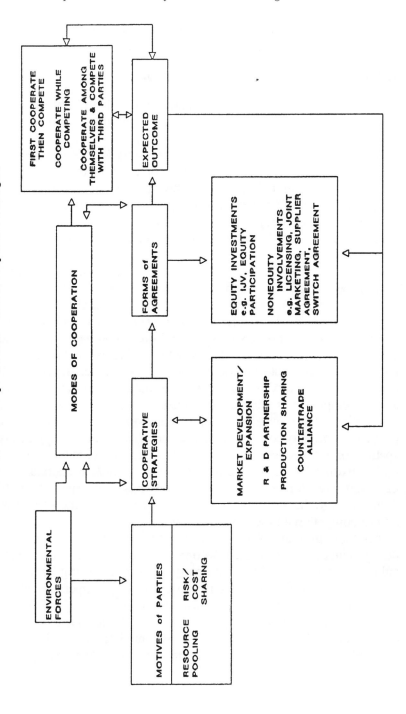

of the parties, (3) cooperative strategies; (4) modes of cooperation, (5) forms of agreements, and (6) expected outcome.

1. Environmental Forces for Cooperation

A continuously evolving market structure and environmental forces leading to cooperative ventures can be classified in three major categories:

a. *Intense International Competition:* Most MNCs have experienced stiff competition in marketing their products and services. Such intensified global rivalry, on the surface, appears to preclude any cooperative effort. Yet interfirm collaboration has increased. To gain a competitive edge, MNCs try unique approaches, including benefitting from their competitors, because competing alone has become extremely difficult.

b. *Technological Advancement:* Today, the level and pace of technological development has forced MNCs to find R&D partners to share know-how and to complement each other's efforts. Technological change is a driving force shaping such cooperations because of the required economies of scale and the accompanying research expenses. Many of modern-day new technologies–electronics, biotechnology, new materials, and new energy sources–represent the leading edge of key developments. One major issue in the research and development of such technologies is cost. Even for a leading international firm, the enormous expenses of development and improvement often become burdensome and risky. For example, Aerospatiale of France, Messerschmitt-Bolkow-Blohm G.m.b.H. of Germany, British Aerospace, and Construccionnes Aeronauticas S.A. of Spain have formed a consortium (Airbus Industries) to enable them to share the enormous costs in building a full line of aircraft, and to compete with the giant Boeing.

Another stimulator for technological cooperation is the fact that new product or technology development may go beyond the technical competence of a single company, thereby requiring some concerted effort. Toshiba, for instance, has joined in cooperative efforts in the area of semiconductors with such innovative and leading corporations as Intel, LSI Logic Corporation, Motorola, and Zilog in the U.S.; SGS Microelectronica in Italy; and Siemens in Germany.

c. *Globalization:* Global corporate strategies have been gaining importance (Chandler, 1986; Levitt, 1983; Porter, 1986). Today, the global-industry, particularly in high-technology areas, requires companies "to capitalize on highly centralized scale-incentive manufacturing and R&D operations, and leverage them through worldwide exports of standardized global products" (Barlett and Ghoshal, 1987, p. 9).

The combined effect of all the factors listed above has led to increases in cooperative ventures.

2. Intermediate Motives of Parties

For analysis, a distinction is made between intermediate and ultimate motives of firms. The former include resource pooling and risk sharing. The latter is discussed under the "expected outcome" subheading below.

International firms involved in cooperation seek either resource pooling or risk- /cost-sharing benefits. Although these two benefits are mutually inclusive, studying them separately helps explain the intermediate motives of parties.

Resource pooling refers to the partners' contribution to a joint project of such resources as capital, know-how, and personnel. A party believes that, in this fashion, it can achieve its objective more effectively and efficiently. For example, a technological breakthrough often requires technical knowledge beyond a single company's domain, as in the case of Philips and Toshiba. Companies can achieve scale advantages in research, production, and marketing through partnerships. Pooling resources can be accomplished through "know-how" licensing, management/marketing service agreement, nonequity cooperative agreements in exploration, research partnership, development/co-production, and equity joint ventures (Contractor and Lorange, 1988).

Risk/cost sharing means parties tend to avoid greater risk by splitting investment with a partner. An international firm may prefer to share the cost of a major project with someone else. The GM-Toyota joint venture illustrates this point. In another example, the Boeing-Japanese consortium, the Japanese hold 15 percent of the 767 airframe in a risk-sharing program (Roehl and Truitt, 1987). Sometimes, to prevent a new product/technology failure, a firm shares its innovation with others, as happened with Matsushita's

VHS format. Occasionally, a firm pursues a retrenchment strategy through cooperation. Volkswagen (VW) agreed to sell Olivetti a 98.4 percent stake in Triumph-Adler, its troubled office equipment unit, and in turn take a 5 percent stake in the Italian company. This accord has relieved VW of a drain of its earnings.

Nevertheless, it must be noted that risk/cost motives may overlap. A firm may try to accomplish both objectives simultaneously.

3. Cooperative Strategies

Environmental forces coupled with a firm's motives have led many multinational firms to develop concerted strategies. As described above, MNCs seeking cooperative ventures may follow a variety of paths. The present model, however, classifies them in relationship to their strategies, as follows:

a. *Market Development and Expansion:* Cooperating firms try to develop and expand the present market to benefit mutually from such progress.

In penetrating hostile foreign markets, international firms may act together to gain better terms, such as easing tariffs and non-tariff barriers, from host governments. For instance, Japan is an extremely difficult market to penetrate by foreign tobacco companies. Yet, with 32 million people smoking 300 billion cigarettes a year, Japan is a crucial market for U.S. and foreign tobacco companies. U.S. cigarette makers cracked the Japanese market only after they had induced the U.S. government to influence the Japanese government to liberalize its trade restrictions.

b. *Research and Development Partnership:* It has become common to see major multinational firms (especially high-technology ones) involved jointly in R&D activities (Fusfeld and Haklish, 1985). According to Morris and Hergert (1987), the largest number of cooperative ventures are formed to engage in joint product development. In semiconductors, for example, Toshiba engaged in technological exchanges with non-Japanese corporations. Toshiba transferred its random-access-memory technology to Siemens. These two companies later continued their cooperation by joint development work on application-specific integrated circuits, including standard cells (Saba, 1986).

Similarly, Samsung Semiconductors & Communications of South

Korea is licensed by Micron Technology to use the latter's technology for VLSI (Very Large-Scale Integrated) circuits design. It also signed a comprehensive technological agreement with Intel, another U.S. firm.

c. *International Production Sharing:* This is another common strategy used by MNCs, and it refers to manufacturing parts of a product in more than one country. A vertical sequence of production-sharing activities can be divided into two main groups of manufacturing operations: the upstream (manufacturing complex components) group and the downstream (further processing and assembly) group. The operations in either group may be conducted by different enterprises. For example, Hyundai Motor and Mitsubishi Motor agreed to jointly produce luxury sedans. Under this agreement, Hyundai manufactures the body for the cars produced by these two automakers. In another area, Mitsubishi makes the major portion of the engines and the transmissions used in the jointly produced luxury car, the Debonair. These examples illustrate how cooperation in manufacturing enables two companies to achieve maximum economic effect with minimum investment. Similarly, Ford, Mazda, and Kia Industrial have agreed to manufacture a subcompact car. Ford intends to use the car to catch up with rival U.S. automakers in the subcompact car market, while Mazda may also import the car to compete with Toyota and Nissan in the Japanese market. Such a production-sharing strategy is changing both industry structure and international competition considerably.

d. *Countertrade Alliance:* Under a countertrade agreement, the seller is partially or fully compensated through counterdeliveries–goods for goods (Culpan, 1986). The seller may look for another firm to market counterdeliveries instead of selling them directly. Then, the firm interested in countertrade seeks out still other firms capable of marketing counterdeliveries, especially when counterdeliveries fall beyond its area of expertise. PepsiCo, for instance, gets vodka in exchange for beverage concentrates it sells to the former Soviet Union. Rather than selling the vodka itself, it has given the rights to import the product to another company, Monsieur Henri Wines Ltd., which specializes in alcohol marketing and pays PepsiCo out of proceeds of vodka sales.

4. Modes of Cooperation

Various modes of cooperation can be divided into three distinct categories:

a. *First Cooperate, Then Compete:* Companies may feel they are not ready for competition in a particular area, so they may choose to cooperate until they build their competence or achieve a common standard. As explained above, Sony, Matsushita, and Hitachi are first trying to establish a standard format for a VCR that would be compatible with high-definition television (HDTV), after which they will continue to compete for their market shares. On the other hand, Matsushita decided to help develop and produce Philips-designed recording tape that can capture and render a much higher quality of sound. Matsushita's support for Philips's digital compact cassette (DCC) in the battle with Sony's digital mini-disc is aimed at shaping the consumer audio market of the future. It is predicted that one format will ultimately dominate the market and that Matsushita's endorsement will benefit the DCC. Also, Philips occasionally has shared its R&D in electronics and pushed for standards with its Japanese competitors. One result of such persistence is that compact disc players now have a standard format worldwide, and are well accepted.

These cooperative ventures go beyond the electronics industry. In the steel industry, National Steel and Nippon Kokan built an alliance through technology transfer. A joint venture in fiber optics between Corning Glass Works and Siemens AG is another example.

Cooperating firms compete among themselves once they achieve their short-run objectives. Such cooperation is a part of their business strategy.

b. *Cooperate While Competing:* Companies may continue to compete while they cooperate. One basic reason for such an alliance is to learn from each other and to overcome one's weaknesses. GM and Volvo set up a joint venture to manufacture heavy trucks in the U.S. while continuing to compete otherwise. GM's partnership with Toyota also illustrates that partners may cooperate while engaging in severe competition at the same time. Similarly, Chrysler has accepted a collaborative plan with Mitsubishi. Thus, a combination of "competition and cooperation" yields a distinctive corporate strategy that leads to continued productivity and growth in the automobile industry. Such a combination capitalizes on the exchange of know-how and "tacit technology."

Such practices are not limited to the automobile industry. For instance, two mighty rivals, IBM and Apple, recently agreed on a broad alliance to share personal computer technology, especially to develop a type of software expected to greatly simplify computer programming.

c. *Cooperate Among Themselves and Compete with Others:* Companies may establish alliances just to compete with third parties. In this fashion, Honeywell, Groupe Bull, and NEC have agreed on a plan formalizing their long-established working relationship. NEC makes the central processing units for both Honeywell's and Bull's largest computers, and it also produces personal computers for Honeywell. Bull makes and markets some Honeywell-model midsize computers outside the U.S., and Honeywell markets NEC's supercomputers line and Bull's networking know-how in the U.S. Honeywell considers this venture a way to become a minor player in the computer business, to cut its losses and to concentrate on businesses where it holds a dominant position, such as in aerospace and defense. Others see the new company as an inexpensive entree to the U.S. market. Moreover, such an accord reflects the united marketing strategy of partners against competitors in the industry.

5. Forms of Agreements

Cooperative strategies are formalized through a variety of agreements, which can be classified in two major categories. The first is investments entailing equity participation of parties in the arrangement. They may take the forms of international joint ventures (IJVs) or stock swaps between partners. IJVs mean the creation of a separate legal entity with shared equity, whereas stock swaps only refer to the exchange of stocks by the partners. Of course, IJVs pose complicated managerial problems, and strategic planning and control are particularly critical in this context (Lorange, 1988). Therefore, they have become the subject of various studies (Franco, 1971; Geringer, 1988; Harrigan, 1985; Hladik, 1985).

The second category of cooperative agreements includes a host of nonequity involvements that do not require equity investments, such as licensing, R&D collaboration, joint marketing, supplier agreements, and switching agreements. They are also called "contractual agreements" (Osborn and Baughn, Chapter 3; Osland and Yaprak, Chapter 4), some of which are described below.

An IJV presents a traditional form used between companies (Berlew, 1984). IJVs mark interfirm partnership involving strategies of market development and expansion, production sharing, and R&D partnership (Franko, 1971; Harrigan, 1986, 1985; Killing 1983, 1982). For example, Nippon Sheet Glass Co., Japan's second largest, has set up a joint venture with the Hankuk Sheet Glass Industry Co. of Korea and the Libby-Owens-Ford Co. of the U.S. to manufacture and market glass efficiently and effectively.

Licensing or cross-licensing is another form of cooperation, which denotes renting or exchanging technologies among firms (Contractor, 1985). "Cooperation through cross-licensing and cross distribution gives firms like Abbott Laboratories and Eli Lilly access to commercialized substances from offshore affiliates like Takeda Chemical and Yamanouchi Pharmaceutical, respectively, more rapidly than they could develop them internally" (Harrigan, 1985, p. 68).

Consortium accords represent a cooperation among several companies jointly undertaking a major project (Morris and Hergert, 1987). The Airbus, mentioned above, is a European consortium competing effectively against U.S. aircraft companies. Consortium arrangements are useful for market development and expansion as well as R&D partnership strategies.

Joint marketing is another collaborative scheme in which partners assume different but complementary marketing responsibilities. The accord among Honeywell, NEC, and Groupe Bull is representative of such a marketing collaboration. Market development and expansion strategy can be realized by joint marketing efforts of companies that complement each other's sale competencies.

Switching agreements are arrangements specifying obligations of parties in a countertrade alliance. The countertrading firm transfers its rights to a third party. Usually, international trade companies are involved in such deals as a third party.

6. Expected Outcome

Of course, the expected outcome from such cooperative ventures are benefits in sales, profits, economies of scale (production and/or marketing), gaining new know-how, reduction of host-country trade restrictions, and achieving trade restrictions against countries that trade unfairly. It must be noted, though, that gains from a cooperative venture may not be equal for each party. The significant point is whether gains are proportional rather than equal. The clarity of expectation of each party is important for continuous relationships between the parties. Unrealistic anticipations held by either party damages the cooperative venture.

IMPLICATIONS AND CONCLUSIONS

A pattern of multinational cooperation is emerging in the global market, creating unprecedented challenges and opportunities for multinational cooperations. To be competitive, MNCs must join "networks of international coalitions" and learn how to manage them (Sharp, 1987; Frunio, 1988).

Potential Drawbacks

Managers of MNCs should be aware of the potential drawbacks of cooperative ventures, which are summarized as follows.

(a) Difficult and Risky Nature: A cooperative strategy is difficult to realize and involves certain risks. Because strategy implementation may be beyond the control of a single party, such a situation may create frustration and delays.

(b) Unequal Gains: Some partners may gain more than the others. Such an outcome should not surprise partners. Nevertheless, unequal benefits may hamper the partnership when the expectations differ and stakes are high.

(c) Cultural Clash: Individual and separate cultures may clash with others, especially within corporations encompassing distinctly differing cultures. For example, the Du Pont-Philips optical-disc venture has been disappointing so far because the partners have experienced "cultural differences" that have slowed the venture, causing it to lose ground to stiff competition from Japanese concerns.

(d) Role Ambiguity: Parties may not be clear about their specific roles. In particular, changing market structures may require unprecedented tasks from partners.

(e) Partner's Alliance with Competitors: A partner may establish cooperative linkages with competing firms. This situation may hamper the present alliance. As a result, an expectation of continuing cooperation with the partner in a series of projects or ventures may result in disappointment. For example, Philips was hoping to get more from its alliance with AT&T, but AT&T had also set up some cooperation with Siemens, the major rival of Philips in Europe.

(f) Facing Antitrust Charges: Antitrust regulations can seriously restrict benefits of an alliance with a major partner and invite governmental intervention. The joint venture between Monsanto and Bayer was allowed to operate for many years before the U.S. Justice Department intervened with an antitrust suit.

Nevertheless, mutual gains from cooperation can outweigh disadvantages. To benefit from a cooperative venture, a firm participating in an alliance should meet certain strategic requirements.

Strategic Requirements

Interfirm cooperation necessitates being open to making changes in: organizational philosophy; corporate culture; the planning process and structure; and managerial techniques (to be able to gear cooperation to the strategic thrust of the firm). These strategic requirements should occur in all of these four key areas:

1. *Corporate Philosophy and Culture:* Cooperative enterprises require a change in corporate philosophy from strict competition based upon "win or lose" to a philosophy of cooperation based upon "win and win." This is a challenging transformation for a company, and only adaptive structures can absorb such a drastic change. Managers planning to undertake a cooperative venture should assimilate it with the concept of "new competition," of gaining mutually, as opposed to "traditional competition" of gaining individually (i.e., the adversarial relationship of "us versus them"). The "cooperation while in competition" mode in particular requires responsibility and openness and fidelity.

2. *Continuous Mutual Commitment and Support:* From beginning to end, cooperative strategy requires mutual commitment among firms as well as the support of top management; the success

of a cooperative strategy depends heavily upon the continuing commitment of each party. Although "environmental and strategic changes over time may shift the relative bargaining power among the partners," (Kogut, 1988b, p. 177), these parties are expected to do their share to provide for the survival and success of cooperation. The formation and implementation of cooperative strategies usually take a longer time and require greater effort than does a unitary strategy. Thus, managers should change their planning perspective from a short-range to a long-range perspective. As Toshiba's technology sharing and Philips' R&D partnership illustrate, long-term strategic commitment is essential for successful cooperative strategy. Such change means waiting patiently for expected gain while continuing to supply the resources and knowledge needed.

3. *Organizational Pattern:* Depending upon the form of cooperation encountered, partners will have to use various organizational arrangements. Since joint ventures, licensing, and switch agreements are more traditional forms, they are covered comprehensively in the literature (Christelow, 1987; Geringer and Hebert, 1989; Hall, 1984; Harrigan, 1985). Technology partnership and joint marketing, on the other hand, are relatively new and require systematic examination. The partners may need a matrix structure composed of specialists representing both partners. Project managers and their relationship with their staff, especially those from other companies, should be clearly defined.

Another alternative arrangement entails the temporary assignment of one's staff to the partner's department. Such cases have not been studied enough in the organizations and management literature. They may raise concerns with reference to authority relations, supervision, and decision making. All of these points should be considered in advance. Specific guidelines should be prepared for the decision-making process, for reporting, for handling of conflicts between members from different companies, and for controlling alliance activities.

4. *A Need for Training:* Companies should train their employees to work on various projects in cooperation with those from allied organizations. Different corporate cultures and methods may clash during such encounters if precautions are not taken. Empathy for differing technical and managerial approaches should be developed

among employees to improve collaboration between partners. This becomes especially important in encounters of employees from totally different cultures, such as in American-Japanese partnerships. It will be useful to provide some knowledge of basic characteristics of the other culture and of its managerial behavior and styles.

It seems that the number of collaborative arrangements among MNCs will surge in the foreseeable future (see Kostelac and Culpan, Chapter 5; Culpan, Chapter 14). Such an increase in interfirm cooperation represents a significant change in the nature of international business (Morris and Hergert, 1987). The present cooperative model provides essential elements to be considered in such an endeavor. Multinational firms should deem cooperative ventures as a viable strategic alternative and prepare themselves for such enterprises.

REFERENCES

Auster, E.R. (1990). The international environment: Network theory, tools, and applications. In F. Williams and D. Gibson (Eds.), *Technological Transfer* (pp. 63-89). Sage Publications.

Barlett, C.A. & Ghoshal, S. (1987). Managing across borders: New strategic requirements. *Sloan Management Review*, Summer, 7-17.

Berlew, F.K. (1984). The Joint Ventures: A Way into Foreign Markets. *Harvard Business Review.* July-August, 48-52.

Chandler, C.H. (1986). The evolution of modern global competition. In M.E. Porter. (Ed.) *Competition in Global Industries* (pp. 405-448). Boston: Harvard University Press.

Christelow, D. (1987). International joint ventures: How important are they? *Columbia Journal of World Business*, 22(2), 7-14.

Contractor, F.J. & Lorange, P. (1987). Competition vs. Cooperation: A benefit/cost framework for choosing between fully-owned investments and cooperative relationships, in Westacott, G., Dexter, C., Yanouzas, J.N., and Boukis, S.D. (eds.) Managing in a Global Economy II, Eastern Academy of Management Proceedings of the Second International Conference, June 14-18, pp. 83-89.

_____. (Eds.). (1988). *Cooperative strategies in international business.* Lexington, MA: Lexington Books.

_____. (1985). *Licensing in international strategy: A guide for planning and negotiations.* Westport, CT: Greenwood Press.

Culpan, R. (1986). Re-emerging countertrade: The case of Brazil. *Issues in International Business.* 3(1), 37-41.

Franko, L.G. (1971). *Joint venture survival in multinational corporations.* New York: Praeger.

Frunio, A. (Ed.) (1988). *Cooperation and competition in global economy: Issues and strategies*. MA: Balinger.

Fusfeld, H.J. & Haklish, C.S. (1985). Cooperation R&D for competitors. *Harvard Business Review*. 11, 60-70.

Geringer, J.M. (1988). *Joint venture partner selection*. Westport, CT: Quorum Books.

Geringer, J.M. & Hebert, L. (1989). Control and performance of international joint ventures. *Journal of International Business Studies*, 20(2), 235-254.

Hall, R.D. (1984). *The international joint venture*. New York: Praeger.

————. (1985). *Strategies for joint ventures*. Lexington, MA: Lexington Books.

Harrigan, K.R. (1986). *Managing for joint venture success*. New York: Lexington Books.

Hladik, K.J. (1985). *International joint ventures*. Lexington, MA: Lexington Books.

Horaguchi, H. & Toyne, B. (1990). Setting the record straight: Hymer, Internalization Theory and transaction cost economics. *Journal of International Business Studies*, 21(3), pp. 487-494.

Hymer, S.H. (1968). La grande 'corporation' multinationale: Analyse de certaines raisons qui poussent a l'integrastion international des affaires. *Revue Economique*, 14(6), 949-997.

Killing, J.P. (1983). *Strategies for joint venture success*. New York: Praeger.

————. (1982). How to make a global joint venture work. *Harvard Business Review*. May-June, 120-127.

Kogut, B. (1988a). Joint ventures: Theoretical and empirical perspectives. *Strategic Management Journal*, 9, 319-332.

————. (1988b). A study of the life cycle of joint ventures. In F. Contractor and P. Lorange (Eds.) *Cooperative strategies in international business* (pp. 169-186). Lexington, MA: Lexington Books.

————. & Singh, H. (1988). Entering the United States by joint venture: Competitive rivalry and industry structure. In F. Contractor and P. Lorange (Eds.) *Cooperative strategies in international business* (pp. 241-251). Lexington, MA: Lexington Books.

Levitt, T. (1983). The globalization of markets. *Harvard Business Review*, May-June, 92-102.

Lorange, P. (1988). Co-operative strategies: Planning and control considerations. In N. Hood and J.E. Vahlne (Eds.) *Strategies in global competition*, (pp. 370-389), London: Croom Helm.

Morris, M. & Hergert, M. (1987). Trends in international collaborative agreements. *The Columbia Journal of World Business*, 22 (2), 15-21.

Neilsen, R. (1986). Cooperative strategies. *Planning Review*, March, 16-20.

————. (1987). Cooperative strategy in marketing, *Business Horizons*, 30 (July-Aug.), 61-68.

Ohmae, K. (1989). The global logic of strategic alliances. *Harvard Business Review*, March-April, 143-154.

Pfeffer, J. & Salancik, G. R. (1978). *The external control of organizations: A resource dependence perspective.* New York: Harper & Row.

————. & Nowak, P. (1976). Joint ventures and interorganizational interdependence. *Administrative Science Quarterly,* 21, 398-418.

Perlmutter, H.V. & Heenan, D.A. (1986). Cooperate to compete globally. *Harvard Business Review,* March-April, 136-152.

Porter, M. E. (1980). *Competitive strategy.* New York: The Free Press.

————. (1985). *Competitive advantage.* New York: The Free Press.

————. & Fuller, M.B. (1986). Coalitions and global strategy. In M.E. Porter (Ed.) *Competition In Global Industries* (pp. 316-343). Boston, MA: Harvard Business School Press.

————.1986. Changing patterns of international competition. *California Management Review,* 28 (2), 9-40.

Roehl, T.W. & Truitt, J.F. (1987). Stormy, open marriages are better: Evidence from U.S., Japanese, and French cooperative ventures in commercial aircraft. *The Columbia Journal of World Business.* 22 (2), 87-95.

Saba, S. (1986). The U.S. and Japanese electronics industries: Competition and cooperation. *Issues in Science and Technology,* Spring, pp. 53-60.

Sharp, D. A. (1987, June 1). Combat protectionism with global alliances, *The Wall Street Journal,* p. 22.

Wall Street Journal, (1990, December 6), p. B3.

Williamson, O.E. (1975). *Market and Hierarchies: Analysis and Antitrust Implications.* New York: The Free Press.

Chapter 2

Hybrid Arrangements as Strategic Alliances: Theoretical Issues in Organizational Combinations

Bryan Borys
David B. Jemison

Observers of the corporate landscape are witnessing an increase in the variety and complexity of organizational forms, many of which represent strategic alliances between organizations, for example, acquisitions, joint ventures, license agreements, research and development (R&D) partnerships, and so forth. These alliances result from strategic and operating moves by firms that have adapted to emerging opportunities as well as those that are repositioning themselves within existing industrial frameworks.

The hybrid arrangements represented by these strategic alliances command our attention for several reasons. From a managerial perspective, they are important because they represent alternative ways of expanding a firm's capabilities or bringing about strategic renewal; yet they present different management challenges than those found in a conventional organization. From a theoretical perspective, hybrids are of interest because they have unique character-

The editor wishes to thank the Academy of Management for permission to reprint this article, which originally appeared in *Academy of Management Review*, 1989, 14(2), pp. 234-249.

The authors extend thanks to Jerry Davis and Sim Sitkin for helpful comments on earlier drafts of this paper. A version of this paper was presented at the 1988 Academy of Management Meeting in Anaheim.

istics that challenge the capabilities of extant theory to both describe and explain their causes and operation. The purpose of this chapter is to explore the uniqueness of these organizational arrangements and to construct a theoretical basis for analyzing them.

First, we define hybrids, illustrating this definition by identifying some common forms and uses and outlining how the unique characteristics of hybrids raise difficult issues for both scholars and managers. Next, we present a model that avoids the shortcomings of existing organizational theories by incorporating the common dimensions of hybrids that make them unique organizational forms: This allows us to build a theory of hybrids sui generis. This is followed by a discussion of differences among different hybrid forms that suggest some implications for managers of hybrid organizations.

THE NATURE OF HYBRIDS

Hybrids are organizational arrangements that use resources and/ or governance structures from more than one existing organization. This definition encompasses a broad range of organizational combinations of various sizes, shapes, and purposes, some of which are formal organizations (e.g., mergers), whereas others are formalized relationships that are not properly organizations (e.g., license agreements). The recent proliferation of these organizational forms appears to be more than a minor and temporary change in the organizational landscape. Powell (1987) claimed that simultaneous pressures toward efficiency and flexibility are pushing more and more firms to experiment with hybrid arrangements. Because these pressures are unlikely to abate, researchers and managers need a more solid analytical framework as they study and use hybrids.

This broad definition allows us to examine the multiple purposes of hybrids while focusing on their common elements, a necessity in building a theoretical framework for hybrids (Kaplan, 1964). Although they arise for many reasons, a generic goal of hybrids is to avoid the disadvantages of conventional (unitary) organizations. Unitary organizations often suffer from, among other things, operational inefficiency, resource scarcity, lack of facilities to take advantage of economies of scale, or risks that are more appropriately spread across several business units. Hybrids offer a wide range of solutions to such problems because they draw upon the capabilities of multiple, independent organizations.

Of the universe of hybrid types, we will, for purposes of illustration, focus on five major ones: *Mergers* are the complete unification of two (or more) organizations into a single organization. *Acquisitions* involve the purchase of one organization by another, such that the buyer assumes control over the other. *Joint ventures* result in the creation of a new organization that is formally independent of the parents; control over and responsibility for the venture vary greatly among specific cases. *License agreements* involve the purchase of a right to use an asset for a particular time and offer rapid access to new products, technologies, or innovations. *Supplier arrangements* represent contracts for the sale of one firm's output to another.

HYBRIDS AS THEORETICAL ORPHANS

In order to adequately address hybrids, a theory should analyze them in a way peculiar to themselves alone, without resorting to theories of particular types (e.g., a theory of mergers, a theory of licensing agreements). The importance of hybrids in competitive strategies demands that a theory identify the qualities that contribute to hybrid survival/success. More generally, a theory should address the multiplicity of issues raised by hybrids, and it should integrate previous research in these areas into a theoretical whole. Existing theory fails on these counts.

The richness of hybrid forms, combined with their distinctive duality, makes them particularly difficult to analyze. A hybrid is simultaneously a single organizational arrangement and a product of sovereign organizations. This conjunctive nature of hybrids and the possibility for multiple levels of analyses call for an open systems approach (Scott, 1987), which allows the researcher to simultaneously address relations among and within organizations. At the same time, however, theories cast at a sufficient level of generalization, for instance, transaction cost analysis (Williamson, 1985), interorganizational relations theory (e.g., Lehman, 1975), and general systems theory (e.g., Boulding, 1956), achieve generality at the expense of the richness of explanation that is required by the variety of issues raised by hybrids. On the other side of the coin is the literature on hybrids, which is sparse (Astley, 1984) and mostly confined to analyses of particular types or isolated disciplinary perspectives (e.g., Killing, 1983).

In one perspective, hybrids are viewed as organizational net-works—arrangements that are "between markets and hierarchies" (Thorelli, 1986, p. 37). In this view, hybrids are seen as networks of relationships of power and trust through which organizations either exchange influence and resources (Thorelli, 1986) or take advantage of economic efficiencies (Jarillo, 1988). In such analyses, the network is viewed as an organizational actor, implying that strategic management of the network yields benefits to be distributed among the network members (Astley, 1984).

Network analysis, however, contributes little to our understanding of the determinants of membership in the network, taking for granted the existence of interorganizational fields (Warren, 1967), organizational communities (Astley and Fombrun, 1983), or non-zero-sum market relationships (Jarillo, 1988) that naturally evolve over time (Aldrich and Wheeten, 1981). Yet hybrids often are formed to disrupt such naturally occurring industry groups and to gain a competitive advantage over their members, rather than to reinforce them.

More important for hybrid analysis, however, is the failure in network theory to recognize that the hybrid-environment boundary is not the only issue. The boundary between the partners and the hybrid is just as important. Thus, we need to understand not only which organizations will become partners but also which part(s) of each partner will belong to the hybrid.

Setting boundaries for hybrids also raises the issue of how to maintain the resulting relationship over time. Powell's (1987) analysis of the historical factors leading to increased use of hybrids suggests that hybrid stability mechanisms are central to using hybrids to reap the benefits of flexibility and efficiency that give them their competitive advantage. Astley and Fombrun (1983) explored organizational analogues to the biological processes that generate stable cooperative dynamics. Their work focused on the environmental conditions that favor cooperative strategies, and it assumed that organizational self-interest will bind partners in such environments. Much of the early work on interorganizational relations focused on mechanisms that maintain orderly relations among competitive organizations, such as coordinating agencies (Litwak and Hylton, 1962) or industry-wide norms (Macaulay, 1963) (see also Benson, 1975; Lehman, 1975; Levine and White, 1961; Pfeffer, 1972). Researchers typically look outside the hybrid for stability mechanisms because hybrid partners often lack the common history necessary to generate such mechanisms internally. Yet because of partner opportunism and the fact that many hybrids are created with short life expectancies, a more robust characterization of hybrid stability is required.

Another perspective on hybrids focuses on the factors that bring two or more organizations together in the first place. Pfeffer, for example, viewed mergers and acquisitions as strategic responses to resource dependencies among organizations (1972; Pfeffer and Nowak, 1976). In a transaction cost perspective (Teece, 1982; Williamson, 1985), hybrids are seen as a way to economize on costly market transactions by incorporating them into a hierarchical framework, or hybrid arrangement. A finance-based analysis focuses on the potential gains from increased access to capital or from diversification (Breeley and Myers, 1981). Others focus on access to technologies (Jemison, 1988) or new markets (Thorelli, 1986). Hybrid theory must, however, move from lists of concrete hybrid purposes to a theory of hybrid purpose.

Uniting around a common purpose is only part of the story; the hybrid must also find a way to achieve that purpose. General organizational theories such as resource dependence (Pfeffer, 1972) and transaction cost analysis (Teece, 1982) do not address the operational issues that often plague hybrids. The difficulties of managing value creation have been studied in certain hybrid types (e.g., acquisitions [Jemison, 1988] and joint ventures [Killing, 1983]). We need, however, to uncover the general characteristics of the process of value creation in hybrids that make achievement of purpose more or less problematic.

Interdepartmental relations theories (for a review, see McCann and Galbraith, 1981) offer some insights into the problems associated with value creation in hybrids, suggesting ways to manage differentiation among partners' attitudes, goals, and perspectives. However, in this perspective an overarching authority is simplistically assumed, and thus it is incorrectly assumed that political coordination problems can be solved through optimal organizational structures, incentives, and procedures. The lack of information and goal consensus that often prevents managers within conventional organizations from applying the insights of interdepartmental relations theory (Pondy, 1970) is magnified in the hybrid case. Moreover, in the interdepartmental relations perspective, the existence of a single organizational technology that provides a guide to coordination is assumed. A central problem for hybrids, however, often is the reconciliation of heterogeneous partner operations.

Our review of extant research on hybrids suggests that this work has focused on four major areas in developing a partial understanding of this phenomenon. Even though each area makes important contributions to our understanding of hybrids, each also provides an incomplete picture. These limitations highlight the uniqueness of hybrid theory:

- First, selection of partners is important; yet it is not only the boundary between the hybrid and its environment that is important but also that between each partner and the hybrid.
- Second, in contrast to unitary organizations, hybrids are composed of sovereign organizations whose continued existence may or may not depend on the hybrid's performance; this sovereignty is a constant threat to the stability and continuity of the hybrid.
- Third, collaboration among sovereign organizations means that different purposes must be reconciled and molded into a common purpose; this means that we need not only a coalitional model of hybrid purpose but also one that recognizes that each partner's commitment to the hybrid's purpose affects the commitments of its own members to its own purpose.
- Fourth, the hybrid often incorporates several technologies. How the partners achieve value creation affects, and is affected by, the operational interdependencies among partners as well as by the other elements of the theory.

In the following section, we address each of these issues in turn, bringing existing theory to bear and suggesting some propositions for further study of hybrids. This approach leads to a discussion of managing hybrids that integrates these four issues.

A THEORY OF HYBRIDS

Hybrid Purpose

Although there is necessarily a common bond that exists before any hybrid is formed, hybrids are still the product of sovereign organizations. It may be convenient to assume that hybrids embody a purpose that is shared by the partners. Yet partners often have different goals, making the resolution of conflicting interests and the maintenance of harmony central to achieving the partners' goals. This harmony and conflict resolution is difficult to achieve because partners often do not share a common environment or domain and, thus, lack a foundation for generating a set of common understandings about the purpose of the hybrid and the process by which that purpose can be achieved. Not only do partners often lack a common domain, but the purpose of the combination may be to actually create that domain. Hybrids have a special need for institutional leadership during formation; this leadership allows them to develop common purpose and understanding (Selznick, 1967).

Although the purpose(s) of organizational combinations have been addressed by scholars in both strategic management and organization theory, neither group has had much to say about the dynamics of hybrid purpose. In his work on mergers and acquisitions, for example, Pfeffer argued that the purpose of combinations is to reduce uncertainty caused by dependency relationships (1972; Pfeffer and Nowak, 1976). In transaction cost theory, it is argued that one purpose of hybrids is to economize on the costs of conducting market exchanges (Teece, 1982; Williamson, 1985). One lesson of the strategy literature, however, is that success often comes from subverting or changing these relationships over time, rather than from following their dictates (Andrews, 1980; Porter, 1985).

The concept of purpose is especially important to hybrid functioning, insofar as it provides institutionalized direction that acts as a legitimating mechanism both among and within the partner organizations (Scott, 1987, p. 32). This legitimating function of hybrid purpose makes breadth of purpose central both to institutional leadership and to the adjudication of political conflict, and it presents a paradox: Although a broad purpose may provide sufficient "glue" for the hybrid in the face of disagreements over narrow interests, a broad purpose may not provide enough detail to adjudicate among these interests. Conversely, although a narrow and focused purpose allows partners to be clearer about what they expect from each other, it may leave many important fringe issues unaddressed. Moreover, it may prove inertial for the hybrid, preventing it from moving into fruitful, yet not-agreed-upon, areas. For example, a joint venture aimed at entering the Japanese market may become incapacitated because of disputes among partners over issues such as speed of entry, the right vehicle, or relative partner commitment. On the other hand, dedicating a joint venture to gaining a dominant share of U.S. automakers' demand for automated transfer line controls may prevent the venture from capitalizing on alternative strategies that may prove profitable.

Breadth of purpose also offers insight into the relationship between the hybrid and the partner's *internal* dynamics. A focus on hybrid purpose often simplistically assumes a stable internal political, economic, and cultural situation on the part of each partner, so that the partners can treat each other as stable, unitary actors (Allison, 1971). This raises problems for negotiation among partners because negotiators may not be able to guarantee the actions of the organizations they represent. Agency theory offers few insights because, according to it, the organization is viewed as a unitary actor and not as a combination of actors who have the potential for dissension (Fama, 1980). Making a clear organizational commitment to a particular hybrid purpose allows top management to legitimate certain actions to its subordinates by claiming that they are required to achieve the purpose; yet this phenomenon is underresearched.

Breadth of purpose is a critical dimension for developing a theory of hybrids, insofar as it affects the nature of hybrid conflict through the way it legitimates agreement among partners at the hybrid level. Moreover, it sheds light on the relations between hybrid and partner at the partner level, identifying one way in which partner management generates hybrid loyalty within the partner organization. Understanding these dynamics is the first step toward understanding hybrids. Table 2.1 outlines research-oriented propositions regarding hybrid purpose (Propositions 1A-1C).

TABLE 2.1. Research Propositions Regarding Hybrid Organizational Arrangements

Purpose

1A. In hybrids in which stated purpose is broader than the actual activities, partners will tend to make unnecessary claims on the hybrid; thus, hybrid resources are likely to be drained off by opportunistic partners.

1B. In hybrids in which stated purpose is narrower than the scope of actual activities, the hybrid will tend to suffer from lack of cooperation from partner employees.

1C. Breadth of hybrid purpose decreases along the following spectrum: mergers and acquisitions, joint ventures, license agreements, and supplier arrangements.

Boundaries

2A. The precision of boundary determination agreements is a key factor in hybrid performance.

2B. In hybrids without well-specified boundaries, partners tend to attach some of their obligations to the hybrid, thus lowering hybrid performance by saddling the hybrid with illegitimate demands on its resources.

2C. Boundary determination problems (e.g., disagreements over access to partner's resources and allocation of hybrid resources) are least frequent in mergers and acquisitions, in which ownership creates clear claims to resources and obligations, and in license agreements and supplier arrangements, in which the origin of the hybrid is determined by the solution to boundary issues. They are most frequent in joint ventures, in which the range of potential claims on partner and hybrid resources is more ambiguous.

Value Creation

3A. In hybrids in which the value-creation process is poorly understood, partner managers will have different assumptions about and understandings of the hybrid's production process, thus interfering with effective cooperation.

3B. In hybrids with pooled interdependence, value-creation problems increase along the following spectrum of shared resources: financial resources, capital equipment, technology, tacit skill (know-how), and human resources.

3C. Hybrids experience more difficulty with management of the value-creation process than do unitary organizations with the same type of interdependence.

3D. In hybrids with sequential interdependence, the key to management of the value-creation process is the quality of technical and administrative coordination mechanisms between partners (e.g., common production philosophy, production machinery, product specifications, delivery schedules, common recordkeeping).

3E. Under conditions of reciprocal interdependence, value creation will be more likely to occur when there is organizational slack within the hybrid and a reciprocal understanding of other partner organization(s).

Stability

4A. Hybrids of any type that face high levels of uncertainty and require close cooperation (e.g., those that have a broad and evolving purpose, face reciprocal interdependence, or rely on transfer of tacit knowledge) rely more on norms (i.e., culture and socialization) than do hybrids that do not face such uncertainty or require close cooperation.

4B. Because the development of normative ties entails closeness and trust, and because contracts are seldom robust against opportunism, hybrids of any type among partners that continue to compete in some markets rely less on contracts or norms than do noncompeting hybrids.

4C. Mergers and acquisitions, insofar as they are long-term hybrids, rely on hybrid-specific norms (i.e., culture, socialization processes) for stability more than do other types of hybrids.

4D. Joint ventures, which often require cooperation in the face of uncertainty and lack of close relations, rely more on institutions such as superordinate goals or "bilateral hostages" for stability than do other types of hybrids.

4E. License agreements and supplier arrangements, insofar as partner contributions tend to be measurable and specifiable in advance, will rely more on contractual mechanisms than will other types of hybrids.

Mergers and Acquisitions

5A. Managerial issues arising from breadth of purpose, interdependence among partners, and their interactions are the key determinants of performance in mergers and acquisitions.

5B. Acquisitions with reciprocal interdependence (e.g., horizontal acquisitions) are more likely to face boundary permeability difficulties than those with sequential (e.g., vertically integrated acquisitions) or pooled interdependence (e.g., unrelated acquisitions).

5C. Acquisitions with reciprocal interdependence are more likely to use institutional and normative stability mechanisms than those with sequential or pooled interdependence.

5D. The broader the acquisition's purpose, the more legitimate is the acquiring firm's involvement in a wider range of the acquired firm's activities and, thus, the greater the boundary permeability.

Joint Ventures

6A. The fit between breadth of stated purpose and actual activities is the key to joint-venture performance. When stated purpose is broader than actual activities, partners are susceptible to unnecessary claims on their resources; when stated purpose is narrower than actual activities, partner managements are unable to get their members to cooperate with the hybrid.

6B. Joint ventures (and license agreements, see below) are more likely than other hybrid types to suffer from problems of boundary definitions; thus, the precision of boundary definition is a stronger determinant of joint-venture performance than of merger, acquisition, or supplier-arrangement performance.

6C. Joint ventures involving pooled interdependencies have less permeable boundaries than do those with sequential or reciprocal interdependence.

6D. Joint ventures with less permeable boundaries use contractual stability mechanisms more than do those with greater boundary permeability.

License Agreements

7A. The key elements of performance for a license agreement are the determination of breadth of purpose and the precision of its boundary definition.

7B. Stability in new license agreements is achieved through contracts more than through other means.

7C. The key boundary determination issue for license agreements is the fit between the amount of transfer of tacit knowledge and the degree of boundary permeability.

7D. As a license agreement ages, its performance is more and more determined by its ability to generate hybrid-specific norms as stability mechanisms.

7E. The more important the transfer of tacit knowledge in a license agreement, the more permeable the boundaries of the licensor and licensee must be for the hybrid to succeed.

Supplier Arrangements

8A. The primary determinant of success in supplier arrangements is management of boundary permeability and the value-creation process.

8B. The performance of supplier arrangements is determined primarily by its ability to create and manage reciprocal interdependencies between supplier and buyer.

8C. New supplier arrangements use contracts more than other mechanisms for achieving stability.

8D. As supplier arrangements age, they rely more on hybrid-specific norms than on contracts as stability mechanisms.

Boundary Definition

Boundary issues in hybrid arrangements are unique in that not only is the hybrid-environment boundary at issue but also the point at which the partner organizations end and the hybrid begins. Decisions must be made about how much of each partner's resources can be legitimately claimed by the hybrid and to what extent each partner's governance structure has legitimate power over the hybrid. Moreover, although recently formed hybrids may be new in legal or organizational fact, they are different from start-ups because they have an immediate size and presence. Hybrid partners already have acquired assets (e.g., human, physical, and financial) and have made commitments to a variety of external constituencies. These commitments may or may not be carried into the hybrid, and they may create constraints on or offer opportunities to the hybrid.

Identification of the resources and obligations that both are and are not part of the hybrid highlights the issue of boundary *permeability*. The key question is: What is the degree and nature of the permeability of the hybrid boundary; what elements–resources, authority, obligations–are allowed to cross it? Extant theory only partly informs this question. In transaction cost analysis (Williamson, 1985), it is suggested that permeability is determined by–all other things being equal–the relative costs of handling a particular element through the hybrid or through one of the partners. Thus, transaction cost analysis offers a rigorous post hoc discussion of the criteria for boundary definition, yet it has little to say about how to identify important factors ex ante or about organizational dysfunctions associated with boundary permeability.

Elements of organizational culture, for example, play a role in defining boundaries by creating barriers to entry of human resources. One function of stories that illustrate the uniqueness of the organization is to allow members to differentiate themselves as a group from other organizations (Martin, Feldman, Hatch, and Sitkin, 1983). Such differentiation can encourage cohesion among hybrid members and allow them to transcend their parochial loyalties to the partner and act in concert for the good of the hybrid. Of course, human resources are not the only resource around which the hybrid must draw boundaries. Partners in joint ventures designed to achieve technology transfer, for instance, often encounter difficulty agreeing on the extent of the supplier's technological know-how to be transferred (Doz, Hamel, and Prahalad, 1986).

The key issue of boundary definition, therefore, is how the hybrid determines which resources and obligations belong to it and which do not. In this light, boundary definition has two important effects. First, it determines both the resources available to the hybrid and the legitimacy of partners' claims on those resources, thus affecting its purpose. It also affects the cohesiveness of hybrid members and, thus, the hybrid's ability to achieve a given purpose. Table 2.1 contains researchable propositions to explore these issues, suggesting conditions in which boundary determination is crucial for hybrid success and placing boundary determination in the context of hybrid purpose and hybrid types (Propositions 2A-2C).

Value Creation

Hybrids are established for a variety of reasons relating to the inability of one of the partners to solve an important problem. Hybrids such as marketing agreements, technology transfer agreements, and some acquisitions often face the possibility that the purpose for which the hybrid was established will be prevented by unforeseen circumstances. Hybrid management is seldom as straightforward as expected because partners often lack reciprocal understanding of the other's operations and, therefore, resistance arises from unexpected sources (Jemison, 1988). *Value creation*, as used here, refers to the process by which the capabilities of the partners are combined so that the competitive advantage of either the hybrid or one or more of the partners is improved. Thus, value creation is a joint effort that occurs after the hybrid is formed, and the operational problems that plague collaboration are central in both hybrid theory and management.

The common theme among these issues is that the hybrid creates value in a way that each of the partners alone could not. The need for cooperation raises the problem of how to coordinate different operations, production philosophies, administrative systems, and so forth. We use Thompson's (1967) typology of technological interdependence to highlight the key aspects of this issue.

Hybrids with *pooled interdependence* are those in which the hybrid provides a common pool of resources from which each of the partners can draw. In such cases, the requirements of fit are simply that each partner can make use of the resources in the pool. In financially motivated hybrids, for example, operational issues have little importance because financial resources are more easily transferable and usable in many different ways. In R&D joint ventures, on the other hand, organizations will be reluctant to join unless they can be certain that the fruits of the venture will be applicable to their operations.

In hybrids with *sequential interdependence*, one partner "hands off" to another (e.g., a supplier arrangement); the key issue is ensuring a fit between the points of contact. Here hybrids face not only technical problems, such as providing detailed enough product specifications to ensure fit among components produced by different partners, but also administrative problems, such as altering delivery schedules.

Reciprocally interdependent hybrids, in which partners exchange outputs between each other and need to learn from each other (e.g., in acquisition in which tacit skills are expected to be transferred), raise a third set of issues. The nature of the hybrid purpose that requires reciprocal interdependence generally calls for fit between a wider range of partner operations than do the other types. Because this fit often cannot be precisely specified ex ante, it must evolve through partner interaction, making organizational slack and flexibility during start-up key issues.

Thus, the interdependence of partners in the hybrid's value-creation process determines whether normal operations management is sufficient, whether special guarantees are required (e.g., product specifications), or whether, indeed, such guarantees are specifiable ex ante or must emerge over time. This complexity is magnified in practice, since hybrid managers often modify their operations to suit new purposes–or even to encourage development of new purposes. Moreover, guarantees of fit between sequentially or reciprocally interdependent units are often inseparable from boundary determination issues. Research on the value-creation process in hybrids has only begun to unravel these factors.

Breakdowns of the value-creation process stemming from problems in managing interdependencies must be identified because such problems are often masked by lack of familiarity with the other firm, distrust, and misunderstanding. Table 2.1 presents researchable propositions that suggest contingencies wherein these problems might be found (Propositions 3A-3E).

Hybrid Stability

The problem of maintaining stability over time is a final issue that must be addressed by hybrid theory. The permanence imputed to organizations by lay observers (Zucker, 1983) is not guaranteed for hybrids; in fact, hybrid arrangements are often used because they do *not* require permanent commitments from the partners. Nevertheless, stakeholders generally demand that performance in a new hybrid be similar to that of an established, permanent organization (Jemison, 1988), and they seldom allow the sort of honeymoon period of less stringent performance requirements generally experienced in other kinds of new enterprise, such as start-ups (Selznick, 1967; Tichy, 1983). These demands raise special problems for hybrids because the mechanisms that provide stability in conventional organizations develop slowly, and partner sovereignty provides a constant strain on hybrid unity. In addressing the question of how (or whether) to maintain the hybrid over time, we take as our starting point the well-known distinction between markets and hierarchies.

Williamson's (1975) market and hierarchies scheme provides our initial characterization of stability alternatives: market-mediated contracts versus organizationally grounded authority. Recent work has extended this notion, recognizing that some market relations have hierarchical characteristics (Granovetter, 1987; Stinchcombe, 1985), and, thus, suggesting that the distinction between contract and hierarchy in hybrids is also one of degree (Thorelli, 1986).

In applying this idea to hybrids, however, we must also recognize that resource to hierarchical mechanisms is different for hybrids than for unitary organizations. Traditional organization theories propose that a conventional organization achieves stability by instituting rules, procedures, and roles that create expectations of stability and dependability among members and stakeholders (Weber, 1946). Organizational institutions arise from the rational adoption of routines (Nelson and Winter, 1982), from acceptance of standard operating procedures (Cyert and March, 1963), or from authority that is taken for granted (Zucker, 1977). A network of institutionalized expectations provides a stable reference point from which organizational members can coordinate their actions.

From a cultural perspective, the power of organizational institutions to provide stability is rooted in shared norms and values (Schein, 1985). However, it may be that sharing per se is not the key to stability (Martin and Meyerson, 1986). The underlying source of cultural cohesion may result from members' expectations that they will be dealt with fairly, which encourages them to submit to organizational authority (Wilkins and Ouchi, 1983, p. 476). This latter formulation suggests that legitimacy and trust are key to nonmarket mechanisms of hybrid stability (Jarillo, 1988). Hybrids, however, often cannot capitalize on such reservoirs of authority and trust because their members lack a common history. Moreover, because some hybrids are not expected to continue over time, their members do not engage in the sorts of behaviors that generate legitimate authority and trust.

A second type of stability mechanism is represented by practices that are common to an industry or economic sector. Although such practices lack the normative force of shared values and legitimate authority, they do create stable expectations among hybrid members. As such, they often are adopted by many organizations whose managers recognize their practical utility and wish to avoid violating standard practices, even though these may not be normatively binding (Macaulay, 1963).

Levine and White (1961), for example, assumed the existence of an outside organization that directs the actions of other organizations. Although applicable in certain cases, such as acquisitions and some forms of cartel, many hybrids lack a strong, central partner. Facing a common outside threat may lead to coordination among organizations (Cummings, 1984). However, we should not overestimate the power of mutual interest to generate cooperation in competitive settings (Axelrod, 1984; Schelling, 1960). Even in situations of mutual advantage, some partners may be able to profit at the expense of other partners, threatening the stability of the hybrid (Doz et al., 1986). Some partners ensure hybrid stability either by tying each partner's parochial interests to the hybrid's success or by exchanging "bilateral hostages," such as key personnel or capital equipment (Kogut and Rolander, 1984). Such practices are easier to undertake than the generation of normatively binding agreements such as organizational culture, but they lack the power of the latter mechanisms.

A third mechanism for stability is the contract, which is guaranteed by forces outside the hybrid (e.g., the courts). One benefit of these mechanisms is that the institutions of contract and exchange that make them possible are generalized throughout the economy and, thus, are readily available and understood by the hybrid partners–although some multicultural hybrids provide important exceptions (Granovetter, 1987). The cost of such available and simple institutions, however, is their lack of flexibility and richness; the shortcomings of contractual transactions are well known in economics (Williamson, 1975, 1985), sociology (Granovetter, 1985), and organization theory (Ouchi, 1980). Contracting problems raised by opportunism and information asymmetries are exacerbated in hybrids; moreover, contracts are problematic in mergers, acquisitions, and some joint ventures in which partner obligations are designed to change over time and, thus, cannot be predicted ex ante (Harrigan, 1985).

Thus, hybrid stability can be achieved by shared norms and expectations of justice, by the adoption of common and general practices, or by relying on extrahybrid institutions, such as the legal system, for enforcement of hybrid contracts. Each of these has disadvantages: Although hybrid-specific norms are powerful and can be quite flexible, they are difficult to develop. Hybrid-specific institutions are more readily available, but they are notoriously weak against opportunistic partners. Contracts are difficult to specify under conditions of uncertainty for which hybrid arrangements are otherwise particularly well suited. Table 2.1 presents a series of propositions that explore the nature and form of hybrid stability mechanisms (Propositions 4A-4E).

GENERATING INSIGHTS INTO HYBRID MANAGEMENT

Our exploration of the uniqueness of hybrid organizations and the theoretical issues they raise suggest that hybrids need not be theoretical orphans. Our theory allows both scholars and managers to consider hybrids in a class of their own and, at the same time, to link the model with previous research. The above discussion has shown that although unitary organizations face the same set of four issues, hybrids face them in different ways because of the need to share resources and governance structures from sovereign organizations; extant theory falls short of addressing this problem. In this section, we extend this theoretical exploration, identifying some important managerial issues and additional propositions for research.

We have made it clear that the four issues in our model–breadth of purpose, boundary permeability, value creation, and stability mechanisms–are mutually determinant and highly interdependent. We have discussed some of the more important interrelationships in our treatment of the individual issues above. For example, we discussed how hybrid purpose can lend legitimacy to claims on partner resources, thereby increasing boundary permeability, and we have discussed how boundaries determine membership and vice versa, thus restricting the range of participants in debates over purpose.

Our discussion of these issues was necessarily abstract because of the prior lack of a theory of hybrids. In what follows, we show that in addition to its contribution to theory building, this model offers insights into the managerial challenges presented by different types of hybrids. We will discuss these challenges in light of the five types of hybrids we used as examples, illustrating in more detail the differences among hybrid types.

Mergers and Acquisitions

The central issues in analyses of mergers and acquisitions are type of interdependence and breadth of purpose, which, in turn, determine the extent of boundary permeability and stability mechanisms. The greater the reciprocal interdependence between the firms, the more permeable their boundaries must be to facilitate this close interaction and the greater their need for institutional forms of stability because contracts cannot guarantee the fulfillment of complex and potentially ambiguous performances. The less interdependent, the more a contractual form of stability becomes useful (e.g., a conglomerate).

The more interdependent the partners in an acquisition, the greater the need for boundary permeability. A long history of organizational research has demonstrated the importance of matching responsibility with authority. We can extend this to the hybrid case by hypothesizing that in successful acquisitions, hybrid managers will have authority over those resources and obligations associated with reciprocally interdependent activities. As a corollary, we suggest that the broader the purpose of the acquisition, the more potentially permeable are the boundaries of the acquired firm, because the acquirer has a claim to a broader set of capabilities (Haspeslagh and Farquahar, 1987).

We suggested above that mergers and acquisitions rely more on hybrid-specific norms than on other types of stability mechanisms. Here we add that, other things being equal, the broader the purpose, the greater the reliance on normative ties, since they are more flexible and can maintain a wider set of relations than can hybrid institutions or contracts. In such close relationships, stability mechanisms and boundaries will change over time, moving toward greater reliance on normative stability and greater boundary permeability. These changes should reveal new possibilities for the merger, and they should lead managers to revise old purposes and discover new ones (March, 1978). Thus, we recognize the interaction between strategy content and strategic processes (Jemison, 1981). We also argue for development of a better understanding of the dynamics of purpose in hybrids, one that transcends simplistic and static notions of strategic fit (Jemison and Sitkin, 1986).

Acquisitions are different from mergers in several important ways, some of which make breadth of purpose particularly salient. One firm is often dominant regarding size and other dimensions. Therefore, a key issue in an acquisition is how to allocate control among the firms. In addition, the management of boundary permeability is important if the purpose of the acquisition is to transfer capabilities and the capability must be preserved (Haspeslagh and Farquahar, 1987). Table 2.1 presents several propositions regarding acquisitions in light of our theory (Propositions 5A-5D).

Joint Ventures

Joint ventures are the most difficult of all hybrid arrangements to characterize because they are simultaneously contractual agreements between two or more organizations and a separate legal (and usually organizational) entity with its own purpose. Despite the inherent necessity for collaboration, joint-venture partners retain organizational sovereignty, thus maintaining differentiation within the hybrid that may hamper cooperation. This problem, combined with the wide range of forms of joint ventures, prevents a simple characterization of the key analytic issues. Here, we indicate the major interconnections among the four elements of hybrid theory, illustrating what effects purpose and value creation have on boundaries and how boundaries and the difficulties of managing them make stability mechanisms important.

Because joint ventures typically are formed by partners that remain independent, partner managers often face difficulties in motivating their employees to cooperate with hybrid management. In response, hybrid managers invoke the hybrid's purpose to legitimate their claims upon partner employees. We can contrast this case with that of mergers and acquisitions, in which hybrid management often has greater organizational authority to back up such claims than it does in a joint venture; whereas in a license agreement or supplier arrangement, the need for collaboration often is not as high as in a joint venture. Thus, the ability of hybrid management to make legitimate claims on partner employees and resources is particularly salient for joint ventures, and it provides an important motivational force.

Purpose clearly affects boundary permeability as well. The relationship between each partner and the joint venture is not bound by clear-cut institutions of ownership, as in mergers and acquisitions or by contract, as in license agreements and supplier arrangements. Moreover, a joint venture often is an evolving collaboration. Thus, the nature of its hybrid-partner boundaries is constantly open to debate, and the legitimating effects of hybrid purpose are key to proper determination of these boundaries.

Hybrid boundaries are also affected by the partner interdependencies involved in the value-creation process. Although joint ventures are often created with the intent of keeping the venture separate from the partner organizations, those with more complex forms of interdependence (sequential or reciprocal) require greater boundary permeability in order to ensure proper coordination.

Yet this degree of permeability is very difficult to specify contractually ex ante. Moreover, the close collaboration typically found in joint ventures requires that the joint venture develop its own identity and institutions. In fact, partner involvement intended either to help the venture or to restrict its activities often threatens its ability to accomplish its purpose.

Thus, the joint venture's purpose and the nature of its value creation affect its boundaries–the determination of which is a key issue for such a flexible organizational form. This dynamic process, as well as the nature of the partner joint-venture relationship, makes institutionalized forms of stability prominent. Table 2.1 contains propositions that explore these insights into joint ventures (Propositions 6A-6D).

License Agreements

License agreements, that is, agreements by which one firm buys the right to use an asset for a period of time (e.g., a particular production process, a patent on a device), typically involve a narrow purpose and limited time frame, and are enforced by a contract. The licensor receives a source of royalties and revenues with little additional investment or return on prior R&D expenditures. Likewise, the licensee is able to lever its activities (e.g., increase its market coverage or overcome a weakness by using someone else's R&D or product development). Licensors often manipulate the boundaries of the agreement to their own advantage by allowing certain innovations to cross the boundary, thereby encouraging the licensee to continue the agreement, and by withholding others.

Interdependence is usually pooled (both parties using the same asset), rather than reciprocal, in such hybrids, leading to little need for extensive operational fit. Some license agreements, however, do allow the licensor access to any technology developed by the licensee through use of the asset (e.g., using a particular production process may generate new capabilities), raising significant operational issues, and in turn, affecting determination of hybrid-partner boundaries.

License agreements may lead to other forms of collaboration as firms increase their knowledge of each other through interaction. But initially, the central issue is specification of purpose through contractual terms (after the initial process of selecting a licensee with the capability to exploit the right once it is licensed). Because license agreements tend to be unstable due to competition, changing technology, and relative rates of partner learning (Doz et al., 1986), the importance of stability mechanisms increases over time. Despite the relative inflexibility of contracts, license agreements tend to rely on them in the absence of the close and broad collaboration required to make other mechanisms feasible. Table 2.1 presents propositions regarding license agreements based on the previous discussion (Propositions 7A-7E).

Supplier Arrangements

Supplier arrangements can be characterized as contractual agreements to provide a particular type or line of goods or services within a specific time frame. Interdependence is usually sequential, with the supplier fitting its piece into the production process of the buyer. Typically, boundary permeability of the supplier must allow inspection of processes to ensure product quality, manufacturing capability, and delivery reliability. In addition, the buyer's boundary must allow the supplier to develop the product to fit the appropriate technical specifications and delivery schedule.

Over time, though, many firms develop more sophisticated supplier arrangements in which reciprocal interdependence becomes strategically important; purpose broadens; and stability mechanisms become institutionally based as well as contractual. Examples of this are Marks and Spencer in the United Kingdom, Benetton in Italy, and many Japanese firms. In these situations, the suppliers have become an integral part of the firm's entire production process, and they work closely with the firm to make suggestions about improving product quality, new materials, new production processes, and so forth. Although contracts still guide production, product specification, and delivery schedules, suppliers in these arrangements have adopted institutional norms that encourage action on behalf of the entire hybrid. Table 2.1 presents propositions designed to explore these insights (Propositions 8A-8D).

CONCLUSION

The pressures firms face to renew their capabilities, to enter new product-market arenas, to deal with resource constraints, and to develop internationally are often well met by hybrid arrangements. These arrangements, in turn, pose new and important challenges to researchers and managers alike. For managers, hybrids are becoming more important as strategic options, yet they are a phenomenon for which managers' past experiences and cognitive maps have not adequately prepared them. For researchers, hybrids challenge existing theory to explain the peculiar dynamics of hybrid purpose, boundaries, value creation, and stability.

Traditional organizational and strategic management theories offer some insights, but they are limited in their applicability to the case of hybrids because they deal with unitary organizations and, therefore, do not address the unique problems raised by an organizational entity composed of two or more sovereign organizations. Although previous attempts at characterizing hybrids have generated some powerful ideas, organizational research has lacked a systematic theoretical framework for hybrid analysis.

Our response to this problem has been to develop a model capable of exploring these issues and to demonstrate some of the insights the model generates. These are centered on four concepts: the breadth of hybrid purpose and the claims and plans that it legitimates; the permeability of hybrid-partner boundaries and the resources and obligations allowed to cross them; the interdependence of partner operations in the value-creation process and the complexity of the arrangements required to manage it; and the nature of the hybrid's stability mechanisms. Not only is each of these issues significant in its own right, but we have also demonstrated that understanding the interactions among them offers insights into hybrids. The ambiguity and complexity of the issues created by hybrid organizations should not deter scholars from pursuing the important questions they raise. We hope that the perspective presented in this paper has provided a first step toward generating a deeper understanding of this increasingly pervasive organizational phenomenon.

REFERENCES

Aldrich, H. E., & Wheeten, D. A. (1981) Organization–sets, action sets, and networks: Making the most of simplicity. In P. C. Nystrom & W. H. Starbuck (Eds.), *Handbook of organizational design* (Vol. 1, pp. 345-408). New York: Oxford University Press.

Allison, G. T. (1971) *Essence of decision.* Boston: Little, Brown.

Andrews, K. R. (1980) *The concept of corporate strategy.* Homewood, IL: Irwin.

Astley, W. G. (1984) Toward an appreciation of collective strategy. *Academy Management Review,* 9, 526-535.

Astley, W. G., & Fombrun, C. J. (1983) Collective strategy: Social ecology of organizational environments. *Academy of Management Review,* 8, 576-587.

Axelrod, R. M. (1984) *The evolution of cooperation.* New York: Basic Books.

Benson, J. K. (1975) The interorganizational network as a political economy. *Administrative Science Quarterly,* 20, 229-249.

Boulding, K. E. (1956) General systems theory: The skeleton of science. *Management Science,* 2, 197-208.

Breeley, R., & Myers, S. (1981) *Principles of corporate finance.* New York: McGraw-Hill.

Cummings, T. G. (1984) Transorganizational development. *Research in Organizational Behavior,* 6, 367-422.

Cyert, R. M. & March, J. G. (1963) *A behavioral theory of the firm.* Englewood Cliffs, NJ: Prentice-Hall.

Doz, Y., Hamel, G., & Prahalad, C. K. (1986) *Strategic partnerships: Success or surrender?* Unpublished manuscript, INSEAD, Fountainebleau, France.

Fama, E. F. (1980) Agency problems and the theory of the firm. *Journal of Law and Economics,* 88, 288-307.

Granovetter, M. (1985) Economic action and social structure: The problem of embeddedness. *American Journal of Sociology,* 91, 481-510.

Granovetter, M. (1987) *Society and economy.* Unpublished manuscript.

Harrigan, K. R. (1985) *Strategies for joint ventures.* Lexington, MA: Lexington Books.

Haspeslagh, P. C., & Farquahar, A. (1987) *Managing acquisition integration: The gatekeeping role.* Working Paper, INSEAD, Fountainebleau, France.

Jarillo, J. C. (1988) On strategic networks. *Strategic Management Journal,* 9, 34-41.

Jemison, D. B. (1981) The contributions of administrative behavior to strategic management. *Academy of Management Review,* 6, 633-642.

Jemison, D. B. (1988) Value creation in acquisition integration: The role of strategic capability transfer. In G. Liebcap (Ed.), *Corporate restructuring through mergers, acquisitions and leveraged buyouts* (pp. 191-218). Greenwich, CT: JAI Press.

Jemison, D. B., & Sitkin, S. B. (1986) Corporate acquisitions: A process perspective. *Academy of Management Review,* 11, 145-163.

Kaplan, A. (1964) *The conduct of inquiry.* New York: Chandler.

Killing, J. P. (1983) *Strategies for joint venture success.* New York: Praeger.

Kogut, B., & Rolander, D. (1984) *Stabilizing cooperative ventures: Evidence from the telecommunications and auto industry.* Working Paper WP 84-11, The Wharton School, University of Pennsylvania.

Lehman, E. W. (1975) A paradigm for the analysis of interorganizational relations. In E. W. Lehman (Ed.), *Coordinating health care: Explorations in interorganizational relations* (Vol. 17, pp. 24-30). Beverly Hills, CA: Sage.

Levine, S., & White, P. E. (1961) Exchange as a conceptual framework for the study of interorganizational relationships. *Administrative Science Quarterly*, 5, 583-601.

Litwak, E., & Hylton, L. F. (1962) Interorganizational analysis: A hypothesis on coordinating agencies. *Administrative Science Quarterly*, 6, 395-420.

Macaulay, S. (1963) Non-contractual relations in business: A preliminary study. *American Sociological Review*, 28, 55-69.

March, J. G. (1978) Bounded rationality, ambiguity, and the engineering of choice. *Bell Journal of Economics*, 9, 578-608.

Martin, J., Feldman, M. S., Hatch, J. J., & Sitkin, S. B. (1983) The uniqueness paradox in organizational stories. *Administrative Science Quarterly*, 28, 438-453.

Martin, J., & Meyerson, D. (1986) *Organizational cultures and the denial, channeling, and acceptance of ambiguity.* Working Paper 807R, Graduate School of Business, Stanford University.

McCann, J., & Galbraith, J. R. (1981) Interdepartmental relations. In P. Nystrom & W. Starbuck (Eds.), *Handbook of organizations* (Vol. 2, pp. 60-84). New York: Oxford University Press.

Nelson, R. R., & Winter, S. G. (1982) *An evolutionary theory of economic change.* Cambridge, MA: Belknap Press.

Ouchi, W. G. (1980) Markets, bureaucracies, and clans. *Administrative Science Quarterly*, 25, 129-141.

Pfeffer, J. (1972) Merger as a response to organizational interdependence. *Administrative Science Quarterly*, 17, 382-394.

Pfeffer, J., & Nowak, P. (1976) Joint ventures and interorganizational interdependence. *Administrative Science Quarterly*, 21, 398-418.

Pondy, L. R. (1970) Toward a theory of internal resource allocation. In M. Zald (Ed.), *Power in organizations* (pp. 270-311). Nashville, TN: Vanderbilt University.

Porter, M. E. (1985) *Competitive advantage: Creating and sustaining superior performance.* New York: Free Press.

Powell, W. W. (1987) Hybrid organizational arrangements. *California Management Review*, 30(1), 67-87.

Schein, E. (1985) *Organizational culture and leadership.* San Francisco: Jossey-Bass.

Schelling, T. C. (1960) *The Strategy of Conflict.* Cambridge, MA: Harvard University Press.

Scott, W. R. (1987) *Organizations: Rational, natural, and open systems.* Englewood Cliffs, NJ: Prentice-Hall.

Selznick, P. (1967) *Leadership in administration.* New York: Harper & Row.

Stinchcombe, A. L. (1985) Contracts as hierarchical documents. In A. L. Stinchcombe & C. A. Heiner (Eds.), *Organization theory and project management* (pp. 121-170). London: Oxford University Press.

Teece, D. J. (1982) Towards an economic theory of the multiproduct firm. *Journal of Economic Behavior and Organization*, 3, 39-63.

Thompson, J. D. (1967) *Organizations in action.* New York: McGraw-Hill.

Thorelli, H. B. (1986) Networks: Between markets and hierarchies. *Strategic Management Journal*, 7, 37-51.

Tichy, N. M. (1983) *Managing strategic change: Technical, political, and cultural dynamics.* New York Wiley-Interscience.

Warren, R. L. (1967) The interorganizational field as a focus for investigation. *Administrative Science Quarterly*, 12, 396-419.

Weber, M. (1946) *From Max Weber: Essays in sociology.* London: Oxford University Press.

Wilkins, A. L., & Ouchi, W. G. (1983) Efficient cultures: Exploring the relationship between culture and organizational performance. *Administrative Science Quarterly*, 28, 468-481.

Williamson, O. E. (1975) *Market and hierarchies, analysis and antitrust implications: A study in the economics of internal organization.* New York: Free Press.

Williamson, O. E. (1985) *The economic institutions of capitalism.* New York: Free Press.

Zucker, L. G. (1977) The role of institutionalization in cultural persistence. *American Sociological Review*, 42, 726-743.

Zucker, L. G. (1983) Organizations as institutions. *Research in the Sociology of Organizations*, 2, 1-47.

Chapter 3

Forms of Interorganizational Governance for Multinational Alliances

Richard N. Osborn
C. Christopher Baughn

Multinational firm alliances are being touted as critical mechanisms for competing in global markets and coping with the increasingly rapid pace of technological development (Ghoshal, 1987; Harrigan, 1987). Yet, although the number of international cooperations appears to be increasing dramatically (Auster, 1987; Hergert and Morris, 1988), they are notoriously unstable, prone to failure, and at best, difficult to govern (Morris and Hergert, 1987; Pucik, 1987). Prior work has suggested that the governance form chosen for these alliances may be particularly important in influencing their success and their ability to meet the objectives of the participating firms (Harrigan, 1988; Rugman, 1981).

The purpose of this study was to provide an empirical analysis of some factors underlying the choice of interorganizational governance form made in newly formed multinational cooperative relationships. We examined joint ventures (which involve creating a new legal entity with shared equity) and contractual agreements that do not involve shared equity (such as licensing, distribution, techni-

Preparation of this manuscript was supported by a grant from the National Science Foundation (No. SES-8504397), Richard N. Osborn, Jon Olson, and Mitsuyo Hanada, co-principal investigators. The authors want to express their appreciation to G. Astley, R. Zammuto, and the many reviewers for their assistance. We determined the order of authorship that appears above by a flip of a coin.

The editor would like to thank the Academy of Management for the permission to reprint this article, which originally appeared in *Academy of Management Journal*, 1990, 33(3), pp. 503-519.

cal assistance, supply, and marketing agreements) as alternative governance modes. Both joint ventures and contractual agreements are commonly used to exchange technology, products, and services across national and firm boundaries (Harrigan, 1987; Hennart, 1988; Porter, 1986).

Our analysis focused on technological factors, building upon previous research in transaction cost economics, international strategy, and organization theory. We examined the interrelationships among form of governance, two technological factors, and parent size for a number of U.S.-Japanese cooperations announced during the three-year period from 1984 to 1986. The technological factors investigated were (1) technological intensity as measured by the ratio between research and development (R&D) expenditures and sales for the product area of the alliance and (2) intent to conduct joint R&D. We emphasized technological factors because they are theoretically important, they help link apparently divergent theoretical perspectives, and they are likely to play an increasingly important role in the future formation and forms of international cooperations (Doz, 1988; Dunning, 1988). Many of the alliances made between firms with headquarters in developed nations are in high-tech areas, and many also involve joint R&D (Auster, 1986; Hladik, 1988).

GOVERNANCE FORMS AND TRANSACTION COSTS

Research in transaction cost economics, international strategy, and organization theory has addressed the development of efficient and effective governance forms for multinational cooperative efforts. According to Williamson's (1975) transaction cost perspective, balancing efficiency and protection leads firms to select a mix of hierarchies and markets to manage transactions. Market transactions, involving exchange between autonomous economic entities, frequently serve as efficient contracting modes. Their use may be hazardous or cumbersome, however, when information regarding circumstances relevant to an exchange is asymmetrically distributed between the parties or when contracts cannot adequately specify the parties' responses to changing conditions over the duration of the contract.

Given the tendency of parties to behave opportunistically under ambiguous conditions and the high costs frequently associated with achieving information parity, the transaction costs of market exchanges may outweigh their benefits. Hierarchical internal organization will become the preferred operating mode under conditions of substantial uncertainty and complexity (Jones, 1983; Williamson, 1975).

Under transaction cost theory, incentives to exploit information differences opportunistically shrink when the parties place transactions in a single hierarchy. Further, such internal organization may enhance information coding, the convergence of expectations, and auditing control, though at greater costs than when price alone can moderate the exchange between parties (Williamson, 1975).

Agreements as Quasi-Markets and Joint Ventures as Quasi-Hierarchies

Full internalization of interfirm transactions through acquisition is, of course, not the only alternative to market-based modes of governance. As several writers have noted, firms may use a wide range of transaction forms in implementing cooperative strategies (Anderson and Gatignon, 1986; Contractor and Lorange, 1988). Following the analysis of Thorelli (1986), we separated various forms of cooperation into market-dominated and hierarchically dominated forms.

Contractual agreements to sell or provide technology, products, or services (e.g., supply and licensing agreements) are market-dominated. Joint ventures, on the other hand, can be seen as quasi-hierarchies.[1] We defined a joint venture as a new legal entity with full status as a corporate entity in which both parents share equity (cf. Auster, 1987; Killing, 1988; Osborn, Hunt, and Jauch, 1980).

Joint ventures provide joint ownership and control over the use and fruits of assets (Kogut and Singh, 1988). They may be used to bypass market inefficiencies. Equity control and both parties' sharing in the profits or losses attained through the venture's perfor-

---

1. As several researchers have noted, a joint venture is both legally and conceptually different from a minority equity participation investment, in which a firm invests directly into a second company (Killing, 1988; Kogut and Singh, 1988). We discuss minority equity investments later in this article.

mance serve to align the interests of the parent firms, reducing the opportunism that may arise in contractual agreements (Hennart, 1988; Stuckey, 1983). Complete ex ante specification of ongoing activities and behavior requirements is therefore not required (Kogut, 1988). The joint-venture form may also allow for a superior monitoring mechanism, since joint-venture owners may be legally entitled to independently verified financial information as well as to information acquired through direct observation.

Though a joint venture does represent a partial internalization, it does not involve complete pooling of the parent's profit streams or the establishment of a single hierarchy. As Harrigan (1988) noted, shared ownership and shared decision-making arrangements can be cumbersome to manage and may reduce the speed with which many actions in pursuit of global strategies can be taken. Although the parties can renegotiate the provisions of both contractual agreements and joint ventures at any time, a joint venture is normally considered more difficult than a contractual agreement to establish, terminate, and fundamentally change (Harrigan, 1988). Finally, differences between home and host cultures in multinational joint ventures may amplify the effort and time required to build a common hierarchy that bridges the gaps in partners' cultural, linguistic, and organizational traditions (Anderson and Gatignon, 1986; Hayashi, 1987; Moroi and Itami, 1987; Zimmerman, 1985).

In short, joint ventures may offer some potential for protection and control, but at substantial administrative costs. The time and costs involved in developing multiparty equity arrangements coupled with the need for give-and-take in jointly managed ventures give the joint-venture form of governance less strategic flexibility than less binding forms of cooperation (Harrigan, 1988).

OPTIMIZING RELATIONS AMONG TRANSACTION, TECHNOLOGY, AND STRUCTURE

Jones (1987) extended the transaction cost perspective, explicitly incorporating technological factors. He argued that "the main imperative facing organizations is three pronged–they must simultaneously optimize the relationship among transactions, technology and structure" (1987: 214). We drew two themes for studying the interorganizational governance forms of international alliances from this interactive view.

Uncertainty, Control, and Governance Form

Several authors have suggested that the recent dramatic increase in multinational alliances represents the emergence of global strategies among firms responding to the internationalization of technological competence and markets (Geringer, 1988; Osborn and Baughn, 1987; Porter and Fuller, 1986). Technological globalization is particularly evident in rapidly advancing areas characterized by high R&D-to-sales ratios. In such technologically intense areas as pharmaceuticals, computers, and semiconductors, specific technical developments in products and processes are likely to come from Japan, North America, or Western Europe.

Uncertainty and control provide a conceptual link between technological intensity and the governance form chosen for an alliance. Technological intensity, as evidenced by a high R&D-to-sales ratio, is likely to reflect high uncertainty, which raises the transaction costs of market-dominated mechanisms. Facing higher costs for monitoring, enforcing, and regulating via market-dominated mechanisms, firms might be likely to select more hierarchical forms of alliance governance as technological intensity increases (cf. Jones, 1987; Williamson, 1975).

In technologically intensive areas, firms are likely to be particularly concerned about control of proprietary knowledge, products, and services. The classic problem of information valuation through market mechanisms may also enhance a preference for transaction forms providing high control. Agreeing upon a price for information is problematic unless a buyer knows what the information is–yet once that knowledge is disclosed, the buyer need not pay for it (Anderson and Gatignon, 1986; Calvet, 1981).

Such arguments explain the relationships that researchers have found between R&D expenditures and a preference for wholly owned subsidiaries over joint ventures (Stopford and Wells, 1972). The quasi-hierarchical joint-venture form does not appear to provide the protection and control attributed to complete internalization. In extending this argument to the choice between the joint-venture form and nonequity forms of cooperation, we might assume that quasi-market arrangements would be the least preferred mode of transaction in technologically intensive product areas.

However, firms may prefer arm's-length contractual agreements. They may use them to control what information is shared, to reduce the chance that knowledge transfer will exceed the scope intended by the parents, and to build interfirm trust before the parties undertake more involved activities (Killing, 1988). Another line of inquiry also suggested that firms forming alliances in technologically intensive areas might prefer agreements.

Technological Positioning and Governance Form

Several investigations of rapidly evolving technological areas have suggested that a key factor for a firm's survival is its positioning within a successful network of suppliers, manufacturers, and distributors. Agreements may be preferable to joint ventures for establishing such an initial position in a new technological area.

In high-tech areas, institutional and interorganizational infrastructures are often poorly developed, likely to change frequently, and particularly weak across national boundaries (Van De Ven and Poole, 1989). Early in the development of new products, several feasible designs having various degrees of governmental support from different nations often compete. Such is currently the case with high-resolution TV and such was the case with nuclear power and VCRs. In such areas, knowledge develops rapidly as various firms move to commercialization, consider entering an area, or merely seek to monitor the development of a technology. In short, firms may be seeking to position themselves. They may still be deciding what portions of the technology to keep, whom they will use as suppliers, and how they might successfully market new products (Skinner, Donnelly, and Ivancevich, 1987; Walker and Weber, 1987). Thus, firms may seek to establish or tap institutional and interorganizational infrastructures and become viable members of a winning network of organizations (Garud and Van De Ven, 1987; Van De Ven and Poole, 1989). Only as a technology stabilizes and it becomes clear that an alliance might be an important source of revenue might firms quasi-internalize such an arrangement through an equity relationship.

In high-tech areas, firms may generate numerous technical spin-offs, many of which are not crucial to their viability. Not all can be commercialized via equity investments. Such spin-offs may also facilitate the eventual establishment of an industry standard by spreading core technological features across apparently diverse products.

Given the need for flexibility, as well as the limited ability of a joint venture to protect a partner's technology, it would seem that involvement in high-tech areas would limit the feasibility of selecting quasi-hierarchical structures as governance forms. Thus,

> Hypothesis 1: To the extent that a cooperative alliance involves areas with high R&D intensity, agreements are more likely than a joint venture to be the chosen form of governance.

Decisions to Engage in Joint R&D

Although quasi-hierarchies like joint ventures may be expensive and time-consuming to develop and may provide only limited protection from exploitation, firms still may prefer them when facing the technological uncertainty associated with joint R&D. Technological commercialization often yields inseparable tasks that favor a hierarchy (cf. Maitland, Bryson, and Van De Ven, 1985). Market-mediated mechanisms may not provide adequate control over the myriad of complex judgmental tasks involved in R&D. In R&D efforts, individuals often need to interact to develop both new ideas and a special language for problem identification and problem-solving (Osborn, Olson, and Hanada, 1985). In joint R&D, the knowledge being exchanged is not yet fully embodied in designs and specifications but embedded in the experience and skills of people–it is what Polanyi (1958) termed "tacit knowledge." Further, information asymmetries may well arise during the R&D process itself, reducing the ability of an a priori agreement to capture the value of each partner's contributions adequately. Equity links increasing the internalization of a transaction would therefore appear to be preferable for transferring noncodified technological know-how (Hennart, 1988).

The decision to engage in joint R&D may also signal a commitment to a long-term relationship between parent firms. Participating firms are moving their joint relationship back up the value-added chain, taking longer to get a payoff and to build an effective organization. Developing new products and services may also allow even the largest multinationals to adjust their global strategies to incorporate the fruits of a joint venture (cf. Porter & Fuller, 1986). Thus,

> Hypothesis 2: The intention to conduct joint R&D increases the probability that firms will adopt the joint-venture form of governance for an alliance rather than agreements.

Parent Size

Organizational size is another of the many other factors we would expect to influence the establishment and form of multinational alliances (Dunning, 1988; Kogut and Singh, 1988; Osborn et al., 1980; Porter and Fuller, 1986). Unfortunately, the theoretical meaning of size remains elusive, since various researchers have interpreted it in quite different ways (cf. Kimberly, 1976). Size also remains outside the theoretical specifications of transaction cost economics. For instance, Jones (1987) questioned whether large organizations might be able to buffer themselves from specific transaction cost requirements, yet he did not incorporate size into transaction cost theory.

Organizational size can be tied to opportunism. Very large organizations may be comparatively invulnerable. With abundant slack resources, multiple technical cores, the ability to retaliate against incursions (alone or in cooperation with government), and a vested interest in protecting its reputation, a very large organization may be less concerned than a smaller firm with a potential partner's possible exploitation (Doz, 1988). Thus, the specific technological factors underlying a cooperation might not receive the same consideration that a smaller firm would accord them. Research on global strategy has suggested that large multinationals will, or should, be more concerned with global strategic positioning than with the transaction costs associated with any one alliance or the tactical adjustments in form stemming from technological factors (e.g., Porter and Fuller, 1986). Several other analyses have suggested that whom a large multinational links with may be more important than how the link is made (see Geringer, 1988, for a review).

Work in organization theory dating back to Blau (1970) and Blau and Schoenherr (1971) has strongly suggested that the structures of very large firms may not reflect the importance of technological factors. More recently, writers such as Hannan and Freeman (1984) and Astley (1985) have also pointed to the intransigence associated with very large organizational size. If internal structures do not vary much with technological factors for very large organizations, the structural forms adopted for multinational alliances might be similarly resistant.

Whether very large size is seen as evidence of invulnerability, a global strategy, or bureaucratic intransigence, one point is clear. The governance form of a cooperative alliance needs to satisfy both parties involved. If only one (or neither one) of the parties is a very large multinational, vulnerability to exploitation may exist, and the economic effectiveness of the transaction itself may be deemed critical. That is, an alliance is more likely to represent a key element in a parent's overall strategy when the parent is not extremely large. In such cases, the interplay among technological factors may be quite important (Jones, 1987). For instance, a comparatively vulnerable, small firm entering a high-tech cooperation in which joint R&D is planned places its sole technical core at risk and may need the expensive protection of the joint-venture form. But when such a firm is not intending to conduct joint R&D, it may well attempt to protect its technical core by using the quasi-market form to control what information is to be shared (Doz, 1988; Harrigan, 1985). Conversely, if both firms are very large multinationals, the interplay among technological factors may be less important. Thus,

> Hypothesis 3: Parent size interacts with technological factors in determining the form of governance firms choose for a cooperative alliance. When both parents are large multinationals, technological factors will be less strongly related to the form the alliance takes than they will be when neither or only one is large.

ALLIANCES, MEASURES, AND STATISTICAL ANALYSES

To examine the hypotheses stated above, we identified 270 new cooperative industrial arrangements between U.S. and Japanese firms announced in the *Asian Wall Street Journal* and in the *Japanese Economic Journal* during the 1984-86 period. This group did not include alliances involving government agencies or universities. The overwhelming majority (248) involved two parent firms. We eliminated alliances involving more than two parents as well as cooperations involving banking firms and trading companies. In the statistical analysis, we did not formally include 22 arrangements that involved equity purchases by one parent in the other, but instead reviewed them separately. Table 3.1 provides some descriptive information on the alliances studied: 153 two-party arrangements with industrial sponsors for which R&D data regarding the product of the arrangement were available.

An alliance was coded as a joint venture when its announcement indicated that the parents had formed a new legal entity with equity contributions. Of the 153 arrangements, 63 (41%) were of this form (see Table 3.2). We coded informal arrangements, cooperative ties, developmental assistance programs, licensing arrangements, and marketing and supply arrangements as agreements.[2]

A cooperation was considered as involving large firms when its consolidated total assets were greater than one billion dollars for the U.S. firm and one hundred billion yen for the Japanese firm. We took data on the parents' consolidated total assets from *Moody's Industrial Manual* (Moody's Investors Service, 1984, 1985, 1986) and the *Million Dollar Directory* (Dun's Marketing Services, 1986) for U.S. firms and from the *Japan Company Handbook* (Toyo Keizai Shinposha, 1984, 1985, 1986) for Japanese corporations. Although the monetary cutoffs were obviously arbitrary, we felt confident that firms of this size were large enough to have the capabilities and to be

---

2. Although the published tracking of announced alliances for this time period may be far from complete, the characteristics of the firms studied appear to be consistent with those given in other published data. For example, Auster's (1986) report on U.S.-Japanese alliances, which she based on Japan External Trade Organization data, shows a similar breakdown by industry and a similarly substantial proportion of alliances (46%) in high-tech industries. Both Hladik's (1988) work on international joint R&D and Takeuchi's (1988) survey of international cooperations involving Japanese firms reported that about 20% of the alliances involved an intent to conduct joint R&D. Finally, Auster's (1987) finding that in recent years joint ventures have accounted for between 20% and 50% of international cooperative linkages is consistent with data reported in Table 3.2.

TABLE 3.1. Characteristics of the Multinational Alliances Studied[a]

Industry or Technology[b]	Frequency	Percentage	Ratio of R&D Expenditures to Sales[c]
Steel	4	2.6	0.5
Textile-apparel	2	1.3	0.8
Food-beverage	4	2.6	0.9
Metals-metal products	10	6.5	1.5
Appliances	4	2.6	1.6
Auto parts	14	9.2	1.9
Tires-rubber	2	1.3	2.5
Miscellaneous manufacturing	5	3.3	2.7
Machines-industrial parts	12	7.8	3.1
Automotive	10	6.5	3.5
Chemicals	19	12.4	3.6
Electronics	7	4.6	4.4
Telecommunications	8	5.2	4.4
Aerospace	2	1.3	4.5
Precision equipment	14	9.2	6.4
Pharmaceuticals	4	2.6	7.6
Computers	19	12.4	7.8
Software	3	2.0	7.9
Semiconductors	10	6.5	10.4

[a] All the alliances studied were between U.S. and Japanese firms. Each involved two industrial firms. The study period was 1984–86. $N = 153$.

[b] The industry or technology areas were derived from the "R&D Scoreboard" of *Business Week* (1985–87).

[c] Percentages shown are three-year averages.

subject to the constraints of very large firms discussed earlier. Nearly half (46%) the alliances involved two large firms.

The technological intensity of an alliance's product was measured as the average ratio of R&D to sales over the three-year study period for U.S. firms in industries producing that product. We took this average from information published in *Business Week* (1985, 1986, 1987), which was based on COMPUSTAT data from that period (see Table 3.1). Only U.S. data were used, since U.S. and Japanese R&D data may not be directly comparable. The financial statements of Japanese firms, for example, do not report the Japanese government's subsidizing of substantial proportions of R&D costs for designated projects or that government's expenditures for technology transfer (Harrigan, 1985).

Evidence of an intention to conduct joint R&D was taken directly from the announcements in the *Asian Wall Street Journal* and *Japa-*

TABLE 3.2. Characteristics of Variables and Intercorrelations[a]

Variables[b]	Mean or Proportion	s.d.	Intercorrelations[c]			
			1	2	3	4
1. Form of alliance	0.41	0.49				
2. Technological intensity	4.48	2.71	−.21			
3. Joint R&D	0.18	0.38	.20	.21		
4. Firm sizes	0.46	0.50	.00	−.17	−.12	
5. Consumer durables	0.26	0.44	−.14	.23	.00	.08
6. Consumer nondurables	0.08	0.28	.03	.02	.04	.04
7. Capital goods	0.56	0.50	−.04	.01	−.01	−.09
8. Producer goods	0.09	0.29	.24	−.38	−.03	.07

[a] Coefficients not calculated are those among levels of a categorical variable. N = 153.

[b] These variables were dichotomously coded, allowing their means to be interpreted as proportions: for form, 0 = some form of agreement and 1 = a joint venture; for joint R&D, 1 = an announced intention to engage in joint R&D, 0 = no announcement; for firm sizes, 1 = both parties large, 0 = otherwise; and for the four industry membership variables, 1 = the association of an alliance's product with the given industry type, 0 = no such association.

[c] A correlation greater than or equal to .14 is needed to achieve significance at the .05 level. A correlation greater than or equal to .19 is needed to achieve significance at the .01 level.

nese Economic Journal. We simply coded the intention as "present" if an announcement mentioned it and as "absent" if it was not mentioned. About 1 in 5 (18%) of the alliances announced such an intent (Table 3.2).

The strategy literature suggests that industry conditions may alter preferences for various forms and types of strategic alliances (Ghoshal, 1987; Harrigan, 1988; Porter and Fuller, 1986). Industry-specific approaches to the introduction of new products and processes as well as differences in the attractiveness of innovation in different industries may alter the impact of technological considerations on the forms agreements take. Industry differences appear to have led to idiosyncratic findings in past organizational research (e.g., Hitt, Ireland, and Goryunov, 1988). It seemed prudent to control for basic industry type. We therefore included the categorical classification of industry type that Hitt et al. (1988) employed as a control (i.e., classifying alliances on the basis of their product). The categories used were: (1) consumer durable goods, (2) consumer nondurable goods, (3) capital goods, and (4) producer goods.

Discriminant function analysis was used to predict the categorical criterion via a series of dichotomous and interval-level predictors (Dillon and Goldstein, 1984). To assess the importance of the technological and size variables over and above that of industry type, we first entered dummy variables (representing the industrial categorization of an alliance) into the equation and then noted the significance of the F-to-enter and the accompanying change in variance accounted for each subsequent variable entered. Similarly, we entered cross-product terms involving the technological and size variables after including their constituent main effects. We chose to look at the significance of the partial Fs rather than the standardized discriminant function weights, since the weights themselves may have provided misleading information when the predictors were correlated (Dillon and Goldstein, 1984). Because we did wish to report the discriminant function weights as well, we conducted the analysis again using the residuals of the cross-product terms calculated by regressing the cross-product terms on their component effects. This procedure, as Lance (1988) suggested, does not affect the overall variance a prediction equation accounts for, or any of the main or interaction effects–the Fs-to-enter and their significance were identical to those obtained without using the residuals. Similarly, the discriminant loadings (structure coefficients) for the main effects remained unchanged. The discriminant function weights and the loadings for the interaction terms, however, more directly reflected the contribution of the variables used to classify the forms of alliances.

RESULTS

Table 3.2 presents the means, standard deviations, and bivariate intercorrelations among the variables used in these analyses. Since industry type was related to alliance form (Table 3.2), we retained it as a control.

As the data in Tables 3.2 and 3.3 show, both the technological intensity of an alliance's product area and the decision to engage in joint R&D were related to the governance form chosen for an alliance. In keeping with previous research on R&D, the intention to conduct joint R&D was somewhat more common as the technological intensity of an alliance's product area increased ($r = 0.21$, $p < 0.01$). Yet, as Hypothesis 1 predicted, agreements were the more

TABLE 3.3. Results of Discriminant Analysis

Step	Variables[a]	F-to-Enter at Step	ΔR²	Final Standardized Discriminant Weights	Final Discriminant Loadings
				.85	.29
1.	Industry categories	3.61*	.07	.81	.08
				.48	−.07
2.	Joint R&D (A)	7.33**	.04	−.63	−.45
3.	Technological intensity (B)	4.56*	.03	.45	.46
4.	Firm sizes (C)	0.00	.00	.00	−.01
5.	A × B	1.68	.01	−.28	−.23
6.	A × C	0.08	.00	−.05	−.03
7.	B × C	0.03	.00	−.05	.04
8.	A × B × C	5.49*	.03	.46	.36
Canonical correlation		.425**			
R²		.18**			
Percent correctly classified		71.9			

[a] Weights and loadings for the industry categories reflect the contribution of the three dummy codes used for the four-group industry typology. Statistics shown for the interactions are residualized cross-product terms.

* $p < .05$

** $p < .01$

common governance form in areas of high technological intensity ($r = -0.21$, $p < 0.01$). The intention to conduct joint R&D was positively related to joint-venture formation ($r = 0.20$, $p < 0.01$), as Hypothesis 2 predicted.

As noted above, there were 22 reported alliances involving one parent's buying equity in the other. Although there were too few of these to formally incorporate them into examination of the hypotheses, we conducted a revealing inspection of these arrangements. Half the minority equity participations involved joint R&D, versus only 11% of the agreements and 29% of the joint ventures. Again, firms chose a more elaborate governance form when conducting joint R&D.

The discriminant function model reported in Table 3.3 yielded a canonical correlation of 0.425 ($p < 0.01$), providing correct classification of 71% of the cooperative arrangements studied. As with the bivariate findings, both the technological intensity of the alliance product and the intention to engage in joint R&D added significant predicted variance; firm size did not.

Although firm size did not interact with the independent effects of the technological factors in influencing governance form, it did interact with the combination of technological factors. The three-way interaction of technological intensity, joint R&D, and firm size did provide a statistically significant increase in the prediction equation (Table 3.3).

Subsequent analysis of the significant three-way interaction (not shown in a table) indicated that engagement in joint R&D in high-tech areas was associated with the joint-venture form if at least one of the firms involved was not large. For the 70 alliances in this study involving two large firms, the two-way interaction of the technological intensity of the product and the intent to conduct joint R&D yielded an increase in R^2 of only 0.01 (n.s). The increase in R^2 with the addition of this interaction for the 83 arrangements involving at least one smaller firm was 0.05 ($p < 0.05$). Thus, it appears that alliances involving at least one firm that is not a large multinational are especially sensitive to the interaction of high technology and joint R&D, and such alliances are likely to employ the joint-venture form of governance when those factors are present.

In summary, the results are consistent with Hypotheses 1 and 2. Hypothesis 3 was supported regarding the three-way interaction of firm size and the two technological predictors, but no significant two-way interactions emerged.

DISCUSSION

When considering the governance form to use for a multinational alliance, parent firms may face conflicting pressures as they move into high-tech areas where joint R&D tends to be common. Although the two measured technological factors were significantly intercorrelated ($r = 0.20$, $p < 0.01$), they were associated with different governance forms: high technological intensity with contractual agreements and the intention to conduct joint R&D with joint ventures.

Our findings are consistent with the technological positioning discussion leading to Hypothesis 1: Contractual forms may not only provide the flexibility and multiple linkages considered so important in technologically intensive areas but also help a firm limit the flow of proprietary information across boundaries. We argued that when joint R&D is present, firms will prefer the joint-venture form because it (1) facilitates information flows, (2) aligns the interests of the partners, reducing opportunism, and (3) provides for day-to-day coordination. Our information concerning a small number of minority equity participations in which one firm bought into its partner is also consistent with these arguments.

The importance of an alliance to its parent firms and its role in their overall strategies may be factors in resolving the conflicting pressures of the related technological factors. Many new high-tech alliances may be devices the partners are using for technological positioning. A decision to conduct joint R&D, however, may well signal a longer-term, more important commitment to the viability of an economic entity. Over time, the role and importance of the alliance may itself evolve, as it becomes more or less important and the parents decide to use it for a different purpose. For instance, an agreement in a high-tech alliance initially used for technological positioning in a network could evolve into an important new business area involving production. Or an initial agreement might yield a consensus to pursue joint R&D. In both cases, we predict that the probability of adopting the joint-venture governance form will increase. As Harrigan (1988) suggested, cooperative arrangements may represent transitional stages in firm positioning. The governance form of an alliance is likely to change as the value of a particular activity to overall firm strategy changes.

The themes of purpose and importance may also be inferred from the interactive findings. Statistically, there was a triple-order interaction among technological intensity, intent to conduct R&D, and firm size in analyses predicting the form of governance. Although several interpretations of these findings are possible, given the various theoretical meanings researchers have attributed to size, we see the following.

In high-tech areas in which partners opt for joint R&D, it is clear that the joint-venture form is preferred when neither or only one partner is a huge multinational. In such cases, it appears that the needs for control, coordination, and protection are particularly strong. The cooperation is important to its parents, and the economic success of the venture itself is likely to be important. For a small parent (worth less than a billion dollars), an alliance is likely to be a geographic diversification move centered on its technical core (presuming, as did Thompson (1967), that smaller firms have only one or a few technical cores). The form of an alliance needs to reflect their requirements for conducting high-tech R&D, or small firms will choose not to participate (cf. Jones, 1987).

When a cooperation involves two huge multibillion-dollar multinationals, however, we see a more complex situation. Even their high-tech R&D alliances might not be central to one of their many technical cores, and the economic success of the alliance itself may not be the most important consideration. For multibillion-dollar multinationals, high-tech R&D alliances might represent a geographic diversification that is not directly related to an existing core business. One or both partners could be exploring new areas or spinning off secondary uses of a new technology. Given the considerable potential market power that combining two multibillion-dollar multinationals can yield, merely establishing an alliance might take precedence over the technical or economic success of the venture itself. Merely establishing a cooperation with the ostensible intent of conducting R&D in a high-tech area may be sufficient to block competitors' entry into that area. Here, the role of the alliance may center on global network positioning to link potentially powerful firms.

In short, this research suggests that technological factors are important for examining multinational alliances, but not necessarily in the manner much current transaction cost theorizing has suggested. Although specific technological dimensions may be correlated, their effects on form may be quite different. Further, the role and importance of an alliance may substantially moderate the collective influence of technological factors on governance forms. Here, parents' size could represent a number of potentially important aspects, such as intransigence, potential combined economic clout, and diversification strategies. In general, we expect that the less central a cooperative alliance is to a parent's core technology and the more that strategic placement in a network is a factor, the less the initial form of governance used for the alliance will reflect technological considerations. Of course, whether the match between technological considerations and governance form is associated with the success of an alliance is a question for future research.

These results also show the need for theoretical integration of the three research streams upon which we drew. Transaction cost theorizing needs to incorporate specific technological factors, and work on technological positioning could benefit from incorporating the economic constraints so dominant in transaction cost economics. Recognition of the conflicting pressures of specific technological factors and the role of corporate global strategy in alliance forms is also needed. Recognizing the technological aspects of interorganizational networks might help economists, strategists, and organizational theorists to both integrate their theoretical positions and begin to isolate the conditions under which theory-specific perspectives apply (cf. Dunning, 1988).

Threads for future research and theorizing concerning the governance forms and evolution of multinational quasi-markets and quasi-hierarchies would include directly measuring such potentially important factors as parents' diversification strategies, market power, and global strategic positioning (in addition to measuring the technological factors emphasized here). Further explorations of the role and importance of alliances do indeed appear warranted, as increasing numbers of firms directly confront the challenge of global technological competence and global markets.

REFERENCES

Anderson, E., & Gatignon, H. A. (1986). Modes of foreign entry: A transaction cost analysis and propositions, *Journal of International Business Studies*, 17(3): 1-25.

Astley, W. G, (1985). The two ecologies: Population and community perspectives on organizational evolution. *Administrative Science Quarterly*, 30: 224-241.

Auster, E. R. (1986). Industrial cooperation between Japan and the U.S. Paper presented at the annual meeting of the Academy of Management, Chicago.

Auster, E. R. (1987). International corporate linkages: Dynamic forms in changing environments, *Columbia Journal of World Business*, 22(2): 3-6.

Blau, P. (1970). A formal theory of differentiation in organizations, *American Sociological Review*, 35: 201-218.

Blau, P., & Schoenherr, R. (1971). *The structure of organizations*. New York: Basic Books.

Business Week. (1985). R&D scoreboard. July 8: 86-106.

Business Week. (1986). R&D scoreboard. June 23: 139-156.

Business Week. (1987). R&D scoreboard. June 22: 139-160.

Calvet, A. L. (1981). A synthesis of foreign direct investment theories and theories of the multinational firm. *Journal of International Business Studies,* 12(1): 4-59.

Contractor, F. L., & Lorange, P. (1988). Why should firms cooperate? The strategy and economics basis for cooperative ventures. In F. L. Contractor & P. Lorange (Eds.), *Cooperative strategies in international business*: 3-30. Lexington, MA: Lexington Books.

Dillon, W. R., & Goldstein, M. (1984). *Multivariate analysis: Methods and applications.* New York: John Wiley & Sons.

Doz, Y. L. (1988). Technology partnerships between larger and smaller firms: Some critical issues. *International Studies of Management and Organization,* 17(4): 31-57.

Dunning, J. H. (1988). *Explaining international production.* Boston: Unwin Hyman.

Dun's Marketing Services. (1986). *Million dollar directory.* Parsippany, NJ: Dun's Marketing Services.

Garud, R. & Van de Ven, A.H. (1987). Innovation and the emergence of industries. Paper presented at the annual meeting of the Academy of Management, New Orleans.

Geringer, M. A. (1988). *Joint venture partner selection.* Westport, CT: Quorum Books.

Ghoshal, S. (1987). Global strategy: An organizing framework. *Strategic Management Journal,* 5: 425-440.

Hannan, M. T., & Freeman, J. (1984). Structural inertia and organizational change, *American Sociological Review,* 49: 149-164.

Harrigan, K. R. (1985). *Strategies for joint ventures.* Lexington, MA: D.C. Heath & Co.

Harrigan, K. R. (1987). Strategic alliances: Their new role in global competition, *Columbia Journal of World Business,* 22(2): 67-70.

Harrigan, K. R. (1988). Joint ventures and competitive strategy. *Strategic Management Journal,* 9: 141-158,

Hayashi, K. (1987). The internationalization of Japanese-style management, *Japan Update,* 5: 20-24.

Hennart, J. (1988). A transaction costs theory of equity joint ventures, *Strategic Management Journal,* 9: 361-374.

Hergert, M., & Morris, D. (1988). Trends in international collaborative agreements. In F. L. Contractor & P. Lorange (Eds.), *Cooperative strategies in international business*: 99-109. Lexington, MA: Lexington Books.

Hitt, M., Ireland, D., & Goryunov, I. (1988). The context of innovation: Investment in R&D and firm performance. In E. Gattiker & L. Larwood (Eds.), *Managing technological development: Strategic and human resources issues*: 73-92. New York: de Gruyter.

Hladik, K. J. (1988). R&D and international joint ventures. In F. L. Contractor &

P. Lorange (Eds.), *Cooperative strategies in international business*: 187-203. Lexington, MA: Lexington Books.

Jones, G. (1983). Transaction costs, property rights, and organizational culture: An exchange perspective. *Administrative Science Quarterly*, 28: 454-467.

Jones, G. (1987). Organization-client transactions and organizational governance structures. *Academy of Management Journal*, 20: 197-218.

Killing, J. P. (1988). Understanding alliances: The role of task and organizational complexity. In F. L. Contractor & P. Lorange (Eds.), *Cooperative strategies in international business*: 55-67. Lexington, MA: Lexington Books.

Kimberly, J. R. (1976). Organizational size and the structuralist perspective: A review, critique, and proposal. *Administrative Science Quarterly*, 21; 571-597.

Kogut, B. (1988). Joint ventures: Theoretical and empirical perspectives. *Strategic Management Journal*, 9: 319-332.

Kogut, B., & Singh, H. (1988). Entering the United States by joint venture: Competitive rivalry and industry structure. In F. L. Contractor & P. Lorange (Eds.), *Cooperative strategies in international business*: 241-251. Lexington, MA: Lexington Books.

Lance, C. (1988). Residual centering, exploratory and confirmatory moderator analysis, and decomposition of effects in path models containing interactions, *Applied Psychological Measurement*, 12: 163-177.

Maitland, I., Bryson, J., & Van De Ven, A. (1985). Sociologists, economists, and opportunism. *Academy of Management Review*, 10: 59-65.

Moody's Investors Service. (1984, 1985, 1986). *Moody's industrial manual.* New York: Moody's Investors Service.

Moroi, K., & Itami, H. (1987). Changing Japan's corporate behavior. *Economic Eye*, 8(3): 18-22.

Morris, D., & Hergert, M. (1987). Trends in international cooperative agreements. *Columbia Journal of World Business*, 22(2): 15-21.

Osborn, R. N., & Baughn, C. C. (1987). New patterns in the formation of US/Japanese cooperative ventures: The role of technology. *Columbia Journal of World Business*, 22(2): 57-65.

Osborn, R. N., Hunt, J. G., & Jauch, L. R. (1980). *Organization theory.* New York: John Wiley.

Osborn, R. N., Olson, J., & Hanada, M. (1985). *Analyzing U.S./Japanese joint research and development units.* Washington, DC: National Science Foundation.

Polanyi, M. E. (1958). *Personal knowledge: Towards a post-critical philosophy.* Chicago: University of Chicago Press.

Porter, M. E. (1986). Competition in global industries: A conceptual framework. In M. Porter (Ed.), *Competition in global industries*: 16-60. Boston: Harvard University Graduate School of Business Administration.

Porter, M. E., & Fuller, M. B. (1986). Coalitions and global strategy. In M. Porter (Ed.), *Competition in global industries*. 316-343, Boston: Harvard University Graduate School of Business Administration.

Pucik, V. (1987). Joint ventures with the Japanese: The key role of HRM. *Euro-Asia Business Review*, 6: 4.

Rugman, A. M. (1981). Internalization and non-equity forms of international involvement. In A. M. Rugman (Ed.), *New theories of the multinational enterprise*: 9-23. New York: St. Martin's Press.

Skinner, S., Donnelly, J., & Ivancevich, J. (1987). Effects of transactional form on environmental linkages and power dependence relations. *Academy of Management Journal*, 30: 577-588.

Stopford, J., & Wells, L. (1972). *Managing the multinational enterprise: Organization of the firm and ownership of the subsidiaries.* New York: Basic Books.

Stuckey, J. (1983). *Vertical integration and joint ventures in the aluminum industry.* Cambridge, MA: Harvard University Press.

Takeuchi, H. (1988). Active pace of global tie-ups belies closed image of Japan firms, *Japanese Economic Journal*, May 7: 22.

Thompson, J. D. (1967). *Organizations in action.* New York: McGraw-Hill Book Co.

Thorelli, H. (1986). Networks: Between markets and hierarchies. *Strategic Management Journal*, 7: 37-51.

Toyo Keizai Shinposha. (1984, 1985, 1986). *Japan company handbook.* Tokyo: Toyo Keizai Shinposha.

Van De Ven, A. H., & Poole, M. (1989). Paradoxical requirements for a theory of organizational change. In A. Van de Ven, H. Angle, & M. Poole (Eds.), *Research on the management of innovation*: 127-148. Cambridge, MA: Ballinger.

Walker, G., & Weber, D. (1987). Supplier competition, uncertainty, and make-or-buy decisions. *Academy of Management Journal*, 30: 577-588.

Williamson, O. E. (1975). *Market and hierarchies: Analysis and antitrust implications.* New York: Free Press.

Zimmerman, M. (1985). *How to do business with the Japanese.* New York: Random House.

Chapter 4

A Process Model on the Formation of Multinational Strategic Alliances

Gregory E. Osland
Attila Yaprak

INTRODUCTION

Perhaps the most significant phenomenon in international business within the last decade has been the dramatic growth in the formation of strategic alliances. While until the 1970s multinational firms typically operated by relying on a network of wholly owned subsidiaries in foreign markets, they have increasingly preferred collaborative arrangements during the 1980s (Dunning, 1988; Gomes-Casseres, 1989). For example, while General Motors owned 100% equity in each of its non-U.S. subsidiaries in 1970, of the 20 new foreign subsidiaries GM established from 1975 to 1988, 12 were joint ventures with other firms. Dunning (1988) reports that between 1983 and 1986, Philips, the Dutch multinational, formed alliances with 236 companies around the world, two of which were with rivals AT&T and Whirlpool. Although the fragmented and incomplete data on strategic alliances inhibit conclusive verification of the patterns of collaborative activity, Contractor and Lorange (1988) report that cooperative arrangements between U.S. and foreign-based firms now outnumber wholly owned foreign subsidiaries four to one.

This explosive growth in the formation of international strategic alliances has led to a flurry of recent research that has explored the phenomenon from a variety of perspectives. These studies have ranged from theoretical contributions (Beamish and Banks, 1987;

Kogut, 1985 and 1988; Kogut and Singh, 1988) to technology and innovation perspectives (Hendryx, 1986; Osborn and Baughn, 1987); from economic explanations such as eclectic theory and transactions costs analysis (Dunning, 1988; Hennart, 1988; Kogut, 1985; Williamson, 1975) to ownership issues (Contractor, 1990; Franko, 1989); and from control and performance concerns (Geringer and Hebert, 1989; Harrigan, 1987 and 1988; Killing, 1983) to strategic perspectives (Jain, 1987; Ohmae, 1989). Yet no comprehensive and integrative theory has emerged. The purpose of this chapter is to help fill this gap by presenting a conceptual model that explains how international strategic alliances are formed. The emphasis of the model is on the logic and process of cooperation, and on the role that trust plays in this process, rather than on the rationale behind alliance formation.

To achieve this purpose, an overview of strategic alliance forms is provided as a foundation for the presentation of the model. Elements of the model are then discussed in the context of situational, process, and outcome variables that lead to satisfaction or dissatisfaction with the performance of the alliance. Implications for future research conclude the chapter.

FORMS OF STRATEGIC ALLIANCES

Strategic alliances have been described as international corporate linkages (Auster, 1987), hybrid arrangements (Borys and Jemison, 1989), strategic partnerships (Hull et al., 1988), international collaborative agreements (Hergert and Morris, 1988), cooperative ventures (Osborn and Baughn, 1987), and strategic alliances (Jain, 1987; Ohmae, 1989; Pucik, 1988). Throughout this chapter, we will use the term "strategic alliance" to describe relationships that are used to exchange technology and goods and services across national and firm boundaries: informal agreements, contractual collaborations, joint ventures, and minority equity alliances.

Lying on a continuum of interdependence between complete mergers and independent spot-market transactions, in each form, the firms voluntarily work together to pursue economic gain. In this context, the term "strategic" implies rational purposes for linking with another firm. While, ideally, one would expect common goals to characterize the relationship, in reality such goals range from shared to mixed to conflicting (Auster, 1987). We begin our discussion with the most interdependent and conclude with the least interdependent form of collaboration.

Minority equity alliances are voluntary relationships between two firms in which one company purchases a substantial, but less than 50%, portion of the other firm to undertake joint activities (Killing, 1988). The global auto industry contains many examples of this type of alliance: Ford owns 25% of Mazda, General Motors 38% of Isuzu, and Chrysler 12% of Mitsubishi (Ingrassia and Graven, 1990). In the Ford-Mazda alliance, the two firms co-design and produce several brands of automobiles, but do not market the cars collaboratively.

A *joint venture* involves the establishment of a new legal, corporate entity in which equity is shared by both parents (Auster, 1987). Joint ventures (JVs) provide joint, but not necessarily equal, degrees of ownership and control over the use and fruits of assets (Kogut and Singh, 1988). Typically, one firm controls the majority of the venture. GM and Toyota's "child," the NUMMI plant in California, for example, is a separate, but linked, organization that produces the GEO line of cars. JVs are the most frequently and most thoroughly researched mode of alliances (see Beamish, 1985; Buckley and Casson, 1988; Contractor, 1990; Franko, 1989; Harrigan, 1985; Hennart, 1988; Hladik, 1985 and 1988; Kogut, 1988; Roehl and Truitt, 1987).

Contractual collaborations are nonequity formal agreements between two or more firms. These include technical training agreements, buybacks, licenses and franchises, and management and service agreements (Contractor and Lorange, 1988). Ciba-Geigy and Eli Lilly, for example, cross-license pharmaceuticals in different markets. Other examples include outsourcing arrangements between firms in the same industry: GM buys cars and components from South Korea's Daewoo, and Germany's Siemens buys computers from Fujitsu. More recently, flexible arrangements between large multinationals have emerged that pool resources or complement one another's strengths in the various functions of business, such as in research and development (R&D), manufacturing, assembly, and distribution (Hamel, Doz, and Prahalad, 1989; Ohmae,

1989). However, each side may agree not to invade the other's key markets.

Informal agreements involve a cooperative association between two or more firms, such as tacit understandings among competitors in an oligopoly. Collusion and anti-trust legislation can become an issue in these informal agreements about pricing, promotion, personnel management, and other activities. A body of literature on informal interfirm cooperation has been developed by the International Marketing and Purchasing Research Group (IMP), which is primarily comprised of scholars in northern Europe. Working on an organized basis since 1976, this group has uncovered a trend toward cooperation and stability in networks of European manufacturer-supplier relationships (see Campbell, 1985; Hakansson, 1982; Hallen, Mohamed, and Johanson, 1989). One study showed, for example, that two-thirds of the cooperative relationships between firms in technical development were informal, rather than contractual (Hakansson and Johanson, 1988).

Although many studies cited above have inductively described the phenomenon of interfirm cooperation and provided a variety of rationale for alliances, no integrative theory has yet emerged. To help fill this gap, a model to explain and predict the formation of strategic alliances is proposed in this chapter.

A PROCESS MODEL TO EXPLAIN STRATEGIC ALLIANCE FORMATION

Our model (Figure 4.1) assumes that organizations are rational systems that actively seek to improve performance in an increasingly competitive environment. While organizations have traditionally pursued improved performance through independent, go-it-alone actions, they have increasingly preferred cooperative arrangements in the 1980s. Globalization of markets, consumer tastes, and knowledge has forced firms to form networks of strategic links to remain competitive and to grow. They have sought opportunities to transform their core capabilities and to reshape the competitive structures of their industries even at the expense of blurring their boundaries. Absorbing new knowledge and capabilities to strengthen core

FIGURE 4.1. A Process Model of Strategic Alliance Formation

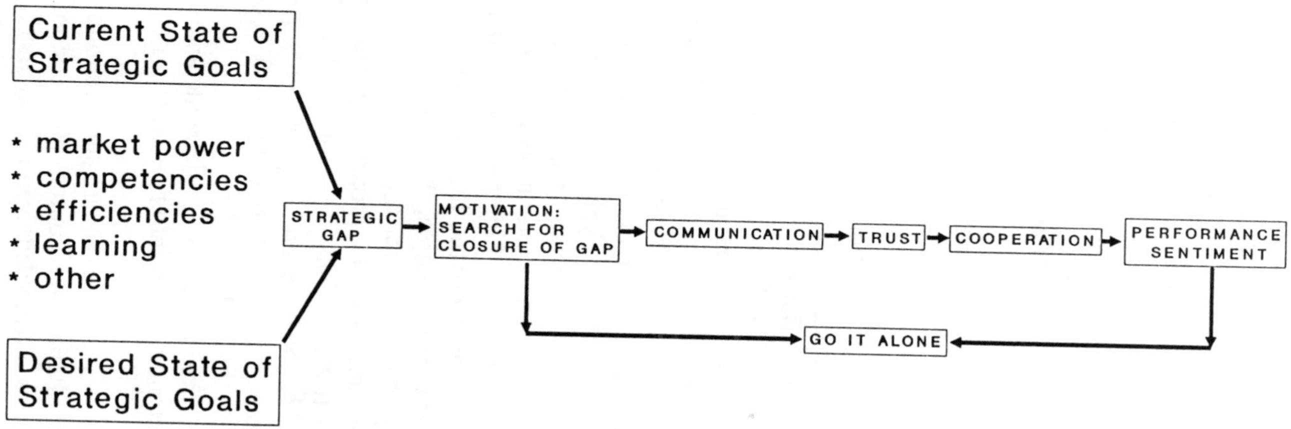

Current State of
Strategic Goals

* market power
* competencies
* efficiencies
* learning
* other

Desired State of
Strategic Goals

STRATEGIC
GAP

MOTIVATION:
SEARCH FOR
CLOSURE OF GAP

COMMUNICATION

TRUST

COOPERATION

PERFORMANCE
SENTIMENT

GO IT ALONE

competencies has become a necessary, indeed an absolutely essential, skill in improving performance in the 1990s.

Our model devotes particular attention to these sets of needs that firms aim to satisfy through strategic alliances. The importance of motivation and harmonious communication between partners is emphasized, as is the increasing role that trust plays in attaining satisfaction. The elements of the model are described next. (See also Figure 4.1.)

Strategic Gap

The profound transformation of the world economy within the last two decades has placed increasing pressure on firms to achieve performance targets (Bartlett and Ghoshal, 1987; Ohmae, 1987; Porter and Fuller, 1986). Thus, as many firms scan the environment and assess their own resources and capabilities, they often discover a gap between what they would like to achieve and what they are able to achieve. Their strategic goals, such as a certain market share or a competitive position, are often unattainable in the new environment of global competition. Tyebjee (1988) calls this occurrence a *strategic gap*. The size and importance of the firm's strategic gap are primary factors in its motivation to enter into a strategic alliance. The greater the size of the gap and the perceived importance of filling it, the more likely the firm will desire to form an alliance with another firm. For example, the firm's desire to bring together complementary resources, to surmount barriers to competitors' markets, to gain access to the proprietary competencies of another firm, or simply to share risks will motivate the firm to enter into a strategic alliance. Such dependency on other firms occurs so the firm may secure the resources it needs to accomplish its goals (Pfeffer and Salancik, 1978).

We classify a firm's needs, or dependencies, that compose the essence of its strategic gaps into three categories:

1. Market Power: Market access and economies of scope.
2. Efficiency: Financial resources and economies of scale.
3. Competencies: Knowledge and skills in activities of the value-added chain of the firm.

Market Power

Strategic management literature emphasizes that firms seek to maximize long-term profits through improving their competitive position vis-à-vis rivals (Kogut, 1988). One way in which firms attempt to accomplish this is by aggressively gaining access to new markets and expanding market share in existing markets.

Linking with host-nation firms to facilitate access to new markets is a major reason that firms form strategic alliances (Dunning, 1988; Harrigan, 1985). Host-country firms may be part of a network of suppliers, distributors, and customers that foreign firms can join through an alliance. Some researchers view this development of interfirm and customer relationships as the critical function of the firm (Hakansson, 1982; Hallen, Mohamed, and Johanson, 1989). Reacting to governmental trade restrictions is another aspect of market access. Killing's research (1983) showed, for example, that this was the primary reason that multinational corporations formed partnerships with host firms and governments in developing nations. Actual or possible government legislation, requiring partnerships with local firms or specifying a minimum percentage of local content, can also prompt a firm to form strategic alliances if it seeks to enter specific markets. However, Beamish and Banks (1987) found that, as an independent variable, government requirements and influence is a much less important explanation for the formation of joint ventures than other factors such as gaining market access or achieving cost economies of scale.

Partnerships with horizontally related competitors offer the potential for many offensive and defensive strategic benefits vis-à-vis other competitors. Two firms may join up to put pressure on the profits and market share of a common competitor. Caterpillar Tractor and Mitsubishi were said to have had this motive in joining together in Japan against Komatsu (Contractor and Lorange, 1988). Vickers (1985) proposed that many R&D collaborations are formed to acquire patents in a large number of nations, thus pre-empting other competitors. In the same vein, joint ventures may be a means by which large corporations increase their control on market power through ties to smaller firms (Kogut, 1988, Hladik, 1988).

As product life cycles become increasingly short and the rate of technological innovation accelerates, strategic alliances become an important means of attaining an initial presence in new product markets that may be of long-term strategic importance to the firm. Through joining with another firm in R&D, for example, synergies can be developed that allow both firms to expand their product offerings. Thus, economies of scope are achieved, enabling additional offensive thrusts. Entry is also gained more quickly, since less capital is required for firms that share costs than for independent firms (Harrigan, 1985). Furthermore, collaborations are a means for firms to diversify from unfavorable businesses to more promising ones. Philips' joint venture with M/A-Com to test the demand for fiber optics exemplifies this market-power motivation. Risks are reduced through cooperative involvement in the development and marketing of a wider array of products.

Efficiency

Firms in highly competitive markets may also recognize a need for greater efficiencies in their activities. Their costs may be too high, relative to competitors, to allow them to attain desired profit margins. For example, a firm's costs for each critical link in the value chain, such as R&D, manufacturing, distribution, and promotion, can be compared with estimates of competitors' costs. Those links where the firm is weakest in a cost sense may suggest activities that can be better performed by a partner in a strategic alliance. When each firm performs the activities that it is most efficient in, costs per unit decline for both.

In this context, Ohmae (1987) argues that the four key elements of a company's business system–innovative R&D, modern production facility, strong sales network, and brand-name establishment–have become very high fixed costs that require most firms to find partners to help maximize contribution margins. These high fixed costs also necessitate expanded volumes on a global scale to enable firms to recover their investment. An example of these *link alliances* (Hennart, 1988), with each firm providing complementary functions, is the joint venture between BASF, a German chemical company, and Dow Chemical. BASF relied on Dow to distribute its proprietary technology in the U.S. market, while for Dow, the JV was a way to reduce R&D costs.

The minimum efficient scale in the activities of the value-added chain is increasing dramatically in most industries. For example, a manufacturer of color televisions has to produce several million sets a year to gain the economies of scale necessary to compete in the global market. This is more than 50 times the minimum efficient scale in the early 1960s (Bartlett and Ghoshal, 1987). Pooling resources with a competitor is a means for firms to achieve such scale. These *scale alliances* (Hennart, 1988) are created when two or more firms join together to perform the same business activity, such as R&D. Illustrating this situation, General Electric and SNECMA, a French manufacturer, combined some of their R&D capabilities to develop a new jet engine. R&D scale alliances in high-technology industries permit firms to keep abreast of innovations by providing a means of sharing development costs (Harrigan, 1985). Harrigan's empirical research found that in the electronic-components, computer, office-equipment, and communications-equipment industries, cooperative strategies were commonplace. Where scale economies were critical, joint ventures occurred; otherwise, licensing and other distribution collaborations were more likely.

More recent research has indicated that firms prefer joint ventures, rather than nonequity agreements, to do scale R&D (Osborn and Baughn, 1990). The joint-venture form is preferred because it facilitates information flows, reduces opportunism through aligned incentives, and provides for day-to-day coordination. According to Osborn and Baughn, data concerning minority equity acquisitions is also consistent with these arguments. Transaction cost analysis suggests, in a similar vein, that the critical dimension of a joint venture is its resolution of high levels of uncertainty over the behavior of the contracting parties, when the assets of one or both parties are specialized to the transaction (Kogut, 1988). Thus, cost efficiencies are a resulting benefit.

Competencies

A growing body of literature has started to address the importance of organizational learning to a firm's success (e.g., Aoki, 1990; Fiol and Lyles, 1985; Fiol, 1989; Hennart, 1988; Itami, 1987; Kogut, 1988). This is because learning is becoming more important for corporations as technology, product, and process life cycles are getting shorter (Bartlett and Ghoshal, 1987). Markets are evolving as consumers and organizational buyers become more sophisticated, and possess new needs and desires. As a process, organizational learning (Fiol and Lyles, 1985) fosters enhanced competencies. For example, on the value-added chain, gaps exist between the level of competence that a firm possesses in a certain function and where it wishes to be. Allying with a partner that is strong in a function where the firm wishes to become more competent is a logical means to help close that gap. Those firms that can become strong in both R&D and manufacturing (product and process innovations), for example, perform best in several critical measures (Kotabe, 1990). In this context, data show that the primary reason Japanese firms link up with American firms is to enhance their technologies and acquire new skills. In contrast, Western firms primarily collaborate with other companies to reduce costs and risks (Hamel, Doz, and Prahalad, 1989). A perception of being the teacher and parent has often hindered U.S. firms' ability to learn from partners and foreign subsidiaries (Bartlett and Ghoshal, 1987).

The knowledge that is acquired from cooperative involvement with another firm may be of several types. Individual-specific knowledge is embedded in the experience and skills of personnel, for which there may be an outside labor market. In contrast, firm-specific knowledge involves complex organizational routines and management systems (Kogut, 1988). Aoki (1990) suggests that Japanese corporations are particularly effective in developing and disseminating this latter tacit knowledge within a corporation through horizontal coordination among operating units and frequent job rotation of personnel. He posits that this emphasis on *integrating* knowledge is more effective than an emphasis on specialized knowledge in today's dynamic environment. In a similar vein, Badaracco (1991) suggests that in a world of knowledge-driven competition and eroding product-based advantages, organizations enter into strategic alliances to enhance their pools of this integrative (or embedded) knowledge and view this knowledge as an asset more fundamental to performance than even patented technology.

Market knowledge that involves an understanding of the sociocultural and competitive environment where a firm intends to distribute its products may also be important in cooperative involvement. Where cultural distance is high, as in a northern European firm seeking to do business in China, firms prefer forming a joint venture with a local firm in order to acquire market knowledge (Beamish and Banks, 1987; Kogut and Singh, 1988). Of particular importance in cooperative agreements is the development of core competencies that spawn a stream of product, process, and marketing innovations. These core competencies are the collective learning in the organization that enable a firm to coordinate diverse production skills and integrate multiple streams of technologies (Prahalad and Hamel, 1990). NEC of Japan formed collaborations with such firms as U.S.-based Honeywell and French-based Bull, for example, to internalize its partners' skills and technology. This ability to learn from others is a key factor in its position as the only global firm with a strong market share in telecommunications, semiconductors, and mainframe computers.

Several problems exist, however, in the process of organizational learning through strategic alliances (Itami, 1987; Kogut, 1988). Reich and Mankin (1986) lament about the apparently one-sided learning on the part of the Japanese that occurred in many U.S.-Japanese strategic alliances in the 1970s and early 1980s. These "bleedthroughs" of knowledge transfer not covered by formal agreements are a benefit as well as a drawback of strategic alliances (Harrigan, 1985). Fiol (1989) argues that CEOs who prefer control and strong boundaries separating their firms from the external environment are unlikely to risk bleedthroughs; thus, they do not tend to form strategic alliances. Firms that do collaborate cope with this problem in several ways. Some perceive knowledge as unguardable; therefore, their focus is on learning from others rather than trying to defend what they possess. Others focus on guarding against competitive compromise. It is best, of course, if each partner believes it can learn from the other and, at the same time, limit access to proprietary skills (Hamel, Doz, and Prahalad, 1989).

Motivation

Motivation, the second element of the model, is closely linked to the notion of strategic gap. It signifies the drive that a firm possesses to satisfy at least one of the three previously discussed perceived needs by the formation of a strategic alliance. It is a cognitive state that channels a firm's energy into the process of finding and developing a partnership. When motivation is manifest, the firm will actively engage in searching for a partner. As a part of the search, a highly motivated firm will begin communicating with potential allies.

Communication

Communication, the formal and informal sharing of meaningful and timely information between firms (Anderson and Narus, 1990), is important in alliance formation because it fosters trust between partners. For one firm to eventually trust another, it must receive evidence of integrity, promises upheld, and opportunistic behavior foregone (Frazier, Spekman, and O'Neal, 1988). Thus, knowledge acquired through communication is an antecedent of trust. Laboratory experiments in the U.S. (Deutsch, Canavan, and Rubin, 1971) and Japan (Yamagishi and Sato, 1986), and mail surveys of multiple firms (Anderson and Narus, 1990; Bialaszewski and Giallourakis, 1985) support this hypothesis.

Trust

Social psychologists have suggested that trust, more than any other single variable, thoroughly influences interpersonal and intergroup behavior (Golembiewski and McConkie, 1975). A consequence of trust is cooperation, evidenced by the formation of a strategic alliance. Trust is likely to be reciprocated if one party takes the initiative to exercise trusting behavior. Mathews and Shimoff (1979) discovered that trust decreases dramatically when the likelihood of reciprocation is reduced. In addition, failure to reciprocate trust decreased the likelihood of future cooperation.

Economists perceive trust as a public good that acts as a social lubricant to make production and exchange possible (Dasgupta, 1988). Thus, in the presence of reasonable alternatives, trust is a precondition of cooperative behavior. The logic of transaction cost analysis (Ouchi, 1980; Williamson, 1975, 1981) helps explain the role of trust in strategic alliances. Williamson's work, concerned with the costs of an exchange, would indicate that costs are incurred in four situations: (1) reaching an agreement satisfactory to both sides, (2) adapting the agreement to unanticipated contingencies, (3) enforcing the terms of the agreement, and (4) terminating the exchange agreement. The costs are linked to the assumption that firms behave opportunistically. Opportunism implies guile, whereby one exchange partner is interested in promoting his own self-interest to the potential detriment of the other (Spekman and Strauss, 1986).

A considerable amount of expense can be avoided if there were complete mutual trust (Lorenz, 1988). Contracts are a feature of most strategic alliances because firms do not completely trust one another, at least initially. However, all possible contingencies cannot be covered in legal contracts, and human rationality is limited. Efforts to protect a firm from opportunism through comprehensive contracting will inevitably be deficient (Lorenz, 1988); some level of trust is still necessary.

Trust is crucial when firms invest in specific assets, locking themselves into a relationship. These transaction-specific investments are highly specialized to the alliance, are not re-deployed easily, and may have little salvage value. They include durable assets, such as production facilities and tooling costs, as well as human assets, such as expert knowledge and technical or human skills (Spekman and Strauss, 1986).

Trust is an underresearched topic that is just beginning to be recognized and studied as a critical construct in interfirm relationships (Dwyer, Schurr, and Oh, 1987). We do know, however, that low levels of trust lead to less favorable communication, attitudes, and bargaining behavior (Schurr and Ozanne, 1985) and that trust develops incrementally over time. It is a present-tense perspective of past behavior that indicates a willingness to engage in future cooperative actions.

That trust is an antecedent to cooperation is supported by many social psychologists' experiments (Axelrod, 1984; Deutsch, Canavan, and Rubin, 1971; Good, 1988; Mathews and Shimoff, 1979; Yamagishi and Sato, 1986). Marketers Schurr and Ozanne (1985) found evidence to support the linkage in a laboratory experiment; while Hallen, Mohamed, and Johanson (1989) discovered a positive relationship between the two constructs in multiple firm interviews in several non-American nations.

Particularly in international business, when physical and cultural distance separate firms, the building of trust is an essential ingredient for successful cooperation (Ford, 1980; Thorelli, 1990). In several Asian cultures, trust and friendships may replace extensive formal contracts. An international comparison of trust in interfirm relationships in the packaged-goods industry revealed that Japanese firms had fewer legal agreements and greater trust of one another than did German firms (Campbell, 1985). If non-Asian firms view trust as relatively unimportant, their potential Asian collaborators often do not. The failure of some American and European firms to plan for lengthy cross-cultural negotiations may indicate a lack of understanding of the need of Asians to take time to develop trust of their potential business partners before making agreements. Chinese negotiators often take a great deal of time determining whether to trust foreign firms and to cooperate with them.

Cooperation

Anderson and Narus (1990) define cooperation as coordinated efforts, based on goal compatibility, that are designed to provide mutual benefits. In our model, cooperation is evidenced by an agreement between two firms to form a strategic alliance. Low levels of cooperation include high levels of conflict, in line with Frazier's (1983) view that factors that reduce conflict, such as communication and trust, increase cooperation.

For several decades, social psychologists have studied cooperation and conflict between competing agents in a laboratory setting. It has been found that subjects' behavior differs according to whether they view the interchange from a short-term or long-term perspective. If subjects believed that they would need to continue to interact over time, their behavior became considerably more cooperative (Axelrod, 1984; Pruitt and Kimmel, 1976). Cooperation is thus more of a feature of long-term interfirm relationships, such as strategic alliances, than of discrete spot-market transactions. For relationships to be maintained, coordinated efforts to provide mutual gains must also exist. Moreover, trust plays an important role in maintaining relationships. When the firms have trust in one another, there will be ways in which the two parties can work out performance difficulties, incompatible goals, and other differences (Dwyer, Schurr, and Oh, 1987).

Performance Sentiment

Performance sentiment is a nominal measure composed of dissatisfaction and satisfaction. Satisfaction is a positive affective assessment of the relationship between two firms; whereas dissatisfaction is a negative affective assessment. These affective outcomes are consistent with previous interorganizational exchange models (Anderson and Narus, 1990; Frazier, 1983; Frazier, Spekman, and O'Neal, 1988). If the goals of the two firms are met, it is logical that the firms will be happier with the relationship. However, in some situations, goals such as increased market power may not be met due to macroeconomic factors outside the control of the firms. If firms perceive that the other party exerted effort and fulfilled their obligations, both sides may still be satisfied with the relationship, even though strategic gaps may remain unfilled.

If the gaps are being filled, satisfaction results from these outcomes and from the process of working together for mutual benefits. Zand (1972) provides empirical evidence for the proposition that trusting, cooperative behavior leads to satisfaction in organizational relationships. In contrast, Frazier (1983) shows that conflict leads to dissatisfaction with the relationship.

Roehl and Truitt (1987), however, indicate a surprising positive relationship between conflict and performance. Yet they describe conflict in terms of tension and disagreement that are resolvable by two firms involved in a joint venture. A possible functional benefit of conflict is more equitable distribution of resources (Dwyer, Schurr, and Oh, 1987). It can be argued that trust is essential for the resolution of this inevitable kind of conflict. Empirical evidence supports this linkage between trust, functional conflict, and satisfaction in manufacturer-distributor working partnerships (Anderson and Narus, 1990).

CONCLUSION

Our model provides rationale for the formation of international strategic alliances. Its tenets are quite simple: a firm must perceive a need to fill a strategic gap through such means as greater market power, increased efficiency, or improved competencies. The motivation to fill the gap leads to communication with at least one potential partner. As the firms gain knowledge about each other's reliability, trust develops. This belief in each other's willingness and ability to do what has been promised helps lead to the formation of a strategic alliance. When firms cooperate with one another, satisfaction with the relationship results.

Undoubtedly, other variables, particularly those exogenous to the two firms, influence the process. Research on cultural influences (such as the affinity for collaboration and regulatory traditions) should help define the effect of these factors on alliance formation. Further, the relevant variables and their relationships need to be operationalized and tested in the context of international strategic alliances. If the present trend of increased collaboration between firms continues, research into the formation and management of strategic alliances will become even more important to both practitioners and scholars of international business.

REFERENCES

Anderson, J.C., & Narus, J.A. (1990). A model of distributor firm and manufacturer firm working partnerships. *Journal of Marketing*, 54(1) January, 42-58.

Aoki, M. (1990). Toward an economic model of the Japanese firm. *Journal of Economic Literature*, 28(1) March, 1-27.

Auster, E.R. (1987). International corporate linkages: dynamic forms in changing environments, *Columbia Journal of World Business*, 22(2), 3-6.

Axelrod, R. (1984). *The Evolution of Cooperation*. New York: Basic Books.

Badaracco, J. (1991), *Knowledge Link: How Firms Compete Through Strategic Alliances*, Boston, MA: Harvard Business School Review.

Bartlett, C., & Ghoshal, S. (1987). Managing across borders: new strategic requirements. *Sloan Management Review*, 29(1), 7-17.

Beamish, P.W. (1985). The characteristics of joint ventures in developed and developing countries. *Columbia Journal of World Business*, 20(3) Fall, 13-19.

Beamish, P.W., & Banks, J.C. (1987). Equity joint ventures and the theory of the multinational enterprise. *Journal of International Business*, 18(2) Summer, 1-16.

Bialaszewski, D., & Giallourakis, M. (1985). Perceived communication skills and resultant trust perceptions within the channel of distribution. *Journal of Academy of Marketing Science*, 13(2), 206-217.

Borys, B., & Jemison, D.B. (1989). Hybrid arrangements as strategic alliances:

theoretical issues in organizational combinations. *Academy of Management Review*, 14(2) April, 234-249.

Buckley, P.J., & Casson, M. (1988). A theory of cooperation in international business. *Management International Review*, 28 Special, 19-38.

Campbell, N.C.G. (1985). An interaction approach to organizational buying behavior. *Journal of Business Research*, 13(1), 35-48.

Contractor, F.J. (1990). Ownership patterns of U.S. joint ventures and licensing negotiations. *Journal of International Business Studies*, 21(1), 55-73.

Contractor, F.J., & Lorange, P. (1988). Why should firms cooperate? The strategy and economics basis for cooperative ventures. In F.J. Contractor & P. Lorange (Eds.), *Cooperative Strategies in International Business* (pp. 3-28). Lexington, MA: Lexington Books.

Dasgupta, P. (1988). Trust as a commodity. In D. Gambetta (Ed.), *Trust: Making and Breaking Cooperative Relations* (pp. 49-72). Oxford, U.K.: Basil Blackwell Ltd.

Deutsch, M., Canavan, D., & Rubin, J. (1971). The effects of size of conflict and sex of experimenter upon interpersonal bargaining. *Journal of Experimental Social Psychology*, 7(2), 258-267.

Dunning, J.H. (1988). *Explaining international production*. London: Unwin Hyman Ltd.

Dwyer, F.R., Schurr, P., & Oh, S. (1987). Developing buyer-seller relationships. *Journal of Marketing*, 51(2) April, 11-27.

Fiol, C.M., & Lyles, M.A. (1985). Organizational learning. *Academy of Management Review*, 10(4), 803-813.

Fiol, C.M. (1989). A semiotic analysis of corporate language: organizational boundaries and joint venturing. *Administrative Science Quarterly*, 34(2) June, 277-303.

Ford, D. (1980). The development of buyer-seller relationships in industrial markets. *European Journal of Marketing*, 14(5/6), 339-353.

Franko, L.G. (1989). Use of minority and 50-50 joint ventures by United States multinationals during the 1970s: the interaction of host country policies and corporate strategies. *Journal of International Business Studies*, 20(2) Summer, 235-254.

Frazier, G.L. (1983). Interorganizational exchange behavior in marketing channels: a broadened perspective. *Journal of Marketing*, 47(4) Fall, 68-78.

Frazier, G.L., Spekman, R.E., & O'Neal, C.R. (1988). Just-in-time exchange relationships in industrial markets. *Journal of Marketing*, 52(4) October, 52-67.

Geringer, J.M., & Hebert, L. (1989). Control and performance of international joint ventures. *Journal of International Business Studies*, 20(2) Summer, 235-254.

Golembiewski, R.T., & McConkie, M. (1975). The centrality of interpersonal trust in group processes. In C.L. Cooper (Ed.), *Theories of Group Processes* (pp. 131-185). New York: John Wiley and Sons.

Gomes-Casseres, B. (1989). Joint ventures in the face of global competition. *Sloan Management Review*, 30(3) Spring, 17-26.

Good, D. (1988). Individuals, interpersonal relations, and trust. In D. Gambetta (Ed.), *Trust: Making and Breaking Cooperative Relations* (pp. 31-48). Oxford, U.K.: Basil Blackwell Ltd.

Hakansson, H. (1982). *International marketing and purchasing of industrial goods.* Chichester: John Wiley & Sons.

Hakansson, H., & Johanson, J. (1988). Formal and informal cooperation strategies in international industrial markets. In F. Contractor & P. Lorange (Eds.), *Cooperative Strategies in International Business* (pp. 369-379). Lexington, MA: Lexington Books.

Hallen, L., Mohamed, N., & Johanson, J. (1989). Relationships and exchange in international business. In S.T. Cavusgil (Ed.), *Advances in International Marketing* Vol. 3 (pp. 7-23). Greenwich, CT: JAI Press.

Hamel, G., Doz, Y.L., & Prahalad, C.K. (1989). Collaborate with your competitors and win. *Harvard Business Review*, 89(1), 133-139.

Harrigan, K.R. (1985). *Managing for joint venture success.* Lexington, MA: Lexington Books.

Harrigan, K.R. (1987). Strategic alliances: their role in global competition. *Columbia Journal of World Business*, 22(2), 67-69.

Harrigan, K.R. (1988). Strategic alliances and partner asymetries. In F. Contractor & P. Lorange (Eds.), *Cooperative Strategies in International Business.* Lexington, MA: Lexington Books.

Hendryx, S.R. (1986). Implementation of a technology transfer joint venture in the People's Republic of China: a management perspective. *Columbia Journal of World Business*, 21(1) Spring, 57-66.

Hennart, J.F. (1988). A transaction costs theory of equity joint ventures. *Strategic Management Journal*, 9(4), 361-374.

Hergert, M., & Morris, D. (1988). Trends in international collaborative agreements. In F. Contractor & P. Lorange (Eds.), *Cooperative Strategies in International Business* (pp. 99-109). Lexington, MA: Lexington Books.

Hladik, K.J. (1985). *International joint ventures.* Lexington, MA: Lexington Books.

Hladik, K.J. (1988). R&D and international joint ventures. In F. Contractor & P. Lorange (Eds.), *Cooperative Strategies in International Business* (pp. 187-204). Lexington, MA: Lexington Books.

Hull, F. Slowinski, G., Wharton, R., & Azumi, K. (1988), Strategic partnerships between technological entrepreneurs in the United States and large corporations in Japan and the United States. In F. Contractor & P. Lorange (Eds.), *Cooperative Strategies in International Business* (pp. 445-456). Lexington, MA: Lexington Books.

Ingrassia, P. & Graven, K. (1990, April 24). Japan's auto industry may soon consolidate as competition grows. *The Wall Street Journal*, pp. A1, A11.

Itami, H. (1987). *Mobilizing invisible assets.* Cambridge, MA: Harvard University Press.

Jain, S.C. (1987). Perspectives on international strategic alliances. In S.T. Cavusgil (Ed.), *Advances in International Marketing* Vol. 2 (pp. 103-120). Greenwich, CT: JAI Press.

Killing, J.P. (1983). *Strategies for joint venture success.* New York: Praeger.

Killing, J.P. (1988). Understanding alliances: their role of task and organizational complexity. In F. Contractor & P. Lorange (Eds.), *Cooperative Strategies in International Business* (pp. 55-67). Lexington, MA: Lexington Books.

Kogut, B. & Singh, H. (1988). The effect of national culture on the choice of entry mode. *Journal of International Business Studies*, 20(3) Fall, 411-432.

Kogut, B. (1988). Joint ventures: theoretical and empirical perspectives. *Strategic Management Journal*, 9(4), 319-332.

Kogut, B. (1985). Designing global strategies: comparative and competitive value-added chains. *Sloan Management Review*, 27(1), (Summer), 15-28.

Kotabe, M. (1990). Corporate product policy and innovative behavior of European and Japanese multinationals: an empirical investigation. *Journal of Marketing*, 54(2) April, 19-33.

Lorenz, E.H. (1988). Neither friends nor strangers: informal networks of subcontracting in French industry. In D. Gambetta (Ed.), *Trust: Making and Breaking Cooperative Relations* (pp. 194-210). Oxford, U.K.: Basil Blackwell Ltd.

Mathews, B.A., & Shimoff, E. (1979). Expansion of exchange: monitoring trust levels in ongoing exchange relations. *Journal of Conflict Resolution*, 23(3) September, 538-560.

Ohmae, K. (1987). The triad world view. *Journal of Business Strategy*, 7(4), 8-19.

Ohmae, K. (1989). The global logic of strategic alliances. *Harvard Business Review*, 89(2), 143-154.

Osborn, R.W., & Baughn, C. (1987). New patterns in the formation of US/Japanese cooperative ventures: the role of technology. *Columbia Journal of World Business*, 22(2), 57-65.

Osborn, R.W., & Baughn, C. (1990). Forms of interorganizational governance for multinational alliances. *Academy of Management Journal*, 33(3), 503-519.

Ouchi, W.G. (1980). Markets, bureaucracies, and clans. *Administrative Science Quarterly*, 25(1) March, 129-139.

Pfeffer, J., & Salancik, G.R. (1978). *The external control of organizations: a resource dependence perspective.* New York: Harper & Row.

Porter, M.E., & Fuller, M.B. (1986). Coalitions and global strategy. In M.E. Porter (Ed.), *Competition in Global Industries* (pp. 315-344). Boston: Harvard Business School.

Prahalad, C.K., & Hamel, G. (1990). The core competence of the corporation. *Harvard Business Review*, 90(3), 79-91.

Pruitt, D.G., & Kimmel, M.J. (1976). Twenty years of experimental gaming: critique, synthesis, and suggestions for the future. *Annual Review of Psychology*, 28, 363-392.

Pucik, V. (1988). Strategic alliances with the Japanese: implications for human resource management. In F. Contractor & P. Lorange (Eds.), *Cooperative*

Strategies in International Business (pp. 487-498). Lexington, MA: Lexington Books.

Reich, R.T., & Mankin, E.D. (1986). Joint ventures with Japan give away our future. *Harvard Business Review*, 86(2), 78-86.

Roehl, T.W., & Truitt, J.F. (1987). Stormy open marriages are better: evidence from U.S., Japanese, and French cooperative ventures in commercial aircraft. *Columbia Journal of World Business*, 22(2), 87-95.

Schurr, P.H., & Ozanne, J.L. (1985). Influences on exchange processes: buyers' preconditions of a seller's trustworthiness and bargaining toughness. *Journal of Consumer Research*, 11(1), 939-953.

Spekman, R., & Strauss, D. (1986). An exploratory investigation of strategic vulnerability and its impact on buyer-seller relationships. In K. Backhaus & D.T. Wilson (Eds.), *Industrial Marketing: A German-American Perspective* (pp. 115-133). Berlin: Springer-Verlag.

Thorelli, H.B. (1990). Networks: the gay nineties in international marketing. In H. Thorelli & S.T. Cavusgil (Eds.), *International Marketing Strategy* (pp. 73-85). Oxford, U.K.: Pergamon Press.

Tyebjee, T.T. (1988). Japan's joint ventures in the United States. In F. Contractor & P. Lorange (Eds.), *Cooperative Strategies in International Business* (pp. 457-472). Lexington, MA: Lexington Books.

Vickers, J. (1985). Pre-emptive patenting, joint ventures and the persistence of oligopoly. *International Journal of Industrial Organization*, 3(1), 261-273.

Williamson, O. (1975). *Markets and hierarchies*. New York: Free Press.

Williamson, O. (1981). The economics of organization: the transaction cost approach. *American Journal of Sociology*, 87(3), 548-577.

Yamagishi, T., & Sato, K. (1986). Motivational bases of the public goods problem. *Journal of Personality and Social Psychology*, 50(1), 67-73.

Zand, D.E. (1972). Trust and managerial problem solving. *Administrative Science Quarterly*, 17(2), 229-239.

II. THE FUNCTIONAL DIMENSION OF GLOBAL BUSINESS ALLIANCES

Chapter 5

Cross-National Corporate Partnerships: Trends in Alliance Formation

Refik Culpan
Eugene A. Kostelac Jr.

INTRODUCTION

Business firms around the world have engaged in cross-national alliances to achieve or sustain competitive advantages in domestic as well as in international markets. Integrated markets and resource dependency in various industries have also stimulated strategic alliances between business firms. For example, the "Single Market" movement in Europe has required non-European companies to consider strategic alliances with European partners to penetrate or expand in this common market (Goette, 1990; Gross, 1989; Wightman, 1988). As a result, companies have been seeking strategic alliances to respond to increased competition, changing market conditions, and rapid technological advances (Culpan, Chapter 1).

This chapter will first review previous studies on strategic alliances in relation to these dimensions: alliance trends, industry settings, types of corporate alliances, purposes, and country of origin of firms engaged in such ventures. Then, according to these same dimensions, the chapter reports the findings of an empirical inquiry. Furthermore, it evaluates cross-national corporate partnership by discussing advantages and disadvantages.

Recent studies have examined domestic and international joint ventures, as well as other forms of collaborations, in an attempt to identify types of companies and industries involved in cooperative ventures (Ghemawat, Porter, and Rawlinson, 1986; Harrigan, 1986;

Hergert and Morris, 1988; Hladik, 1985); the reasons for engaging in such ventures (Berg, Duncan, and Friedman, 1982; Contractor and Lorange, 1988; Porter, 1985; Negandhi and Savara, 1989); and how to negotiate and manage a successful cooperative alliance (Carter, Cushman, and Hartz, 1988; Harrigan, 1986).

Janger (1980), for example, reports that most of the Fortune 500 companies with more than $100 million in sales were engaged in one or more international joint ventures. Such a frequent use of joint ventures among large U.S. multinational companies suggests that these companies are attempting to improve their competitive position in international markets through strategic alliances. Janger also notes that the primary reasons given by companies for using joint ventures were to develop new markets and gain access to materials. Killing (1983), however, reports that joint-venture activity between U.S. firms occurred more frequently (approximately twice the number of ventures, compared with ventures between U.S. firms and foreign partners) than ventures between U.S. and foreign partners. This observation suggests that U.S. firms were more concerned with protecting local markets than with expanding overseas.

However, most of these research studies primarily concentrated on joint ventures, so that other forms of cooperative alliances, especially non-equity arrangements, including research and development (R&D) partnerships, marketing agreements, and supplier agreements now warrant further attention.

TRENDS AND PATTERNS
IN CROSS-NATIONAL ALLIANCES

Frequency of Interfirm Cooperations

Views conflict over the number of alliances formed in the last two decades. Ghemawat, Porter, and Rawlinson (1985) found that annual coalition formations fluctuated between a high of 120 in 1974 and a low of 55 in 1978. These researchers, therefore, concluded that no clear change is evident in the number of international coalitions formed over the 1970-82 period.

In contrast, some other researchers reported increases in cooperative agreements (Harrigan, 1985; Hladik, 1985; Hergert and Morris, 1988). For example, by examining characteristics of international joint-venture activity between 1974 and 1982, Hladik (1985) concluded that the absolute number of international joint-venture formations increased significantly during the period studied. The number of international joint ventures observed in the last four years of her study doubled in comparison with those observed over the first five years. Similarly, Hergert and Morris (1988) reported an increase in the use of collaborative agreements between 1975 and 1986.

Still, some other researchers claim that strategic alliances present a cyclical pattern. For example, Berg, Duncan, and Friedman (1982) observed that joint-venture formations were less sensitive to economic changes reflected in capital markets than in changes in production within the U.S. economy. The researchers noted that the growth rate in domestic joint ventures declined during recessionary periods (1969-70 and 1972-75), suggesting that the formation of joint ventures are cyclical in nature. Hladik (1985) also noted that the formation of international joint ventures seems to occur in cycles. Similarly, Gomes-Casseres (1988) argued that international alliance formations are of a cyclical nature and closely correspond to economic cycles. Joint ventures appear to expand when economic conditions encourage companies to expand abroad, reach a peak as local partners hinder global coordination; and then decline in the final phase after the company realizes that it can compete better with a wholly owned subsidiary rather than with a joint venture (Gomes-Casseres, 1988).

Conflicting observations about the number of alliances formed during the past two decades may be attributable to the differences in the methodology used by these researchers in selecting their samples, or it may have resulted from the actual variations in alliance formations that occurred over time.

Industry Settings of Cooperations

Ghemawat, Porter, and Rawlinson (1986) reported that alliances were concentrated in certain industries. Alliances within the chemicals, computers, and other electronics industries have increased during the 12 years of their study. Berg, Duncan, and Friedman (1982) observed that joint ventures were not uniform across industries. Alliance activity was especially varied in the chemical and tobacco industries. Berg et al. found 282 alliances reported by chemical companies, as compared with five by tobacco companies. Between 1964 and 1975, the heaviest incidence of joint-venture activity was observed in the mining, chemicals, electrical machinery, and non-electrical machinery industries. These researchers concluded that this high incidence of alliance activity was primarily due to "the importance of natural resources for mining and the need for risk pooling among participants in the other industries" (Berg, Duncan, and Friedman, 1982, pp. 15-16).

Types of Alliances

Cooperative ventures between two or more firms include both equity and non-equity arrangements (Culpan, Chapter 1, and Osborn and Baughn, Chapter 3). A joint venture, the most common form of equity arrangement, "implies the creation of a separate corporation, whose stock is shared by two or more partners, each expecting a proportional share of dividends as compensation" (Contractor and Lorange, 1988, p. 7). A joint venture is one of several productivity-enhancing forms of economic organization that permit a firm to capitalize on inventions, take advantage of complementary technologies, or reduce time lags in product introduction (Berg, Duncan, and Friedman, 1982).

Other alliances that represent non-equity forms of cooperation between two or more firms include supply agreements, licensing, marketing agreements, exploration consortia, research partnerships, and co-production agreements. Both the equity and non-equity forms of alliance represent long-term relationships that provide individual firms with the means to broaden the scope of a firm without expanding the firm. Equity and non-equity alliances also allow a firm to share activities without the inherent risks of going it alone (Porter, 1985).

Purposes of Participating Firms

The motives of participating firms in a cooperative venture may vary according to their resource dependency and involvement in certain activities in the value chain. Some firms form alliances because they face too much risk in their competitive environments or possess too few internal skills to cope with these challenges alone. Therefore, it appears that most successful cooperative ventures are being formed between firms possessing specific strengths that complement those of their partners and between firms with compatible objectives. Usually, these objectives are related to strategies set to obtain resources and skills that individual firms lack internally. Culpan, in Chapter 1, combines a variety of reasons for strategic alliances into two principal motives: resource pooling and risk/cost sharing. He argues that a firm in partnership with another firm either complements its weakness with its partner's strength or tends to share an augmented risk and the costs of operations.

With reference to R&D joint ventures, Hladik (1988) listed spreading costs and risks, access to technology and technical know-how, access to markets, and competitive positioning as the primary purposes given by partners for forming a joint venture. On the other hand, Hergert and Morris (1988) identified the strategic rationale behind international collaboration as (in descending order): joint product development, production, marketing production and/or marketing, development and marketing, and a combination of all of them. They argued that "cooperative behavior begins to occur very early in the product-development cycle" (p. 107), because it is easier to manage at this stage than during the marketing stage.

A review of the purposes stated for cooperative ventures implies that they can be categorized as market entry and expansion, joint R&D, production partnership, and a combination of these individual purposes. This categorization will be used for our empirical inquiry.

Country of Origin of Partners

The number of collaborative agreements between the three major trading blocks has increased steadily from 1979 to 1985 (Hergert and Morris, 1988). Hergert and Morris noted that "a majority of the collaborative agreements are struck between partners within European Community or between U.S. and European firms. The Japanese are less active in cooperative ventures than their U.S. and European counterparts" (p. 102). Of the European firms, the French are the most active ones in forming cooperative ventures. Although the British come next, they collaborated less with European partners and more with Japanese partners. (Hergert and Morris, 1988).

Of course, these kinds of findings depend upon the methodology used for the inquiry. For example, the findings of Hergert and Morris are based on the INSEAD data base, which might be biased toward European firms and certain kinds of collaborative activities. Our investigation, on the other hand, covers strategic alliances between mostly U.S. and non-U.S. firms.

AN EMPIRICAL INVESTIGATION

Method

The data base of new alliances formed between U.S. and non-U.S. firms was created from published announcements in the Three-Star Eastern Edition of *The Wall Street Journal* for the four-year period 1986-89. The sample of alliances were identified by scanning the general news abstracts listed in *The Wall Street Journal* Index under the subject headings of joint ventures, licensing, and other interfirm cooperations. The sample only includes announcements that stated that the firms agreed to, formed, entered, or completed an alliance with another company. Announcements of a future planned alliance were excluded from the data base unless the actual agreement was subsequently reported in the index.

The data base contains the following information:

- The date the alliance was cited in *The Wall Street Journal* Index.
- The name of the parent firm and home-country location of parent firm. (This information was obtained from the index citation or, when necessary, from references citing information included in *The Wall Street Journal* article.)
- The four-digit Standard Industry Classification (SIC) code for the U.S. parent company. A SIC code was assigned to a company–based on the major industry of the parent company–in those cases where a SIC code could not be referenced from the Predicast's F&S Index.

- The form of the alliance was identified, either as a joint venture, joint R&D, licensing, or other type of alliance.
- The principal activity of the alliance was classified, either as manufacturing, sales, R&D, or other activity. A manufacturing category embraced any alliance where the primary activity involved production, assembly, or packaging. Sales includes marketing, repairs and maintenance, finance, transportation, or other sales and service-related activities. R&D consists of activities associated with product or process R&D. Other activities encompass any activity not fitting into these categories–including farming, raw material extraction and exploration, etc.

Since the primary focus of this study is on alliances between U.S. and non-U.S. firms, the methodology used assumes that information obtained from *The Wall Street Journal* is representative of current alliances and formed by U.S.-based companies.

The research design for this study is similar to the one used by Ghemawat, Porter, and Rawlinson (1986) in their study of international coalition activity from 1970-82 and to that used by Hergert and Morris (1988) in their study of trends in international alliances from 1976-86.

RESULTS

A growing number of alliances were observed for the four-year period cited; in all, 391 alliances were reported in 38 industries. The frequency of alliances is presented in Figure 5.1. The findings show that the overall number of partnerships between U.S. and foreign firms has increased more than the partnerships between U.S. firms. While the U.S.-foreign partnerships demonstrated stability as a percentage of the total number of alliances over this period, the domestic alliances decreased in number.

Frequency in Alliance Formations

Figure 5.1 shows the trend of new alliance formations observed during the 1986-89 period. The data suggest that there was a signifi-

FIGURE 5.1. Alliance Trends

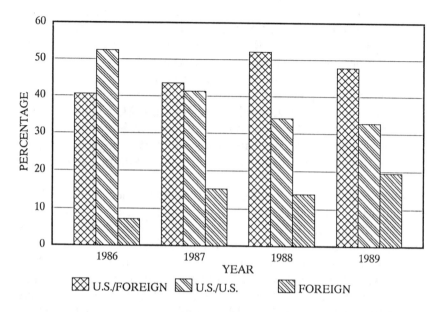

cant increase in alliance activity during the latter two years. The number of alliances reported in 1988 and 1989 were more than three times the number reported during the 1986-87 period. Based on an absolute number of occurrences, the data indicate that there was an observed explosion in alliance formations in 1988, compared with the activity in 1986 and 1987. The percentage of U.S.-foreign partnerships increased as a percentage of total alliances for the 1988-1989 period, compared with the percentage of total alliances during the years 1986-1987. (See Table 5.1.)

Industry Setting

Although cross-national alliances are being used more frequently (as shown in Figure 5.1), they are concentrated within relatively few industries. For example, several major industries account for approximately 65% of the alliances reported. The highest number of alliances were observed in the electric and electronics industry. Other industries that reported a high frequency of alliance formations

TABLE 5.1. Industry Listing of Corporate Partnerships

SIC CODE	INDUSTRY	1986	1987	1988	1989	TOTAL
1000	MINING & EXTRACTIVE	1	1	2	5	9
1500	CONSTRUCTION	– –	1	2	– –	3
2000	FOOD & KINDRED PRODUCTS	1	2	2	5	10
2100	TOBACCO	– –	– –	– –	1	1
2300	APPAREL	– –	– –	– –	1	1
2600	PAPER & ALLIED PRODUCTS	– –	1	3	2	6
2700	PRINTING & PUBLISHING	1	– –	7	3	11
2800	CHEMICALS & ALLIED PROD	4	8	15	17	44
2900	PETROLEUM & ENERGY	1	– –	8	2	11
3000	RUBBER & PLASTIC	– –	– –	3	4	7
3100	LEATHER	1	– –	– –	– –	1
3200	STONE, CLAY & GLASS	– –	1	6	1	8
3300	METALS	– –	2	5	1	8
3400	FABRICATED METAL	– –	1	3	2	6
3500	MACHINERY (excluding electric)	4	4	15	14	37
3600	ELECTRICAL & ELECTRONIC	7	7	14	20	48
3700	TRANSPORT EQUIPMENT	5	3	13	9	30
3800	INSTRUMENTS	3	3	1	2	9
3900	MANUFACTURING NEC	– –	1	– –	1	2
4000	TRANSPORTATION	– –	1	1	5	7
4800	COMMUNICATIONS	3	2	8	11	24
4900	ELECTRIC, GAS & WATER	1	– –	2	5	8
5000	WHOLESALE & RETAIL TRADE	1	2	7	1	11
6000	FINANCIAL SERVICES	1	3	10	11	25
7000	SERVICE INDUSTRIES	5	3	12	25	45
8000	MEDICAL & HEALTH SERVICES	1	– –	1	1	3
8500	SCIENCE, R & D	1	– –	– –	1	2
8900	PROFESSIONAL SERVICES NEC	– –	– –	2	3	5
9100	NATIONAL GOVERNMENT	– –	– –	1	1	2
9900	BUSINESS	1	– –	1	5	7
	TOTAL	42	46	144	159	391

(in descending order) were: miscellaneous service industries; chemicals and allied products; machinery, excluding electric (this category includes computer-equipment manufacturers); transportation equipment; financial services; and communications. With the exception of the miscellaneous and financial service industries, these industries characteristically display substantial operating risks, high entry costs, and rapidly changing technology. The increases in service industry alliances can be traced primarily to financial industry (banking) alliances formed in 1988-89 and to increases in alliance activity within the hotel, advertising, and entertainment industries. This trend can possibly be explained in terms of the increasing risks and costs associated within these industries during the latter part of the 1980's.

Form of Alliances

Figure 5.2 categorizes the various types of strategic alliances by legal form. Sixty-nine percent of the alliances reported in the sample were joint ventures. The remaining non-equity forms of alliances consist of R&D licensing, and various other agreements (including co-production and marketing agreements). As depicted in Figure 5.2, it can be concluded that the joint-venture form of alliance appears to be the most popular form of alliance. Also, the number of joint ventures reported as a percentage of total alliances appears relatively stable during the four-year period, with a slight increase noted in 1988. Therefore, we conclude that there was no significant change in alliance trends during this four-year period.

FIGURE 5.2. Form of Alliance

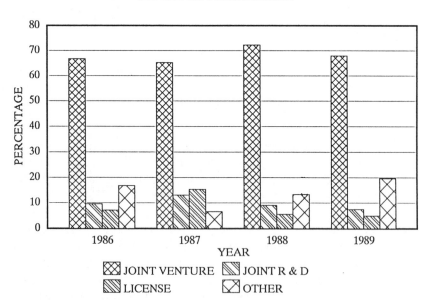

Purposes of Alliance

The reasons firms gave for forming alliances are presented in Figure 5.3. The largest number of cooperative ventures, approximately 41%, were formed to engage in joint sales and marketing activities. It is surprising that there were relatively few R&D alliances. R&D strategies were noted as the primary reason for forming an alliance in 10.8% of the cases, while joint manufacturing and production were reported in 32.7% of the alliances. Technology-sharing arrangements were used primarily by U.S. companies, to gain expertise from Japanese electronics firms. For example, Texas Instruments formed a joint development agreement with Hitachi of Japan to gain expertise in the production of memory chips (*The Wall Street Journal*, December 23, 1988). VLSI Technology Inc. also formed a technology-sharing arrangement with Hitachi to gain expertise in producing semiconductors (*The Wall Street Journal*, May 11, 1988).

FIGURE 5.3. Alliance Purpose

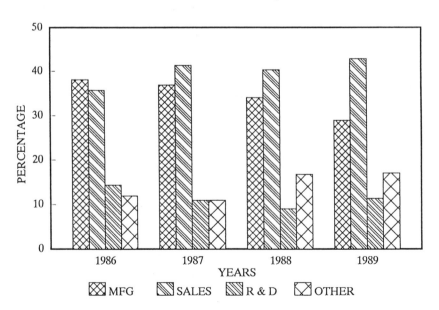

Country Origin of Partners

Figure 5.4 summarizes the alliance partners' country of origin, according to their parent company location. The country of origin of the participating firms varies widely. In over 80% of the reported alliances, at least one participant was a U.S.-based company. This finding is understandable in light of the inherent U.S. bias of the sample. Nevertheless, more than one-half of the alliances reported by U.S.-based companies involved a foreign partner. This may show an increasing trend for US-foreign partnerships. U.S. alliances with European and Japanese firms account for almost 65% of the partnerships reported. The percentage of U.S. partnerships with Japanese and East Asians reached 43%. Notable in the last two years is an obvious surge in U.S.-East European alliances.

AN EVALUATION OF STRATEGIC ALLIANCES

After examining alliance activities theoretically and empirically, we conclude that business firms across the borders must have a purpose for their engagements in interfirm partnerships. We believe

FIGURE 5.4. Country Origin of U.S. Partner

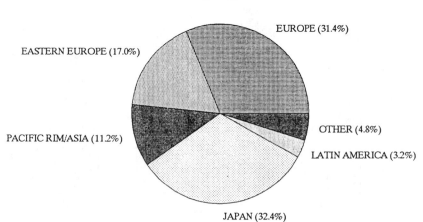

that this purpose is to gain or sustain a competitive advantage. However, any competitive edge a firm holds may change as industry conditions change. Porter (1990) asserts that "the possibilities for new ways of competing usually grow out of some discontinuities or change in industry structure" (p. 45). According to Porter, the "most typical causes of innovations that shift competitive advantage" are new technologies; new or shifting buyer needs; the emergence of a new industry segment; shifting input costs or availability; and changes in government regulations (p. 45). Such industry changes provide the impetus for seeking new strategic alternatives (and strategic alliance happens to be one). In placing alliances in a proper perspective, Kanter (1989) shares our view:

> In the face of heightened competitive pressures and the worldwide scope of both technology and markets, many U.S. firms have established new cooperative agreements with other organizations at home and abroad that involve unprecedented (for them) levels of sharing and commitment. While American firms, particularly small ones, have always allied with other firms for specific purposes, the extent as well as diversity of such activity has grown in recent years, moving from the periphery to take a central place in some companies' strategies. (p. 119)

Of course, as is true for any strategic option, forming a strategic alliance has its own advantages as well as disadvantages. Therefore, firms should be aware of benefits and limitations of such strategies. In other words, there are several factors that must be evaluated by companies considering the establishment of an alliance with a foreign firm as part of their overall corporate strategy. The determining factors for strategic alliances are defined by referring to the literature.

Advantages

Cooperative ventures can provide strengths by creating vertical linkages to decrease dependency on outsiders, improve access to foreign technology, circumvent market imperfections, and exploit scale economies. These vertical linkages may afford firms the benefits of integration, diversification, or international market entry without the apparent resource commitments (Thorelli, 1986). This means cooperative ventures provide competitive strength by consolidating a firm's existing market position.

With respect to joint ventures, Harrigan (1986) defined the advantages into three principal categories: internal benefits, competitive benefits, and cooperative benefits. Internal benefits are obtained from risk sharing, acquiring access to resources, developing scale economies, acquiring better information and production practices, and reducing employee turnover. Companies do not want to risk their financial assets on a project that involves uncertainties or costly expenditures to develop the required technology. Competitive benefits are derived from exerting influence over normal industry evolution, preempting competitor strategic moves, gaining timing advantages when entering a market, and developing defensive strategies in response to industry globalization (Harrigan, 1986). Strategic benefits include creating and exploiting synergies with owner's activities, gaining know-how through technology transfers, and entering new businesses (diversification) or expanding internationally (Harrigan, 1988). International cooperative ventures could increase in importance as a strategic weapon for effective competition in the global market place. Whether they are used for market power or sourcing advantages, cooperative ventures enable participants to acquire an edge over competitors.

The most likely candidates for alliances are firms that have difficulties in pursuing a go-it-alone strategy because of their lack of capabilities or resources. As a result, firms consider an alliance as another strategic option. In this respect, Harrigan (1986) points out that strategic alliances will enable partners to share financial and operating risks and costs, obtain benefits associated with scale economies and operating synergies, and increase market share.

Berg, Duncan, and Friedman (1982) also identify a number of advantages associated with forming joint ventures. These include improved transfer of technology, reduced capital expenditures, scale economies, rapid commercialization of new products, and reduced financial and operational risks.

Furthermore, Kanter (1989) offers this explanation:

Another justification for partnerships is their dynamism. Some partnerships that begin as an alternative route to gaining a capacity or a resource may end with at least one organization better able to provide that resource itself, so that it no longer requires the partner. Dependence is decreased over time, and the partnership dissolves. But other partnerships have the opposite dynamic. What begins as a limited alliance may move toward greater degrees of interdependence, and with organizations merging. Some analysts have compared 'strategic alliance' to marriages, but they are really more similar to living together. (p. 122)

Alliance formation can also be a means to overcome protectionist or nationalistic attitudes and measures in target countries. For example, some European countries have become increasingly protectionist and nationalistic, especially in their demonstrated preference for local suppliers over foreign suppliers. In such cases, joint-venture participation can become a necessity. This protectionist attitude may trigger an increase in the percentage of joint ventures being formed in countries that adopt protectionist policies.

Strategic alliance can pave the way for entry into strictly controlled markets or for changing host-government regulations concerning foreign investment and competition (Hladik, 1985). More permissive governmental regulations adopted by Mexico, China, and the former U.S.S.R. have encouraged Western firms to establish a number of joint ventures with local firms.

Probably the most convincing argument for alliances and partnerships is the benefit to be gained from organizational learning, also called "tacit knowledge," which refers to the reciprocal knowledge acquired by partners (Borys and Jemison, Chapter 2). Stressing emphasis on interfirm knowledge exchange, Badaracco (1991) contends that

[k]nowledge links can help one company learn special capabilities from another; they can help a company combine its special capabilities with those of another organization to create new embedded knowledge; and they can enable one company to help another organization build up its skills and capabilities in ways that will benefit both companies later on. (p. 14)

Disadvantages

Yet, despite the advantages listed above, formation and management of partnerships involve enormous problems: "Independent studies by McKinsey & Company and Cooper & Lybrand show that perhaps 70 percent of joint ventures or formal 'strategic alliances' are disbanded or fall short of expectations" (Kanter, 1989, p. 121).

A major limitation for formation of a successful alliance is the problem of finding a compatible partner. Koot (1988), for example, concluded that finding and selecting a compatible partner are the most difficult tasks. Likewise, Harrigan (1985) argued that ventures are more likely to succeed when partners have complementary missions and capabilities. These capabilities can include resource and managerial capabilities and other attributes that create a strategic fit. Harrigan (1988) also concluded that ventures are more successful when partners have similarities in relationship to venture formations, products, markets, and technology.

Disadvantages usually result from problems concerning the satisfaction of the demands of at least two unrelated parties. Obviously, having a partner will make the decision-making and control processes more cumbersome. Killing (1983) argued that having multiple parents in a joint venture is a major source of problems manifested in two specific areas. First, problems are encountered at the level of the board of directors. "The board of directors of a joint venture contains representatives from each parent and it is here that differences in priorities, direction, and perhaps in values will emerge. The result can be confusion, frustration, possible bitterness, and resulting slowness to make decisions" (Killing, 1983, p. 9). Second, problems develop in relationship to staffing. A joint venture generally employs both general and functional managers drawn from its parents. "Not surprisingly, the working relationship between the two managers in this situation tends to be strained, cumbersome, and inefficient" (Killing, 1983, p. 10).

Major hurdles that successful joint ventures must overcome include setting up adequate safeguards to protect patents, products, and know-how. It is always helpful to keep the mission of a venture limited to a set of boundaries, so that the venture does not become its sponsors' competitor (Harrigan, 1986). Shared ownership arrangements can also create problems that result from the roles partners assume in the venture. Killing (1983) contended that the more similar the skills and the more equal the contributions between the partners, the greater the likelihood of shared decision making and of success for the alliance. Similarly, Harrigan (1986) advised that the best relationships are established between firms of similar size or culture. Potential problems become real problems when one partner dominates and exploits the other partner (Mascarenhas, 1989). Other problems can develop within the relationship when, for example, through a state of unequal ownership, control or influence is exerted by a dominant partner and consequently results in loss of proprietary knowledge and assets to a potential competitor should the alliance be terminated (Root, 1988).

With reference to the asymmetrical size of allied companies, we believe that a small company can lose out considerably if the larger partner unexpectedly changes its strategy. In any case, the large partner tends to dominate the small partner and shape their relationship. Moreover, sheer size often causes the small partner to become very frustrated.

Other problems can arise from pitfalls inherent in a successful alliance (Carter, Cushman, and Hartz, 1988; Hladik, 1985; Killing, 1983) and also from disproportionate contributions of resources, information, and capital (Fuller and Porter, 1986; Harrigan, 1985). In addition, problems arise when partners are unable to manage a venture effectively due to restrictive government policies regarding economic regulations (Harrigan, 1986).

Another often-cited obstacle to strategic alliance is antitrust regulations. Antitrust problems normally result from government policies aimed at regulating local economic competition. Some countries have strict antitrust laws that prohibit certain business cooperations among firms. This situation occurs especially when two large companies competing in the same industry form an alliance that creates an unfair advantage over other firms in the same industry. Harrigan (1986) warned that failure to consider antitrust issues when forming an alliance can result in costly and unnecessary litigation, wasteful use of company resources, and possible loss of one's competitive position.

The purposes given for forming a joint venture can serve as

important indicators when analyzing joint-venture behavior, because they provide a basis for determining the economic benefits expected from an alliance. Difficulties arise, however, when trying to make assumptions about alliance activity across industries. Although the above discussion about the merits of cooperative arrangements is based primarily on joint ventures, the same arguments can easily be extended to most other forms of alliance.

At the same time, because they are unlike a joint venture, non-equity forms of alliance have not been studied extensively; we need to develop new conceptual models and managerial guidelines dealing with the special problems of non-equity alliance. For example, while an R&D partnership presents issues pertaining to configuration of sharing proprietary know-how, agreements on design specifications, and minimum efficient scale in R&D (Hladik, 1988), a countertrade partnership involves the problems of late deliveries of goods and inferior product quality (Culpan, 1989). Such issues need to be addressed within the context of an alliance.

CONCLUSION

This study has attempted to provide some insight into recent international strategic alliances across industries. It has also sought to provide a summary of the benefits and risks associated with cross-national alliances. The authors' conclusion is that the use of strategic alliances can vary widely across industries. Typically, strategic alliances in the electronics industry were developed to obtain economies of scale in production, distribution, and marketing as well as to reduce costs associated with R&D required to expand such activities beyond a single country. More often, these alliances are formed to obtain access to technology and to establish and strengthen market share on a global basis.

The increasing interest of firms in developing strategies for competition in international markets calls for further research in the use of cross-national alliances within specific industries to determine if any significant advantages are present when entering, protecting, or expanding market shares under changing economic conditions. A recent survey of Chief Executive Officers of electronics firms (*Electronic Business*, 1990) showed that manufacturing and technology alliances are expected to grow, while marketing agreements are expected to decline. Increasing costs of manufacturing and technological development were stated as the primary reasons for forming alliances to compete on a global scale.

While this study has addressed some of the issues involved in using cross-national alliances as part of a firm's global corporate strategy, the increasing popularity of cross-national alliances and complex factors entering into the decision to form an alliance require further research. A thorough analysis of individual industry characteristics is needed to fully understand the similarities and the differences present in alliances between international firms. In addition, managers must consider how a cooperative venture will affect the competitive position of participating firms. To do so, they should examine the benefits and the costs of an alliance and also compare these factors with those associated with a strategy of going it alone.

REFERENCES

Badaracco, Jr., J.L. (1991). *The knowledge link.* Boston: Harvard Business School Press.

Berg, S.V., Duncan, J., and Friedman, P. (1982). *Joint Venture Strategies and Corporate Innovation.* Cambridge: Oelgeschlager, Gunn & Hain, Publishers, Inc.

Carter, J. D., Cushman, R.F., and Hartz, C.S. (1988). *The Handbook of Joint Venturing.* Homewood, IL: Dow Jones-Irwin.

Contractor, F. J., and Lorange, P. (1988). Why should firms cooperate? The strategy and economics basis for cooperative ventures. In F.J. Contractor and P. Lorange, (Eds.), *Cooperative Strategies in International Business* (pp. 3-30). Lexington, MA: Lexington Books.

Culpan, R. (1989). Strategic use of countertrade in multinational business. *Journal of Business Strategies,* 6(1), 22-32.

Electronic Business. (March 19, 1990). Shift in focus for strategic alliances. pp. 58-60.

Fuller, M. B., and Porter, M.E. (1986). Coalitions and global strategy. In M. E. Porter (ed.), *Competition in Global Industries* (pp. 315-342). Boston: Harvard Business School Press.

Goette, E. E. (1990). Europe 1992: Update for business planners. *The Journal of Business Strategy,* (March/April): pp. 10-13.

Gomes-Casseres, B. (1988). Joint venture cycles: The evolution of ownership strategies of U.S. MNEs, 1945-75. In J. Contractor and P. Lorange (Eds.), *Cooperative Strategies in International Business* (pp. 111-128). Lexington, MA: Lexington Books.

Ghemawat, P., Porter, M.E., and Rawlinson, R.A. (1986). Patterns of international coalition activity. In M. E. Porter (Eds.), *Competition in Global Industries* (pp. 345-365). Boston: Harvard Business School Press.

Gross, T. F. (1989). Europe 1992: American firms blaze the hottest frontier. *Management Review*, September, 24-29.

Harrigan, K. R. (1985). *Strategies for Joint Ventures*. Lexington: Lexington Books.

Harrigan, K. R. (1986). *Managing for Joint Venture Success*. Lexington, MA: Lexington Books.

Harrigan, K. R. (1988). Joint ventures and competitive strategy. *Strategic Management Journal*, 9, 141-158.

Hergert, M., and Morris, D. (1988). Trends in international collaborative agreements. In F. J. Contractor and P. Lorange (Eds.), *Cooperative Strategies in International Business* (pp. 99-110). Lexington, MA: Lexington Books.

Hladik, K. J. (1985). *International Joint Ventures*. Lexington: Lexington Books.

Hladik, K.J. (1988). R&D and International joint ventures, in F.J. Contractor and P. Lorange (Eds.), *Cooperative Strategies in International Business* (pp. 187-203). Lexington, MA: Lexington Books.

Janger, A. R. (1980). *Organization of International Joint Ventures*. The Conference Board, New York.

Kanter, R. M. (1989). *When Giants Learn to Dance*. New York: Simon and Schuster.

Killing, P. K. (1983). *Strategies for Joint Venture Success*. Praeger Publishers.

Koot, W. T. M. (1988). Underlying Dilemmas in the Management of International Joint Ventures. In F. J. Contractor and P. Lorange (eds.), *Cooperative Strategies in International Business* (pp. 347-368). Lexington: Lexington Books.

Mascarenhas, B. (1989). Transnational linkages and strategy. In A. R. Negandhi and A. Savara (Eds.), *International Strategic Management* (pp. 29-52). Lexington: Lexington Books.

Negandhi, A. R. and Savara, A. (1989). (Eds.) *International Strategic Management*. Lexington: Lexington Books.

Porter, M. E. (1985). *Competitive Advantage: Creating and Sustaining Superior Performance*. New York: The Free Press.

Porter, M. E. (1990). *The Competitive Advantage of Nations*. New York: The Free Press.

Root, F. R. (1988). Some taxonomies of international cooperative arrangements. In F. J. Contractor and P. Lorange (Eds.), *Cooperative Strategies in International Business* (pp. 69-80). Lexington: Lexington Books.

Thorelli, H.B. (1986). Networks: Between markets and hierarchies. *Strategic Management Journal*, July, 37-51.

The Wall Street Journal. (1988, December 23). p. 2B.

The Wall Street Journal. (1988, May 11). p. 5.

Wightman, D. R. (1988). Joint venturing in Europe. In J. D. Carter, R. F. Cushman and C.S. Hartz (Eds.), *The Handbook of Joint Venturing* (pp. 247-263). Homewood, IL: Dow Jones-Irwin.

Chapter 6

Technology-Based Cross-Border Alliances

Philippe Gugler
John H. Dunning

INTRODUCTION

Firms, particularly transnational corporations (TNCs), operate through a global network of related enterprises. One of the main characteristics of these networks is the creation, diffusion, and commercialization of technological innovations. Although the transnationalization of research and development (R&D) activities by TNCs is a comparatively new phenomenon, it is fast becoming an important one. Japanese companies, for example, have sent thousands of engineers to be trained at European and American universities and have set up R&D units in Europe (e.g., Sharp, Sony, Canon, and Hitachi in Ireland)[1] and in the United States (e.g., NEC in Princeton; Kobe Steel and Fujitsu in Silicon Valley). European and American companies have also set up innovatory centers overseas. For example, Dow, Corning, IBM, TI, DuPont, and W. R. Grace are actively pursuing basic research, and Kodak, Dow Chemical Pfizer, and Digital Equipment are actively pursuing applied R&D activities in their Japanese laboratories.[2] Ciba Geigy has innovatory capacity in the United States and Japan, as well as in Europe (e.g., France, Italy, Germany, and the Netherlands) and in some developing countries (e.g., Brazil, Mexico, and South Africa). In 1990, a Canadian multinational enterprise (MNE)–Northern Telecon–transferred part of its domestic R&D facilities to the southern U.S.

Figures 6.1 and 6.2 are reprinted from *Long Range Planning,* Volume 25(1), Philippe Gugler, "Building Transnational Alliance to Create Competitive Advantages, pp. 90-99, Copyright 1992, with permission from Pergamon Press Ltd, Headington Hill Hall, Oxford OX3 OBW, UK.

Some of these international R&D operations are realized through cooperative agreements. Over the past decade, technology-intensive industrial sectors have been affected by a wave of joint ventures and strategic alliances. Many of these involve large TNCs working together on different continents. By cooperating with foreign partners, firms may benefit from the sharing of risks and the pooling of assets, based on their allies' competitive advantages, and on the resource capabilities and markets of the nations in which they operate.

Cross-border strategic alliances, which differ from traditional collaborative arrangements in that they are concluded to advance the global strategy of the participating firms,[3] have increased dramatically in the past few years. For example, cooperative agreements concluded between U.S. and foreign firms are believed to outnumber fully owned foreign subsidiaries by a factor of at least four to one.[4] In the 1980s, U.S. firms formed over 2000 agreements with European corporations. A recent McKinsey study reveals that the number of U.S. international joint ventures (i.e., the creation of a new entity) established annually increased sixfold from 1976 to 1987.[5] In the European Commission (EC) as well, the number of cross-border coalitions also increased in the 1980s. Further details are set out in Table 6.1.

Tables 6.2 and 6.3 reveal that cooperative agreements have tended to be concentrated in high-technology industries (micro-electronics, aeronautics, new materials, biotechnologies) and in industrial sectors that are using more and more sophisticated technologies (e.g., robotics in the automobile sector). Thus, for example, over half of the firms in the fields of biotechnology and machine vision are engaged in strategic alliances,[6] and most of these agreements are R&D-related.

The data bases suggest that most alliances are concluded by large corporations that are headquartered in the U.S., Western Europe, or Japan. These corporations operate through a large web of formal and informal coalitions, most of which are in the advanced industrialized countries. These developments induce the formation of oligopolistic networks, with the major world producers at the hub of these networks. In the words of an Organization for Economic Cooperation and Development (OECD) report:

TABLE 6.1. Evolution of Cooperative Agreements Established Annually (1974-1989)

	(a)	(b)	(c)	(d)	(e)	(f)	(g)
1974			37				
1975	3		14				169[1]
1976	7		16			31	
1977	7		15				
1978	7	2	14				
1979	13	1	27				317[2]
1980	22	4	34	85		94	
1981	28	22	40	169			
1982	23	19	35	197			
1983	39	16		292	46		
1984	66	42		346	69		1504[3]
1985				487	82		
1986				438	81		
1987					90	180	
1988					111		
1989					129		2629[4]

Sources :
(a) Alexis Jacquemin, Marleen Lammerant and Bernard Spinoit, Compétition européenne et coopération entre entreprises en matière de recherche-développement, Commission des Communautés européennes, Document, Luxembourg, 1986 : data on 212 cooperative agreements formed between 1978 and 1984 by at least one EC's firm.
(b) C.S. Haklisch, Technical Alliances in the Semiconductor Industry, Mimeo, New York University, 1986 : Cooperative agreements formed by the 41 major world's semiconductors producers.
(c) Karen J. Hladik, International Joint Ventures, Lexington Books, Lexington Mass., 1985 : U.S. International Joint Ventures created in high income countries between 1974 and 1982.
(d) G.C. Cainarca, M.G. Colombo, S. Mariotti, C. Ciborra, G. De Michelis, M.G. Losano, Tecnologie Dell'Informazione E Accordi Tra Imprese, Fondazione Adriano Olivetti, Edizioni di Comunità, Milano, 1989 : Arpa data base on 2014 agreements formed between 1980 and 1986 in the Information technologies sectors (semiconductors, computers and telecommunications)
(e) Commission's Reports on the EC's Competition Policy. See for example : Commission des Communautés européennes, Dix-huitième Rapport sur la politique de concurrence, Bruxelles-Luxembourg, 1989.
(f) Karen J. Hladik et Lawrence H. Linden, "Is an International Joint Venture in R&D For You ?", Research Technology Management, Vol. 32, No. 4, July-August 1989, page 12 : McKinsey Studies on U.S. International JVs created in 1976, 1980 and 1987.
(g) John Hagedoorn et Jos Schakenraad, Leading Companies and the Structure of Strategic Alliances in Core Technologies, MERIT, University of Limburg, 1990 : Cati data base on 9000 agreements formed until July 1989.
[1]: before 1974; [2]: 1975-1979; [3]: 1980-1984, [4]: 1985-1989.

TABLE 6.2. Distribution per sectors of U.S. International Joint Ventures created in 1980 and in 1987 (per cent)

Sector	1980	1987	R&D JVs 1987
Transport equipments	10	12	14
Computers	3	8	14
Semiconductor & optical disks	8	8	18
Other electric & electron. equip.	4	7	4
Pharmaceutical	3	7	21
Other chemicals	19	21	14
Instruments	7	7	11
Others	46	30	4

Source : Laren J. Hladik and Lawrence H. Linden, "Is an International Joint Venture in R&D For You ?", **Research and Technology Management**, Vol.32, No.4, July-August 1989, page 12.

TABLE 6.3. Distribution per sectors of JVs in the EC* (1984-1989)

Sector	Number	Per cent
Food & beverages	30	6,10
Chemicals, rubber, glass and ceramics	101	20,50
Electric and electronic equipments	102	20,70
Instruments, machines	60	12,15
Information technologies equipments	20	4,05
Metal products and manufacturing	48	9,75
Transport equipments	27	5,45
Wood, furnitures, paper	34	6,90
Extractive industries	15	3,05
Textile, leather, shoes	7	1,40
Construction materials	27	5,45
Others	22	4,45
Total	493	100,00

* JVs among firms : (i) from the same Member State; (ii) from more than one Member State; (iii) from Member States and outside States but with a significant effect on the EC market.

Source : Commission des Communautés européennes, **Dix-neuvième rapport sur la politique de concurrence**, Bruxelles-Luxembourg, 1990, page 332.

in the case of agreements between large firms in "world market" or global industries, the arrangements must be set in the context of the mutual recognition and interdependence of decisions on the part of firms, which characterize concentrated industries in which oligopoly prevails.[7]

Nevertheless, smaller companies are becoming more involved in strategic alliances, particularly with their larger customers. According to the Arpa data base in Italy, asymmetrical agreements between large and small enterprises are growing more rapidly than those between large firms.[8] For example, in the computer sector, IBM is collaborating with Microsoft to exploit its growing expertise in software for desk-top computers. In the biotechnology sector, the Swiss TNC Hoffmann La Roche has links with smaller firms such as Genentech, Immunex/Ajimoto, Centocor, Cal Bio, Amgen, Cetus, and Synergen.[9] Alliances among small- and medium-sized enterprises are also quite frequent, particularly in the EC, where these operations are promoted by the Commission.

The causes, mechanisms, and consequences of these new organizational forms are still uncertain, since most cases of strategic alliances are very recent. In this chapter, attention will be given to these topics in order to evaluate the importance of R&D-related alliances in the general context of the internationalization of technological activities. The discussion is divided into four sections. The first examines the determinants of R&D alliances; the second deals with the management of strategic alliances; the third studies the mechanisms of R&D cooperative agreements; and the fourth contains some reflections on the potential impact of R&D alliances.

THE ANALYTICAL FRAMEWORK
OF THE DETERMINANTS OF STRATEGIC ALLIANCES
AND SOME EMPIRICAL EVIDENCE

According to Bruce Kogut[10] the motivations for strategic alliances can be classified under three main headings: the enhancement of market power, the evasion of small number bargaining, and the transference of organizational knowledge. A cost/benefit analysis of cooperative agreements may help to understand when, where, why, and which types of firms cooperate. According to the main studies on strategic alliances, interfirm coalitions are intended to achieve the following benefits:

- Sharing of the cost of large investments needed for specific activities, such as R&D.
- Access to complementary resources (e.g., synergistic technologies).
- Acceleration of return on investments through a more rapid diffusion of the firm's assets.
- Spreading of risks.
- Efficiency creation through economies of scale, specialization, and/or rationalization.
- Co-opting competition.

Nevertheless, strategic alliances may also involve costs to one or the other of the participating partners. Foremost among these is the possibility that the other partner (who is also often a major competitor) may gain a *relative* strategic advantage.

A no less pertinent question is why other organizational forms may fail to achieve the same results as alliances at the same, or lower, net costs. Contractor and Lorange[11] present a comparison in terms of costs and benefits to answer this question. But one of the problems that still remains unsolved is why, and under what conditions, strategic alliances are likely to provide a more efficient form of operation than other modes (such as a complete integration or a market transaction).

The theories of games, oligopoly, the firm, international production, competitive strategies, marketing, and numerous theoretical developments may also help us to understand why firms are cooperating instead of pursuing a go-it-alone strategy or choosing a spot-market relation.

The theory of non-cooperative games may help to explain under what conditions cooperation may emerge and survive in a world of egoists without central authority (imposing the cooperative solution). Analysis of the prisoner's dilemma[12] and specific developments of this dilemma, such as the study of the tit-for-tat strategy,[13] shows that a non-cooperative agreement is possible when: (1) the game is repeated indefinitely; (2) the interests of the players are not in total conflict; and (3) the future is sufficiently important, relative to the present. Non-cooperative games theory also assumes that the partners to any coalition have similar needs and a willingness to share the risks of a particular venture and that reciprocity and the retaliation play an important strategic role.[14]

Cooperative games theory studies the negotiation tactics among the partners who have to decide the partition of the cooperative payoff. Under the development of model negotiation for two-person games[15] and n-person games,[16] it is possible to understand the rival interests among allies, particularly in the formation of interfirm coalitions. The interface between transaction costs (including negotiation costs) and the cooperative payoff varies according to: the relative power of the partners (conditioned by the relative position) when the firms don't cooperate; the maximum cooperative payoff available to each partner;[17] and the likely costs of the agreement relative, for example, to its duration.[18] The risk aversion of each partner to support a non-cooperative solution[19] determines all of these factors and under which conditions a potential partner will cooperate. Other developments, including studies of the characteristic function, the Shapley value,[20] and the bargaining set[21] are also useful in understanding the emergence of interfirm networks and the intra- and inter-network rival and cooperative interests. Thanks to these kinds of theoretical models, it is possible to evaluate complex situations and several kinds of joint-venture agreements, which strengthen all partners against outsiders while it weakens some partners vis-à-vis the others.

According to their main hypotheses, non-cooperative games (noncommunicability and unenforceable agreements) and cooperative games (communicability, enforceable agreements) are unable to fully cover the complex problems of strategic alliances whenever these occur in a market where rival behaviors coexist with cooperative behavior. In other words, where companies join forces in some areas, while pursuing go-it-alone strategies in others. New developments such as the almost non-cooperative games[22] and the almost cooperative games[23] simultaneously integrate rivalistic and cooperative behaviors into strategic models. Such models help (1) to evaluate strategic alliances in the context of the competitive incentives among allies and the competitive rivalry within industrial sectors[24] and (2) to provide a useful taxonomy of the transaction costs of the cooperative benefits related to the adhesion to specific coalitions.[25] Among other things, this approach also shows that a cooperative agreement is a constantly evolving bargain among the partners and that a long-term view is necessary for cooperation to emerge and survive in a non-zero-sum game situation.

The transaction cost problems, applied specifically to the firm, are studies in the theory of the firm and of the internalization. According to Ronald Coase, a firm will tend to expand until the cost of organizing an extra transaction becomes equal to the costs of acquiring this transaction on the open market.[26] This dichotomy between the market and the hierarchies, as organizational instruments, has been criticized in that it fails to acknowledge the fact that firms sometimes cooperate rather than compete with each other.[27] For example, G. B. Richardson suggests that complex networks of cooperation and association exist because of the need to coordinate closely complementary but dissimilar activities.[28] Likewise, David Teece argues that cooperative agreements may be explained by the need of firms to combine the use of different specific and co-specific assets to commercialize an innovation.[29] Thus, the comparison of transaction costs and governance costs is a possible way to understand why firms wish to cooperate with each other. They choose strategic alliances to minimize the costs of transaction and control, and to reduce risks. For example, Kogut writes:

> In summary, the critical dimension of a joint venture is its resolution of high levels of uncertainty over the behavior of the contracting parties when the assets of one or both parties are specialized to the transaction and the hazards of joint cooperation are outweighed by the higher production or acquisition costs of 100 percent ownership.[30]

Thus, R&D alliances may be concluded in order to avoid the control costs of an in-house development, a merger, or an acquisition (such as rigid structures, which prevent switching research capability, strategy, development orientation, etc.). The alliances may also be concluded to avoid high capital costs, investments, and risks as well as pure market transaction costs (such as costs induced by moral hazard and adverse selection).[31] Finally, the emergence and growth of generic technologies, while breaking down the traditional boundaries between industries, is creating additional pressures on firms to cooperate with their rivals in oligopolistic sectors. Indeed–and we are indebted to Francois Chesnais of the OECD for this point–future global competition may be as much between a collection or cluster of technology-related industrial or service firms as between firms according to the end products they produce.[32]

The above analysis, however, does not explain why firms choose to cooperate with *foreign*-based partners. The theory of international production argues that to invest abroad, firms must find it more profitable, or strategically worthwhile, to engage in foreign rather than domestic production. Similarly, cross-border strategic alliances may be presumed to offer *additional* advantages to the partnering firms than their intra-country counterparts. Comparative models developed, for example, by Hirsch,[33] Rugman,[34] and Buckley and Davies[35] are designed to compare the costs associated with the different organizational modes considered. The theory of transaction costs, applied to the internationalization of value-added activities, gives a good framework to: (1) compare the costs and benefits of foreign direct investment (FDI) and non-equity agreements;[36,37] (2) analyze "scale" and "linked" equity joint ventures;[38] (3) study firms' horizontal and collaborative joint ventures;[39] and (4) to explain vertical integration and collaborative agreements.[40]

However, it is questionable whether purely economic theories can adequately explain why firms cooperate and why they collaborate on an international level. Peter Buckley, for example, argues

> despite listing of these costs and classification (information costs, bargaining costs, enforcement costs, governance costs), nowhere do we find estimates of such costs. How significant are they in relation to transport costs, production costs, marketing distribution costs? Casual empiricism suggest that they are very high, and there are some wild estimates of the proportion of transaction costs in GDP. However, estimates are es-

sential if we are to move beyond heuristic models to concrete predictions about market configuration.[41]

Thus, many costs associated with the organizational forms compared are underestimated, as shown in a study on the transaction cost approach to the make-or-buy decisions in the automobile sector.[42] Furthermore, as noted by Farok Contractor, transaction cost minimization does not necessarily result in strategic optimization in the long run, or in profit maximization in the short run.[43] The static orientation of most of the transaction costs theoretical developments may explain this analytical weakness. Thus, as noted by Teece, transaction cost economics must be married to organizational decision theory if the dynamics of channel selection are to be properly appreciated and understood.[44]

The comparative models of choice of an organizational mode and the theory of transaction costs may be completed by John Dunning's eclectic paradigm of international production. This paradigm embraces the main vehicles of foreign involvement by enterprises (including several forms of strategic alliances) and suggests which route of exploitation is likely to be preferred.[45] The paradigm, also known as the OLI paradigm, suggests that it is the interaction between the level and pattern of a firm's ownership ("O") (or competitive advantages) and a country's location ("L") (or competitive advantages)–together with the strategy the firm chooses to adopt to organizing its cross-border activities in light of these advantages and those that arise from hierarchical control ("I" advantages)–that will determine its propensity to engage in FDI or some other form of international economic involvement.[46] For example, Dunning explains the more pronounced propensity by Japanese firms to engage in cross-border joint ventures relative to U.S. firms by observing that

> . . . their ownership advantages are of a kind that makes full internalization an inappropriate way to organize foreign manufacturing. They need the intangible assets of indigenous firms (e.g., better access, to local inputs, knowledge of product markets, law and customs, and how to negotiate with governments), while the technology they transfer is less idiosyncratic, more mature, and more readily marketable than that of US MNEs.[47]

The dynamic application of the eclectic paradigm of international production,[48] which takes into account the contribution of the literature on global strategic management,[49] offers a powerful framework for analyzing the different types of cross-border value-added activities.[50] Figure 6.1 presents a simple model, showing the contribution of the OLI parameters as explanatory tools of strategic alliances, particularly in the R&D field. The figure sets out the major factors that help to explain the emergence and growth of alliances in the 1980s and 1990s, according to the OLI configuration of the participating firms. In fact, new developments such as globalization of business, the development of cross-border organizational networks, and the emergence of core technologies (or technological systems) affect the way in which firms might create, maintain, and improve the "O" advantages and, consequently, the "L" and "I" parameters.

The eclectic paradigm may also be widened to take into account some new theoretical contributions such as the study of Charles Hill, Peter Hwang, and Chan Kim, which considers the major categories of variables influencing the entry mode choice of a firm.[51]

The distinction between structural and transactional market failures, identified by the eclectic paradigm, is particularly useful in analyzing the determinants of cooperation in specific sectors. Weijian Shan considers cooperative agreements to be the product of a double failure of the market. The first is the transactional difficulty in transferring the services of specialized assets. The second embraces the transactional problem of internalizing the functions of both production and transaction.[52]

At the same time, Shan and others also emphasize the role played by structural market failures such as entry barriers, government intervention, and recent changes in the world economy (such as globalization and unification of markets, increased investment risk and uncertainty, technological breakthroughs, convergence of system products, and faster rate of development [and obsolescence] of new products and processes). An overview of the main factors influencing the emergence of R&D alliances–technological innovation, convergence of technologies, and globalization of markets– seems relevant in understanding this issue. These three factors are related, but for analytical purposes, they are presented separately.

FIGURE 6.1. The Value of Strategic Alliances

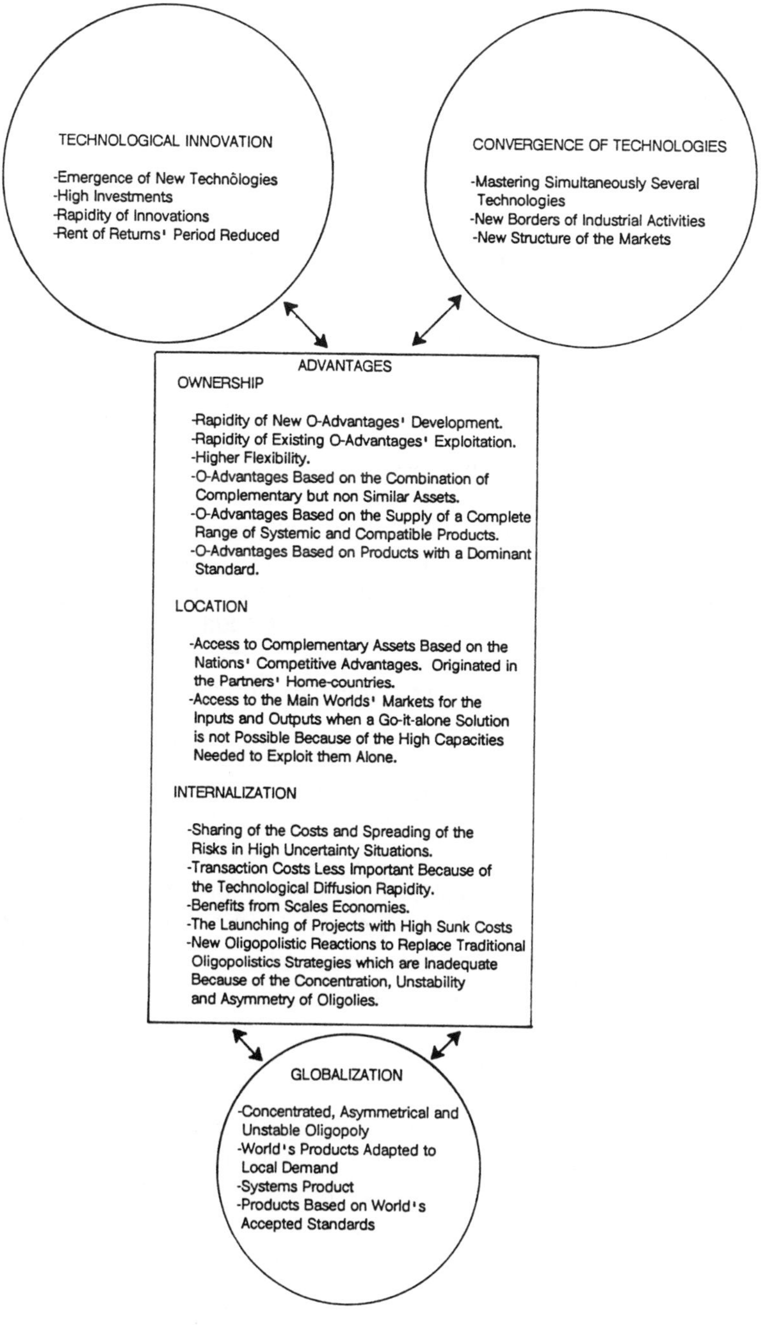

TECHNOLOGICAL INNOVATION

-Emergence of New Technôlogies
-High Investments
-Rapidity of Innovations
-Rent of Returns' Period Reduced

CONVERGENCE OF TECHNOLOGIES

-Mastering Simultaneously Several
 Technologies
-New Borders of Industrial Activities
-New Structure of the Markets

ADVANTAGES

OWNERSHIP

-Rapidity of New O-Advantages' Development.
-Rapidity of Existing O-Advantages' Exploitation.
-Higher Flexibility.
-O-Advantages Based on the Combination of
 Complementary but non Similar Assets.
-O-Advantages Based on the Supply of a Complete
 Range of Systemic and Compatible Products.
-O-Advantages Based on Products with a Dominant
 Standard.

LOCATION

-Access to Complementary Assets Based on the
 Nations' Competitive Advantages. Originated in
 the Partners' Home-countries.
-Access to the Main Worlds' Markets for the
 Inputs and Outputs when a Go-it-alone Solution
 is not Possible Because of the High Capacities
 Needed to Exploit them Alone.

INTERNALIZATION

-Sharing of the Costs and Spreading of the
 Risks in High Uncertainty Situations.
-Transaction Costs Less Important Because of
 the Technological Diffusion Rapidity.
-Benefits from Scales Economies.
-The Launching of Projects with High Sunk Costs
-New Oligopolistic Reactions to Replace Traditional
 Oligopolistics Strategies which are Inadequate
 Because of the Concentration, Unstability
 and Asymmetry of Oligolies.

GLOBALIZATION

-Concentrated, Asymmetrical and
 Unstable Oligopoly
-World's Products Adapted to
 Local Demand
-Systems Product
-Products Based on World's
 Accepted Standards

Technological Innovation

The development and emergence of new technologies (defined as an industry paradigm shift) can trigger changes in the existing market structures.[53] A study conducted some years ago by International Management revealed that keeping pace with new technologies was the biggest problem affecting the performance of companies from 20 countries.[54] As earlier underlined by Raymond Vernon, competitive threat and/or profit opportunities are the main forces behind oligopolistic actions and reactions.[55] New technologies induce both a response by competitors and offer new profit opportunities. Consequently, they seem to be important in the choice of competitive strategies.

The commercialization of emerging technologies (such as microelectronics, biotechnologies, new materials) is characterized by more intensive competition in innovatory activities (first-mover advantage). Once an innovation is made, the innovator needs to commercialize it quickly, because of the erosion of its monopoly position (shorter product life cycles, diffusion of technology, new innovations, etc.) and the need to promote standards. In this context, strategic alliances may help to accelerate the marketing process (first-mover advantage) and provide the innovator with the maximum rent on his innovation.[56]

Furthermore, as uncertainty about the success of the commercialization of innovations is high, the development and production costs of technology are huge—for example, £2 billion for a new global car model and £500 million for a new mainframe computer.[57] Designing and manufacturing the new four-megabit dynamic random access memory (DRAM) cost $2 billion, while the current world market for all types of DRAMs is worth less than $10 billion in annual sales.[58] Thus, firms have to increase their investments, particularly in R&D.

In the electronics sector, the top-100 publicly held U.S. companies spent $18.2 billion on R&D in 1988, a 15.7% increase from the $15.7 billion logged in 1987.[59] Even large firms cannot muster the necessary financial resources and take the risks inherent in such huge R&D investments.[60] For example, a *Financial Times* survey in 1990 indicated that even with the growing concentration of European producers, the three largest chip-makers, Philips, Siemens, and SGS-Thomson Group, are still far from generating the return needed to fund the larger R&D investments necessary to remain competitive against their U.S. or Japanese rivals.[61] Thus, strategic alliances may be a relevant response to these challenges. For example, in the aeronautics sector, General Electric is seeking to spread the $1.2 billion to $2 billion cost of developing the world's largest commercial jet engine by negotiating risk-sharing partnerships with European and Japanese engine producers.[62]

Convergence of Technologies

Innovation increasingly depends on combining incremental advances across a wide range of disciplines. The convergence of technologies, particularly of new technologies, is one of the major new trends in technological developments since the beginning of the 1980s.[63] This convergence may be observed within and between technological clusters. Thus, different technologies have to be mastered at the same time and, consequently, R&D expenditures for developing the latest generation of core products are higher.

Moreover, new core technologies tend to be more generic (i.e., more widespread in their use) than those that they replaced. This fact provides new opportunities for strategic alliances to benefit from synergistic technologies.[64] For example, between 1984 and 1989, Olivetti (computers and office automation) and AT&T (telecommunications) formed an agreement that was intended to exploit the maximum synergies from their complementary assets. AT&T is also collaborating with IBM for the development of network systems. The increasing use of optoelectronics in telecommunications has made it necessary for the major producing firms to master know-how and technologies in the field of optical fibers. Thus, Corning Glass, a leading firm in this field, is now at the center of an international alliance network.[65] Ciba Geigy, a leading Swiss chemical company, is cooperating with the U.S. firm Olin for the development of special chemicals used in the production of high-performance semi-conductors, and with the Chinon Corporation of California on research into human immune deficiency.

The robotics industry is also based on the integration of a multitude of sectors (e.g., computers, machine tools, software, etc.).

Firms have to acquire various knowledge and, thus, make large investments in R&D in order to maintain their global competitive positions. As noted by the Economic Commission for Europe/ United Nations Center on Transnational Corporations (ECE/ UNCTC) Joint Unit on TNCs, the main robotic producers have been driven to achieve economies of scale through collaborative agreements.[66]

Globalization

One of the main forces behind strategic alliances is the need to compete internationally. As underlined by Fortune,

> for many major companies, going global is a matter of survival, and it means radically changing the way they work.[67]

Globalization changes both the motivation for and the pattern of foreign direct investments,[68] and it creates a need for more flexible production and marketing systems and new forms of organization.

Firms trying to position themselves as global players face several problems, such as the cost of building a simultaneous presence in several product areas and foreign markets. For example, the limited size of the U.K. market, and the problems Apricot encountered in selling hardware abroad, convinced the company that it was necessary to have a partner who could offer both market access through new marketing channels and access to technology that Apricot felt unable to develop on its own.[69]

Globalization of markets mainly takes place in an oligopolistic competitive structure, characterized by high concentration and instability, and sometimes of asymmetry as well (e.g., in the computer sector, with IBM as the major producer). These oligopolistic features induce new kinds of actions and reactions. For example, in the case of market concentration, strategic alliances may be thought of as a new kind of "follow the leader" strategy, when the costs of hierarchical entry into a new market are too high.[70] Asymmetry may involve collaborative strategies such as technology leveraging and the protection of market positions.[71] For example, WordPerfect and Lotus signed a technological alliance with each other, in part because they were worried about Microsoft, which is cooperating with IBM.[72] Oligopolistic instability may also induce strategic alliances to meet the challenge of new competition; the major collaborative programs launched in the EC and U.S. are also aimed at competing against Asian producers.

Global markets may also be characterized by the convergence of consumer needs and preferences.[73] As noted by Kenichi Ohmae,

> for a firm with a good grasp of the shared needs of 630 million people and the courage to launch a product in the Triad market, it is essential to have networks that can deliver a newly developed product nearly simultaneously to scores of different points on the globe. . . . Presently, the most pragmatic and productive method of expanding a product's market is the formation of a consortia alliance.[74]

The emergence of product systems is another feature of a global market that may also increase the attraction of cooperative operations.[75] For example, in 1991, Silicon Graphic signed two R&D agreements–one with Microsoft and the other with the computer producer Compaq. These deals have helped create a powerful technological core in the computer industry, because they have linked together three leaders: one in software, the second in exploitation systems, and the third in computers.

The promotion of worldwide standards is another important factor to be considered. For example, European firms like Philips are cooperating for the promotion of a European standard for European high-definition television (HDTV). In May 1990, Philips and Thomson-CSF signed an agreement that involved joint R&D on integrated circuits, flat screens, liquid crystal displays, and broadcasting equipment. (This agreement aims to improve new standards.[76]) In 1991, AT&T and IBM signed an agreement to make their competing systems compatible.[77]

The completion of the European Single Market by the end of 1992 will also aid the path toward globalization of value-added activities. Europe 1992–involving a market of 340 million people– will modify the OLI parameters of many MNEs or prospective MNEs. For example, it will no longer be necessary for a firm to be located in every EC country to avoid non-tariff barriers. As a result, some kinds of intra-EC defensive investment may well be replaced by increased intra-EC exports. At the same time, non-EC firms will increasingly seek to establish a presence in the EC to counteract the possible emergence of "Fortress Europe"; harmonization of regimentations and the introduction of new legal structures (e.g., antitrust policy) are likely to influence the form of that presence. Confronted with the new conditions of the Single Market, firms are currently reconsidering their corporate strategies to create or sustain their "O" specific advantages. In this respect, strategic alliances are a means by which the exploitation of the new opportunities and challenges–including those of penetrating world markets–follow from the removal of intra-EC barriers.[78]

R&D strategic alliances have, then, to be studied in the context of the technology strategies that are concerned with exploiting, developing, and maintaining the sum of the company's knowledge and abilities.[79,80] The regionalization of market globalization frequently creates a need for the reorganization and restructuring of value-added activities, which involve interfirm links. The rising costs and uncertainty of R&D call for the sharing and pooling of risks. Convergence of technologies drives firms to seek quick access to know-how and capabilities they do not possess. All of these factors pose a threat to hierarchical growth and control. They are new parameters that need to be added to the explanations of a firm's expansion limits that have been suggested by several scholars, including Penrose,[81] Robinson,[82] and Chandler.[83] They require a new approach to the internationalization of production, since it may be that only by strategic alliances can firms properly create, exploit, and sustain their particular competitive advantages.

MANAGING STRATEGIC ALLIANCES

Strategic alliances may provide unique opportunities to share the assets and capabilities of a wide web of partners, including customers, suppliers, competitors, distributors, universities, etc. But cooperative agreements are not risk-free. Howard Perlmutter and David Heenan, for example, found that in a number of U.S.-Japanese alliances,

Japanese colleagues took advantage of valuable US technology and marketing know-how only to discard their American partners.[84]

Robert Reich and Eric Mankin assert that the Japanese partners of U.S. firms keep the higher-paying, higher value-added jobs in Japan and gain the project-engineering and production-process skills that underlie competitive positions, whereas their American partners are losing their competitive strength.[85] History has shown that cultural differences; lack of agreement about the objectives of the partnership, and/or of the right managerial handling of it; poor communications; and partner opportunism have been among the frequent causes of failure of collaborative arrangements. By cooperating, a firm may have access to some information without paying the market price for it; yet it may use this knowledge to out-compete its partner.

Such risks are likely to be especially high in R&D alliances. For example, Daimler, which is cooperating with General Electric, concluded an alliance–through its MTU subsidiary–in 1990 with UTC's Pratt and Whitney division. Immediately after the announcement of this agreement, General Electric accused Daimler of fraud and misappropriation of trade secrets by cooperating with UTC, one of GE's competitors in the aero-engine market. GE alleged that this alliance broke its agreement with MTU to cooperate in developing the next generation of high-thrust engines. It also asserted that it had provided MTU with comprehensive business and technological information, which would help a competitor develop an alternative to the GE90 engine. Pratt and Whitney argued that the agreement with MTU to develop a rival to the GE90 was a logical extension of the close collaboration that had developed between the two firms over many years.[86]

This kind of conflict is not unusual, and it seems to be becoming increasingly frequent with the development of inter-organizational networks. Firms often cooperate with other firms in one network, while competing with them in other networks. For example, in 1974, Snecma (France) signed an agreement with GE for the production of a new type of engine, even though UTC's Pratt and Whitney division held 10% of the Snecma stock. Aeritalia (Boeing's partner) and Aerospatiale (Airbus industries' member) are cooperating in the development, production, and marketing of the commercial aircraft ATR. Boeing's Japanese partners (for the production of the 767) are now considering an alliance with McDonnell Douglas.

The case of GE-Daimler is an example of the kind of conflict that may occur between partners of a technologically-based strategic alliance. In his study of a group of collaborative ventures involving U.S. and non-U.S. firms, David Mowery concluded that the way in which technological development was managed by the partner firms was critical to their success or failure.[87]

In order to minimize the risk of one company using its partner's unique technological advantages to that partner's own disadvantage, firms have adopted various protective devices, five of which we will now briefly describe.

Restrictive and Exclusivity Clauses

According to Jordan Lewis,

> one useful tactic, when law permits, is to agree to limit undesired market entry by a partner, an alliance, or product of the alliance.[88]

In 1986, Texas Instruments concluded an agreement with Hitachi to develop a 16-megabit dynamic RAM chip. The agreement precisely catalogued the intellectual property that belonged to each company. It was also agreed that whatever technological advances stemmed from the alliance would be jointly owned, but would not be shared with outsiders without the express permission of each partner.[89] To give another example, in January 1990, Siemens signed an agreement with IBM to jointly develop a chip capable of storing 64-million bits of information. One clause of this agreement prohibited either company from cooperating with any Japanese company in memory-chip development.[90]

In some cases, of course, such restrictions run counter to national or regional (EC) anti-trust provisions. Lewis quotes the interesting example of General Electric and Rolls Royce, which in 1989 formed an alliance to produce a pair of each other's jet engines.

Each firm also obtained access to the other's markets. The deal came apart when Rolls modified one of its engines to compete with the GE engine they shared. Beyond that point, further cooperation became impossible, since Rolls would have had access to sensitive GE sales information. While there was some feeling within GE that Rolls was obliged *not* to compete with GE, there was no denying that Rolls had an expected sales opportunity that created a strong incentive to move on its own. Anti-trust constraints had precluded a formal agreement on this.[91]

Limitations Placed on Technology Transfer

Information is always pooled when firms cooperate. Yet, as noted by Hamel, Doz, and Prahalad, companies must carefully select the skills and technologies they pass on to their partners; they should also develop safeguards against unintended informal transfers of information.[92] Firms may also be tempted to minimize the transfer of technology to avoid a disclosure of their core know-how. This may be done, for example, by sharing only the *results* of applying the product or process technology. In the case of the consortia International Aero Engines (which includes Pratt and Whitney, Rolls Royce, Fiat, MTU, Ishigawajima-Harima Heavy Industries, Kawasaki Heavy Industries, and Mitsubishi Heavy Industries), Pratt and Whitney and Rolls Royce minimized the contribution of their own cutting-edge technology by designing the engine in modular form and by assigning the development of different modules to different partners.[93]

The Division of Control and Responsibilities in Collaborative Ventures

The division of control is also an important issue that needs to be resolved prior to the commencement of any alliances. The partners must also find an organizational solution to minimize the uncertainties in their relationship. Some legal forms may ensure more policy control than others. Thus, collaborating firms may choose legal forms through which (1) the partners are more able to exercise significant control over the other's relevant activities and (2) "free riding" behaviors are avoided and the alliance is stabilized through the creation of mutual hostage positions, whereby all the parties stand to lose if the agreement is breached. Each kind of organizational mode implies a different level or kind of governance, which has to be optimized, depending on the resource commitments and the way in which risks are shared.

Efficient Alliance Planning

Firms entering into alliances will wish to be clear of the terms of the agreement and to be able to monitor its consequences. In planning an alliance, each partner needs to form a precise picture of the agreement's implications (in terms of rights and duties) for each partner and to use this as a guide for partner choice and alliance design. The clarity of goals is vital. According to Robert Lynch, ambiguous goals, fuzzy directions, and uncoordinated activities are the primary causes of failure in cooperative ventures.[94] No issue of concern to either party should be taken on trust when it can be reasonably formalized. At the same time, trust and forbearance are critical ingredients of any successful alliance.

However, while it may be easier to cooperate when partner's non-competitive interests and partners are far apart, this does not mean that collaboration among competitors is necessarily an undesirable strategy. Alliances between rivals may be profitable for each partner, but the conditions to succeed (as identified by games theory, for example) have to be respected.

Selection of Alliances Based on Trust, Commitment, and Compatibility

This selection could be a successful way to avoid insurmountable conflicts of interest among the partners. As one Chief Executive Officer has noted:

> you've got to be sure you're working with earnest and ethical people who aren't trying to undermine your company. Usually, a partner will have access to your trade secrets. He might attempt to complete a few projects, learn what you do, then exclude you from a future deal.[95]

Firms may also be more cautious of their potential partners' stability. This issue is also important to bolster trust and commitment. For example, the president of a Japanese company, complaining about its American partner (which had gone through three ownership changes over the preceding decade) remarked that "we never know who we are dealing with."[96] The purchase of MTU by Daimler may have also contributed to the destabilization of MTU's collaborative ventures. As suggested by the games theory, successful cooperation develops only with efforts over time.

THE MECHANISMS OF R&D ALLIANCES: A NETWORK APPROACH

The Various Kinds of Alliances

The literature identifies several different kinds of cooperative ventures. These include formal and informal alliances; vertical, horizontal, and conglomerative links; equity and non-equity agreements; production R&D, marketing, supply, or multiple agreements; and national, regional, or transnational alliances.

R&D alliances may be classified under four main headings. These are:

- University-located R&D strategic alliances that involve more than one industrial firm: the Semi-conductor Research Corporation (SEMTEC) in the U.S. falls into this category.
- Private strategic alliances negotiated and organized without the intervention of government.
- Interfirm agreements organized through governmental agreements (e.g., European Spatial Agency, and Airbus).
- National or international collaborative programs such as ESPRIT in the EC, Eureka in Europe, ICOT in Japan, Alvey in the U.K., etc.

As seen previously, R&D strategic alliances may involve the exchange and pooling of existing technology and/or the development of new technologies. For example, Hitachi is selling Texas

Instruments (TI) the secrets of how to stack semi-conductors on a single silicon chip, in exchange for TI's expertise in software.[97] In 1990, Siemens and IBM concluded a joint venture to develop a new generation of chips,[98] while AT&T and Tandem Computers agreed to jointly develop and market computer systems that combine Tandem's "fault tolerant" designs and AT&T's Unix operating system software.[99] Under the terms of another alliance between AT&T and NEC (concluded in 1990), the American company has the right to market, design, and produce chips licensed by NEC. In return, the Japanese firm will receive computer-aided design tools that AT&T has developed.[100] In the computer software sector, WordPerfect and Lotus have been working together since 1988 to develop a common interface for the next generation of their products.[101] In the aeronautics sector, Rolls-Royce (U.K.) and Snecma (France) signed a new cooperation agreement in 1989 to jointly develop a new-generation supersonic engine.[102]

However, in the majority of R&D-related agreements, technology is transferred in exchange for "something else," such as access to new markets or to financial resources. Coalitions involving the use of corporate-venture (CV) capital are frequent in some industrial sectors, such as biotechnologies. As noted by S. Mariotti and E. Ricotta,

> for a large company, CVC is an additional investment and in some cases, it is particularly well suited to take advantage of the continuous flow of new technologies produced by small and medium-sized companies. Through the CVC, a company can appraise its interest in a business in formation in "real time." It is the flexible financial activities of the small innovative units, which remain completely autonomous.[103]

In other cases, each partner contributes a different kind of value-added activity. For example, in 1990, AT&T and Mitsubishi signed an agreement covering technology sharing, worldwide marketing, and manufacturing of static random-access memory (SRAM) chips. Through this agreement, AT&T will have the right to manufacture and market SRAM chips designed by its Japanese partner—including current and future generations of products.[104] In April 1991, Toshiba and General Electric announced a wide-ranging alliance for the joint development and marketing of home appliances and the establishment of two joint ventures. In participating in this agreement, Toshiba is hoping to prevent, or bypass, any trade restrictions resulting from a possible surge in protectionism and anti-Japanese sentiments.[105]

Some R&D agreements, which are initially formed to pool technological assets and capabilities, are later extended to the manufacturing and/or marketing stages of production. For example, in 1990, British Aerospace and Aerospatiale (France) agreed to undertake a five-year feasibility study on a supersonic commercial airplane to replace the Concorde. The decision on whether to launch a $10 billion production program is to be made in 1995, based on the results of the study.[106] A questionnaire related to the strategies of 750 U.S. electronics firms showed that interfirm manufacturing and technology agreements will probably grow in the first half of 1990, while marketing alliances may decline. Some details are set out in Table 6.4

R&D agreements have also been formed as part of governmental collaborative programs. For example, more than 300 companies are involved in the ESPRIT program launched in 1984 by the EC. Around 1600 firms (99% of them are European) participate in the Eureka Projects (around 300 projects). Previously closed to "foreign" firms, national and inter-governmental collaborative programs are becoming more and more open to them. For example, AT&T and IBM participate in some EC programs through their affiliates established in Europe. In Japan, foreign companies have been invited to participate in a $195 million governmental project to develop jet engines for supersonic passenger aircraft.[107]

Small and medium-sized companies are also involved in several collaborative programs. For example, firms employing up to 500 people participated in 49% of the first round of the BRITE program and in 60% of the second round.[108] Nevertheless, EC-related programs represent only 4% of the private and public R&D investments in Europe.[109]

The Dynamics of Networks

Firms are often involved in both private and public cooperative ventures within complex networks, which, like consortia, may have vast potential for affecting entire industries.

TABLE 6.4. Major types of Agreements formed by 750 U.S. Electronics firms in 1990 and expected for 1990-1995 (percentage of total respondent)

Types of agreements	1990 (A)	1990-1995 (B)	(A)-(B)
Marketing agreements	67	61	- 9
Providing technology licensing	45	54	+ 20
Research contracts	38	43	+ 13
Receiving technology licensing	36	43	+ 19
Receiving equity	34	42	+ 24
Manufacturing agreements	33	44	+ 33
Providing equity	14	28	+100

Source: Electronic Business, March 1990, page 58.

In these networks, R&D links involve complex relations based on the coexistence of cooperative and competitive interests. Such networks have to be studied within the general context of (1) inter-firm networks, which are both stable and changing and (2) the business transaction among firms that generally takes place within the framework of established relationships.[110] While these networks portray the interaction of the participants, they also provide the framework within which the interactions take place. Thus, any analysis of them must include the social environment as well as the intra- and inter-organizational interactions.[111]

According to K. S. Cook and R. M. Emerson,[112] an alliance may be defined as a "set of two or more connected exchange relations." Interfirm networks are articulated by a time structure, a power structure, an interest structure, and a capacity structure. The capacity structure determines the synergistic surplus that results from the web of connections.[113] As shown in games theory, the payoff for cooperation by any one firm in the network depends on several factors, including the "status quo" position (which means the firm's payoff when it doesn't cooperate). In most cases, the relationship between the assets controlled by the participating firms sets the basis for, and interaction within, a network.[114]

Industrial markets are, in fact, complex systems of formal and informal relations between economic, political, and social agents. Alliance networks are a particular kind of inter-organizational network. As observed by Lars Engwall and Jan Johanson,[115] in every exchange relationship within a network, there is a potential conflict between the participating firms over both the distribution of economic rent earned by the network and the course of its future development. At the same time, there are powerful forces making for cooperation and mutual forbearance.

Several kinds of industrial networks may be identified. These include intrafirm networks, non-cooperative interfirm networks, and cooperative interfirm networks. The relative importance of each kind of network depends on the country, industry, and firm-specific characteristics. For example, more than half of Corning Glass's profits are from its 23 joint ventures.[116] In 1988, 60% of Aerospatiale's sales were derived from operations realized in cooperation.[117] According to a recent survey, Japanese firms obtain 5%

of their supplies through non-cooperative transactions, 40% from their internal networks, and about 55% from cooperative networks. In contrast, only 6% of supplies of U.S. firms come from alliance networks in the United States.[118]

In many industrial sectors (aeronautic, semiconductor, telecommunications, computers, semi-conductors, etc.), it is possible to identify hierarchical galaxies, in which a pivotal group of firms are surrounded by satellite partners.[119] For example, as illustrated in Figure 6.2, the major world producers of semi-conductors have a focal position in a complex web of alliances. At the same time, new coalitions may induce new market structures. For example, Figure 6.3 reveals that in the international telecommunications sector, the market is dominated by a limited number of interfirm clusters, each of which comprises a network of affiliated or allied firms. These companies are joined around systemic technological clusters and/or technological trajectories. The result is the emergence of a network of international oligopolists who perceive that their individual interests are best served by some degree of technological collaboration with each other.

Alliance networks originate from a complex market structure in which it is more and more difficult to discern rivalry from cooperation. By participating in several programs, one firm can be active in various forms of strategic alliances, each involved with its own cluster of partners, which often overlap.[120] Thus, a firm may cooperate with some partners in a specific network, and compete with them in another.

Networks and Innovation

As has been noted by David Teece, innovation demands complex interactions and de facto integration among a multiplicity of organizational units.[121] One of the major effects of the emergence of transnational alliance networks is their role in technological innovation. Hakan Hakansson has argued that an innovation should be seen not as the product of only one actor but as the result of an interplay between two or more actors; in other words, as a product of a "network" of actors.[122] For example, in the semi-conductor sector, new generations of chips have been developed through al-

FIGURE 6.2. Alliances Networks in the Semiconductor Industry (1990)

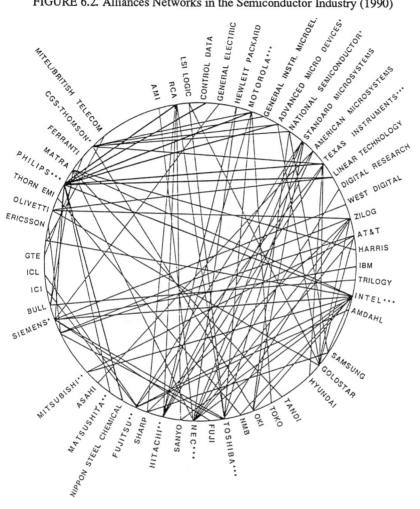

FIGURE 6.3. Interfirms Clusters and Networks in the Telecommunication Industry

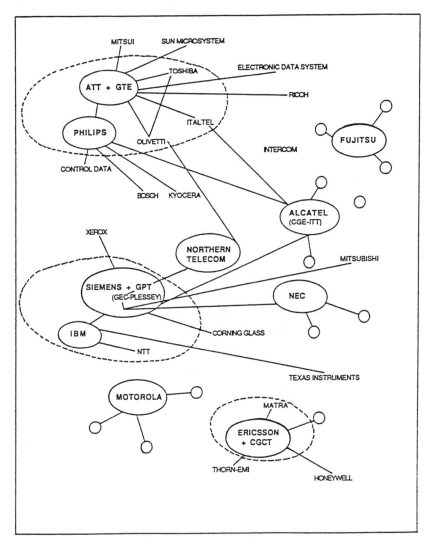

Source: Philippe Gugler, **Les alliances stratégiques transnationales**, Editions Universitaries Fribourg Suisse, Fribourg, 1991.

liances between Siemens and IBM, Siemens and Philips, Motorola and Toshiba, and Hitachi and Texas Instruments.

Formal and informal alliance networks may not only lead to more innovations, they may also help to diffuse existing technologies, know-how, and capabilities. In particular, linkages between firms belonging to different national collaborative programs–such as the European Eureka, Esprit, Race, or Jessi programs; the U.S. Sematech programs; and the Japanese VLSI and ICOT programs–may help promote an inter-network technological exchange and induce a greater synergistic surplus.

Nevertheless, interfirm agreements do not always induce new innovations or major technological transfers. In fact, there are some risks of this type of collaboration, the purpose of which is to delay or frustrate new innovations or to slow down the rate of technology diffusion.[123] Furthermore, knowledge sharing among partners may be limited because the firms do not wish to reveal too much of their cutting-edge technologies to potential competitors. For example, in the aeronautics sector, in several cooperative agreements, transfers of technology are minimized by assigning the development of different modules to different participants.[124] As a result, it took several years to negotiate how technology would be transferred between General Dynamics and Mitsubishi on the FSX fighter plane, in order to minimize technology transfer from the U.S. to Japan.[125]

In Japan, companies taking part in national R&D programs have been known to keep information about their own technologies in sealed envelopes, which are to be opened only in case of disagreement over the allocation of the results.[126] In some cases, alliance clauses prevent technological diffusion from the partners to other firms. For example, Siemens and IBM, who are cooperating in the development of a new generation of chips, have signed a clause that prohibits either company from cooperating with any Japanese firm in memory-chip development.[127] Thus, competition among interfirm networks may help preserve innovative vitality and prevent collusive restraint of technological innovation and diffusion. Nevertheless, networks' potential anti-competitive effects may be significant and need to be closely maintained by the authorities.

SOME REFLECTIONS ON THE EFFICIENCY
OF R&D ALLIANCES

Clearly, technological alliances have implications for the competitiveness of both firms and nations. Unfortunately, it is difficult to measure the impact of alliances in terms, for example, of the input and output related to R&D joint activities. What is the share of R&D jointly realized, as compared with all R&D activities? What is the importance of international technological alliances in the globalization of technological activities? What is the role of technical cooperation in new innovations? To what extent can one attribute any success of the commercialization of a particular innovation to its particular organizational structure? What is the contribution of each partner in terms of assets exchanged and/or shared? What share do foreign firms have in the local innovation realized through strategic alliances? In what location are R&D joint activities undertaken and what is their impact on the local economy?

According to the available data, it seems difficult to find an answer to these questions. Nevertheless, as we already mentioned, it is possible to glean some hints from specific industrial cases. For example, new generations of semi-conductors have been developed through alliances among the major world producers. The European HDTV standards may compete with the Japanese standard, thanks to collaborative ventures, particularly in the Eureka framework. Without the Airbus project–which involves intra-European technical, production, and marketing cooperation–it would have been difficult for the countries involved to have maintained an independent commercial aircraft industry.

Some years ago, Robert Hawkins observed that technological cooperation may be positive or negative for global industrial productivity, or it may be both good and bad from the national point of view. He went on to suggest that much will depend on the conditions of the individual case and upon the perspective from which goodness or badness is judged.[128]

The rising popularity of strategic alliances has not occurred without a measure of skepticism. Some scholars refer to the disappointing history of cooperative ventures in the past and point out the organizational problems incurred because of the incompatibility of goals and differing "corporate cultures" of the partners.[129] Furthermore, some consortia, particularly in the U.S. (e.g., Sematech, Semi-conductor Research Corp. [SRC], and Micro-electronics and Computer Technology Corp. [MCC]), have been a major disappointment to their supporters. In encouraging the collaboration of firms that are strong competitors, some R&D consortia seem to have failed because of a lack of confidence and trust among and between partners.[130] In the U.S., opponents of government involvement assert that federal programs, far from encouraging innovation, may have stifled entrepreneurial efforts.[131] In Europe, some critics argue that the EC programs are spread among too many projects and/or too many firms to be efficient.

London's *The Economist* has been particularly scathing about government support for commercial R&D consortia. In an article published in January 1990, it argued that such consortia would

> neither improve education nor reduce the interest-rate-boosting federal budget deficit. Instead of encouraging the heartening trends in R&D, consortia refill the troughs of big-company lobbyists.[132]

Yet there is some evidence to suggest that some cooperative projects do seem to have succeeded. One example is the VLST program in Japan, which has played an important role in helping Japanese companies to overtake U.S. competitors in semi-conductor memory technology and production.[133] Another is the Eureka Project on HDTV for the development of an international standard, which may well help European producers to head off the threat of Japanese domination.[134] In some cases, government projects may also stimulate R&D; according to the EC, the European information technology industry doubled in the past four years, due in part to collaborative programs.[135]

Furthermore, it seems that the major criticisms of national consortia are more directed to their political management and organization than to the concept of R&D collaboration per se. The possible pitfalls of some government projects could also be attributed to the firms themselves. Some experts argue that certain companies are collaborating only on technologies that are not crucial to the competitiveness of the ultimate product. Sometimes, firms are partici-

pating in a given project only to keep an eye on competitors. Therefore, the cooperative goals are insufficiently determined, and the
partners fail to achieve a successful commercialization of the
technologies jointly developed.

Other critics point to the anti-competitive effects of cooperative
agreements, and they advise governments to restrict some kinds of
alliances, such as horizontal agreements.[136] On the other hand,
strategic alliances may well fill a real need to share costs that are
beyond the scope of many firms. As noted by Davidson,

> anti-trust policies that were appropriate in a domestic econo-
> my with few linkages to the international system can be self-
> destructive in an internationally competitive environment.[137]

Confronting this debate, governments adopt "reason rules" in their
anti-trust regulations. Cooperative agreements are generally autho-
rized whenever they appear to offer enough economic benefits to
compensate for their possible anti-competitive effects. In fact, as we
have seen, R&D alliances are rarely initiated to restrict competition
but rather to counteract endemic market failure. Viewed from a
national perspective, R&D collaboration may also induce higher
productivity, avoid a duplication of research investment, reduce
structural overcapacity, and improve the competitiveness of their
national champions.

The socially beneficial effects of R&D strategic alliances depend
upon the industry, market, and firm-specific characteristics. For
example, as noted by Alex Jacquemin, R&D alliances are most
likely to have positive effects in markets where there are strong
externalities or spill-overs in the absence of cooperation, and in
markets where a high rate of R&D sharing or between-member
spill-over is feasible.[138]

Technological alliances seem to involve higher positive effects in
the basic research field. In fact, it is usually hard to make a profit
from basic research. For example, neither AT&T's introduction of
the transistor nor IBM's Nobel Prize-winning discovery of higher-
temperature superconductors seems to have revitalized their competitive positions.[139] Thus, private and public collaborative projects
in basic research may promote innovations that otherwise wouldn't
have been developed. For example, AT&T has joined with its rival

IBM to support a long-term research project into super-conductivity, at the Massachusetts Institute of Technology.[140]

Still, there are circumstances in which R&D agreements do involve high economic or strategic social costs. Where, for example, collusive behavior stifles future innovation or restricts the diffusion or dissemination of technology, or creates additional barriers to the entry of competitors, it might reduce the social product. It may also result in a strategically unacceptable technology drain from the home country. For example, in the information technology sectors, Sun, Hewlett-Packard, and MIPS conceded licenses to its Japanese partners Fujitsu, NEC, Sony, Toshiba, and Hitachi–all of whom are now able to build RISC-based workstations.[141] Some U.S. experts are opposed to these kinds of alliances. In the Boeing-Japanese firm links, experts argue that by cooperating, Boeing will lose its technological edge by helping its Japanese partners to acquire the know-how to develop and produce airplanes.[142] In the U.S., the FSX Fighter case (already mentioned above) also underlines the risk of technological drain to the benefit of the partners. The source of the debate was the project of the co-production with Japan (Mitsubishi was the prime contractor) of a new tactical fighter plane, based on the American F-16 produced by General Dynamics. Critics of this alliance feared it would lead to an erosion of American technology and add to the ability of Japan to launch a civilian aerospace industry that would directly compete with the American firms.[143]

The probable impact of technological strategic alliances on both the firm's and the nation's competitiveness is indeed complex. Clearly, much depends on the opportunity cost of such alliances and whether or not the alternative alliances, which might have been concluded, would have operated to the (net) disbenefit of the non-participating partner.[144] However, it can safely be concluded that technological cooperative agreements play an important role in both the ownership and location of innovatory activities. The potential impact of R&D joint activities may be appreciated from a private and public point of view. It constitutes a new factor to consider in the bargaining game between firms and governments, and particularly so in cases where the private interests related to strategic alliances oppose the social, economic, and political goals of governments.

CONCLUSIONS

Within a web of strategic alliances, companies perceive they gain valuable technological synergism and risk-reducing benefits. This chapter has made an attempt to provide a broad overview of major developments related to strategic alliances, particularly in innovatory activities. It has also tried to indicate the probable impact of technological cooperative agreements from a private and a social point of view. Obviously, such an overview cannot be conclusive and comprehensive–if for no other reason than the reality it tries to analyze is complex, dynamic, and inadequately documented. Despite this caveat, we believe this chapter has demonstrated four main things:

1. International inflows and outflows of technologies organized through strategic alliances vary between industries.
2. Strategic alliances have to be understood not only as a substitute but also as a complementary organizational form necessary to create, maintain, and enhance the technological advantages of the firms and the location of their innovatory activities.
3. R&D cooperative ventures are part of complex intra- and inter-organizational networks in which technologies are created, disseminated and, improved upon on an international basis.
4. It is possible to incorporate strategic alliances into the mainstream economic and business theories, which have attempted to explain the internationalization of value-added activities, and to the level and pattern of both intra/interfirm exchanges and intra/inter-industrial exchanges.

ENDNOTES

1. ECE/UNCTC Joint Unit on Transnational corporations, *Les sociétés transnationales japonaises en Europe: structures, stratégies et nouvelles tendances*, Geneva and New York, 1991.

2. Susan Moffat, "Picking Japan's Research Brains," *Fortune*, March 1991, pp. 54-59

3. Christopher Clarke and Koeron Brennan, "Allied Forces," *Management Today*, November 1988, p. 128.

4. Farok J. Contractor and Peter Lorange (eds), *Cooperative Strategies in International Business*, Lexington Books, New York, 1988, p. 4.

5. Karen J. Hladik and Lawrence H. Linden, "Is an International Joint Venture in R&D For You?," *Research Technology Management*, Vol. 32, No. 4, July-August 1989, p. 12.

6. Frank Hull and Gene Slowinski, *Strategic Partnerships Between Small and Large Firms in High Technology: A Theoretical Framework for Analysis*, Mimeo, Rutgers University, 1987, p. 1.

7. *Technical Co-operation Agreements Between Firms: Some Initial Data and Analysis*, DSTI/SPR/86.20, Part I, Paris, 1986, p. 3.

8. Gian Carlo Cainarca, Massimo G. Colombo, and Sergio Mariotti, *Cooperative Agreements in the Information and Communication Industrial System*, Milan, 1988, p. 5.

9. *Business Week*, February 19, 1990, p. 38.

10. For the strategic context, see Bruce Kogut, "Joint Ventures: Theoretical and Empirical Perspectives," *Strategic Management Journal*, Vol. 9, 1988, pp. 319-332.

11. Farok J. Contractor and Peter Lurange, op. cit.

12. Martin Shubik, "Game theory, behavior, and the paradox of the Prisoner's Dilemma: Three solutions," *Journal of Conflict Resolution*, Vol. XIV, No. 2, 1970, pp. 181-931.

13. Robert Axelrod, *The Evolution of Cooperation*, Basic Books, New York, 1984.

14. See, for example, Jordan D. Lewis, *Partnerships For Profit: Structuring and Managing Strategic Alliances*, The Free Press, 1990, p. 1.

15. John F. Nash, "The Bargaining Problem," *Econometrica*, Vol. 18, No. 2, April 1950, p. 152-162. John F. Nash, "Two-Person Cooperative Games," *Econometrica*, Vol 21, No. 1, January 1 953, pp. 128-140.

16. John Von Neumann and Oskar Morgenstern, Theory of Games and Economic Behavior, Princeton University Press, Princeton, 1947.

17. Ehud Kalai and Meir Smorodinsky, "Other Solutions to Nash's Bargaining Problem," *Econometrica*, Vol. 43, No. 3, May 1975, pp. 513-518.

18. Ariel Rubinstein, "Perfect Equilibrium in a Bargaining Model," *Econometrica*, Vol. 50, No. 1, January 1982, pp. 97-109. Ariel Rubinstein, "A Bargaining Model with Incomplete Information about Time Preferences, *Econometrica*, Vol. 53, No. 5, September 1985, pp. 1151-1172.

19. Frederik Zeuthen, *Problems of Monopoly and Economic Warfare*, Routledge and Kegan Paul Ltd., London, 1930.

20. L. S. Shapley, "A Value for n-person Games," *Annals of Mathematic Studies*, Vol. 28, 1953, pp. 307-371.

21. Robert J. Aumann and Michael Maschler, "The Bargaining Set for Cooperative Games," *Annals of Mathematic Studies*, Vol. 52, 1964, pp. 443-476.

22. John C. Harsanyi, *Rational behavior and bargaining equilibrium in games and social situations*, Cambridge University Press, Cambridge, Mass., 1977, pp. 273-288.

23. Philippe Gugler, *Les alliances stratégiques transnationales*, Editions Universitaires Friborg Suisse, Friborg, 1991.

24. Bruce Kogut, op. cit.

25. See also Peter J. Buckley and Mark Casson, "A Theory of Cooperation in International Business," in Farok J. Contractor and Peter Lorange (eds), *Cooperative Strategies in International Business*, Lexington Books, 1988, pp. 31-53.

26. "The Nature of the Firm," *Economica*, New Series, Vol. IV, November 1937, pp. 386-405.

27. M. A. Adelman, "The Large Firm and its Suppliers," *The Review of Economics and Statistics*, Vol. 31, No. 2, May 1949, p. 113-118. P. W. S. Andrews, "Industrial Economics as a Specialist Subject," *Journal of Industrial Economics*, Vol. 1, No. 1, November 1952, p. 72-79. Jacques Houssiaux, "Le concept de 'quasi-intégration' et le rôle des sous-traitants dans l'industrie," *Revue Economique*, No. 2, March 1957, p. 221-247 and "Quasi-intégration, croissance des firmes et structures industrielles," *Revue Economique*, No. 3, May 1957, pp. 385-411.

28. G. B. Richardson, "The Organization of Industry," *Economic Journal*, Vol. 82, No. 327, September 1972, p. 282.

29. David J. Teece, "Profiting from technological innovation: Implications for integration, collaboration, licensing and public policy," *Research Policy*, Vol. 15, No. 1, February 1986, pp. 288-290.

30. Bruce Kogut, op. cit., 1988, p. 321.

31. Alexis Jacquemin, "Cooperative Agreements in R&D and European Antitrust Policy," *European Economic Review*, Vol. 32, 1988, p. 552.

32. As is particularly the case in the strategic networking of firms in different branches of the telecommunications and biotechnology sectors. The notion of strategic business groups is also relevant for understanding the changing characteristics of oligopolistic competition.

33. Seev Hirsch, "An International and Trade Investment Theory of the Firm," *Oxford Economic Papers (New Series)*, Vol. 28, No. 2, 1976, pp. 258-270.

34. Alan Rugman, *Inside the Multinationals*, Columbia University Press, New York, 1981, pp. 54-60.

35. Peter J. Buckley and Howard Davies, *The Place of Licensing in the Theory and Practice of Foreign Operations*, University of Reading Discussion Papers in International Investment and Business Studies No. 47, November 1979.

36. David J. Teece, "Transaction Cost Economics and the Multinational Enterprise: An assessment," *Journal of Economic Behavior and Organization*, Vol. 7, 1986, p. 21-45, and "The Multinational Enterprise: Market failure and Market Power Considerations," *Sloan Management Review*, Vol. 22, No. 3, 1981, pp. 7-10.

37. Charles W. L. Hill and W. Chan Kim, "Searching for a Dynamic Theory of the Multinational Enterprise: A Transaction Cost Model," *Strategic Management Journal*, Vol. 9, 1988, pp. 93-104.

38. J. F. Hennart, "A Transaction Cost Theory of Equity Joint Ventures," *Strategic Management Journal*, Vol. 9, July-August 1988, pp. 361-374.

39. Paul W. Beamish and John C. Banks, "Equity Joint Ventures and the Theory of the Multinational Enterprise," *Journal of International Business Studies*, Vol. 19, Summer 1987, pp. 1-16.

40. Erin Anderson and Hubert Gatignon, "Modes of Foreign Entry: A Transaction Cost Analysis and Propositions," *Journal of International Business Studies*, Vol. 17, Fall 1986, pp. 1-26.

41. Peter J. Buckley, "The Limits of Explanation Testing the Internalization Theory of the Multinational Enterprise," *Journal of International Business Studies*, Vol. 19, No. 2, Summer 1988, p. 184.

42. G. Walker and D. Weber, "A Transaction Cost Approach to Make-or-Buy Decisions," *Administrative Science Quarterly*, Vol. 29, No. 3, 1984, pp. 373-391.

43. Farok J. Contractor, *Contractual and Cooperative Modes of International Business: Towards A Unified Theory of Model Choice*, Graduate School of Management Working Paper, No. 89-15, Rutgers University, August 1989, pp. 13-14.

44. David J. Teece, "Multinational Enterprise, Internal Governance, and Industrial Organization," American Economic Review, Vol. 75, No. 2, May 1985, p. 237.

45. John H. Dunning, *Explaining International Production*, Unwyn Hyman, London, 1988.

46. For a discussion of some strategies toward the internationalization of production see David Lei, "Strategies for Global Competition," *Long Range Planning*, Vol. 22, No. 1, 1989, p. 102.

47. John H. Dunning, "Non Equity Forms of Foreign Economic Involvement and the Theory of International Production," in R. W. Moxon, T. W. Roehl, J. F. Truitt (eds), *Research in International Business and Finance*, Vol. 4, JAI Press Inc., 1984, p. 34.

48. John H. Dunning, *Explaining International Production*, London, Unwin Hyman, 1988, Chapters 1 and 2, and *Multinational Enterprises and the Global Economy*, Reading, Mass., Addison Wesley, 1991, Chapters 3 and 4.

49. John H. Dunning, *Global Strategy and the Theory of Industrial Production: An Exploratory Note*, Reading and Rutgers University, 1990.

50. John Cantwell, *Technological Advantage As a Determinant of the International Economic Activity of Firms*, University of Reading Discussion Papers in International Investment and Business Studies, No. 105, October 1987, p. 3.

51. Charles W. L. Hill, Peter Hwang and W. Chan Kim, "An Eclectic Theory of the Choice of International Entry Mode," *Strategic Management Journal*, Vol. 11, 1990, p. 117-118.

52. Weijian Shan, "An Empirical Analysis of Organizational Strategies by Entrepreneurial High-Technology Firms," *Strategic Management Journal*, Vol. 11, pp. 129-131.

53. Alice M. Sapienza, "R&D collaboration as global competitive tactic–Biotechnology and the ethical pharmaceutical industry." *R&D Management*, Vol. 19, No. 4, October 1989, p. 285.

54. *International Management*, December 1984, p. 58.

55. Raymond Vernon, "International Investment and International Trade in the Product Cycle," *Quarterly Journal of Economics*, Vol. LXXX, 1966, p. 200.

56. Weijian Shan, op. cit., p. 131.

57. Christopher Clarke and Kieron Brennan, op. cit., p. 128.

58. *The Economist*, February 3, 1990, p. 66.

59. *Electronic Business*, August 1989, p. 50.

60. ECE/UNCTC Joint Unit on Transnational Corporations, *Recent Developments in Operations and Behavior of Transnational Corporations: Towards New Structures and Strategies of Transnational Corporations*, ECE/UNCTC Joint Unit Publications Series 7, Geneva, 1987, p. 19.

61. *Financial Times*, March 11, 1991, p. 1.

62. *Financial Times*, January 17, 1990, p. 26.

63. Rob van Tulder and Gerd Junne, *European Multinationals in Core Technologies*, John Wiley/IRM, 1988.

64. Margaret Sharp, "Europe: Collaboration in the High Technology Sectors," *Oxford Review of Economic Policy*, Vol. 3, No. 1, Spring 1987, p. 60.

65. *Fortune*, March 27, 1989, p. 58.

66. ECE/UNCTC Joint Unit on Transnational Corporations, op. cit., 1987, p. 20.

67. *Fortune*, August 28, 1989, p. 70.

68. Gaston Gaudard, "Transnationalization and Global Financial Equilibrium," in Zuhayr Mikdashi, *Bankers' and public authorities management of risks*, Macmillan Press Ltd., Londres, 1990, p. 234.

69. *Financial Times*, January 10, 1990, p. 23.

70. Frederick T. Knickerbocker, *Oligopolistic Reaction and Multinational Enterprise*, Harvard University Press, Cambridge, Mass., 1973. Knickerbocker study concerns national market concentration, but his contribution may easily be applied to an international market concentration.

71. ECE/UNCTC Joint Unit on Transnational Corporations, op. cit., 1987, pp. 22-23.

72. *The New York Times*, December 3, 1989, p. 14.

73. Kenichi Ohmae, "The Global Logic of Strategic Alliances," *Harvard Business Review*, March-April 1989, p. 144.

74. Kenichi Ohmae, *Beyond National Borders: Reflections on Japan and the World*, Dow Jones-Irwin, Homewood, Illinois, 1989, pp. 86-87.

75. OCE/UNCTC Joint Unit on Transnational Corporations, op. cit., 1987, p. 19.

76. *The New York Times*, May 17, 1990, p. D5.

77. *Financial Times*, March 27, 1991, p. 25.

78. Pierre Buigues et Alexis Jacquemin, "Strategies of Firms and Structural Environments in the Large Internal Market," *Journal of Common Market Studies*, Vol. XXVIII, No. 1, September 1989, p. 65.

79. *Business Week*, July 4, 1988, p. 109.

80. For an analysis of technology strategy, see David Ford, "Develop Your Technology Strategy," *Long Range Planning*, Vol. 21, No. 5, 1988, pp. 85-95.

81. Edith T. Penrose, *The Theory of the Growth of the Firm*, M. E. Sharpe Inc., New York, 1980 (reedition), pp. 43-63.

82. Austin Robinson, "The Problem of Management and the Size of Firms," *The Economic Journal*, Vol. XLIV, June 1934, pp. 242-257.

83. Alfred D. Chandler, *Strategy and Structure: Chapters in the History of the American Industrial Enterprise*, IT Press, 1962, pp. 7-17.

84. Howard V. Perlmuter and David A. Heenan, "Cooperate to compete globally," *Harvard Business Review*, March-April 1986, p. 142.

85. Robert B. Reich and Eric D. Mankin, "Joint Ventures with Japan give away our future," *Harvard Business Review*, March-April 1986, pp. 78-86. See also "Joint Ventures may damage your health," *Financial Times*, September 9, 1987, p. 8; "Are Foreign Partners good for U.S. Companies?," *Business Week*, May 28, 1984, pp. 48-52; "Corporate odd couples: Beware the Wrong Partner," *Business Week*, July 21, 1986, pp. 98-103.

86. *Financial Times*, April 7-9, 1990, p. 10, and *The New York Times*, March 28, 1990, p. D1 and D9.

87. David C. Mowery, "Collaborative ventures between U.S. and foreign manufacturing firms," *Research Policy*, Vol. 18, 1989, p. 26.

88. Jordan D. Lewis, op. cit. 1990 p. 60.

89. Louis Kraar, "Your rivals can be your allies," *Fortune*, March 27, 1989, p. 58.

90. *The New York Times*, February 2, 1990, p. D1 and D9.

91. Jordan D. Lewis, op. cit., 1990, p. 60.

92. Gary Hamel, Yves L. Doz, and C. K. Prahalad, "Collaborate with your competitors–and win," *Harvard Business Review*, January-February 1989, p. 136.

93. David C. Mowery, 1989, p. 23.

94. Robert Porter Lynch, "Building Alliances to Penetrate European Markets" *The Journal of Business Strategy*, March-April 1990, p. 8.

95. Cited in J. Michael Geringer, "Partner Selection Criteria For Developed Country Joint Ventures," *Business Quarterly*, Vol. 53, No. 1, Summer 1988, p. 61.

96. Cited in Jordan D. Lewis, op. cit., p. 250.

97. *The Economist*, May 20, 1989, p. 104.

98. *The Economist*, February 3, 1990, p. 72.

99. *The New York Times*, March 13, 1990, p. D4.

100. *The New York Times*, March 8, 1990, p. D9.

101. *The New York Times,* December 3, 1989, p. F14.

102. *Financial Times*, December 19, 1989, p. 14.

103. S. Mariotti and E. Ricotta, "Diversification, Agreements Between Firms and Innovative Behavior," paper presented at the Conference on Innovation Diffusion, Venice, 1986, p. 39.

104. *Financial Times*, February 16, 1990, p. 6.

105. *Financial Times*, April 14, 1991, p. 10.

106. *Financial Times*, May 10, 1990, p. 3.

107. *The New York Times*, December 1, 1989, p. D5.

108. *Financial Times*, January 1, 1990, p. 13.

109. Peter Kuentz, "Expériences réalisées en matière de coopération technologique européenne," *Vie Economique*, 6/1990, p. 13.

110. Jan Johanson and Lars-Runnar Mattsson, "Interorganizational Relations in Industrial Systems: A Network Approach Compared with the Transaction-Cost Approach," *International Studies of Management and Organization*, Vol. XVII, No. 1, 1987, p. 35.

111. Michael E. Porter and Mark B. Fuller, "Coalitions and Global Strategy," in Michael E. Porter, *Competition in Global Industries*, Harvard Business School Press, Boston, Mass., 1986, p. 316.

112. K. S. Cook and R. M. Emerson, "Power, Equity, and Commitment in Exchange Networks," *American Sociological Review*, Vol. 43, 1978, p. 725.

113. Dirk-Jan F. Kamman and Dirk Strijker, "Concept of Dynamic Networking in Economic and Geographical Space and their Application," in GREMI, *Innovative Milieux and Transnational Firm Networks: Towards a New Theory of Spatial Development*, International Workshop, Barcelone, March 1989.

114. Björn Aexlsson, "Supplier Management and Technological Development," in Hakan Hakansson, *Industrial Technological Development: A Network Approach*, Croom Helm, 1987, pp. 128-176.

115. Lars Engwall and Jan Johanson, *Banks in Industrial Networks*, Working Paper 1989/2, Uppsala University, 1989, pp. 4-5.

116. *Fortune*, March 27, 1989, p. 56.

117. Aerospatiale, *Le Groupe*, Paris, 1989, p. 25.

118. Frank Hull, Gene Slowinski, Robert Wharton, and Toya Azumi, "Strategic Partnerships between Technological Entrepreneurs in the United States and Large Corporations in Japan and the United States," in Farok J. Contractor and Peter Lorange (eds), op. cit., p. 451.

119. John H. Dunning, *Multinationals, Technology and Competitiveness*, Unwin Hyman, London, 1988, p. 177.

120. George Ferné, R&D "Programmes for Information Technology," *The OECD Observer*, August-September 1989, p. 10.

121. David J. Teece, "Inter-organizational Requirements of the Innovation Process," *Managerial and Decision Economics*, Special Issue, Spring 1989, p. 41.

122. Hakan Hakansson, *Industrial Technological Development: A Network Approach*, Croom Helm, 1987, p. 3.

123. Barry E. Hawk, "La recherche-développement en droit communautaire et en droit anti-trust américain," in Jacquemin Alexis and Rémiche Bernard (eds), *Coopération entre enterprises: Enterprises conjointes, stratégies industrielles et pouvoirs publics*, De Boeck/Editions Universitaires, Brussels, 1988, pp. 230-231.

124. David C. Mowery, "Collaborative ventures between U.S. and foreign manufacturing firms," *Research Policy*, Vol. 18, 1989, p. 23.

125. *The Wall Street Journal*, March 21, 1990, p. A3.

126. George Ferné, op. cit., p. 10.

127. *The New York Times*, February 6, 1990, pp. D1 and D9.

128. Robert G. Hawkins, "Technical Cooperation and Industrial Growth: A Survey of the Economic Issues," in Herbert I. Fusfeld and Carmela S. Haklisch,

Industrial Productivity and International Technical Cooperation, Pergamon Press, 1982, p. 17.

129. Peter F. Drucker, "From Dangerous Liaisons to Alliances for Progress," *The Wall Street Journal*, September 8, 1989, p. A14.

130. *Electronic Business*, January 22, 1990, pp. 46-52.

131. *Business Week*, January 8, 1990, p. 25.

132. *The Economist*, February 3, 1990, p. 66.

133. *Financial Times*, December 3, 1990, p. V.

134. *International Management*, April 1990, p. 49.

135. *Financial Times*, March 11, 1991, p. VI.

136. Michael E. Porter, "The Competitive Advantage of Nations," *Harvard Business Review*, New York, The Free Press, 1990.

137. William H. Davidson, "Ecostructures and International Competitiveness," in Negandhi Anant R. and Savara Arun, *International Strategic Management*, Lexington Books, 1988, p. 20.

138. Alexis Jacquemin, op. cit. pp. 553-554.

139. *The Economist*, February 3, 1990, p. 66.

140. *The Economist*, February 3, 1990, p. 66.

141. *Business Week*, October 23, 1989, p. 110.

142. *The New York Times*, November 3, 1989, p. D1 and D5.

143. B. R. Inman and Daniel F. Burton, "Technology and Competitiveness: The New Policy Frontier," *Foreign Affairs*, Spring 1990, pp. 122-125.

144. For a general discussion of the social costs and benefits of the export of technology through joint ventures and foreign direct investment, see John H. Dunning, *Multinationals, Technology and Competitiveness*, Unwin Hyman, London, 1988.

Chapter 7

Protection of Competitive Advantage in U.S./Asia-Pacific Joint Ventures from High-Technology Industries

John D. Daniels
Sharon L. Magill

INTRODUCTION

International joint ventures have long been important for United States firms, and such ventures were noted to have become a major form for the conduct of U.S. business abroad by the mid-1950s (Friedmann and Kalmanoff, 1961). There is, nevertheless, conflicting evidence on whether this use has grown or remained fairly stable as a portion of U.S. firms' total international business operations (Kobrin, 1988; Harrigan, 1988). Furthermore, very little is known about international joint ventures between U.S. high-tech firms and companies from the Asia-Pacific area. Therefore, the purpose of this study is to provide some preliminary information and hypotheses regarding these partnerships, with an emphasis on the motivation for, and management of, the ventures. This subject is important because of the proprietary nature of the products designed and manufactured by most high-technology firms.

A chronological perusal of previous works highlights several trends that are pertinent to our study. Probably the most notable impression is that firms view joint ventures more favorably today than in the past. For example, although Friedmann and Kalmanoff (1961) listed joint-venture benefits, they concluded that "if a project calls for a joint venture, this is at times a sufficient reason for its rejection by an investor who would not even take the trouble to analyze its profitability." In contrast, Ohmae (1989) recently stated, "Properly managed alliances are among the best mechanisms. . . . In today's uncertain world, it is best not to go it alone." One gets the impression, therefore, that joint-venture receptiveness has gone from a reluctant compliance with outside requirements (usually governmental) to that of a preferred means of meeting global strategic objectives.

A second significant development concerns attitudes, particularly within the United States, that joint ventures abroad will speed the foreign appropriability of technology, thus impairing the future competitiveness of the donor country (Reich and Mankin, 1986). This argument is somewhat counter to the emergence of technology treatment within joint-venture literature, which has evolved since the 1960s from a view that technology flows were one-way (i.e., from home countries to the foreign locations where joint ventures were established). Early examination of the technology flow was almost entirely from the standpoint of the technology suppliers' bargaining power. More recently, the technology transfer process has been viewed increasingly as two-way, with synergies in research capabilities between U.S. firms and their foreign joint-venture partners, in the United States or abroad (Osborn and Baughn, 1987; Auster, 1987).

A third stream of literature has discussed joint-venture staffing. Early studies (Friedmann and Kalmanoff, 1961) included staffing only in the context of the motivation for U.S. joint ventures abroad (e.g., to obtain management skills and to maintain employee morale in host countries). More recently, home-country nationals in a foreign joint venture have been viewed as a control mechanism (Shenkar and Zeira, 1987) and as an instrument to affect the appropriability of the joint venture's or foreign partner's technology (Harrigan, 1986). There has also been an increased interest in the impediments that joint ventures impose on organizational development objectives of the partners (Shenkar and Zeira, 1987).

METHODOLOGY

Although various arbitrary measurements are often used to classify firms as high-tech, the distinctions are not that clear in practice.

We felt that the logical means of selecting a sample for our study would be to concentrate on firms within high-technology industries, because firms therein presumably share–and are able to survive–because of long-term technical entry barriers. We used research-and-development (R&D) expenditures as a percentage of sales as a proxy of technological intensity, and relied on data in the *Business Week* 1987 annual "R&D Scoreboard," which included 915 companies in 44 industry categories or sub-categories. We selected the six industries with the highest R&D expenses as a percentage of sales, ranging from 8.2% to 9.6%. The choice of six industries was arbitrary, but seemed a natural break in the data, inasmuch as the next highest industry category had a figure of only 6.9%. These six industries contain 187 firms, or 20.4% of the *Business Week* list. They include the following: (a) drugs and research, (b) semi-conductors and electrical components, (c) graphic and laser, (d) software and services, (e) office automation, and (f) computers. Because we found few firms with joint ventures and because we offered anonymity to respondents, we have combined our reporting of categories b through f, which we call "office automation and components."

We examined descriptions in *Moody's Industrial Manual* for all 187 firms and phoned all those with some type of shared ownership arrangement. We determined that 16 firms had a total of 20 joint ventures with Asia-Pacific firms. We wrote to the Chief Executive Officer or a Senior Vice President in these 16 firms, explaining our study and saying that we would phone to set appointments to discuss their operations. Nine of the 16 firms (56.3%) participated in our study and supplied information on 11 of the 20 joint ventures (55%). Three participants with four joint ventures are in the drug and research group, and six with seven joint ventures are in office automation and components. In each case, we were able to interview management with direct responsibility for their companies' activities in the ventures.

Joint Venture Descriptions

Of the eleven joint ventures we studied, seven are in Japan, three in Korea, and one in the United States (with a Japanese partner). Most of the joint ventures in our study are relatively young, having been established in the 1980s; only one was established in the 1960s, with another three in the 1970s.

The foreign partners of U.S. firms in high-technology industries vary by size, type of ownership, scope of operations, products, skill levels, and reasons for entering joint ventures with U.S. partners. In fact, this variance is so great that few patterns emerge.

In six of the joint ventures, the foreign partners produce similar or complementary products to those of the U.S. partner; thus, the ventures are aimed to strengthen both firms' positions within an existing-product group focus. In two, the foreign partner is a related distributor, thus the joint ventures serve as a means of expanding control along the value chain. In another three, the local partners are in completely different lines of business. For them, the joint ventures provide diversified financial returns.

The skills of the joint-venture partners were generally described as being complementary to those of their U.S. partners. Specific skills that were repeatedly cited as valuable included: access to distribution channels; personal contacts with key customers and influential government employees; the ability to hire key personnel for the joint ventures; and (in the case of drug firms) the knowledge of how to gain regulatory product approval. It appears that partners are chosen, in large part, because they can provide some form of personal contact that the U.S. partner would find it difficult, or impossible, to establish.

Overall, U.S. firms have chosen a diverse group of individuals and foreign firms as their joint-venture partners. On a prescriptive note, it appears that firms considering the establishment of an international joint venture would be wise to consider a variety of individuals and firms as potential partners. Many firms stressed that one of the keys to the successful establishment and maintenance of an international coalition was the wise choice of any foreign partners. Our data suggest that the optimal partner can come in many different forms.

Some form of production occurs within 10 or 11 joint ventures. Seven of these are basically full-production units; two are merely assembly operations for parts exported from the United States; and one makes components in Japan that are sold entirely to the U.S. parent. (This is the only instance where exports are significant for the joint venture.) The remaining joint venture is in distribution, handling only the U.S. firms' wholly owned output. Two primary factors account for the high incidence of production: (a) governmental regulations often make exports impractical, and (b) product adaptations and modifications are needed to serve certain foreign customer needs, thus scale economies by exporting from the United States are not possible.

All the joint ventures in our sample have an indefinite life span. Our respondents typically viewed their joint ventures as not being of strategic importance to them, of remaining operative only as long as they are profitable, and of being in fairly tenuous positions. However, these opinions seem to contradict their actions. For example, one of the respondents noted that its joint-venture contract specifies dissolution in 30 days if either parent grows dissatisfied; yet this joint venture is now ten years old.

Short-term profitability is a key factor in U.S. firms' establishment of these joint ventures. All but one of the respondents noted an expectation that the joint venture would become self-sustaining within three years; and many felt that the new organization should be profitable almost immediately. This expectation has been met for the majority of joint ventures in this study.

LOW INCIDENCE OF JOINT VENTURES

Although much of the current literature proclaims joint-venture benefits in a global environment, a mere 12.3 percent of firms in high-tech industries report their utilization anywhere, and only 9 percent of firms have them with Asia-Pacific partners. Even among the firms using joint ventures, the form is seldom the dominant or preferred method of international operations. Instead, these firms conduct most of their foreign business through other operating forms, such as wholly owned subsidiaries, licensing agreements, or sales/purchase contracts. A combination of factors seems to explain the low usage of joint ventures: perceived transaction costs, shortness of the product life cycle, and the bargaining strength of high-tech firms.

Perceived Transaction Costs

Sometimes joint ventures are viewed as representing the worst of both markets (externalization) and hierarchies (internalization). The transaction cost argument is based on a company's preference for saving resources, thus leading it to "farm out" all possible activities that cannot be performed more cheaply within the organization (Williamson, 1975). The "farming out" would lead to such operating forms as distributorships, manufacturing contracts, and licensing agreements; in fact, these are the forms most frequently used by our sample firms. However, transaction cost theory notes that the costs of handling activities internally may be cheaper because the parent and the subsidiary are likely to have a common culture; a company can use its own managers who understand its objectives; protracted negotiation with another company are avoided; and possible problems of enforcing an agreement are evaded (Teece, 1985).

The perception that may cause high-technology firms to avoid the use of joint ventures is simply that such arrangements entail both substantial costs (similar to wholly owned operations) and substantial demands to control and monitor the activities of the joint venture (similar to the transaction costs associated with wholly externalized operations). Furthermore, the cost of start-up negotiations may be high; the negotiations commonly took two years to complete in the ventures we studied. In addition, the company may lose some control over revenues and over the flexibility to deal with global competitors and customers (Giddy and Rugman, 1979). These fears are, no doubt, exacerbated when an alliance is contemplated with a foreign partner whose culture and business practices may be perceived as very different from those found in U.S. firms.

Rapid Obsolescence

Studies testing the product life-cycle theory have shown that the manufacturing location does not likely move abroad for products with very short life cycles because there is no time to achieve the cost reductions (Giddy, 1978; Lutz and Green, 1983). For many high-technology products, particularly in office automation and components, product obsolescence occurs too rapidly for the international diffusion of production; therefore, these products depend more on exports than on foreign production to tap foreign markets.

Government Regulations and Bargaining Strength

Even when highly satisfied with their joint ventures, almost half of respondents disclosed that they probably would not have shared ownership had they not been driven to do so by government actions. Markets seemed too promising to forgo; but respondents could not serve the foreign markets adequately through exports. In fact, in only three cases were respondents able to export successfully prior to the joint ventures' establishment, and these respondents felt they needed a greater commitment through direct investment to keep sales from plateauing. Once firms knew they needed to invest, the ownership-sharing requirements were primarily governmental, through legislation or entry negotiations; these involved all the joint ventures in Korea as well as two in Japan.

The low overall incidence of joint ventures by high-technology firms is due in part to their strong bargaining position with host governments, which is influenced by the resources brought in by the investors and by the number of firms offering similar resources. This is consistent with earlier findings that foreign investors are more likely to be able to gain a high percentage of ownership—even 100 percent in countries with ownership-sharing requirements—when they bring in advanced technology (Fagre and Wells, 1982). However, given the apparent high overall bargaining capabilities for high-tech firms, why did our respondents nevertheless opt for their specific joint ventures? Part of the answer seems to lie in the weak technical bargaining position for office-automation and components companies in Japan. All the participants within this category have a joint venture in Japan; four of six have their only joint venture in Japan. Their bargaining strength is weak in Japan because the Japanese market for these products is so large that firms must sell there to be competitive globally (Ohmae, 1986) and because low competitive lead time over Japanese companies necessitates their early entry into the market, which is consistent with existing international expansion theories (Stobaugh, 1969; Ayal and Zif, 1979). Shared ownership sometimes speeds U.S. firms' entry, while excluding potential Japanese competitors from entering the market on their own.

The companies within the drugs and research category also possess a strong global bargaining position based on technology. In fact, they seem to have a stronger bargaining position in Japan than the office-automation and components group. One reason is that the drugs and research industry generally has longer product life cycles because of the ordinarily higher time and cost of bringing a new product to market and the greater reliance on patents–as opposed to industrial secrecy programs–to protect the technology. These factors lower the potential appropriability by local firms and help explain drug companies' prevalence of foreign sales through wholly owned production facilities in general (Weber and Smith, 1989). Only one of the four joint ventures by drug firms is in Japan, and this operation is for sales of a branded non-drug consumer product.

RATIONALE AND ADVANTAGES
OF OWNERSHIP SHARING

Firms wishing to sell most of their output in Japan felt that Japanese partnership was mandatory to gain access to the market, which has historically been difficult to penetrate. By being "perceived as Japanese" and staffing almost entirely with Japanese nationals supplied by the partners, respondents felt they could gain access to local distribution and cultural expertise.

The reasons for sharing ownership were different for the United States partners whose joint-venture outputs are sold primarily in the United States. For the one in Japan, the U.S. firm wanted the combination of low-cost and high-quality production from Japanese employees, but needed a partner to supply capital. For the one in the United States, the U.S. firm wanted to access its Japanese partner's product technology.

Once the U.S. partners saw the need or desirability to establish joint ventures, they negotiated an array of partner contributions that greatly exceeded the narrow rationale that we have just described. For example, although only two respondents mentioned the need for capital as a reason for sharing ownership, all foreign partners have supplied capital to the ventures.

Firms in drugs and research tend to have high fixed distribution costs; thus, there are substantial distribution scale economies to be gained through accessing a wider product line, either through internal development or through contractual arrangements with other firms. In three of the four joint ventures by drug firms, the non-U.S. partners have substantial and closely related product technology, some of which is contributed to the joint ventures; consequently, the ownership sharing provides the potential of product-line expansion. This experience contrasts substantially with the joint ventures in the office automation and components group, where only one of seven non-U.S. partners is supplying significant product technology to the venture.

All of the U.S. parent firms are satisfied with the performance of the joint ventures we studied. Contrary to the possibility of high operating and transaction costs, the specific alliances that our respondents have entered appear to offer advantages of both markets and hierarchies: resource inputs are complementary and, once the agreement has been negotiated, there have generally been minimal transaction costs of dealing with the foreign partners.

CONTROL

Mechanisms

In partially owned operations, companies may increase their control over an operation by holding key resources outside the operation; owning an equal or majority of voting shares; dispersing other voting shares when holding a minority; making frequent contacts; standardizing reports; building of a corporate culture; staffing key positions with one's own personnel; and assuring sufficient representation within the board of directors. All of these methods were used by at least one of our respondents. However, only four mechanisms were used by a majority of the firms we contacted: maintaining at least equal ownership with partners whenever possible, establishing at least an equal representation on boards of directors, requiring standardized reports from the joint-venture management, and holding a key resource (R&D) outside the joint venture.

Ownership by the U.S. partners ranged from 45% to 70% with the U.S. partner retaining less than 50% ownership in only one operation. Although a few firms noted, somewhat unhappily, that their ownership percentage was restricted by local law, an equal number stated that they hoped for joint-venture partners who were equal to them in size, power, and percentage ownership.

The interface between management from the U.S. partners' corporate headquarters and management in the joint venture was deemed very important, especially through joint ventures' boards of directors, which meets only several times per year. When the boards are equally divided between the partners, the joint ventures tend to be fairly autonomous regarding day-to-day decisions. However, the joint-venture management must go to the board of directors for decisions concerning policy and key decisions. Although equal board representation does not give control to the U.S. partners, the U.S. partner is assured that the foreign partner cannot take strategic actions without its concurrence.

Three joint ventures stand in sharp contrast to these relatively autonomous operations. For these, interaction tends to be very frequent, sometimes several times per day. One of these joint ventures was noted as being of "extreme strategic importance" to its parent firm, which helps explain such desire for tight control.

Another form of contact is through visits by U.S. headquarters' personnel to the joint ventures; however, this control mechanism is not heavily utilized. Although there is wide variation, trips to the joint ventures tend to occur between two and four times per year, generally as part of a broader overseas visit to various joint ventures, subsidiaries, and licenses. In contrast, the non-U.S. partners in three of the joint ventures have no direct interface at all with management within the ventures.

Monthly financial reports from the joint ventures to the U.S. parents are standardized in over 70% of cases. One firm requires reports only on a quarterly basis. Clearly, such reports do not represent an intensive control mechanism.

Staffing and Personnel Policies

Because high-technology firms generally depend on proprietary information for competitive advantage, we expected that respondents would attempt to protect their technologies by staffing most key positions, especially in R&D, with expatriate home-country nationals in order to control intellectual property. This expectation proved to be incorrect except for two joint ventures, both created by the same U.S. parent. Initially, the parent firm sent only a few managers overseas. Over time, however, the firm came to fear that the local partners might not adhere to the Foreign Corrupt Practices Act; therefore, this U.S. firm has increased the number of expatriate managers in these joint ventures until, today, they hold at least half of the key positions. Although the base salaries for these managers are paid by the joint venture, any additional compensation, such as private schools for dependents and home leaves, must be borne by the U.S. parent firm.

The initial staffing of most joint ventures involved the use of a few key expatriates during the start-up phase for the new enterprise, while the bulk of the employees were supplied by the local partner. A notable variation to this pattern was found in a Japanese joint venture in which the U.S. and Japanese partners both chose the president of the joint venture and then delegated all hiring and staffing decisions to that president. (It is interesting to note that this Japanese president still heads the joint venture ten years later.) Another variation occurred in two joint ventures, which have no full-time personnel of their own. Instead, the local partners handle all operations with their own people and allocate a portion of their expenses to the ventures.

Following the start-up, most expatriates have returned home as soon as possible so that, at most, two expatriates remain in any single joint venture. The top managers, usually local nationals with long tenure records, are appraised by the joint ventures' boards of directors. Compensation for joint-venture employees has usually been handled in two distinct phases. During the establishment of the joint venture, any salaries and other expenses for expatriates have been charged to the parent firm. Once functioning, however, the joint venture is considered to be a self-sustaining unit and, thus, pays any salaries and compensation for all employees assigned to it.

Who Controls the Joint Ventures?

Joint ventures may be controlled jointly by the partners, by one of them, or be independent of both. Or each partner may seek to control only certain aspects of the venture that are most important to it. Control is seldom an either-or situation, since each partner may exert degrees of influence over certain practices, and these degrees may fluctuate over time.

In spite of the complexity, we classified the joint ventures from an overall control standpoint. The locus of control depends highly on the ventures' relative importance to the parents. Specifically, control goes to one parent when it is more important to that parent; to both when the operation is significant for both; and to neither when operations will have little impact on either parent. Although a number of different control mechanisms may exist, we found that the degree of ownership closely paralleled the extent to which other mechanisms are used.

Since two-thirds of the firms participating in this study have only one international joint venture, it is understandable that control practices are generally devised on a case-by-case basis rather than being based on an all-encompassing policy. A respondent with six international joint ventures, of which one is included in this study, is attempting to establish an overall policy based on two critical guidelines: that all such ventures will be managed by locals and that all partners will be equal in terms of ownership share. Although the other two firms with more than one joint venture have some overall concerns about control, they feel that each joint venture is simply unique, so that they cannot be guided by any sort of a "cookbook" approach.

PROTECTION OF TECHNOLOGY

The competitive advantage for most high-tech firms is, obviously, their technology. We were surprised, therefore, that only one firm initially noted technology to be the primary factor it sought to control; however, additional probing yielded a near consensus that sufficient actions are undertaken so that partners do not usurp proprietary technology. Firms tend to use a combination of mechanisms to assure this control.

Mechanisms for Controlling Technology

Location of R&D. Although the product lines manufactured within the host-country joint ventures are usually not as broad as those in the partners' home countries, some leading-edge products are manufactured in all but one of the full-production joint ventures. At the same time, there is evidence that some new products are initially exported from the United States until there is demonstration that scale economies are possible in more than one production location. Thus, the product life-cycle explanation of international trade and investment may be in decline, but it is not fully in demise.

Little R&D takes place within the joint ventures; consequently, new developments could be withheld if the partners reach a conflict situation. Most efforts are developmental, especially by drug firms' joint ventures, because of government requirements for clinical trial work. The size of joint-venture R&D departments is small compared with those of the U.S. parents'. The ownership of any output from these units is unclear, but since most of the R&D is adaptive, its use outside the host country is questionable. Most firms noted that the joint ventures owned their own research output, but that partners could probably have free access to that output to exploit elsewhere if they so desired.

Low Partner Appropriability. Large firms with highly related technology and established international operations are better equipped to appropriate the joint venture's technology than small firms with less related technology and purely domestic sales. In only two of the eleven joint ventures do the foreign partners have all three attributes–related technologies, large in size, and international in scope–that would most enhance their competitive capabilities. One of these is the joint venture in the United States, where the Japanese partner is the technology supplier. In the second, the U.S. partner has increased its holdings from 50% to 60% of the operation and now staffs all key positions with its own personnel. The fact that almost half of our respondents alluded to their partners' shortcomings suggests that their partners were chosen, in part, because of their lack of capabilities to appropriate the technology.

Development of Trust. Another prevalent response regarding the control of technology centered around one theme–trust. Several firms noted that the primary requirement for a successful joint venture is choosing, and then trusting, the right partner. Therefore, once the proper "mate" is found, the rest of the relationship is relatively worry-free. This parallels the characterization of joint ventures as uneasy alliances that must depend on trust (Harrigan, 1984) and that lowered transaction costs occur when there is trust in an alliance partner (Jarillo, 1988).

Two means were used to find these ideal joint-venture partners. One was to develop long-term dealings with their partners (either via licensee relationships or distributorships) before the joint venture was established. A second way was to look for partners who place great value on their reputations. This is understandable since the protection of the firm's reputation was the largest response to our question on what factors U.S. firms hope most to protect within their international joint venture(s).

Non-High Technology Activities. When one thinks of firms in high-technology industries, one immediately thinks of the high-tech parts of their operations, which constitute their major competitive advantages. However, many of their products, components, and functions do not involve the development and production of leading-edge products. When joint ventures are involved in these non-high-tech areas, there is less concern about a partner's usurpation of competitive positions. In three situations, the joint ventures are involved in no production of high-technology products; instead, they merely assemble components or distribute. In a fourth situation, the joint venture uses foreign technology to produce in the United States. In a fifth case, the operation produced highly standardized components (wafers) that are sold to the U.S. parent. In the remaining six cases, there is some leading-edge product output from the joint ventures, but much of the production involves mature product technology.

Build Interdependence. One firm has a wary attitude toward its foreign partner because that partner is equal to itself in both "muscle" and capabilities. Through the joint venture, the foreign partner has access to many of the U.S. partner's critical technologies; thus, it has the capability to become a major rival. Both firms have been extremely careful in terms of the strategic direction of their relationship. Thus far, both have monitored the venture very closely. But now the two partners are establishing a second joint venture, this time in the United States, by using the foreign firm's technology. The interdependence on each other's technology is expected to lessen the need to monitor technology usage within the joint ventures abroad.

Separate Licensing Agreements. Since many international licenses are given to companies connected in ownership with the licensor, we expected that our respondents would volunteer that these arrangements are an additional way of protecting the technology they transfer to the ventures. We asked open-ended questions about concerns and methods of protecting technology within the ventures. That none mentioned licensing agreements leads us to believe that they are of low importance for protection within the ventures. Where used, they are mainly a means of compensating for contributions beyond the mere investment in capital and managerial resources.

CONCLUSIONS

The explicit and implicit practices that our participants have used to assure that partners do not usurp their assets indicate that foreign joint ventures are not ceding the future U.S. competitive situation. Furthermore, some respondents are receiving technology from their partners. But firms from high-tech industries depend on the propriety of their technology to maintain their competitive viability. Companies that depend primarily on other competitive assets, such as marketing or capital intensity, may not attempt as much to control the appropriability of the newer and higher-tech products within their portfolios.

REFERENCES

Auster, E. R. "International Corporate Linkages: Dynamic Forms in Changing Environments," *Columbia Journal of World Business*, Vol. 22 (Summer, 1987), pp. 3-6.

Ayal, I. and J. Zif. "Market Expansion Strategies in Multinational Marketing," *Journal of Marketing*, Vol. 43 (Spring, 1979), pp. 84-94.

Fagre, N. and L. T. Wells, Jr. "Bargaining Power of Multinationals and Host-Governments," *Journal of International Business Studies*, Vol. 8 (Fall, 1982), pp. 9-23.

Friedmann, W. G. and G. Kalmanoff. *Joint International Business Ventures* (New York: Columbia University Press, 1961).

Giddy, I. H. "The Demise of the Product Life Cycle in International Business Theory," *Columbia Journal of World Business*, Vol. 13 (Spring, 1978), pp. 90-97.

Giddy, I. H. and A. M. Rugman. "A Model of Trade, Foreign Direct Investment and Licensing," Working Paper No. 274A (New York: Columbia University Graduate School of Business, 1979).

Harrigan, K. R. "Joint Ventures and Global Strategies," *Columbia Journal of World Business*, Vol. 12 (Summer, 1984), pp. 7-14.

Harrigan, K. R. "Joint Ventures and Competitive Strategy," *Strategic Management Journal*, Vol. 9 (March-April, 1988), pp. 141-158.

Harrigan, K. R. *Managing for Joint Venture Success* (Lexington, MA: Lexington Books, 1986).

Jarillo, J. C. "On Strategic Networks," *Strategic Management Journal*, Vol. 9 (January-February, 1988), pp. 31-41.

Kobrin, S. J. "Trends in Ownership of American Manufacturing Subsidiaries in Developing Countries: An Inter-Industry Analysis," *Management International Review*, (Special Issue, 1988), pp. 73-84.

Lutz, J. M. and R. T. Green. "The Product Life and the Position of the United States," *Journal of International Business Studies*, Vol. 14 (Winter, 1983), pp. 77-93.

Ohmae, K. "Becoming a Triad Power: The New Global Corporation," *International Marketing Review*, Vol. 3 (Autumn, 1986), pp. 36-49.

Ohmae, K. "The Global Logic of Strategic Alliances," *Harvard Business Review*, Vol. 89 (March-April, 1989), pp. 143-154.

Osborn, R. N. and C. C. Baughn. "New Patterns in the Formation of US/Japanese Cooperative Ventures: The Role of Technology," *Columbia Journal of World Business*, Vol. 22 (Summer, 1987), pp. 57-65.

Reich, R. B. and E. D. Mankin. "Joint Ventures with Japan Give Away Our Future," *Harvard Business Review*, Vol. 86 (March-April, 1986), pp. 78-86.

Shenkar, O. and Y. Zeira. "International Joint Ventures: Implications for Organization Development," *Personnel Review*, Vol. 16, No. 1 (1987), pp. 30-37.

Stobaugh, R. B., Jr. "Where in the World Should We Put That Plant?" *Harvard Business Review*, Vol. 47 (January-February, 1969), pp. 132-134.

Teece, D. J. "Transactions Cost Economics and the Multinational Enterprise," Berkeley Business School International Business Working Paper Series, No. IB-3 (Berkeley, CA: University of California Business School, 1985).

Weber, J. and E. T. Smith. "Merck Wants to Be Alone—But with Lots of Friends," *Business Week*, No. 3130 (October 23, 1989), p. 62.

Williamson, O. E. *Markets and Hierarchies: Analysis and Antitrust Implications*, (New York: Free Press, 1975).

Chapter 8

Building Partnerships
with Japanese Corporate Groups

Douglas N. Ross

The popularity of strategic alliances among managers has increased over the past 20 years primarily because of their usefulness in creating new competitive options. The push for expanded global business alternatives can be attributed to various factors, including increasing international competition, globalization of industries, improved information/communication capabilities, rapid change in technologies, large-scale economies that extend beyond the capability of a single firm, desire to share risk, and trade restraints (Contractor and Lorange, 1988; Harrigan, 1985; Hall, 1984). Further, the prospects are that new links and new forms of joint endeavor will continue to spread across the business horizon (Morris and Hergert, 1987).

CONTEXT: THE NETWORK OF RELATIONS
OF THE PARTNER FIRM

Any cooperative relationship, and strategic alliances and joint ventures in particular, can only be understood in the context of its total set of relations (Kogut, 1988; Thorelli, 1986; Walker, 1988). Nowhere does that observation apply more than in dealing with a Japanese corporate group member. In practical terms, industry analysis needs to be expanded to include a "contextual" analysis as a prelude to any relationship with a Japanese company. This

The author wishes to thank Refik Culpan and an anonymous reviewer for helpful comments and suggestions. Errors of commission and omission remain my own.

chapter focuses on the importance of context for a strategic alliance, that is, an examination of the established network of relationships of the potential Japanese partner.

STRATEGIC ALLIANCES

Many international corporate linkages such as joint research and development (R&D), technology transfers, joint ventures, and licensing represent a choice for a firm's managers to achieve competitive ends. These strategies refer to collaborative relationships among firms or groups of firms who work together to attain their strategic objectives (Berg, Duncan, and Friedman, 1982; Harrigan, 1985; 1988; Killing, 1983). An important manifestation of cooperative strategy is the set of interrelationships among firms such that they become loose confederations of firms with interdependent economic objectives (Taoka and Beeman, 1991).

Scholars and managers alike have directed much useful discussion to the motivations, successes, failures, and potentials of interorganizational arrangements. For example, Harrigan (1985, 1988) examined partner asymmetries and concluded that ventures are more likely to succeed when the bargaining power of the venture's sponsors is evenly matched and when missions, resource capabilities, and managerial capabilities are complementary. On the other hand, most interfirm alliances fail (Kearney Associates, 1987) because of multinational partners limiting a joint venture's autonomy (Franko, 1971); the drive for unambiguous control causing conflicts (Stopford and Wells, 1972); significant challenges to management that are posed by dual or shared control (Beamish, 1985; Killing, 1983); difficulties in managing networks of interdependent organizations in long-term relationships (Thorelli, 1986); parent motives playing a determining role (Kogut, 1988); and pre-venture strategy development inadequacies (Roos, 1989). Most of these reasons for failure are probably valid for the Japanese-U.S. alliances examined. Another reason for failure may be important but have nothing to do with the partners themselves. Rather, it may be attributed to a partner's other commitments and relationships that have a higher priority than the success of an often temporary joint venture. The following example illustrates the point. The share of foreign-affiliated joint enterprise in the industrial output of many industrialized countries ranges from 20% in some European countries to 50% in Canada. In the United States, the ratio has recently doubled to about 9%, while in Japan, it is less than 5% and based primarily on petroleum and rubber companies established soon after World War II (Christelow, 1987).

From the perspective of the single firm, network analysis has been utilized to delineate the firm's frame of operation (Hakansson and Johanson, 1988) and to describe unique combinations of strategy, structure, and management process (Miles and Snow, 1986). Kogut (1988) suggests context as an important variable in studying interfirm relationships. Nevertheless, the effect of a network of relationships on new international cooperative arrangements has not been studied adequately. These existing network relations may be the critical variable in the success or failure of a strategic alliance, particularly with a Japanese company.

The following sections explore the strategic importance of a possible partner firm's set of interrelationships, utilizing (1) Japanese industrial context and corporate networking practices as an illustration, (2) present case examples, and (3) suggested guidelines for foreign firms in establishing collaborations with Japanese corporate groups.

THE NATURE OF CORPORATE GROUPINGS

Corporate groupings in Japan (*keiretsu* and *kigyo shudan*) emerged, at least in part, as a response to the post-World War II breakup of the holding company-centered industrial combines (*zaibatsu*). The main *zaibatsu* banks were left intact, however, and around them formed six huge alliances: Mitsui, Mitsubishi, Sumitomo, Fuyo, Sanyo, and Dai-ichi Kangyo. They have been variously described as loosely linked political confederations (Christopher, 1983); stable, strategically coordinated alliances (Ferguson, 1988; 1990); coherent mini-economies (Gerlach, 1987); bank-centered or industrially linked business groups (Kotler, Fahey, and Jatusripitak, 1985); a closely tied complex of industrial and financial corporations (Miyazaki, 1980a); inter-market groups (Nakatani, 1984); industrial clusters of related and supporting industries (Porter, 1990); hierarchically ordered systems of subsidiaries, suppliers, subcontractors, and distributors associated with a particular manufacturer (van Wolferen, 1990); ostensibly independent companies, cooperating voluntarily with each other for important financial, commercial, and strategic reasons (Wright, 1989); and as a network of small, independent manufacturing firms loosely organized by a large trading company or manufacturing firm to complement one another's skills in performing a variety of manufacturing and distribution functions (Yoshino, 1976).

Thus, a working definition emerges: a bank-centered, industrially linked, strategically coordinated, inter-market, political-financial alliance of businesses (Ross, 1991). How greatly do corporate groupings affect Japanese business? "Not a single soul can live outside their influence" (Kiyonari and Nakamura, 1980, p. 250). This peculiarity of Japanese industrial organization must be understood in order to properly comprehend the Japanese competitive regime as a whole (Nakatani, 1984).

From the above listing, it may be apparent that there is some confusion about corporate groupings. Popularly, they may be known as *keiretsu,* technically vertical, intra-market groups, or they may be referred to as *kigyo shudan,* which are horizontal inter-market groups. Sometimes they may be confused with *sogo shosha,* or trading companies, whose relationships may be "diagonal," in the sense that they can serve many markets and many activity chain levels. The essential point is that corporate groupings are very important, whichever manifestation they take.

Table 8.1 shows the hierarchically and horizontally interrelated Japanese political business system that forms the context for the set of interrelationships composing a corporate grouping. In the table *keiretsu* member companies are designated "G-form" corporations to distinguish them from single-hierarchy, standalone companies (see Williamson and Bhargava's descriptions [1972] of U-form, H-form, M-form companies).

Intra-National Policy Umbrella

Corporate groupings are themselves embedded within a reciprocal context of governmental influence. Mechanisms exist to assist in the working out of overall national direction. These inter-sectoral

TABLE 8.1. Context for Japanese Corporate Groupings

Features	Relationships
Intra-national policy umbrella ...	inter-sectoral groups eg MOF, MITI, <u>Keidanren</u>.
• political-financial.......	Inter-alliance groupings of business leaders, trade associations comprised of industry members.
Dual Structure:	
Upper Echelon	
Intra-alliance cooperation.......	Inter-company groupings
• strategically-coordinated.	G-form focus; access to resources; support for strategic direction
• bank-centered.............	long term capital access
• industrially-linked.......	resource leverage due to focus on value chain link
• inter-market..............	friendly markets; each alliance tends to have a company in each industry
Intra-G-form company.............	Inter- work group groupings.
• corporate focus	value chain specialization, functional specialization
• people & management systems	visible, real time management systems
Lower Echelon	
Suppliers/ subcontractors.......	risk takers, innovators

arrangements tend to include at least those at the top from various corporate groups.

Political-financial component. Some commentators stress the importance of an inter-sectoral government-business cooperative approach (Johnson, 1982; Prestowitz, 1988). A recent example is a chemical laser system developed by Kawasaki Heavy Industries, with financial assistance from the government's Research Development Corporation (RDJC) (*Tokyo Business Today*, 1991). The Japanese market is protected from foreign intrusion by both government neo-mercantilist policy and *keiretsu* practice (Woronoff, 1986; Wright, 1989). As a result, market entry by foreigners may often be gained only at great long-term expense (Magnusson and Gross, 1990). The Structural Impediments Initiative is a U.S. effort to overcome some of the more obvious obstacles, such as department store ownership and financial reporting requirements (Chipello and Brauchli, 1991).

In a sense, government sanction helps maintain an oligopolistic market structure in a given industry, with firms from each major *keiretsu* competing vigorously among themselves, primarily on quality and service. The pattern is to encourage stable relationships on prices, but vigorous competition on product quality (Henderson, 1973). Many "precompetitive" arrangements on research are allowed (*Business Week*, 1990), such as the electric car consortium (Patterson, 1991).

Business groups not only greatly influence economic policy but also greatly influence politics and foreign policy, usually through business associations such as the Federation of Economic Organizations, the Japan Federation of Employer's Associations, the Japan Committee for Economic Development, and the Japan Chamber of Commerce (Kiyonari and Nakamura, 1980). Japanese trade policies and practices exist in their present form because Japanese business wants them that way. A foreign partner must understand that the role of the Japanese government is to support Japanese interests.

Intra-Alliance Cooperation

Strategically coordinated. The corporate grouping context of a Japanese firm is important because of financial and trade dealings, interlocked ownership and directors, and shared personnel. Presidents of the major companies in a corporate grouping develop directions for the group as a whole, including joint investments. In Sumitomo, for example, this club is called the *Hakasui Kai*; in Mitsui, it is the *Nimokukai*. In the Sumitomo group, there are some ten different types of interfirm councils, such as those for R&D vice presidents, which meet regularly to coordinate their efforts. The main goals of overall alliance strategy are to increase both sales and market share.

Bank-centered. Bargaining power is maintained through interlocking shareholdings, directors, and banking connections (Miyazaki, 1980b). Japanese strategic alliances often form around a major international company, such as NHK Spring, the largest manufacturer of springs for the automobile industry. A partial listing of the ownership structure, including Daido Steel, Nissho Iwai (trading company), Nomura Securities, Bank of Yokohama, and Sogo Taxi (retailer) reflects the NHK network of connections to suppliers, commercial and investment banks, distributors, and other complementary-product companies. These are the types of relationships that must be considered by a prospective NHK partner.

Only 13 major banks control 52% of Japan's total bank lending to corporations, and these financial institutions act as conduits of funds to borrowing companies (Imai & Itami, 1984). Banks compete among themselves, but provide access to a stable, long-term source of capital for their *keiretsu* members (Ohmae, 1982); these banks form the center of the groups, linking them horizontally to the enterprises, both through lending and cross-holdings of shares (Miyazaki, 1980a).

A long-term focus is the norm. An Organization for Economic Cooperation and Development (OECD) study underscored the benefits derived by the Japanese economy from a long-term perspective. The study (1972) concluded that industrial policies encouraging computers and industrial machinery, for example, "are precisely the industries where income elasticity is high, technological progress is rapid and labor productivity rises fast" (OECD, 1972:15). Compare this measured approach with profit-taking of Chrysler Motors in selling out its 9.7% share of Mitsubishi Motors; or with Honeywell, selling its 23.5% stake in Yamatake-Honeywell; or with General Motors, selling its 2% of Isuzu (Holden and Reed, 1990). To quote Sony's chairman Morita (1987): "We feel that a company that sells its assets has no future." One must ask: Is it any wonder Japanese give much higher priority to stable, long-term relationships than to short-term "deals"?

Industrially linked. Small- to medium-sized manufacturing firms are typically given a limited number of production operations by large companies, which provides a value chain focus (Tsurumi, 1976). Additional manufacturing company (production) resource leverage is achieved in other functional areas, such as marketing and finance, by relying heavily on trading companies and banks (Tsurumi, 1976; Ohmae, 1982).

A group safety net provides the stability to retrench or to persevere. For example, Nissan's supporting Fuji Heavy Industries (in which it holds a 4.5% share) with orders for 60,000 Nissan Pulsars and production equipment to build them on the same line as the Fuji-built Subaru (White, 1991), or an NEC supercomputer subsidiary, HNSX, being supported by NEC and the Sumitomo group through a five-year sales drought (Bulkeley, 1991).

Inter-market. Corporate groups acquired a set of growing businesses in every industry (Miyazaki, 1980b) and, with them friendly markets (although there are now numerous large postwar independent companies, such as Sony and Honda, who have grown up primarily with an export focus). These function as a hedge against market uncertainty. Estimates range that from 10% to 50% of Japanese business is intra-alliance (Wright, 1989).

Lower Echelon: Suppliers/Distributors

Numerous small supplier-subcontractor enterprises form the base of an industrial alliance pyramid–a single electronics company reportedly can have 6,000 subcontractors in its industrial group (Sakai, 1990). It has been suggested that this base is the lower platform of a "dual" structure of the Japanese industrial economy (Miyazawa, 1980) and forms a cushion for the more visible upper echelon during times of economic retrenchment; however, many shared institutions assist these suppliers in their relentless pursuit to cut costs, continuously innovate, and improve product quality.

The corporate grouping (*keiretsu*) firm has potent, close allies. Any prospective partner must closely assess its "fit" into the whole network of relationships in order to determine what any gains are likely to be and which firm is likely to receive them.

EXPERIENCES WITH INTERNATIONAL STRATEGIC ALLIANCES

This section explores two major sets of international business relationships. First, we focus on an important Japanese company, Toshiba, and its interrelationships. Its context includes the support available to Toshiba from the Mitsui group (Bank, Trust, Insurance, Mitsui Trading, and so on) and the extensive, intricate Toshiba-U.S. network set out in Figure 8.1. Second, U.S-Japan collaborations

FIGURE 8.1. Toshiba's Global Strategic Alliances

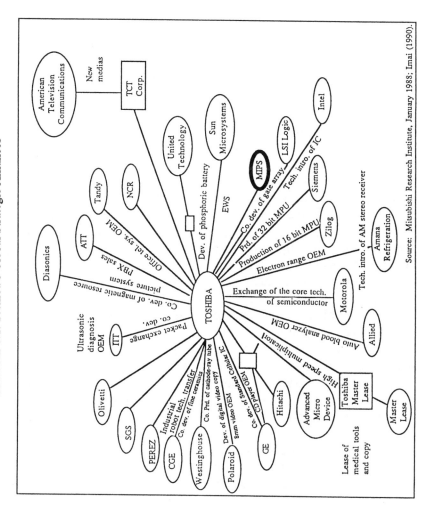

Source: Mitsubishi Research Institute, January 1988; Imai (1990).

191

have occurred in many industries–integrated circuits, biotechnology, pharmaceuticals, robotics, and steel. Examples from the commercial aircraft industry and the auto industry will be examined in more detail.

Toshiba is a major global high-tech company at the center of many cross-border, interfirm interactions. For example, in the semiconductor industry, a trend is emerging toward the decoupling of design and manufacturing. A response is illustrated in the Toshiba-MIPS alliance in Figure 8.1. The interfirm linkage on the production of a RISC-type (restricted instruction set computer) microprocessor was established to exploit the growing market. Recent Toshiba strategic alliances include: Zilog (microcomputer); LSI Logic (co-development of next generation of semicustom integrated circuits); Hewlett Packard (HP) (1M DRAM); Seimens (1M DRAM); Motorola (DRAM, microprocessor); Siemens (co-development of standard cellular); and Motorola (semiconductor partnership). Of course, each of the corporate groups has a major firm in the industry entering into many comparable alliances–Hitachi, NEC, Mitsubishi Electric, and others. In terms of specific interfirm collaborations, the chances for success are dependent upon the strategies of the firms concerned (Imai, 1990); however, in formulating and implementing its strategy, the Japanese G-form organization partner always considers the interests of its group.

International cooperative ventures in the commercial aircraft industry, as in all industries, involve both benefits and costs. Often the advantages are easier to calculate–sharing risks and resources, accessing national markets, and reducing competing products. While there may be a net gain to alliance participants, questions must be answered as to how the interests of the partners will be protected and how the gains will be shared.

The Boeing-Japan relationship illustrates an alliance designed to produce a product for the use of a participant. Of the world's five commercial airframe builders, only Boeing offers a full family of aircraft. The cooperation between Boeing and the Japanese consortium began with a subcontracting agreement in the early 1970s, which was very much weighted in Boeing's favor, and later developed through the sequence of Boeing aircraft: 747, 757, 767, and the 7J7. It was not until after the success of the 747, however, that

Boeing turned to international partnerships with the Japanese to ease the resource demands of simultaneous development of two aircraft, the 757 and the 767 (Roehl and Truitt, 1987). The cost of new product development is high–$1.5 billion for the 767, plus $1.5 billion for the V2500 high-bypass engine (Mowery, 1988). The Japanese Aircraft Development Consortium–Fuji Heavy Industries (FHI), Kawasaki Heavy Industries (KHI), and Mitsubishi Heavy Industries (MHI) and the Japanese government–took over about 15% of the airframe on the 767, including production on fuselage, panels, doors, and composite structures. (The V2500 engine is being developed by International Aero Engines, a complex venture involving Pratt and Whitney, Rolls Royce, Fiat, MTU, and a consortium of Japanese companies (KHI, MHI, and Ishikawajima-Harima Heavy Industries). Participation on the 7J7 may approach 25% (Moxon, Roehl, and Truitt, 1988). The strategic directions are clear. The Japanese Ministry of International Trade and Industry (MITI) has targeted the commercial aircraft industry for development. Boeing wants to continue its full line of aircraft and even maintain full control over the 7J7 design to assure a product fit (although the Japanese have a larger share of the design, development, and manufacturing). Technology transfer and information sharing may have significant long-term consequences for the Boeing competitive position. While price and definition of technology (i.e., what is "off limits") have been worked out, the depth of technological access has been problematical. Obviously, the Japanese consortium wanted complete information on a part; however, Boeing obviously wanted to regulate the flow because a future competitor may be being created.

Roehl and Truitt (1987) claim that the proper approach to a long-term collaboration is to expect the best, but prepare for the worst. Changes may cause a reconfiguration of the joint venture, with continuous bargaining based upon the changing relative powers of the players. The key to success may lie in an appropriate, realistic process of negotiation and implementation.

The General Motors/Toyota venture in the New Universal Motor Manufacturing Company (NUMMI) illustrates an additional alliance aim: organizational learning. NUMMI is ostensibly a temporary alliance to assist GM in learning how to improve efficiency in small-car production and to assist Toyota in learning how to market more effectively (Weiss, 1987). This is being accomplished by GM managers being loaned to NUMMI to work under more senior Japanese managers; preparing videotapes on NUMMI techniques; a computer-accessible database for all GM assembly plants; and plant visits for managers and union officials. Already, the GM Saturn project is benefitting (Womack, 1988). Obviously, only time will tell whether such aims are achieved.

GUIDELINES FOR A JAPANESE PARTNERSHIP

The most common mode of entry into the Japanese market is a strategic alliance, although to date returns from many such alliances have been marginal at best (Sadamoto, 1982). Still, increasingly cooperative ventures are being utilized by U.S. firms to meet new economic and technological demands (Osborn and Baughn, 1987). Table 8.2 offers a summary guide for prospective foreign company collaborative ventures with any "ostensibly independent" Japanese company (because usually they are not).

Contextual Analysis

This section provides practical suggestions for future strategic alliance participants. As stated above, cooperative relationships can be best understood in the context of its total set of relations (Kogut, 1988; Thorelli, 1986; Walker, 1988). That insight is particularly valuable in relation to dealings with a Japanese corporate group member. What it means for the foreign manager is that a "contextual" analysis should be included along with an industry analysis prior to any relationship with a Japanese company. The Japanese G-form company (where G-form organization includes the *keiretsu* formal support network), such as Mitsui's Toshiba, must be seen as pursuing–and having the wherewithal to pursue–long-term, technology-driven strategies.

Strategic alliances are arranged marriages. Participants need to understand each other's "family" background and interests as a first step in the relationship. As illustrated, the Japanese partner always considers its group interests before and during relationships

TABLE 8.2. Guidelines for Partnering with a Corporate Group Firm

Contextual analysis:	Ascertain your role in the other partner's network of relationships.
Cooperative process:	Establish alliances when synergy exists (that is, a positive sum relationship for both parties); learn and practice managing cooperative relations.
Innovation process:	Understand strategic role of your firm in other partner's innovation process.
Market access:	Use alliances to augment your core strength and be alert that technologies transferred do not foreclose your participation in the products and production technology of the next generation.
Authority relations:	Share strategy-making but develop a clear dominant-subordinate relationship for day to day operations; keep contact at high levels; and work to build credibility on both sides.

with outsiders. Still, the situation may not be as dense and monolithic as it appears. For example, Table 8.1 above shows the "dual" structure of the economy as an important fact (Miyazawa, 1980; Sakai, 1990). Thus, at a minimum, cooperative strategy toward a Japanese entity will depend upon its location in the upper or lower echelon of a corporate grouping. Sakai (1990:48) suggests that joint ventures or licensing with upper-echelon firms may later result in complaints of technology being "robbed." This is because the foreign company does not understand the dual structure: an upper-echelon firm contracts production to a lower-echelon group firm that supplies the product and, at the same time, learns how to produce a competing clone. A solution is to work directly with lower-echelon firms, bypassing upper-echelon commissions and establishing direct working relations, which can lead to a much higher likelihood of success.

Collective Strategy and the Process of Cooperation

Collective strategy (Astley and Fombrun, 1983; Dollinger, 1990) deals with joint actions undertaken by interorganizational collectivities. It is a "systematic response by a set of organizations that collaborate in order to absorb the variation presented by the interorganizational environment" (Astley and Fombrun, 1983: 580). For a systematic response to occur, collective relationships are needed to establish and maintain synergy (i.e., to attain goals not achievable by a firm acting independently). Collaboration suggests that the decision-making process itself is collective, involving negotiation and bargaining among interests, rather than a purely rational economic process. This certainly describes decision processes in both the corporate grouping (*keiretsu*) and the member companies.

Pucik (1988) identified the primary reason for low performance of American partners–low capability in managing cooperative relationships. Thus, an important management skill for strategic alliances, and one that must be learned, is the ability to balance numerous stakeholder interests to achieve their mutual satisfaction. In any event, there is no substitute for practice, even though new skills, particularly for Americans, are needed (Kearney Associates, 1987).

Network Relationships, the Innovation Process, and Partner "Fit"

For foreign cooperators, a major challenge posed by the Japanese G-form is to understand and position themselves appropriately in this Japanese pattern. The Japanese corporate-group support network enables a firm to focus on its area of special expertise–research, product design, development, production, marketing, etc.– and maintain industrial competitiveness. The innovation process requires a wide range of capabilities and related functional complementarities (Teece, 1986), which Japanese industrial organization appears to have achieved. Thus, it is critical for a prospective collaborator to understand not only where in the network of relationships it will "fit" but also what its strategic role will be in the group's innovation process. Then, some real assessments can be made for joint-venture durability and for possibilities of satisfying all parties.

Market Access and Technology Transfer

In most international linkages, a main motive for collaboration boils down to access to markets, whether in the U.S. or in Japan.

Foreign firms usually search for opportunities to enter and to expand within markets. When market access is restricted or closed altogether, the foreign firm has a particular incentive to enter because real competition is artificially limited. Thus, a firm may be forced to trade away its technology–organizational and technical–to overcome the barrier.

Access to markets is usually achieved by trading technology. The Japanese seem to have a history of negotiating for themselves the part of the value-added chain that has the greatest potential for controlling the next generation of production technology (Reich and Mankin, 1986), although more recent work does not support so general a proposition (Mowery, 1988). Often, the joint ventures that turn out poorly have been established for the wrong reasons. For example, a firm may attempt in an alliance to compensate for its weakness rather than seek to bolster its core strength. Since technology transfer (and organizational learning) are likely to be at the center of many strategic alliances, managers must understand the processes of both technology development and its transfer. Cooperative relationships, however, can help even a single firm specialize to maintain competence in specific technical areas. In this, long-term alliance relationships are important but difficult.

Authority Relations

From a traditional perspective, the joint venture is inherently unstable because of shared authority. For example, Killing (1983) hypothesizes that the simpler the tasks of management are, the more a joint venture can be run as if it had only one venture parent. Therefore, to his view, a dominant parent is most preferred; a shared parent role would be least preferred. Thus, his focus is on parent firms' roles with respect to influence on venture decision making and activities. Corporate-group companies have almost complete autonomy in their competitive market place; strategic direction, however, is a group or multi-hierarchy process, with the dual aims of growth in market share and long-term growth for the group. From a group perspective, shared authority at the strategic level may not be that undesirable. The open question is whether an outside firm can truly participate in the shared authority structure, within a reasonable strategic risk tolerance. If the foreign firm is unable to share in overall strategy making, then ventures should be within a dominant-subordinate framework.

CONCLUSIONS

This chapter has dealt with the importance of "context" for a strategic alliance, as illustrated by the established network of relationships in the Japanese industrial structure. These existing network relations may be a critical variable in the success or failure of a strategic alliance, especially within reasonably similar competitive regimes (such as South Korea and Taiwan).

Japan–for reasons of history, geography, culture, and character–has developed original, if not entirely unique, industrial organizations. Other Asian nations, such as Korea (with its mercantilist policies and big-business groups, or *Chaebol*) and Taiwan, have emulated Japan's industrial structure at least to some extent. Therefore, contextual analysis is extremely important for any foreign firm seeking collaborative relations within a corporate-group-dominated competitive regime.

Changing circumstances cause pressures for reconfiguring a strategic alliance. Thus, managers should recognize that their involvement in alliances will entail continuous bargaining based upon the changing relative powers of the players. Success may lie in appropriate processes of negotiation and implementation, and in never losing sight of the need to build core competencies over the long term.

REFERENCES

Astley, G. & Fombrun, C. (1983). Collective strategy: a social ecology of organizational environments. *Academy of Management Review, 8* (4), 576-587.

Beamish, P. (1985). The characteristics of joint ventures in developed and developing countries. *Columbia Journal of World Business, 20* (Fall), 13-20.

Berg, S., Duncan, J. Jr., & Friedmann, P. (1982). *Joint venture strategies and corporate innovation.* Cambridge, MA: Oelgeschlagera, Gunn & Hain.

Bulkeley, W. (1991). NEC steals Cray thunder at weather center. *Wall Street Journal.* July 2, B1.

Business Week (1990 September 24). Maybe the U.S. could use a keiretsu or two. p. 162.

Chipello, C. & Brauchli, M. (1991). U.S. officials pressure Japan on cartels, markets. *Wall Street Journal,* January 21, 1991. A7.

Christelow, D. (1987). International joint ventures: how important are they? *Columbia Journal of World Business. 22* (2), 7-14.

Christopher, R. (1983). *The Japanese mind.* New York: Simon & Schuster.

Contractor, F. & Lorange, P. (1988). Why should firms cooperate? In F. Contractor & P. Lorange (Eds), *Cooperative Strategies in International Business,* Lexington, MA: Lexington Books. 3-28.

Dollinger, M. (1990) The evolution of collective strategies in fragmented industries. *Academy of Management Review. 15* (2), 266-285.

Ferguson, C. (1988). From the people who brought you voodoo economics. *Harvard Business Review,* May-June, 17-24.

_____ (1990). Computers and the coming of the U.S. keiretsu. *Harvard Business Review,* July-August, 55-70.

Franko, L. (1971). *Joint venture survival in multinational corporations.* New York: Praeger.

Gerlach, M. (1987). Business alliances and the strategy of the Japanese firm. *California Management Review.* Fall, 126-142.

Hakansson, H. & Johanson, J.(1988) Formal and informal cooperation strategies in international industrial networks. In F. Contractor & P. Lorange (Eds.), *Cooperative strategies in international business* (pp. 369-379). Lexington, MA: Lexington Books.

Hall, R.D. (1984). *The international joint venture.* New York: Praeger.

Harrigan, K. (1985). *Strategies for joint ventures.* Lexington, MA: Lexington Books.

_____ (1988). Strategic alliances and partner asymetries. In F. Contractor & P. Lorange (Eds.), *Cooperative strategies in international business* (pp. 205-226). Lexington, MA: Lexington Books.

Henderson, D. (1973). *Foreign enterprise in Japan.* Tokyo: Tuttle.

Holden, T. & Reed, S. (1990). Saying sayonara is sweet sorrow. *Business Week.* March 12, 52.

Imai, K. (1990). Japan's business groups and keiretsu in relation to the structural impediments initiative. Paper presented to the symposium on the "U.S.-Japan Relationships Entering a New Phase: Issues of Structural Impediments," held in Tokyo March 26, 1990, and Washington DC, April 9.

Imai, K. & Itami, H. (1984). Interpenetration of organization and market: Japan's firm and market in comparison with the U.S. *International Journal of Industrial Organization. 2,* 285-310.

Johnson, C. (1982). *MITI and the Japanese miracle.* Stanford: Stanford University Press.

A. T. Kearney Associates. (1987). *Making strategic alliances work for your company.* Chicago: author.

Killing, J. (1983). *Strategies for joint venture success.* New York: Praeger.

Kiyonari, T. & Nakamura, H. (1980). The establishment of the big business system. In K. Sato (Ed.), *Industry and business in Japan,* (pp. 247-284). White Plains, NY: Sharpe, 247-284.

Kogut, B. (1988). Joint ventures: theoretical and empirical perspectives. *Strategic Management Journal. 9* (4), 319-332.

Kotler, P., Fahey, L., & Jatusripitak, S. (1985). *The new competition: What theory Z didn't tell you about marketing.* Englewood Cliffs: Prentice-Hall.

Magnusson, P. & Gross, N. (1990). Japan's latest end run around free trade, *Business Week,* October 1, 32.

Miles, R. & Snow, C. (1986). Network organizations: new concepts for new forms. *California Management Review,* 28, (3), 62-73.

Miyazaki, Y. (1980a). Excessive competition and the formation of *Keiretsu.* In K. Sato (Ed.) *Industry and business in Japan,* (pp. 53-73). White Plains, NY: Sharpe.

_____ (1980b). The Japanese-type structure of big business. In K. Sato (Ed.) *Industry and business in Japan* (pp. 25-34). White Plains, NY: Sharpe.

Miyazawa, K. (1980). The dual structure of the Japanese economy and its growth pattern. In K. Sato (Ed.), *Industry and business in Japan* (pp. 22-52). White Plains, NY: Sharpe.

Morita, A. (1987). *Made in Japan.* London: Fontana.

Morris, D. & Hergert, M. (1987). Trends in international collaborative agreements. *Columbia Journal of World Business. 22* (2), 15-21.

Mowery, D. (1988). Joint ventures in the U.S. commercial aircraft industry. In Mowery, D. (Ed.), *International Collaborative Ventures,* (pp. 71-110). Cambridge, MA: Ballinger.

Moxon, R., Roehl, T. & Truitt, J. (1988). International cooperative ventures in the commercial aircraft industry: gains, sure, but what's my share? In F. Contractor & P. Lorange (Eds), *Cooperative strategies in international business,* (pp.255-277). Lexington, MA: Lexington Books.

Nakatani, I. (1984). The economic role of financial corporate grouping. In M. Aoki (Ed), *The economic analysis of the Japanese firm,* (pp. 227-258). New York: Elsevier Science Publishers.

Ohmae, K. (1982). *The mind of the strategist.* New York: McGraw-Hill.

Organization for Economic Cooperation and Development (OECD). (1972). *The industrial policy of Japan.* Paris: OECD.

Osborn, R. & Baughn, C. (1987). New US/Japanese cooperative ventures: the role of technology. *Columbia Journal of World Business. 22* (2), 57-65.

Patterson, G. (1991). U.S. auto firms say joint effort is the way to gain electric-car edge. *Wall Street Journal,* January 21.

Porter, M. (1990). *Why nations triumph.* Fortune, March 12, 94-108.

Prestowitz, C. (1988). *Trading places: How we allowed Japan to take the lead.* New York: Basic Books.

Pucik, V. (1988). Strategic Alliances with the Japanese: Implications for human resource management. In F. Contractor & P. Lorange (Eds.), *Cooperative strategies in International Business,* (pp. 487-498). Lexington, MA: Lexington Books.

Reich, R. & Mankin, E. (1986). Joint ventures with Japan give away our future, *Harvard Business Review.* March-April, 78-86.

Roehl, T. & Truitt, J. (1987). Stormy open marriages are better: Evidence from US, Japanese and French cooperative ventures in commercial aircraft. *Columbia Journal of World Business*. Summer, 87-94.

Roos, J. (1989). *Cooperative venture formation processes: Characteristics and performance*. Stockholm: Institute of International Business/Stockholm School of Economics.

Ross, D. (1991). Japanese keiretsu: Global managers' unseen competitors. *Advances in International Comparative Management*, Vol. 6, Greenwich, CT: JAI Press.

Sadamoto, K. (Ed.) (1982). *Breaking the barriers*. Tokyo: Survey Japan.

Sakai, K. (1990). The feudal world of Japanese manufacturing. *Harvard Business Review*, November-December, 38-49.

Stopford, J. & Wells, L. (1972). *Managing the multinational enterprise*. New York: Basic Books.

Taoka, G. & Beeman, D. (1991). *International Business*. New York: HarperCollins.

Teece, D. (1986). Profiting from technological innovation: implications for integration, collaboration, licensing, and public policy, *Research Policy*. 15, 285-305.

Thorelli, H. (1986). Networks: between markets and hierarchies. *Strategic Management Journal*, 7, 37-51.

Tokyo Business Today. (1991). Laser for autos. 59 (1), 19.

Tsurumi, Y. (1976). *The Japanese are coming: A multinational interaction of firms and politics*. Cambridge, MA: Ballinger.

van Wolferen, K. (1990). *The enigma of Japanese power*. New York: Vintage Books.

Walker, G. (1988). Network analysis for cooperative interfirm relationships. In F. Contractor & P. Lorange (Eds.), *Cooperative strategies in international business*, (pp. 227-240). Lexington, MA: Lexington Books.

Weiss, S. (1987). Creating the G.M.-Toyota joint venture: A case in complex negotiation. *Columbia Journal of World Business*. 22 (2), 23-38.

White, J. (1991). Nissan broadens ties with Fuji in production pact. *Wall Street Journal*. January 22, 1991, C8.

Williamson, O. & Bhargava, N. (1972). Assessing and classifying the internal control structure of the modern corporation. In Cowling (Ed.) *Market Structure and Corporate Behavior Theory and Empirical Analysis of the Firm*, (125-148). London: Gray-Mills.

Womack, J. (1988). Multinational joint ventures in motor vehicles. In D. Mowery (Ed.), *International Collaborative Ventures in U.S. Manufacturing*, (pp. 301-348). Cambridge, MA: Ballinger. 301-348.

Woronoff, J. (1986). Japanese industrial collusion and trade. *Joint Economic Committee, Congress of the United States*. Washington, DC: US GPO, January, 1986.

Wright, R. (1989). Networking–Japanese style. *Business Quarterly*, Autumn, 20-24.

Yoshino, M. (1976). *Japan's multinational enterprises*. Cambridge, MA: Harvard University Press.

Chapter 9

Ownership and Control in East-West Joint Ventures

J. Michael Geringer

Joint ventures (JVs), which involve shared ownership and decision making by two or more parent organizations, have become an increasingly pervasive phenomenon in international business during the past decade. This trend is especially pronounced in terms of the incidence of East-West JVs, those ventures that involve Western firms and partner organizations from the former U.S.S.R. or the five Eastern European nations that composed the recently terminated Council for Mutual Economic Assistance (CMEA): Poland, Hungary, Bulgaria, Romania, and Czechoslovakia. Recent changes in regulations regarding foreign investment have resulted in dramatic increases in the number of joint ventures formed in these nations and in those involving Western firms (Goldman, 1989; Nigh, Walters, and Kuhlman, 1990). Despite continued uncertainty regarding the nature and extent of forthcoming political and economic changes in the former CMEA countries, the dramatic changes brought on by free market transformation seem likely to foster significant levels of JV activity in the foreseeable future.

The recent expansion of East-West JV activity can be partly attributed to regulatory requirements, which have often reduced the attractiveness–or totally precluded the use by Western firms–of other investment options (such as wholly owned subsidiaries). For example, until January 1, 1989, the former Soviet Union prohibited foreign partners from owning more than 49 percent of a venture, and several of the Eastern European nations have similarly imposed limits on the extent of foreign ownership in certain strategic industries. However, even when full ownership has been permitted, Western firms have often voluntarily chosen to utilize JVs because of the additional benefits that these ventures can provide, including reduction of risk; access to, and knowledge of, local markets; and improved ability for overcoming bureaucratic or cultural barriers. Besides enhancing prospects for the JV being treated as a "local" firm, minority participation can help the Western firm avoid the necessity for financial consolidation of what may be essentially an entity with unknown value and performance prospects.

In addition to their frequency, East-West JVs represent an increasingly important managerial concern because of changes in their strategic orientation. Initially, many of these ventures had been viewed as a means of exploiting potentially profitable peripheral markets or outdated technologies, and their activities were considered to be of marginal importance to the maintenance of a parent's competitive advantage.

However, an increasing number of East-West JVs involve products, markets, or technologies that represent the parents' primary or "core" activities, and they often involve host-country firms that may constitute existing or potential competitors. Indeed, a principal objective of many of these ventures is to increase the efficiency of the Eastern European and former Soviet companies to a level more comparable with the West. The development of an enterprise that can be economically viable within the former U.S.S.R. or Eastern European context, and possibly in Western markets as well, has proven to be a major challenge for many firms, due to a host of cultural and infrastructural factors. To the extent that these barriers can be overcome, and to the extent that economic reforms continue to be successfully introduced within these former CMEA countries, there is potential for significantly altering the regional or global structure of entire industries. Thus, from a strategic perspective, developments in East-West JVs require increased scrutiny and understanding.

Yet, despite their increased popularity and strategic importance, East-West JVs have frequently failed to fully satisfy the strategic objectives of one or all of their parent firms (Goldman, 1989; Artisien and Buckley, 1989; Barrett, 1987; Geringer and Hebert, 1991). Many of the performance problems experienced by these ventures have been linked to the complexity associated with the presence of two or more parent organizations, which often embody widely disparate ideologies and goals (West, 1959; Franko, 1971; Killing, 1982; Moxon and Geringer, 1985). This complexity is captured by an expression used by the Chinese to describe JVs: "*Tung chuang, yi meng*," meaning "same bed, different dreams." For example, conflicts of interest have often arisen among partner organizations due to a divergence of priorities regarding production for export (and the generation of hard currency) versus import substitution. This complexity often causes the ventures to be difficult to manage and can result in substantial transaction costs associated with coordination of, and communication between, the parent organizations, as well as between parents and the JV. The complexity is often further compounded by the continuing rapid and radical changes in the political, social, and economic environment confronting East-West JVs, as well as by incompatibilities associated with differences in partners' languages, corporate or national cultures, organizational size and operating policies, and so forth. These performance problems constitute a major concern, particularly for the Western parents. Besides consuming large amounts of management time, money, and other scarce resources, a JV may also expose critical aspects of the parent's strategy, technology, or other know-how to partner or non-partner firms, thereby threatening to compromise the Western parent's long-term competitive position.

Clearly, there are many challenges associated with successful formation and management of East-West joint ventures. However, the control exercised by parents and the venture managers over a JV's activities has repeatedly been identified in other settings as an important variable influencing JV performance and the attainment of parent organizations' objectives (Killing, 1983; Schaan, 1983; Geringer and Hebert, 1989). However, the issue of control of East-West JVs has previously received minimal attention from management scholars. Based on over two dozen interviews with executives and government officials in North America, Eastern and Western Europe, and the U.S.S.R., as well as a review of case studies, control also appears to be a critical determinant of East-West JV performance. Therefore, this chapter's objective is to examine the importance of JV control, and to identify several key issues associated with the exercise of effective strategic control in East-West JVs.

THE IMPORTANCE OF CONTROL
IN EAST-WEST JOINT VENTURES

Control is a complex and multidimensional concept that has challenged managers and scholars for decades. The concept refers to the process by which one organization influences, to varying degrees, the behavior and output of another entity through the use of formal or informal mechanisms (Geringer, 1989). Formal control typically relies on authority-based power arising from such institutionalized mechanisms as ownership or organizational structure. However, control can also be exercised through a broad range of informal mechanisms that can influence behavior and thus affect the probability of achieving specific outcomes. The popular conception of control is in its deterministic form, wherein one entity has sufficient power (such as through full ownership) to fully dictate behavior or outcomes. Nevertheless, control can represent a continuum, ranging from complete control to no control over outcomes. Particularly in the case of JVs, it is much more common for parents to have only partial control.

Control plays an important role in determining a firm's ability to achieve its strategic objectives, since it affects the organization's ability to monitor, coordinate, and integrate the activities of its various business operations. Without effective control efforts, firms are likely to experience increased difficulty in successfully managing their operations and achieving their objectives. This is a particular concern in the case of JVs since, due to the shared-ownership and decision-making nature of these ventures, each partner must relinquish some control over the JV's activities. For reasons intimately related to their corporate strategy and objectives, parents often avoid relinquishing control over some or all of their activities.

Attainment of a firm's objectives over the long term is contingent upon its ability to implement a strategy that exploits its distinctive competencies along one or several critical dimensions of corporate activity. Because it may decrease the probability of achieving a desired behavior or outcome, insufficient or ineffective control over a JV can limit the parent's ability to coordinate its activities, efficiently utilize its resources, and effectively implement its strategy (Stopford and Wells, 1972; Lorange, Scott Morton, and Ghoshal, 1986; Anderson and Gatignon, 1986). In contrast, exercising control over some or all of a JV's activities may protect the parent from damaging leakage of critical dimensions of its strategy, technological core, or other proprietary innovations or know-how. Such leakage, between the partners or to firms outside the venture, may have serious competitive effects, possibly creating new competitors or otherwise limiting the parent's or venture's overall efficiency (Reich and Mankin, 1986; Hamel, Prahalad, and Doz, 1989). Indeed, the threat of technological pirating, knock-off products and the like–often without effective response by partners or host-country governments–has been a concern for many firms involved in East-West JVs.

In addition, JV control is important due to the fundamental weakness of centrally planned economies such as those that characterized the CMEA: low productivity. This situation is attributable to a lack of market orientation among many managers and employees in these countries; uncertainty regarding relevance of market and cost data associated with centralized planning systems; frequent scarcity of adequately skilled labor; an inefficient and sometimes corrupt supply-and-distribution system; and the high level of political and economic uncertainty associated with the transformation of these centrally planned economies. Particularly if the JV is attempting to export its goods, ineffective control can harm performance because of such factors as product engineering or quality control procedures that fail to meet Western standards. As a result, a critical issue is how East-West JVs should be controlled in order to promote successful performance and the attainment of the parents' strategic objectives. In this regard, the first concern commonly expressed by managers is how to divide the JV's ownership among the partners.

THE OWNERSHIP-CONTROL DILEMMA IN EAST-WEST JOINT VENTURES

When determining how East-West JVs' equity will be divided among the parents, managers have typically chosen one of the following two alternatives: *majority/minority* (where one partner has over 50 percent of the venture's equity) or *50/50* (where the partners have equal or approximately equal shares, with no clear majority held by any one partner). A fundamental issue associated with this decision is the impact that ownership may have on how the JV is managed. Prior studies showed that firms frequently sought majority ownership to achieve effective management control (Tomlinson, 1970; Friedmann and Beguin, 1971; Stopford and Wells, 1972; Nigh, Walters, and Kuhlman, 1990). The rationale was that a majority owner would be able to exercise dominant control over a JV, allowing decisions to be made rapidly in response to market or product developments and thus avoid the costly compromises or decision-making deadlocks that a 50/50 JV might confront (Killing, 1983; Geringer and Woodcock, 1989). Majority ownership might also limit unintended diffusion of technology or other know-how to partners or other organizations if the dominant partner could exercise tighter control over the JV's activities.

Host-country preferences and regulations have often hindered the pursuit of majority ownership by Western firms interested in forming East-West JVs. These hurdles to majority ownership have been the cause of substantial consternation for many Western firms, which have often responded by either deciding not to invest in the host country or to invest in a much more modest manner. Indeed, since January 1989, when majority foreign ownership was first allowed, over 20 percent of all new U.S.-former U.S.S.R. JVs have involved this option, with another 42 percent involving 50 percent foreign ownership (Nigh, Walters, and Kuhlman, 1990). However, although rules regarding JV ownership by Western firms are beginning to ease in the former U.S.S.R. and most of the Eastern European nations, the argument here is that the emphasis of many executives on achieving majority ownership may be overstated.

While majority ownership may provide a parent with some control, it will rarely enable the parent to dictate all of the JV's decisions all of the time. In many instances, particularly for major decisions of the JV's board, decisions tend to be made by consensus. Thus, distinctions such as a majority on the Board, or the ability to nominate the General Manager versus the Deputy General Manager, can be relatively unimportant. If a parent attempts to force its will upon its partners merely on the basis of relative ownership, then the JV's prospects for long-term survival will be sharply diminished. A majority owner may be able to successfully outvote its partner on critical decisions once, or even twice. However, even if the majority partner feels that its skills and decision-making abilities are "clearly" superior to the other partner's, a minority partner who is systematically outvoted on important issues is likely to feel that its objectives are not being achieved and its trust in the partner's actions and intentions may erode rapidly (Habib, 1987; Geringer and Frayne, 1990). The result is typically a heightened level of conflict and confrontation. Unless the situation is quickly rectified, such a venture will generally be terminated within a short time.

Thus, regardless of the division of equity, in order for a JV to operate successfully over the long term it must be operated on a "win-win" basis. Demanding majority ownership, and then managing the JV to exploit this ownership advantage, is likely to result in *lower* performance. Even if the host country's regulations mandate dominant ownership by local firms, this often will not ensure that the local partner has *full* control over the JV, or even control over the venture's strategically critical activities. Therefore, instead of merely focusing on how the ownership will be divided, the critical concern for executives should be how the JV will be *managed* so that each partner's objectives are likely to be attained. In this regard, it may not be necessary to exercise control over the *entire* JV, but only over selected dimensions of its activities in order for a parent's objectives to be achieved.

EXERCISING EFFECTIVE CONTROL OVER EAST-WEST JOINT VENTURES

In attempting to successfully control East-West JVs, it is necessary to design and implement a control system that will permit effective control to be exercised over critical JV decisions. From an individual parent organization's standpoint, an effective JV control system is one that promotes the attainment of the parent's strategic objectives for the venture. However, the unique feature of JVs is the shared nature of their ownership and decision making. Therefore, in order to develop a truly effective control system, the parent must not focus solely on its own self-interests. Rather, the parent must also ensure that the control system it proposes to implement will not prevent the other major stakeholders in the JV–particularly the other partner, as well as venture management, employees, and the host government–from also achieving *their* objectives. Differences in objectives among participants in East-West JVs are common and, unless the venture is designed and managed so that each of the stakeholders perceives that its objectives will be attained, the JV is likely to encounter conflicts, bureaucratic delays, and other performance problems. Thus, it is imperative that the parents be aware of, and take into consideration, the objectives of the JV's other stakeholders when attempting to design and implement an effective JV control system.

In attempting to design an effective control system, it is necessary to distinguish three underlying dimensions that compose JV control: focus, extent, and mechanisms (Geringer and Hebert, 1989). These dimensions, and their relationship to strategic control of East-West JVs, are discussed below.

Focus of Control Efforts

The term "focus" refers to the scope of activities over which a parent seeks to exercise, or to *not* exercise, control. A parent may be able to achieve its strategic objectives by exercising dominant control over only a few activities of the venture, rather than attempting to control all of the JV operations. This is a particularly important issue when the JV's equity is equally divided, or when a parent only has a minority equity position, as commonly occurs in East-West JVs. It is also critical when a parent wants to extensively integrate specific JV activities–such as raw materials procurement, manufacturing, or marketing–with its other operations (Geringer, 1989).

In this regard, each parent must determine what JV activities it needs to have control over. This decision will be an outgrowth of the parent's strategic objectives for both the short and long term, and should reflect the key success factors that are critical to maintaining the parent's competitive advantage, as well as ensuring the economic viability of the JV (Geringer, 1991). For example, problems with the quality of output from the Eastern-nation partners have arisen in many East-West JVs. While the partner's traditional domestic products might have been acceptable in an undersupplied Eastern market, they often fail to meet international quality requirements. Specifically, low quality levels are often a reflection of a combination of contextual factors, including a relatively low quality requirement in a market in which industrial and especially consumer goods are scarce; a lack of feedback from the market under a system of central planning and state allocation; low individual and organizational motivation; and a scarcity of high-quality raw materials and purchased components. Thus, particularly for JVs concerned with exporting in order to generate hard currency, effective control of product quality is essential.

In identifying these key activities and decisions, parent managers must distinguish between what they *want* and what they *need* to control. Many firms, particularly in the West, have fallen into the trap of believing that more control is always better. Unfortunately, this type of thinking ignores the direct and indirect costs associated with exercising that control, particularly over JV activities that are of limited importance to the success of the venture or the parent firm, or in which the parent's resources or capabilities are insufficient.

It should be apparent that there is a fit between the control requirements and capabilities of the individual partner organizations in order for JV formation to proceed. For example, current accounting principles in the Soviet Union and Eastern European countries are generally perceived as inadequate by Western standards. The debate on LIFO versus FIFO methods for inventory valuation is just beginning, and current cost-accounting practices essentially fail to distinguish fixed from variable costs. In addition, the existence of non-market prices for key raw materials or JV outputs may diverge substantially from comparable market-based figures in the West. This can result in dramatic changes in costs and bottom-line performance as prices in formerly centrally planned economies are adjusted to more accurately reflect their values in the outside world, possibly endangering the JV's long-term viability. For reasons such as these, it is common for Western partners to retain primary control over the accounting function, at least until the local partner or the venture's employees can develop adequate expertise.

This type of compatibility among the partners' objectives, capabilities, and responsibilities can thus facilitate successful performance of East-West JVs by reducing the level of transaction costs associated with inter-partner conflict and compromise (Geringer, 1988). In the absence of such a fit, the strategic and economic viability of the venture may be threatened and the pursuit of a different, more compatible partner or of a non-JV form of operation (e.g., licensing or long-term contracting) may be warranted.

An example of this type of fit is a recently formed JV between IMAX Systems Corporation of Canada, the developer of giant-screen/large-format film technology, and Znanie, a Russian organization involved in educational and cultural activities. The JV would enable IMAX to access a large market with one of the highest rates of movie attendance in the world, as well as the opportunity to produce a series of films about the former Soviet Union that could be shown worldwide. The JV would provide Znanie with access to the innovative IMAX technology and films. While both partners would participate in filmmaking and theatre operations in the former U.S.S.R., Znanie would have dominant control over marketing and government relations within the former U.S.S.R.; IMAX would control marketing and distribution of Soviet-produced IMAX films elsewhere in the world. This division of control was consistent with the parents' respective strengths and objectives, as well as with the operational requirements of the joint venture.

A parent may also specifically desire *not* to exercise extensive control over particular JV activities. This is particularly likely when the activity is not central to the parent's strategic focus, or if the partner has a much stronger competitive position on that particular dimension. Similarly, if efforts to effectively control an activity would entail high administrative or learning costs, or would utilize scarce management time and force the firm to divert its attention from its principal operations, then delegation of control to the partner or to the JV's managers might be a more appropriate option. For example, many of the Western companies that have entered into East-West JVs during the late 1980s have been relatively small (Nigh, Walters, and Kuhlman, 1990). Because of the dramatic changes taking place in the former CMEA countries, government regulations, as well as the local ministries and their policies and executives, are constantly changing. Keeping track of these changes, and maintaining a feel for who the decision makers are, thus represents a constant challenge. It is virtually impossible for most smaller firms to devote the resources necessary to accomplish this task. Instead, the most common approach is to delegate most of the responsibility for local issues, such as monitoring of regulatory and political changes and the maintenance of government relations, to the local partner. This enables the Western firm to focus its limited resources toward those areas that are critical to the JV's success and in that it has the necessary expertise.

Extent of Control Efforts

"Extent" of control refers to the degree of control exercised by a parent over individual JV activities. It ranges from complete control by one parent, to equal control by each parent and/or the venture's managers, to complete control by the JV's managers.

The presence of two or more parents constitutes the major source of management difficulties in most JVs (Young and Bradford, 1977; Janger, 1980; Killing, 1983; Geringer, 1988). Domination of JV activities by a single parent or the venture's managers may reduce the costs and uncertainties associated with coordination among parents, as well as the risk of unintended disclosures of proprietary know-how to a partner or other outside organizations. Dominant control structures often make JVs easier to manage and may be more successfully executed than when the decision-making control is shared by the parents (Killing, 1983; Anderson and Gatignon, 1986). For example, a basic tenet of McDonald's strategy is that the same levels of quality, service, cleanliness, and value (QSC&V) will exist across all of their restaurants worldwide. Maintaining this uniformity is so critical that it took McDonald's 12 years to negotiate an acceptable JV agreement with the food service division of the Moscow City Council to serve the Moscow market. George Cohen, Vice Chairman of Moscow-McDonald's, commented that, "We negotiated long and hard with the Soviets, but our philosophy of QSC&V was the one item that was non-negotiable." Despite a minority 49 percent share, McDonald's retains control over all key operational aspects of the JV. To ensure that their rigid specifications and standards for food are maintained, McDonald's constructed a fully integrated, strictly controlled, state-of-the-art food-processing and distribution center at a cost of over $40 million. To control quantity and quality of inputs while maintaining its policy of buying from local suppliers, McDonald's shipped in its own seed potatoes and high-quality bull semen, taught farmers how to raise the beef and other agricultural products, and even picks up milk from local Russian farms in its own refrigerated dairy trucks. It only depends on its Russian partner to win it sugar and flour allocations in the Russian economic planning system. Yet despite ceding almost complete control, the Russians with their crippling distribution problems and neglected service sector, stand to benefit from learning McDonald's foolproof food technology and management methods.

However, as discussed above, it may not be necessary for a parent to dominate the *overall* JV in order to achieve these benefits. Rather, as in the IMAX-Znanie example, it may be possible to have a split control structure, where each parent or the JV managers exerts dominant control over one or several different activities of the JV (Geringer and Hebert, 1989; Geringer, 1989). Yet, the decision to use either overall or selective dominant control structures is appropriate only if the controlling party has the skills and resources necessary to satisfy the market requirements, such as sufficient manufacturing expertise, financial acumen, or relationships with distributors or government regulators. In addition, it is essential that the partner having dominant control does not abuse this privilege. Otherwise, an erosion of trust and escalation of conflict among partners is likely to result, often with significant implications for JV performance.

Mechanisms of Control

Control "mechanisms" represent the means by which parents exercise control over a JV. Two main types of mechanisms are available to parents for exercising effective control over East-West JVs (Schaan, 1983). *Positive* control mechanisms, which parents employ in order to promote certain behaviors, can be distinguished from *negative* control mechanisms, which are used by a parent to stop or prevent the JV from implementing certain activities or decisions. Positive control tends to be exercised through informal mechanisms, including staffing, reporting relationships, and participation in the planning process. In contrast, the more bureaucratic negative control includes reliance on such mechanisms as formal agreements, approval or veto by parents, and the use of the venture's board of directors.

Decisions regarding what control mechanisms to employ, and how to employ them, have important implications for a JV's operation. In this regard, it is essential that the important interrelationships between control mechanisms and both the extent and focus of control be fully appreciated. For example, due to differences in ideology and a scarcity of personnel with adequate technical and managerial capabilities, human resource management often represents a crucial strategic control mechanism in East-West JVs (Frayne and Geringer, 1987, 1990; Geringer and Frayne, 1990; Schaan and Beamish, 1988; Pucik, 1988). Indeed, for the example discussed earlier, the effective management of human resources was viewed by McDonald's as one of the–if not *the*–most important factors in achieving JV success in Moscow. As Bob Hissink, Vice President of Operations working with the Moscow JV, said, "The really important part of developing a McDonald's crew lies in the training." As a result, McDonald's insisted on the ability to employ part-time workers, in opposition to the Soviet labor laws existing at that time, and it installed its full company system of bonus payments for productivity. The top four Soviet managers spent ten months in North America undergoing the same intensive training program that all managers in the McDonald's system worldwide must successfully complete. Another 24 assistant managers each received 3 months of on-site training in Toronto. All other employees were put through similar rigorous training programs in Moscow.

Yet, even if it is a minority partner, a parent may be able to influence relative allocation of control over a JV by influencing staffing of the venture's top management positions. The means of selecting, training, evaluating, and rewarding the performance of general managers and other key JV personnel can significantly affect not only the venture itself but also its relationship with each parent. The JV general manager's position, in particular, can affect the venture's operations, since the general manager is responsible for maintaining relationships with each of the parents, as well as running the JV. For example, even if it is unable to appoint the JV's director general, the Western parent may still be able to exercise control over the venture by influencing the training and performance evaluations of the director general as well as the other key JV positions. This can be especially valuable in attempting to overcome the deficient levels of personal motivation and lack of experience with financial accountability that have been a traditional outgrowth of centralized systems of planning and management.

Contrary to initial appearances, these three dimensions of control–focus, extent, and mechanisms–are not incompatible, but rather complementary and interdependent. They each examine a different aspect of JV control. Parent organizations must simultaneously consider all three of these dimensions in order to design and implement effective control systems for an East-West JV. Failure to do so will often prevent the parents from achieving the full benefits of their cooperative endeavor.

ACHIEVING AND MAINTAINING A CONTROL "FIT" IN EAST-WEST JOINT VENTURES

It is readily apparent that there can be benefits from the exercise of control in East-West JVs. Without such control, parent firms may encounter difficulties in achieving the full potential of their strategies and in attaining their objectives. On the other hand, the exercise of JV control is not without drawbacks; it indeed has a cost. Control often implies a commitment from a parent in terms of both responsibility and resources, and may lead to increased overhead costs. It can also increase the risks to which a firm is exposed. Consequently, particularly in East-West JVs involving geographically dispersed and culturally dissimilar partners, the exercise of extensive control over a venture's activities and decisions can generate important coordination and governance costs and limit the JV's efficiency. This may be especially true for control efforts oriented toward activities and decisions having little importance for performance of either the JV or the parent.

Therefore, the critical issue for a parent is to exercise control–in terms of focus, extent, and mechanisms–over the JV in a manner that will enable it to successfully implement its strategy without incurring a level of administrative or organizational inefficiencies that outweighs the gains from its cooperative endeavor. In other words, there is a "fit" between the parents' strategies and the JV's control structure when the benefits outweigh the costs of control; this fit is best when the margin between benefits and costs is optimized. For example, a U.S. manufacturer of agricultural implements wanted to form a JV in the former U.S.S.R. to access the large Russian domestic market and to provide a base for exporting to Europe. The Russian partner wanted to tightly control production scheduling in order to coordinate the JV's activities. However, the extent of control sought by the Russian partner would limit the JV's ability to respond to fluctuations in export market demand, and thus its ability to generate the level of hard currency desired by both parents and necessary to pay for imports of critical raw materials and components. In this case, in order to allow the JV to be economically viable, achieving a control fit required a *reduction* in the extent of control desired by the Russian partner.

Sometimes it is necessary for the control structure to evolve over time in order to maintain this fit. For instance, a mid-sized German manufacturer of industrial equipment negotiated a JV with a Polish firm to produce machinery and components for domestic and export markets. From a strategic standpoint, the German company's principal objectives were to exploit its technical expertise in product design and manufacturing, as well as to improve access to the Polish and other Eastern European markets, while overcoming the constraints imposed by high labor costs in its German plant. The Polish partner had access to substantial amounts of relatively inexpensive skilled labor, as well as to the Eastern European markets, but lacked the manufacturing technology necessary to produce high-quality machinery. When the JV was first formed, the German firm wanted to exercise very tight control over the venture's Polish manufacturing operations in order to ensure effective technology transfer. It insisted on designing the layout of the JV's plant and sent a team of engineers to Poland to oversee the installation of equipment and to help train employees. It also sent a group of Polish supervisors and technicians to Germany to observe its domestic operations and receive specialized training in an operating facility. During the JV's first year of production, the German firm maintained very close supervision of the Polish operations to minimize the defect rate and to ensure that the skill transfer was success-ful. Since that time, it has been gradually shifting control of manufacturing to its Polish partner. Although the German firm keeps technical managers on-site, the individuals are assuming more of an advisory role than a supervisory role over the JV's manufacturing activities.

CONCLUSIONS

As firms increasingly utilize East-West JVs as tools for attaining strategic objectives within a rapidly changing competitive environ-ment, the issue of *control* of these ventures is experiencing a corre-sponding increase in attention from managers and academics alike. Yet, understanding of JV management lags behind the demands of practice. Managers have received minimal guidance regarding how East-West JVs should be controlled, or about the requirements for exercising effective control. As a result, many firms have chosen to bypass use of these ventures, or have entered them ill-prepared. These firms may not only be missing potentially valuable opportu-nities but they may be ultimately eliminating themselves as viable contenders within entire industries or regions of the world. By addressing strategic control in East-West JVs, this chapter has at-tempted to bring into focus a critical issue influencing JV manage-ment and performance, and provide a base for improved under-standing and management of these ventures.

REFERENCES

Anderson, E. & Gatignon, H. (1986). Modes of foreign entry: A transaction cost analysis and propositions, *Journal of International Business Studies*, Fall: 1-26.

Artisien, P. & Buckley, P. (1989). Joint ventures in Yugoslavia: Opportunities and constraints, *Journal of International Business Studies*, Spring: 111-136.

Barrett, M., (1987). Risks of East-West joint ventures, *Euromoney*, September: 476+.

Franko, L.G., (1971). *Joint venture survival in multinational corporations*, New York: Praeger.

Frayne, C.A. & Geringer, J.M. (1987). Self-management: A key to improving international joint venture performance. *Proceedings of the First Conference on International Personnel and Human Resource Management*, Singapore, B1-5.

Frayne, C.A. & Geringer, J.M. (1990). The strategic use of human resource management techniques as control mechanisms in international joint ventures. In G. Ferris & K. Rowland, (Eds.), *International Human Resources Management*, Supplement Volume 2 of *Research in Personnel and Human Resources Management*, Greenwich, CT: JAI Press: 53-69.

Friedmann, W.G. & Beguin, J.P. (1971). *Joint international business ventures in developing countries*, New York: Columbia University Press.

Geringer, J.M. (1988). *Joint venture partner selection: Strategies for developed countries*, Westport, CT: Quorum Books.

Geringer, J.M., (1989). Parent strategy and division of control in international joint ventures, *Proceedings of the Administrative Sciences Association of Canada*, Montreal: 45-54.

Geringer, J.M., (1991). Strategic determinants of partner selection criteria in international joint ventures. *Journal of International Business Studies*, 22 (1): 41-62.

Geringer, J.M. & Frayne, C.A. (1990). Human resource management and international joint venture control: A parent company perspective. *Management International Review*, 30: 103-120.

Geringer, J.M. & Hebert, L. (1989). Control and performance of international joint ventures, *Journal of International Business Studies*, Summer: 235-254.

Geringer, J.M. & Hebert, L. (1991). Measuring performance of international joint ventures, *Journal of International Business Studies*, 22 (2): 249-263.

Geringer, J.M. & Woodcock, C.P. (1989). Ownership and control of Canadian joint ventures, *Business Quarterly*, Summer: 97-101+.

Goldman, M.I. (1989). Joint ventures return to Communist China and the Soviet Union, *Business in the Contemporary World*, Winter: 84-92.

Habib, G.M. (1987). Measures of manifest conflict in international joint ventures, *Academy of Management Journal*, 30 (4): 808-816.

Hamel, G., Prahalad, C.K. & Doz, Y.L. (1989). Collaborate with your competitors–and win, *Harvard Business Review*, January-February: 133-136+.

Janger, A.R., (1980). *Organization of international joint ventures*, New York: Conference Board.

Killing, J.P. (1983). *Strategies for joint venture success*. New York: Praeger.

Lorange, P., Scott Morton, M. & Ghoshal, S. (1986). *Strategic control*, St. Paul: West.

Moxon, R.W. & Geringer, J.M. (1985). Multinational consortia in high technology industries: Commercial aircraft manufacturing. *Columbia Journal of World Business*, 20 (2): 55-62.

Nigh, D., Walters, P. & Kuhlman, J.A. (1990). US-USSR joint ventures: An examination of the early entrants. *Columbia Journal of World Business*, Winter: 20-27.

Pucik, V., (1988). Strategic alliances with the Japanese: Implications for human resource management. In F. Contractor & P. Lorange, (eds.), *Cooperative strategies in international business*, (pp. 487-498). Lexington, MA: Lexington.

Reich, R.B. & Mankin, E.D. (1986). Joint ventures with Japan give away our future, *Harvard Business Review*, March-April: 78-86.

Schaan, J.L., (1983). *Parent control and joint venture success: The case of Mexico*. Unpublished doctoral dissertation, University of Western Ontario.

Schaan, J. & Beamish, P. (1988). Joint venture general managers in LDCs. In F. Contractor & P. Lorange, (eds.), *Cooperative strategies in international business*, (pp. 279-299). Lexington, MA: Lexington.

Stopford, J. & Wells, L. (1972). *Managing the multinational enterprise*, New York: Basic.

Tomlinson, J.W.C., (1970). *The joint venture process in international business: India and Pakistan*, Cambridge, MA: MIT Press.

West, M.W., (1959). Thinking ahead: The jointly-owned subsidiary, *Harvard Business Review*, July-August: 31-32+.

Young, G.R. & Bradford, S., Jr., (1977). *Joint ventures: Planning and action*, New York: Financial Executives Research Foundation.

Chapter 10

Strategic Alliances in the Global Container Transport Industry

Mary R. Brooks
Robert G. Blunden
Cheryl I. Bidgood

INTRODUCTION

Strategic alliances have been common in the shipping industry for more than a century. The past ten years have witnessed a dramatic shift in the strategies of ocean carrier firms, as they have engaged in mergers, acquisitions, and strategic alliances, seeking to develop integrated door-to-door capabilities in response to a rapidly changing environment and the requirements of increasingly demanding customers.

This chapter will examine the nature of strategic alliances in the global container transport industry and the forces that are driving the current round of strategic alliance activity. It begins by defining the types of strategic alliances common in the container transport industry. This is followed by a model of the forces that encourage firms to enter into strategic alliances or develop door-to-door distribution networks in other ways. The chapter then reviews the strategies, as reported by the public press, pursued by five of the largest container shipping companies to establish integrated distribution networks. The chapter concludes with a discussion of the use of strategic alliances by carriers as they attempt to position themselves advantageously for the future.

COMMON FORMS OF STRATEGIC
ALLIANCES IN OCEAN TRANSPORT

The ocean transport industry employs a variety of types of strategic alliances to grow cooperatively or, as is often the case, to limit competition. Because some of these arrangements are unique to the industry or the terms are not self-explanatory, this section explains some of the most prevalent forms of strategic alliance employed. Each of the alliances noted below may or may not accompany other interfirm arrangements. They all imply a commitment made between firms to complement and support each other's activities for as long as it serves a mutually beneficial purpose.

Conferences

Sturmey (1962) has defined a conference as

> . . . an association of competing liner owners engaged in a particular trade who have agreed to limit the competition existing among themselves. As a minimum, they will have agreed to charge freight rates or passenger fares for each class of traffic according to an agreed schedule of charges and to show no discrimination between shippers. To the agreement foreswearing all forms of price competition may be, and usually is, added an agreement to regulate sailings according to a predetermined pattern and to recognize the berth rights of other members. A further step may be to add a full pooling agreement under which profits and losses on the trade covered by the conference are shared between the member lines. (p. 322)

Conferences, the original interfirm agreement of the shipping industry, grew out of the excess cargo capacity prevalent in the Europe-Far East trades in the latter half of the 19th century, with the first conference created for the U.K./Calcutta trade in 1875. Through coordinated sailings, pre-determined prices, and cargo volume ceilings, the industry was able to restore profitability and control predatory pricing and cut-throat competition. The agreements forged then form the base for conference operations today (Brooks et al., 1983).

However, the future of the conference as an interfirm partnership is in doubt. Regulatory agencies have relaxed their vigilant watch of conference activity; perhaps that is because they note that the conference system, particularly since the passage of the U.S. Shipping Act of 1984, has been less than effective in its efforts to control prices and operating conditions on the major trade routes. It has often been argued that non-conference carriers provide an effective check on the power of the conferences. Many in the industry argue that the conference system is unlikely to see the dawn of the next century.

Slot Charters, Co-ordinated Services, and Equipment-/Chassis-Sharing Agreements

The ability to mount a credible service requires the carrier to be able to provide weekly service to the client. This mandates an investment in three ships (if a return voyage takes 21 days; four ships are needed if the cycle is 28 days), plus a minimum number of containers to carry the goods and possibly chassis for their inland transport to a railhead or intermodal terminal. It is this equipment investment that may easily exceed the firm's financial capability, thereby necessitating the use of an alliance. Informed industry estimates are that fixed costs have risen since the early 1980s from 30% (largely vessel-related) to 70% due to the investment in Electronic Data Interchange (EDI), containers, and chassis now necessary.

In the case of the slot charter (vessel space-sharing agreement), a carrier on a route may offer to another carrier (which may be a competitor) a fixed number of spaces, or slots, per sailing for a fixed period of time at an agreed price. Although both firms may still be competitors, the firm offering the slots secures revenue for those slots it may not be able to sell otherwise, thereby financing the investment in the ship. In this case, the shipper may have contracted with Carrier A to move his goods, when in fact they are carried on Carrier B's vessels without his knowledge, because Carrier A took advantage of a slot chartered on B's ship.

Slot charter agreements are common in coordinated services where the financial arrangement for the space is often distinctly separate from the contribution of the ship servicing the route. In this combination, not only are slots bought, sold, or traded, but the two firms coordinate sailing schedules so as to jointly offer a regular fixed-date sailing schedule. A recent illustration is the integrated service launched by P&O and Maersk on the Europe-Far East route in March of 1991; the joint scheduling will provide two sailings a week, but each company will retain its separate identity and marketing organization.

A second illustration would be the St. Lawrence Coordinated Service run by Canada Maritime and Orient Overseas Container Line (OOCL). Until the renegotiation of the agreement in 1990, each partner's share of the slots available was not equal to the slots it contributed to the service; this required a complex slot charter contract (in addition to the coordinated service agreement) and that Canada Maritime purchase slots from OOCL. The new agreement brings contributed slots closer to slots offered to the customer by each partner. Yet each company, although dependent on the other, still competes more than cooperates.

Carriers may also form alliances in the non-core (e.g., not vessel-owning or -operating) part of the business. The need for containers or other equipment may prompt strategic alliances for investments in these support areas. Equipment-sharing agreements–to share the costs and utilization of port-side cranes in company-owned terminals for example–are similar to slot charters and may or may not be part of the package when a slot charter agreement is negotiated. The degree of cooperation in these ventures depends very much on the perception of the firm as to the marketing benefits of a "rolling billboard" to the individual carrier's image with the customer. Highly competitive firms often view this to be a neutral ground where the savings from better asset management can be substantial and risks to the core business minimal.

Consortia

The shipping industry has always had difficulty defining what is meant by consortia. Helmut W.R. Kreis of the Commission of the European Communities Directorate General–Competition has gone on record as defining consortia as specialized joint ventures encompassing many different arrangements. He notes that the industry has "no common views . . . even on the definition of what constituted a consortium–except that the shipping industry claimed antitrust immunity for them" (*The Journal of Commerce*, October, 1990, p. 1A).

Consortia have been common practice in the liner shipping industry during the past 20 years. Prior to that, most firms joined a conference and otherwise competed for cargo on the basis of service. The mounting capital cost of ships and the aggressive marketing of Oriental shipping companies in the 1970s drove many Western operators to rethink their strategies. The result, in some cases, was vessel-pooling consortia–instances where shipping companies contributed ships and other resources to create a new jointly owned entity offering more frequent service than could be offered by any of the companies alone. Three of the top-30 container operators are multinational consortia–United Arab Shipping Company, Scandutch, and Gearbulk–but none of these is in the top ten. However, this type of alliance is declining as individual firms lose their identity to the consortium. In addition, consortia have proven to be slow to respond to the rapidly changing needs of the marketplace. The past year has witnessed announcements of the demise of both the Scandutch and Trio consortia, which are major players on the Europe-Far East route. Later in this chapter, the restructuring of Atlantic Container Line, a once very successful North Atlantic consortium, is described.

CONCEPTUAL BASES

Much of the literature on strategic alliances focuses on those driven by market access requirements, not a major issue for this industry. Because many industries are globalizing, strategic alliances offer an important mechanism for achieving this objective quickly. Shipping has been a global industry for centuries. More relevant is the research that focuses on the strategic use of alliances to share benefits such as economies of scale, co-opting competition, or raising barriers to entry.

Although all strategic alliances comprise cooperative arrangements between firms, they may be used for different purposes. In some cases, they are between firms that are in direct competition and are designed to lessen the level of competitive rivalry and/or improve capacity utilization and service levels. In other cases, they are between firms whose service capabilities complement each other and jointly make a complete, integrated service possible. Figure 10.1 arrays the strategic alliance vehicles common in the transport industry along a competition-cooperation continuum. This framework is a simplification of one proposed by Denham (1991).

Conferences may be the least cooperative (i.e., most competitive) of strategic alliances, since in their simplest form they may be no more than price-fixing agreements to eliminate price competition among members. Slot charters and other forms of asset sharing require greater cooperation, but also hold the potential for increased benefits as equipment utilization is maximized; however, firms engaged in these are often in head-to-head competition on the same trade route. Vessel-sharing consortia with joint marketing agreements and management committees, like equity joint ventures, require even more cooperation as firms become partners in the new venture.

Denham's competition-cooperation continuum provides insufficient explanation for firms' strategic behavior. The Contractor and Lorange (1988) paradigm provides another dimension on which to evaluate the strategic behavior of firms. The degree of inter-organizational dependence partners in a coordinated service or slot charter agreement perceive is greater than for those participating in a conference, but less than for those with a common marketing entity, even though they may be similarly positioned on a cooperation-

FIGURE 10.1. Range of Strategic Alliances in the Container Transport Industry I

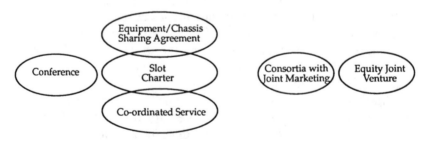

competitive continuum. The relative position of each form of alliance in terms of its inter-organizational dependence is illustrated in Figure 10.2.

As Contractor and Lorange (1988) point out,

> it may also be critical to assess the degree to which the relationship leaves the partners mutually interdependent and, thus, potentially vulnerable later on. This question must be assessed differently depending on whether the industry is characterized by global production-interaction efficiencies or by adaptation to the unique country-level circumstances. (p. 8)

The shipping industry, characterized by capital-intensive and highly mobile assets, is by no means country-based. It is clear that the partners in strategic alliances in this industry are highly vulnerable. Other than Electronic Data Interchange (EDI), there is very little technology that is not already well diffused, making it difficult to maintain competitive advantage in the face of intense cutthroat competition. Therefore, it is not surprising that strategic alliances are used only when viewed as absolutely necessary because of their benefits–economies of scale, co-opting the competition, or raising the barriers to entry.

Finally, carriers have always been wary of alliances from a regu-

FIGURE 10.2. Range of Strategic Alliances in the Container Transport Industry II

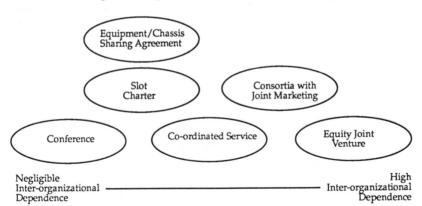

Negligible
Inter-organizational
Dependence

High
Inter-organizational
Dependence

latory point of view. Since the earliest days of the conferences, carriers have been eyed as collusionists and therefore concerned that cooperation might be branded by the authorities as anti-competitive. One of the reasons why the slot charter is viewed as an acceptable strategic alliance alternative by both regulators and carriers is its position on the competition-cooperation continuum (i.e., very close to the competition end). It enables carriers to retain their individual marketing identities and compete vigorously in the marketplace while they gain the advantages of sharing costs. Such competition allays the regulators' fears of an anti-competitive environment. While competitive, it is quite difficult for such competitive entities to cheat on the cooperative part of the agreement without jeopardizing the arrangement.

Over the past decade, the use of strategic alliances has grown and the reasons for that growth can be found in the environment in which the container transport industry finds itself. The model that follows is an attempt to map the factors that influence the strategic behavior of international container carriers. It uses a strategic management perspective to identify and describe the environment and industry factors that are driving changes in individual firm's strategies. The theory is simple: trends and forces at work in the environment lead to new opportunities and threats in the industry. As managers perceive these, they anticipate their likely effects on their firm's performance and may choose to respond by changing their strategies. (One possible response is to develop strategic alliances.) In any event, the subsequent performance of the firm, or its competitors, all interact with industry and environmental forces to shape the industry. That environment and the forces at work in it are detailed in the model that follows (Figure 10.3) and in the next section.

Driving Forces in the Container Transport Industry Regulatory Factors

It is generally agreed that the liberalization of trade regulations, the reduction or elimination of tariffs, and the harmonization of rules and regulations can only lead to trade creation. The Canada-U.S. Trade Agreement, the Single Market Initiative in Europe, and the liberalization of Eastern Europe are all predicted to lead to a

FIGURE 10.3. A Model of Strategic Behavior in the Container Transport Industry

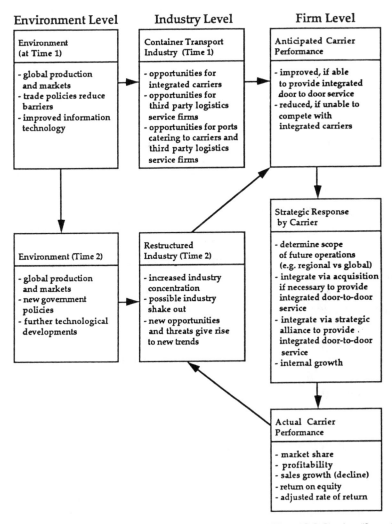

Source: This model is a later version of the one presented in Brooks, M.R. and R.G. Blunden, "Strategic Alliances vs. Ownership in the Container Transport Industry: An Exploration of the Issues," Saskatoon: Canadian Transportation Research Forum *Proceedings*, 1990, p. 1-13.

greater volume of trade; in the case of the latter, the experts reviewing the state of trade resulting from the liberalization of Eastern
Europe are in agreement that increased trade will be likely, but they
expect reduced trade in the short-term, with a longer timeline for
trade growth. The jury is still out on the ability of the Canada-U.S.
Trade Agreement to generate increased trade, since it is difficult to
separate the effects of the agreement from the effects of the current
recession. In theory, trade liberalization should increase trade opportunities and, hence, further the growth of secondary industries,
like transport, that depend on trade.

Trade policy is not the only environmental factor affecting the
transport industry, however. Governments exert a significant degree
of control over a firm's strategic choices through its competition
and mergers policies. Mergers policy investigation thresholds used
by the Commission of European Community (EC) are much higher
than they are in North America. In Canada and the U.S., liner
conferences are exempt from competition (anti-trust) regulation as
long as they meet certain conditions; likewise, Regulation 4056
essentially exempts EC liner conferences from the Competition
Rules (Articles 85 and 86) of the Treaty of Rome (Erdmenger and
Stasinopoulos, 1988). All of these countries accept that shippers
want to move goods of any size and type at their convenience and
that liner conferences are the most efficient way of doing this.
Nevertheless, developments in Europe have now left most EC
countries with only a few major liner carriers. (The extent of corporate concentration within the industry will become apparent later in
this chapter.)

Although consortia in the liner industry receive little attention
from competition watchdogs in North America, because consortia
are often conference members and conferences are well scrutinized,
the Directorate General–Competition for the EC has been reviewing
its policy on consortia since 1986. Although an interim report is-
sued in January 1988 concluded that there was no evidence to
justify a block exemption from competition rules for consortia, the
1990 U.K. House of Lords Select Committee (1986) has called for
urgent clarification. The British Shippers' Council favors an individual rather than a block exemption and has convinced the British
government to support efforts in this direction. The primary argu-

ment is that consortia represent a current market practice that acts as a counterbalance to the market clout of the megacarriers (Bott, 1990). The uncertainty surrounding the application of Competition Rules in Europe has apparently not hampered the existence of consortia, the largest of which are based there.

Global Production and Markets

Increasingly, competitive pressures are forcing manufacturing companies to look at their operations and their markets as global in nature. In terms of markets, global commonalties facilitate the standardization of products sold to differing markets worldwide. The ability of a firm to undertake a global strategy has been fostered by both technology and telecommunications advances that were not available in previous decades. In addition, decreases in overall transport costs arising from logistical technological innovations have encouraged companies to develop new strategies and consider global sourcing of products, components, and services.[1]

The globalization of industry underscores the need for an efficient and cost-effective world distribution system. Transportation and communication are the links that allow the global corporation to develop competitive advantage internationally. The effects of this situation are downward pressure on transportation rates and an increased customer orientation (Porter, 1986). The transport literature has noted that this trend reduces the overall demand for ocean transport; the declining demand for bulk carriage of raw resources has not been matched, in tonnage terms, by the increase in containerized finished goods moved.

Increased competition on a global scale is also forcing firms to consider greater integration of their production processes with suppliers and markets as a means to gain competitive advantage. Just-in-Time (JIT) systems, a natural by-product of such integration, is highly dependent on precise international delivery schedules. With a JIT approach to manufacturing, raw materials and goods in transit are considered inventory and the carrier is viewed as a stage in the manufacturing process.

In order for JIT to work effectively, manufacturers and carriers need to cooperate closely. Since reliability is critical, the building of trust between parties is essential to a JIT approach. With this in mind, enhanced integration between some carriers and manufacturers is taking place through strategic alliances (Bowersox, 1990). Logistics alliances are expected to grow in the coming decade, as manufacturers secure their market position through alliances with carriers; these relationships commonly have built-in performance standards that must be met in order for such an alliance to continue (Brooks and Kindred, 1990). This chapter does not focus on that type of alliance but on the ones that take place within the container transport industry.

Technological Developments

The increasing trend towards globalization of production and markets and the demands from cargo interests for speedier delivery and improved cargo tracing have forced the shipping industry to respond to these requirements in their pursuit of cargo. EDI has helped carriers meet these needs by eliminating the paperwork associated with the transfer of containers between modal carriers and, in the process, expediting delivery and lowering costs. EDI is of critical importance because of the high-value nature of the cargo, and it is gradually evolving for many lines from a tool of competitive advantage to one of competitive necessity. Shipping lines, after several years of going it alone to develop proprietary EDI systems, are realizing the benefits of cooperation. The impatience of carriers to see EDI networks in place has led to the development of EDI-SHIP, a joint venture of the world's largest shipping lines, and a network, software, and message standard for the industry launched in the fall of 1990 (*The Journal of Commerce*, August, 1990).

Other technological developments in the industry, such as the development of doublestack rail cars, have led the way to even greater integration within the industry. The capital-intensive nature of both railroads and shipping has meant that this is another area ripe for the development of strategic alliances. Railroads can gain the volume necessary to make doublestack rail cars and unit trains cost-effective for long-haul container moves by feedering overseas container lines. Significant cost savings are possible using doublestack technology, and this can create further competitive advantages for ocean operators aligning themselves with American railroads, where costs per loaded mile in 1985 ran at $0.79 for traditional

TOFC (trailer on flat car) moves and $0.56 for doublestack container moves (Grimm and Smith, 1985).

The New Industry Environment

The factors described above come together to significantly influence the international container transport industry. New opportunities for carriers have emerged. Carriers may seek to cater to the demands of JIT-oriented customers with an integrated door-to-door service backed up by EDI container tracing and documentation systems. Technology and regulation have combined forces to make such services possible. The better the service a particular carrier offers, the more likely it is to secure the business. How to improve service offerings then becomes the question carriers are asking, and strategic alliances offer one vehicle for achieving that goal. The Chairman and Chief Executive Officer of Sea-Land, Alex Mandl, expresses the following thoughts on the issue: "It is not essential for the company to own the assets. What is critical is the ability to offer a seamless service to the customer" (*Lloyd's Shipping Economist*, 1990, p. 33).

In the marine transportation industry, fixed costs are high and the product is perishable. Large container ships cost tens of millions of dollars, and when they leave port with unfilled capacity that potential revenue is lost forever. Door-to-door capabilities imply an ability to move cargo over both land and sea and therefore require carriers with land and sea capabilities. Firms historically focused on either land or sea transportation with costly capability in order to offer a service to customers. The EDI networks that promise reduced clerical costs, improved cargo tracking, and speedier delivery are costly capital investments that require systems integration among all carriers in the delivery channel if their benefits are to be realized. And so the opportunity for further growth through strategic alliances with other carriers is there. The choice remains–alliance or go it alone.

Strategic Responses: Alliance or Ownership?

Carriers can develop integrated door-to-door services on their own or cooperatively with other firms. Those that choose to go it alone must fill the gaps in their distribution networks through acquisition or internal growth and expansion. For a marine container transport company, that may mean adding routes, ports of call, and/or port facilities in addition to securing inland transportation capabilities. By going it alone, they exercise greater control over the network, but the costs are significant.

An analysis carried out by *Containerisation International* (1990) showed that 38% of contracted capacity in TEU (Twenty-foot Equivalent Unit) slots was for ships of greater than 3000 TEU, and by 1990 the editor saw "no reason why owners should not go for vessels of 5,000 TEU and over in the 1990s" (p. 5). Parallel to this trend is an increased use of larger feeder vessels to ensure that the fullest utilization possible is made of the larger mainline vessels (*Containerisation International*, 1990). The mammoth capital investment required by vessels of this size has added more fuel to the trend to grow through either acquisition or strategic alliance. The cost efficiencies supporting larger vessels are quite clearly illustrated in Table 10.1.

A smaller vessel does not generate the per-TEU cost efficiencies

TABLE 10.1. Cost Comparison Between Two Trans-Atlantic Service Alternatives

	Alternative "A"	Alternative "B"
Fleet	4 X 500 TEU	1 X 2,000 TEU
Annual Vessel Capital and Operating Costs	$14,100,000	$8,000,000
Annual Port Charges	$3,600,000	$1,800,000
Annual Fuel Consumption	$5,100,000	$1,810,000
Annual Total System Costs	$22,800,000	$11,300,000
Total Capacity Offered	52,000 TEU	52,000 TEU
Slot Cost Per Leg		
at 100% Utilization	$438	$223
at 85% Utilization	$515	$263

"A":   4, second hand, 500 TEU cellular vessels with a 28 day round-trip, an 8 year life expectancy. Price: $6 million each. Fuel consumption: 45T/day, at $90 /T.
"B"   1, new 2,000 TEU cellular vessel, with a 28 day round-trip, depreciated over 10 years. Price: $40 million for the ship. Fuel consumption: 70T/day, at $90/T.
Annual Interest Rate: 10%. All $ are US$.

Source: Louis J. LeGendre, Compagnie General Maritime, Presentation: "Partnerships in Liner Shipping: CGM–French Line's Perspective," Halifax, September 10, 1990.

possible with larger vessels. Therefore, larger vessels offer significant cost advantages to operators with the financial capacity to invest in such vessels. For those without such financial clout, strategic alliances of the slot charter or consortium variety give them some of the cost advantages previously only available to the mega-carriers. Rather than operate 400-500 TEU vessels, a number of smaller operators can each buy a 2,000 TEU vessel and, by taking advantage of one or more alliance options on a shared route, offer a service equivalent to that offered by the giants like Maersk or Sea-Land, assuming that the market demand will support the capacity injected.

In the broadest of terms, these capabilities can be added by the company itself or by securing access to another firm's capability through some form of strategic alliance. Integrated door-to-door systems development is costly both in financial and time terms. In the time it takes a firm to develop its own door-to-door capabilities, others may build defensive market positions in those very markets by speedier means. Acquisition may be a much speedier way to develop an integrated door-to-door capability, but suitable candidates are not always available or the buyer may be forced to pay a substantial premium to acquire a suitable firm. Acquisitions are not guaranteed successes in any event. The difficulties of integrating acquiring and acquired firms are legendary, and on routes where there are only two primary carriers–the premium operator and the discount one–such integration is not only extremely difficult but subject to allegations of anti-competitive behavior.

This leads us to the strategic alliance as a means of developing an integrated door-to-door carrier. Strategic alliances may be the only way for a firm with limited financial resources to compete with others developing integrated transportation systems–or they may be the fastest way for firms to take advantage of present opportunities and develop defensible competitive advantage. This is becoming even more critical, since the major lines are moving to consolidate their worldwide market position. See Figure 10.4 for strategies of selected container careers.

An analysis carried out by *Containerisation International* has shown that the largest 20 operators have increased their market share of global capacity throughout the 1980s; these carriers con-

FIGURE 10.4. Strategies of Selected Container Carriers

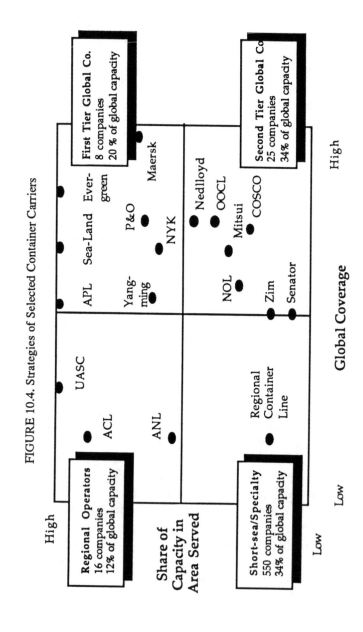

Source: James Brennan, Temple Barker & Sloane, Inc., *Intermodalism in the 1990's* (Speech: Halifax Port Days '89, September 18, 1989).

236

trolled 26% of the world's slots in 1980 and, by 1990, that share had grown to 39%. Booz Allen predicts that by 1995 these 20 carriers will control 50% of the world's slots (Booz Allen & Hamilton Inc., 1990). Of these, a select number of companies have emerged to service the global distribution needs of shippers. At the same time, a number of carriers have opted for a niche strategy, concentrating on particular markets, but not necessarily offering a less sophisticated transport alternative; Zim, ACL and Senator Line are examples of this strategy (*Containerisation International Yearbook*, 1990).

Looking to the future, the availability of adequate capital and the managerial capability to ensure long-term market presence are critical factors in the further evolution of the megacarriers. This does not, however, mean that the trend has slowed. Further concentration in the industry is still underway, as strategic alliances between megacarriers supplement service expansion and vertical integration activities in the search for global dominance of the industry. The following section examines five companies: four top-20 carriers and one regional operator, Atlantic Container Line (ACL), a consortium.

CASE STUDIES

The preceding discussion of the container transport industry led to several conclusions. First, that the industry is in a period of significant change and that that change is customer-driven. The regulatory environment and technological innovations of the day are enabling carriers to meet these demands through the provision of fully integrated logistical services. Second, carriers that move decisively in this direction may be able to create sustainable competitive advantage in their markets. Finally, carriers that are slow to respond may be forced to develop similar capabilities to protect their competitive position.

However, it is less clear how carriers will attempt to develop such capabilities. Will they go it alone, developing the required capabilities through internal growth and expansion or acquisition, or will they seek to fill the missing links in their networks through strategic alliances? There are clear advantages to each path. In an effort to develop further insight into this issue, we will examine five companies' strategies in greater detail.

Five case studies were developed through a review of the trade press. They were not randomly selected and do not necessarily represent a balanced view of the total industry. Rather, they were expressly chosen to provide insight into strategic responses of carriers perceived to be using alliances to position themselves to compete in an environment increasingly seeking an integrated transportation network. In addition to the trade press review, each of the following companies' vessel holdings were assessed for the type of cargo-carrying capacity and vessel management strategy (owned and managed; owned and chartered-out; managed and chartered-in; or agency) recorded in *Lloyd's List of Shipowners*. The data were analyzed to ensure that there was consistency between the media reports of carriers' strategies and their operating structures.

Sea-Land Service Inc.

Since its early years as the pioneer of containerization under the leadership of Malcolm McLean, Sea-Land has grown to become a global intermodal organization with a fleet of 60 ships and annual revenues in excess of US$2 billion. In May 1986, CSX moved to gain control of Sea-Land in its bid to become the world's premier transportation company. The Sea-Land purchase enabled CSX to move into the international spotlight from its strong U.S. domestic position, and it saved Sea-Land from the unwelcome attentions of corporate raider Harold Simmons.[2] CSX is proud of its efforts to consolidate its position in the worldwide transport industry.[3] By 1988, it ranked third in containership tonnage after Evergreen and Maersk.

Sea-Land has recently changed its emphasis from "being a liner company–that circles the globe–to a full service transportation company offering global logistics packages that can be competitive with firms providing contract logistics" (Middleton, 1990). In order to accomplish this goal, Sea-Land Services Inc. has adopted a proactive strategy, an integral part of which is the use of vessel-sharing arrangements with other lines in order to improve asset utilization and reduce costs. For example, in the North Atlantic trades, Sea-Land Services Inc. has a strategic alliance with Nedlloyd and P&O

Containers Limited, whereby efficiency is enhanced through vessel sharing. This alliance has existed since 1986 and was renewed, in the fall of 1989, for another ten years. In late August 1990, Sea-Land and P&O expanded their alliance to include Maersk Line for vessel sharing on the route between Europe and the U.S. West Coast. This arrangement with Maersk had originated with Maersk's discussions with CSX for the purchase of Sea-Land. While not willing to sell its ocean carrier line, CSX favored a strategic alliance with Maersk as one way to boost Sea-Land's refrigerated traffic business (*The Journal of Commerce*, September, 1990). Sea-Land reports that, prior to vessel-sharing agreements, the cost of operating the Sea-Land fleet accounted for 27% of its total costs; by 1990, that had dropped to 12.9% (Middleton, 1990).

Sea-Land's proactive strategy also includes slot exchange programs that increase their access to ports not on their schedule and open their ports of call to other liner companies. To further improve asset utilization and drive down costs, alliances have also been formed for the purposes of joint equipment interchange and joint inland management (Middleton, 1990).

In 1988, Sea-Land entered into a strategic alliance with Norasia to form an Asia-Middle East-Europe (AME) service (Middleton, 1990). Again, this alliance was formed for the express purpose of improving asset utilization and reducing costs. Sea-Land provides the terminal facilities and EDI systems, while Norasia provides a fleet of ten state-of-the-art vessels. Increased penetration of the Asian market was desired, since it had become the second-fastest-growing market in the world.

Liner services to the former Soviet Union are also in their plans. Again, Sea-Land will look to gain expertise in that market and reduce its investment risk through strategic alliances with other distribution firms. In September 1990, Sea-Land announced that it had signed connecting carrier agreements with two of the Soviet Union's largest regional shipping companies–the Baltic Shipping Company based in Leningrad and the Black Sea Shipping Company, or Blasco, based in Odessa.[4] According to *The Journal of Commerce*: "These arrangements place Sea-Land in the leading position to carry cargoes, not only between Europe and Asia, but in the developing trade routes under the terms of the new U.S.-former

U.S.S.R. bilateral maritime agreement. . . . "[5] In conjunction with these new strategic alliances, Sea-Land has opened offices in Moscow and Brest, and the possibility of including intermodal facilities in the Soviet transportation network is being discussed.

Sea-Land's U.S.-based operations are supported by their CSX/ Sea-Land Logistics divisions. In the Pacific Rim, Sea-Land operations are supported by their subsidiary, Buyers Consolidated. Sea-Land's European logistics operation is rooted in two joint ventures with Frans Maas of Dusseldorf. The first, involving equal equity participation, concentrates on logistics management and is available globally through Sea-Land's affiliated companies, while the second provides dedicated trucking services within Europe, focusing on meeting specific customer needs (*Container News*, 1990).

These strategic responses are evidence of a marked departure from its traditional philosophy; Sea-Land Services had been described as "private, competitive and committed to a go-it-alone philosophy" (Middleton, 1990, p.12). The company has, however, become a strong advocate of strategic alliances and uses the full range of alliance options to meet the needs of an industry in transition.

Maersk Line

Maersk is a division of the giant Danish shipping firm A.P. Moller, which includes holdings in intermodal services. If the A.P. Moller holdings are included, Maersk is the second-largest container carrier, based on TEU slots in service at the end of 1989.

In 1987, Maersk expanded its operations into the North Atlantic container trade. The *Journal of Commerce* referred to this as "the single biggest event in the North Atlantic container trades, in the last five years."[6] Maersk's target for this North Atlantic operation was to capture in excess of 10% market share. In order to achieve this objective, Maersk planned an aggressive pricing strategy: lower freight rates by 15% in the first year and 10% in the second year, with the expectation that prices would level out in the third year.[7] At that point, Maersk counted on the route becoming profitable. Although Maersk captured more than 10% of the market in the three years, profitability eluded the company. As a result, in 1990 the line announced a rationalization of its operations in order to boost profitability. This rationalization included negotiations with CSX for the possible purchase of Sea-Land Services. While these negotiations did not result in a Maersk purchase of the U.S.-flag carrier, they produced a vessel-sharing agreement. Under this arrangement, Maersk provides space to Sea-Land Services Inc. and P&O Containers on all of its ships serving the U.S. West Coast from Europe. In exchange, Maersk receives space on Sea-Land and P&O vessels calling on East Coast and Gulf Coast ports.

The signing of this vessel-sharing agreement coincided with Maersk's decision to finally join the North Europe-USA Rate Agreement, the rate-making group for steamship lines carrying cargo from Europe to the United States. Maersk had joined the rate-making conference for the U.S.-to-Europe direction in 1987, but had operated as a non-conference member in the westbound trade. Sentiment within the industry was that Maersk deliberately postponed entry into the conference for the westbound direction in an effort to capture significant market share on this more lucrative leg of the route.[8] However, the signing of the vessel-sharing agreement with two major carriers of the rate-making group necessitated a commitment in both directions because "a vessel-sharing agreement with a carrier that did not follow conference pricing guidelines would be awkward."[9] Maersk's membership in the North Europe-USA Rate Agreement conference took effect on October 1, 1990, and is still active.

Maersk has long been a proponent of the shipping conference system and holds memberships in many of them. Recently, however, Maersk's president, Alfred Ruhly, has made public some doubts about the viability of them under the current American legislation. In an interview in August 1990, he criticized the American system and called for its dissolution: "In the American trades they allow the conference chairman . . . to speak for all the lines. (But) he isn't speaking for Maersk . . . especially when he argues with the shippers, our customers."[10] Ruhly believes that the only solution is to withdraw the antitrust immunity the U.S. currently grants steamship conferences. He predicts that would cause the conference system to collapse and result in a multi-year global rate war that would force weaker shipping companies out of business.[11] Although many would agree with him, no one seems prepared to fire the first shot, and conference membership remains in the range of available strategic alliances.

Hapag-Lloyd

As part of its 1980s restructuring program, the German carrier Hapag-Lloyd adopted a competitive pricing policy for its services and began looking for possible cooperative arrangements with other carriers. One such cooperative arrangement that developed was the Trio consortium on the trade route between Europe and Asia. This consortium, formed in the early 1980s, was comprised of 5 lines and 27 vessels. The other four members were P&O Containers Ltd. (British), Ben Line Containers Ltd. (British), Mitsui O.S.K. Lines Ltd. (Japanese), and Nippon Yusen Kaisha (Japanese). This consortium operated effectively, capturing as much as 17% of the container traffic on the Europe-Far East trade.[12]

In 1990, the five members of Trio announced that their consortium would be dissolved and replaced with two new ones. The two British carriers decided to form their own alliance, while Hapag-Lloyd opted to join the two Japanese members. The five lines plan to continue cooperating closely with each other in such matters as shared terminal facilities and EDI systems. They feel that two smaller consortia will be more flexible and able to respond more quickly to the needs of the market place.[13]

Hapag-Lloyd is also a member of the Far Eastern Freight Conference. In 1990, this conference controlled 50% of the traffic (an estimated 1.8 million TEU) on the Europe-Far East route.[14] Membership in this conference requires that Hapag-Lloyd comply with the conference-established rates; in the past, this had not been a problem, since Europe-Asia was the most lucrative of the three major trade routes. Within the past year or two, profit margins have declined drastically.[15] In 1989, Hapag-Lloyd lost over DM20 million (US$12 million) from liner shipping, compared with a profit of about DM50 million (US$29 million) a year earlier. According to Hans Jakob Kruse, board spokesperson for Hapag-Lloyd and the Far East Freight Conference chairman, this devastation is entirely attributable to a deterioration in market conditions on this Europe-Far East route that is largely the result of competition from non-conference carriers and increasing capacity from new ships being delivered.[16] The situation is likely to worsen as Hapag-Lloyd takes delivery of several large container ships in 1991 and 1992.

Hapag-Lloyd also has a partnership on the North Atlantic route with ACL. When asked about Hapag-Lloyd's future in such strategic alliances and partnerships, Kruse "predicted the end of revenue-pooling partnerships and a growth of much looser groupings based on space-sharing arrangements."[17] The Hapag-Lloyd of the early 1980s had been criticized for its indecisiveness and cumbersome management structure; that problem appears to have been overcome.

Compagnie Generale Maritime[18]

In the view of *The Journal of Commerce*: "There is a limited number of companies which can be said to be worldwide operators. The world market will continue to divide the global operators from the regional operators, and we have no intention of being regional."[19] Compagnie Generale Maritime (CGM), as of September 1990, operated 34 ships with a total slot capacity of 41,512 TEU, or approximately one-half the ships and one-third the capacity of the market leader Evergreen. By CGM's own reckoning, this ranked them in 15th position worldwide in September 1990. They provide liner services on 24 trade routes and are a member of some 20 partnership or vessel-operating agreements. Their strategic focus is one that relies on quality partnerships with customers and suppliers and includes a stated intention to share capital intensive assets, including vessels, containers, and possibly other components in the future. Their need to establish a separate identity was one of the prime factors in their three-year effort to withdraw from the ACL consortium.[20]

In spite of CGM's sale of its shares in ACL, Claude Abraham, chairman of CGM, indicated in a *Journal of Commerce* interview[21] that there was still a future for the shipping consortium. He reported that a growing number of shipowners were opting out of strategic marketing alliances in favor of going it alone because of the need to differentiate their services in the eyes of shippers. In his view, the consortium still had a role to play on the lighter trade routes, such as those running north to south, where a single line does not have the ability to offer the required frequency of departures. In October 1989, CGM sold its share in one consortium (ACL) and in June

1990 joined Italia di Navigazione SpA, Costa Container Lines, and Evergreen Marine Corporation to provide weekly service between North America and the Mediterranean. However in the new consortium (known as Med-Atlantic), CGM maintained its own marketing identity.

Atlantic Container Line (ACL)–A Consortium

The restructuring of ACL affords some insight into the effectiveness of consortia in today's market. Bilspedition AB, a trucking and forwarding firm based in Gothenburg, Sweden, has acquired both Cool Carriers AB, in the refrigerated shipping business, and Transatlantic Shipping Co. Ltd, a large container shipping company. Shortly after its acquisition of Transatlantic, the company moved to secure its current dominant position on the North Atlantic through a restructuring of ACL, one of the largest shipping lines on the North Atlantic. ACL was in financial difficulty and later posted a loss of US$40 million for 1989. In November 1989, Transatlantic gained full control of ACL through the purchase of the shares held by Cunard Steam-Ship Co. A month prior to this, Bilspedition AB, Transatlantic's parent, acquired the ACL shares held by Sweden's Wallenius Lines and France's CGM.[22] Bengt Koch, President of ACL Services Limited at the time of the acquisition, indicated that the purchase of the French and Swedish shares was a competitive necessity:

> While our original shareholding has served us well for the past 20 years or so, it was becoming increasingly evident that we need to run ACL with a simpler structure that is able to respond quickly and effectively to the demands of an ever-changing marketplace.[23]

Cunard's sale of the shares was part of a strategy by Trafalgar House PLC, Cunard's parent; it no longer participates in shipping consortia where it does not have majority control.

ACL is a strong advocate of alliances and has been reported to be looking for a strategic alliance to provide cargo to feeder its North Atlantic operation; one target is the global-carrier American President Lines (APL).[24] Based in Oakland, California, APL is ranked sixth in terms of slot capacity, but has not competed with ACL. APL's advantage lies in its Pacific operations and strong U.S. West Coast presence–a perfect complement to ACL's East Coast niche for Far East-Europe trade via a U.S. landbridge. An equipment and slot charter alliance could provide significant competitive advantages, but a deal has not yet been reported in the trade press. ACL believes equipment sharing could substantially improve its profitability, and in May of 1991, it announced that it and Hapag-Lloyd would each undertake a slot-charter agreement with Canada Maritime for the movement of Canadian cargo via the Montreal gateway (a port neither carrier serves).

DISCUSSION

The 1980s have been tumultuous for the ocean carrier industry, and this trend is likely to continue as the industry evolves. Carriers have adapted their strategies and rationalized their operations in response. A variety of strategic alliances have played a key role, as carriers scramble to lower their operating costs through higher vessel utilization.

However, not all forms of strategic alliance have been embraced. Some carriers have reassessed their stance toward shipping conferences–conference membership that represents both the least effort to cooperate with other carriers and the oldest form of strategic alliance in the industry. Some carriers that have traditionally been strong supporters of the conference system have recently incurred substantial losses as a result of competition from non-conference carriers. Conversely, some traditionally conference-shy carriers, such as Evergreen (the largest of the container carriers), have also had to rethink their attitude toward the conference system. Although the company has a track record of short-term involvement with both the Asia North America Eastbound Rate Agreement (ANERA) and the Transpacific Westbound Rate Agreement (TWRA) (Canna, 1987), it has been reluctant to join conferences in the past. Evergreen was coerced into joining the Mediterranean westbound conference, SEUSA, when the Italian government threatened to deny the company access to its markets unless it became a conference member. Recently, Evergreen has revised its involvement in shipping conferences through the consideration of new or renewed memberships.

Other than traditional conferences, strategic alliances between shipping companies often take the form of slot-chartering agreements, such as that which existed between ACL and Hapag-Lloyd on the North Atlantic since 1986, or vessel-sharing agreements, like the ACL consortium that lasted two decades. Vessel-sharing agreements have proven to be less flexible in highly competitive environments. If the restructuring of ACL and the demise of the Scandutch and Trio consortia are the more prominent indicators of the growing disenchantment with consortia, it is likely that future strategic alliances will take the form of slot-charters and equipment-sharing agreements rather than consortia. Such alliances permit firms to retain their flexibility and marketing identity, while realizing the benefits of sharing ships or equipment.

Judging from the strong preference by market leaders for strategic alliances that focus on the middle range of options–equipment alliances or slot charters–strategic alliances are key to developing that "seamless" distribution service referred to by Mandl. The cost savings are clear from the Sea-Land experience and the CGM cost analysis presented in Figure 10.4 strengthens the case for alliance in this industry.

Although strategic alliances are often not the preferred route of companies, they are often the only affordable option. Maersk wanted ownership of Sea-Land, its closest competitor, but when it could not dominate the market through ownership, the option of a strategic alliance was preferable to the continuation of the existing competition. Clearly, strategic alliances will remain an important option for ocean container carriers, and given the advantages of the middle range of options, it seems that they will play an ever-increasing role in the global container transport industry.

ENDNOTES

1. Refer to Table 2 of *The business implications of globalization*. Ottawa: Investment Canada, 1990. (This has been adapted from T. Wacher and R. Koxen, *Going Global*, Business Intelligence Program Report No. 782, Fall 1989, p.4).

2. Company Analysis: Sealand (1989, October). *Lloyd's Shipping Economist*, pp. 26-31.

3. As cited in *The Journal of Commerce*, (1988, October 1), p. 1A.
4. *The Journal of Commerce*, September 14, 1990, p. 1A.
5. Ibid.
6. *The Journal of Commerce*, August 2, 1990, p. 1A.
7. Ibid.
8. *The Journal of Commerce*, August 28, 1990, p. 8B.
9. *The Journal of Commerce*, August 27, 1990, p. 10B.
10. *The Journal of Commerce*, August 2, 1990, p. 1A.
11. Ibid.
12. *The Journal of Commerce*, April 19, 1990, p. 1A.
13. Ibid.
14. Ibid., p. 1B.
15. Ibid., p. 1B.
16. *The Journal of Commerce*, May 30, 1990. p. 1A.
17. Ibid.
18. L.J. LeGendre (1990, September 10). *Partnership in liner shipping: CGM-French Line's perspective.* Presentation at Halifax Port Days, 1990, Halifax, Canada.
19. *The Journal of Commerce*, September 25, 1989, p. 5T.
20. Ibid. p. 1T.
21. *The Journal of Commerce*, February 13, 1989, p. 1B.
22. *The Journal of Commerce*, December 11, 1989, p. 6C.
23. *Canadian Sailing*, October 16, 1989, p. 5.
24. *The Journal of Commerce*, May 7, 1990, p. 1A.

REFERENCES

Booz Allen & Hamilton Inc. (1990, September 10). Strategic shifts in world liner markets. Presentation at Halifax Port Days 1990, Halifax, Canada.
Bott, A. (1990, September). Playing field imbalances. *Transport*, pp. 207-11.
Bowersox, D.J. (1990). The strategic benefits of logistics alliances. *Harvard Business Review*, 67 (4), 36-45.
Brooks, M.R., Brown, M.G., Gold, E., McDorman, T., and Power, M.E. (1983). *The nature and operation of liner shipping conferences in a Canadian context.* Halifax, Canada: Canadian Marine Transportation Centre, Dalhousie University.
Brooks, M.R. and Kindred, H.M. (1990). The incidence and effects of marine cargo delays in law and commerce. *Maritime Policy and Management*, 17, (3), 189-197.
Canna, E. (1987, August). Evergreen goes public. *American Shipper*, p. 32.
Containerisation International Yearbook 1990, pp. 5.-6.
Container News, March 1990, p. 10.
Contractor, F.J. and Lorange, P. (1988). Why should firms co-operate? The strategy and economic basis for co-operative ventures. In F.J. Contractor and P.

Lorange (Eds.) *Co-operative Strategies in International Business*, (pp. 3-28) Lexington, MA: Lexington Books.

Denham, M. (1991, Winter). Strategic alliances: partnering for global success. *McKinsey on Management*, pp. 32-36.

Erdmenger, J. and Stasinopoulos, D. (1988). The shipping policy of the European Community. *Journal of Transport Economics and Policy*, September, pp. 355-360.

Grimm, C.M. and Smith, K.G. (1985). Impact of deregulation on railroad strategies and performance. In *TRF Proceedings*, (pp. 540-544). Proceedings of the 26th Annual Meeting of the Transportation Research Forum.

The Journal of Commerce, August 2, 1990, p. 1A.

The Journal of Commerce, September 29, 1990, p. 1.

The Journal of Commerce, October 25, 1990, p. 1A.

Lloyd's Shipping Economist (1990, February). p. 33.

Middleton, W. (1990, October). Sea-Land goes global. *Container Management*, p. 12.

Porter, M.E. (1986). Competition in global industries, a conceptual framework. In M. Porter (Ed.) *Competition in global industries*, (pp. 15-60) Boston: Harvard Business School Press.

Sturmey, S.G. (1962). *British shipping and world competition*. London: University of London, The Athlone Press, p. 322.

U.K. House of Lords Select Committee on the European Communities (1986). *European maritime transport policy*. London: HL Paper 106, Her Majesty's Stationery Office.

III. THE BEHAVIORAL AND HUMAN RESOURCES MANAGEMENT DIMENSIONS OF INTERNATIONAL JOINT VENTURES

Chapter 11

Planning International Joint Ventures: The Role of Human Resource Management

Deepak K. Datta
Abdul M. A. Rasheed

INTRODUCTION

The last decade has witnessed an increasing globalization of the business environment, manifested in part by the rapid integration of the economies of industrialized nations, and the globalization of products, markets, consumer tastes, and lifestyles. This phenomenon has brought home the realization among firms in developed countries that, in order to remain competitive, they need to more aggressively pursue opportunities in other countries. Cooperative ventures provide an important strategic option, and although they have been more common in developing countries in the past, the number of such ventures among firms in industrialized countries has been on the increase in recent years. This increase has been promoted, in part, by greater global competition, larger and riskier projects, and research and development (R&D) requirements that go beyond the capabilities of any one firm (Ohmae, 1989). Examples of such ventures include FujiXerox, a 50-50 joint venture between Fuji Film of Japan and Rank Xerox of U.S., and the recent collaboration by Mitsubishi of Japan and Daimler-Benz AG of Germany in a variety of projects ranging from autos to aircrafts.

The authors wish to thank Anthony J. Daboub, Gregory Dess, and two anonymous reviewers for their helpful comments on earlier versions of this chapter. Partial funding for this project was provided by the University of Kansas General Research Fund–Allocation #3127200038.

Cooperative ventures cover a broad range of alliances, including jointly owned enterprises, various forms of licensing agreements, and contracts relating to supplies and technology exchange. However in this chapter, we focus on the most common form of cooperative ventures, namely, joint ventures or jointly owned enterprises. Such ventures have been enjoying increasing popularity, as borne out by U.S. Department of Commerce statistics that indicate a consistent increase in their number (Christelow, 1987). Even as far back as 1979, a Conference Board study found that "most of the Fortune 500 companies were engaged in one or more international joint ventures" (Janger, 1980). Paradoxically, however, empirical studies on the performance of international joint ventures (or IJVs) indicate that such ventures are plagued by problems, with failure rates often in excess of 40% (Kogut, 1988). The high failure rates, the complexities of managing an IJV, and the irreversible nature of the substantial financial and non-financial resources often committed to such ventures point to the importance of systematic planning for IJVs (Devlin and Bleackley, 1988). Also, given that failure can often be attributed to human resource management (HRM) issues, it points to the importance of giving such issues adequate attention in the planning process. Unfortunately, this attention is often very limited. Human resource (HR) dimensions are often treated as short-term implementation issues rather than as important long-term considerations in the planning of such ventures. This situation is evident from the findings of an interesting study of 38 alliances by Coopers et al., who found that of the 100 to 5000 hours spent in the creation of an alliance, on the average, a mere 2%-4% of the time was spent discussing, analyzing, and resolving human resource issues (cited by Revesz and de la Sierra, 1987). However, after experiencing management problems linked to human resource issues, most managers in the survey readily admitted that they should have spent much more time on such issues (Revesz and de la Sierra, 1987).

In this chapter, we seek to identify the key HRM issues associated with the planning of IJVs and discuss why a careful consideration of such issues is critical to the eventual success of a venture. While HR issues are undoubtedly very important in considerations involving the implementation and management of a potential IJV, they also play a key role in other steps of the planning process. The framework provided in this chapter and discussion of key HR issues should be valuable to both practitioners involved in the making of IJV decisions and to researchers interested in studying the implications of HR issues in such ventures. This chapter concludes with a summary of key HRM questions that need to be addressed at each step of the IJV planning process.

THE IJV PLANNING FRAMEWORK

Joint ventures, if carefully planned and executed within the context of a company's overall strategic plan, can offer a broad array of benefits. In addition to facilitating entry into attractive markets, IJVs can offer synergistic benefits by combining complementary skills and capabilities. They also help to lower costs associated with labor, transportation, overheads, and taxes. Additional benefits can accrue from increased economies of scale, particularly in industries such as automobiles where the "critical mass" is very high (Datta, 1988). In addition, IJVs often result in a reduction of political and business risks (Reynolds, 1984) and in increased opportunities to gain competitive advantage through a partner's relationship with local government and institutions. These connections are particularly useful in obtaining privileged access to local resources and in reducing a bias in favor of local firms.

To attain these benefits, IJVs must be carefully planned. Although each IJV might have certain unique characteristics, there is an underlying commonality among the issues that needs to be examined and analyzed in planning for an IJV. These common dimensions have been integrated in the form of a framework (Figure 11.1) that provides a systematic approach to the analysis and evaluation of IJVs by delineating the various tasks, activities, and factors influencing the performance of IJVs.

The steps in the planning of IJVs include: (1) the evaluation of environmental forces, (2) examination of objectives of the joint-venture partners and their congruity, (3) evaluation of partner capabilities, (4) deciding on the appropriate joint-venture form, and (5) identification and assessment of the issues relating to the implementation and management of the joint venture. Each of these issues is discussed more fully in the following pages. Also considered are

FIGURE 11.1. IJV Planning Framework

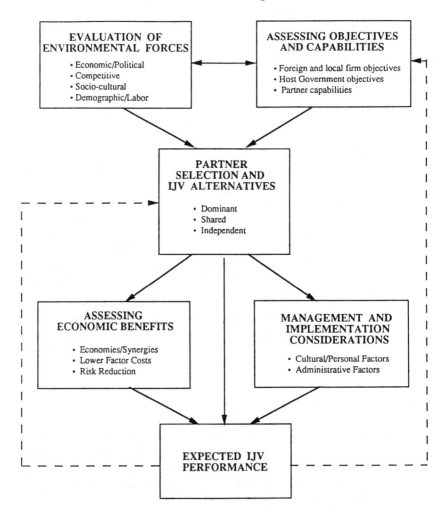

many of the human resource issues that are important for the successful accomplishment of tasks at each stage of the IJV planning process.

Evaluation of Environmental Forces

Environmental and competitive factors figure prominently in IJV decisions, including the choice of IJV partners and the location of the venture. These factors include, among others: the size of the market, its projected growth, the level of current competition, and the currency position of the country. Particularly critical are issues related to the political environment, involving factors such as the stability of the host government, attitudes towards foreign investment, extent of discrimination against foreign companies, patent protection, and regulations pertaining to foreign investment. Also, it is important to evaluate changes or trends in the economic, legal, and social environments of the prospective host country along with an assessment of their human resource implications and the potential impact on human resource policies.

In addition, a firm involved in setting up an IJV must carefully assess the local labor market and its characteristics from a human resource perspective. For example, given that the majority of the employees in an IJV are likely to be host-country nationals, the availability of necessary skills locally is important to the success of most IJVs. Also, it must be recognized that different countries are in different stages of evolution in terms of available technical and managerial skills. IJV planning should, therefore, take into account not only the current availability of skills but also the future availability and the related issue of cost. Moreover, careful consideration should be given to the prevailing work ethic in a country. A poor work ethic, coupled with a lack of adequate incentives, can result in extremely poor productivity in some countries, which can more than offset the benefits of low labor rates.

The role of HR planning in IJVs certainly extends to a careful evaluation of existing labor laws and policies. These include laws and policies pertaining to the hiring and firing of employees, collective bargaining, mandatory worker participation in management, the activism and power of trade unions, and labor-management relations. For example, in many developing countries, local government policies encourage the division of job functions in order to aid employment (Conway, 1986). The resulting overstaffing can drive down productivity and put into question the desirability of an IJV. In addition, in some countries, local labor laws might make it difficult to temporarily lay off employees in response to short-term declines in market conditions, or the power of local trade unions might make it virtually impossible to dismiss even very poor performers.

The socio-cultural environment is especially relevant to international joint ventures. Considerable differences exist in cultural characteristics across countries, the impact of which must be carefully studied in the selection of IJVs. Employees in an IJV may come from different countries and, thus, hold diverse values and norms of behavior, which pose major management challenges (Shenkar and Zeira, 1990). Failure to address issues of cultural compatibility can, therefore, easily contribute to the eventual failure of an IJV (*Business Week*, 1989). Cultural differences in the context of IJVs can take many forms. As observed by David S. Tappan, CEO of Fluor, when planning and negotiating a joint venture in China, it is important to realize that the Chinese ostensibly place greater emphasis on friendship than on business relationships. This is contrary to practices in the U.S. and many Western countries (Tappan, 1986). Local culture also influences aspects of everyday life, including the quality of the available workforce and the prevailing work ethic, both of which are critical to the success of an international joint venture. In addition to the above, an understanding of the local cultural environment also helps the foreign firm to identify the skills required of expatriate managers who might be sent to manage the venture.

Assessment of Partner Objectives

Along with the analysis of environmental factors, a systematic evaluation of IJV opportunities requires that each partner consider the objectives of the other partner and their compatibility. As mentioned previously, there are a number of reasons why firms choose to participate in joint ventures. This often results in considerable diversity in partners' objectives. For example, a firm may be interested in a joint venture because local laws limit foreign equity participation and an IJV may be the only option available to the firm if it wants to enter a promising foreign market. In many countries, there may not be any formal legal difficulties associated with entry, but a joint venture may be preferable due to the country-specific skills that a partner can bring. These may include the ability to cut through the bureaucratic delays inevitable in many countries through the careful use of contacts and relationships that the local partner enjoys with influential members of the government. In some cases, a firm may seek a joint venture in order to reduce resource commitments and risks, especially political risks stemming from factors such as fluctuating currencies, unstable local governments, rising economic nationalism, and formal and/or informal restrictions on foreign companies.

The objectives and expectations of the local firm upon entering an IJV may be very different. For a firm in a developing country, these often include the acquisition of new technology (Lasserre, 1984), access to the use of well-known brand names and trademarks, or potential access to foreign markets. In addition, IJV planning involves identifying and addressing the objectives of the host government, especially in situations where the joint-venture option is chosen primarily to satisfy host-government objectives. Such objectives can include increased local employment, import substitution, conservation of foreign exchange, technology transfer, and the reduction of foreign control over local industry (Wright and Russell, 1975).

The mere existence of differences in objectives does not mean that they are incompatible. However, it is important to understand the partners' objectives before embarking on an IJV, given that they determine the partners' attitude toward the venture and also reflect the strategic importance that they attach to the joint venture, including the resources they are willing to commit to it. An example would be human resources: A partner would be willing to assign its best people to an IJV only if it perceives the venture as being strategically important. Objectives will also influence future strategies and policies, including the appropriate human resources strategy (e.g., the choice of reward and evaluation mechanism, staffing strategy, and approach to management-labor relations). A good understanding of partners' objectives also means that differences can be identified and addressed and mutually acceptable compromises reached all in the planning stage. The result is generally better rapport and increased likelihood of venture success. Moreover, an acceptable level of compatibility in partner objectives is important in any IJV if the partners are to work together despite differences in management styles and philosophies, access to resources, and organizational cultures (Geringer, 1988). Without this compatibility, the firms may be wise to abandon the idea of an IJV and turn instead to another form of strategic alliance, such as licensing.

Evaluation of Partner Capabilities

In addition to examining the partners' objectives, one needs to evaluate the partners' skills and capabilities in the planning of IJVs. IJVs provide excellent opportunities to overcome deficiencies in knowledge of local markets, customs, business practices, and bureaucratic procedures. An IJV agreement is most beneficial when the skills and capabilities of the partners complement one another toward the realization of synergistic benefits. This is particularly true in the case of employee skills available in the two firms. It is therefore important to assess the capabilities and the competencies of people likely to be involved in the venture. Also, such assessment should not be confined to lower-level employees, but should be extended to include the competencies of managerial personnel. Managerial capabilities also have important implications on the autonomy that will eventually be provided to the IJV. The extent to which such autonomy can be given obviously depends on the capabilities of the IJV management team, which is generally comprised of managers from both parents.

In the preceding sections, we have discussed how the analysis of the environment and the evaluation of potential partners' objectives and capabilities provide the basis for selecting joint-venture partners and the form of the IJV. In the following section, we identify the different forms that joint-venture agreements can take, and we discuss their implications for HRM. It must be remembered that the selection of the joint-venture form should be based, in part, on human resource considerations.

Choice of the IJV Form

Killing (1982) provides a typology of IJVs, which is based on the nature of equity participation and the degree of parental involvement and control. The three forms are: (1) the dominant partner joint venture, (2) the shared-management joint venture, and (3) the independent joint venture. As will be explained later, the choice of a specific IJV form depends to a large extent on HRM considerations.

The *dominant parent* joint venture comes closest to the concept of a wholly owned subsidiary; the dominant partner typically selects most of the venture managers. The IJV board of directors, comprised of executives from each parent, plays a largely ceremonial role, while most of the venture's strategic and operating decisions are made by executives of the dominant firm. The second, and perhaps most common joint-venture form, is the *shared management* or "50-50" venture. In this type of venture, both parents own the joint venture equally and are both actively involved in its management. The third, the *independent* joint venture, involves ventures that are relatively free of interference from either parent.

The choice of the desired joint-venture alternative is obviously constrained and influenced by environmental factors and the partners' capabilities and objectives. For example, laws in a number of countries (e.g., the Soviet Union, India, Korea, and Indonesia among others) limit foreign equity participation in IJVs to less than a controlling interest, making it impossible for the foreign firm to establish a dominant parent IJV. Moreover, a firm may not wish to yield controlling interest to its partner or even enter into a 50-50 joint venture if it perceives the partner as having only limited capabilities. Alternatively, in a situation where the local partner has only limited interest in being actively involved in the management of the venture, the foreign firm might prefer the dominant parent IJV strategy, if local laws permit this option.

Personnel and HRM issues and their implications should play an important role in the selection of the appropriate IJV form. For example, while the dominant IJV strategy has the advantage of providing a firm with greater control over the venture's strategic direction, it may not necessarily be the most desirable alternative. Foreign control in the joint venture can generate feelings of hostility among host-country nationals, who might view themselves as being dominated by "foreigners." Second, there is the important question of whether the foreign firm has an adequate number of qualified managers whom they can assign to manage such a venture. There are additional human resource and organizational considerations that play an important role in the choice of the IJV alternative (e.g., differences in culture and business practices), in the operating styles of the management groups, and also in the policies (especially the HR policies) of the two organizations. The shared or 50-50 alternative might be particularly vulnerable to such differences and can be especially difficult to manage where significant differences exist between the parents.

Management and Implementation Considerations

One of the most talked about alliances of the 1980s, the partnership between AT&T and Olivetti & Co. proved to be a failure from the very beginning. One of AT&T's top executives later attributed most of the problems to cultural differences between the two companies (Wysocki, 1990). In contrast, General Electric's jet engine partnership with Snecma, a French government-controlled aerospace company, has proved to be one of the most successful joint ventures. This success was achieved in spite of several cultural, linguistic, and logistical problems because both companies have taken several steps to minimize the potential for conflict. These include delegating considerable responsibility to senior joint-venture managers and clearly allocating the responsibilities of the partners to areas in which they are competent.

In planning and analyzing IJVs, firms typically emphasize the technical, legal, and financial aspects of the venture. Unfortunately, the attention given to human resource considerations is often minimal, resulting in frequent implementation problems and unfulfilled expectations.

Cultural and Personal Factors

There are a number of cultural and personal factors that significantly influence the performance of an IJV. These include: (1) cultural differences, (2) management styles, (3) loyalty conflicts, (4) staffing and training, and (5) career and family considerations. These are briefly discussed in the following paragraphs.

1. Cultural differences. Many of the problems and misunderstandings in IJVs can be traced to cultural differences that exist both at the national and organizational level. HRM practices are probably the most sensitive to cultural diversity. For example, Japanese organizations are characterized by lifetime employment, group decision making, paternalism, and promotion and pay based on seniority. The American system, on the other hand, emphasizes contractual relationships, high labor mobility, individual decision making, and compensation based on performance. Not surprisingly, a study by Peterson and Schwind (1977) of IJVs in Japan found that cultural differences often cause communications breakdown among partners and contribute to IJV failure. Further corroboration is available in a recent *Business Week* (1989) article, which attributes the failure of many U.S.-Japanese IJVs to unresolved cultural differences that made it impossible for the parent companies to work together.

It is apparent, therefore, that planning an IJV requires an appreciation and understanding of cultural differences. It also requires a respect for the people of the host country, their aspirations, and their customs. Because of cultural differences, many host governments and local firms, particularly in developing countries, often have considerable misgivings about entering into IJV relationships. Consequently, unless the foreign firm displays requisite understanding and sensitivity, misunderstandings and feelings of distrust emanating from such differences can derail even the most promising of ventures. In this connection, it is also important to consider the form of the joint venture. Although cultural differences need to be addressed in any joint venture, special attention should be given to ventures that require greater interaction among parent company managers and where the incidence of joint decision making is likely to be high (e.g., in 50-50 ventures).

2. Management styles. Planning for joint ventures should account not only for cultural differences but also for potential differences in management styles (Datta, 1988; Scanlon, 1986). For example, differences in attitudes toward risk might result in conflict between partners–with one partner willing to take risks toward seeking high returns, while the other insists on greater security. Another example of differences in management styles is attitudes on subordinate participation in decision making. Such differences lead to conflicts over what is appropriate leadership. Some differences in style are to be expected in most IJVs. However, it is important to understand the nature and effects of such differences as early as possible in the planning phase. It is only through mutual understanding and dialogue that these differences can be managed.

3. Loyalty conflicts. Does the manager of an IJV owe his primary loyalty to the IJV or to his parent company? Loyalties among IJV employees sometime remain with their parent companies, which then receive priority over joint-venture goals (Shenkar and Zeira, 1990). Loyalty issues can be particularly sensitive. Consequently, even a perception among local firm officials that expatriate managers in an IJV are more loyal to the foreign firm can result in continued suspicion, distrust, and conflicts. Similarly, foreign firms sometimes view managers from its local partner as being "agents" of the local firm, looking out only for the local firm's interests. Given their disruptive potential, loyalty issues should be brought out and discussed during the planning and negotiations phase so that mechanisms for resolving conflicts can be built into the human resource management of the IJVs (Lorange, 1986). At the extreme, it may even be necessary to hire outsiders for key positions in order to avoid loyalty conflicts and bridge resultant communication gaps.

4. Staffing and training. A central issue in IJV planning should be personnel selection and staffing. This involves deciding on the criteria to be used for employee selection, the relative contribution of personnel by the partners, and positions that will be filled by each. Staffing decisions, especially those related to the selection of key managers, should be made well in advance of the conclusion of an IJV agreement. This will help minimize the scramble, that often follows the consummation of an IJV to locate appropriate personnel, with staffing decisions being based on expediency rather than prudent planning. More importantly, early selection of key managers means that they can be involved in the crucial negotiations process. In this way, one avoids the undesirable situation where one team does the negotiating leading to the formation of the IJV, while another is involved in its subsequent implementation.

Another HR issue that warrants careful consideration in the planning of IJVs is the use of expatriate managers in managing such ventures. While the number of executives willing and able to work abroad is steadily increasing, extensive use of expatriates can be both costly and risky for a firm. Harvey (1983), for example, estimates that the average cost to the parent company for each unsuccessful expatriate assignment can be as high as three times the domestic salary, plus the cost of relocation. Since U.S. firms have the highest expatriate failure rates, finding ways to reduce the failure and recall rate of expatriates assumes much greater importance (Tung, 1982; Desatnick and Bennett, 1978). The situation is further complicated by the negative reactions of host-country nationals to the appointment of a large number of expatriates in an IJV. Not only do nationals sometimes see the expatriates as blocking their career paths, they also question their commitment to the venture and their sensitivity to local attitudes and customs. It may, therefore, be prudent to have both partners involved in identifying the selection criteria and, preferably, even in the selection of expatriate managers. While technical competence is undoubtedly important, selection should take into consideration a number of other factors. These include: proficiency in the local language; knowledge of the business environment in the host country; intercultural, diplomatic, and interpersonal capabilities; and flexibility and adaptability of the manager's family. As Menderhall, Dunbar, and Oddou (1987) found, personnel selection based on technical competence alone can be an important cause of joint-venture failure. Yet, a study by Tung (1981) found that only 5% of firms formally assessed a candidate's relational abilities. By ensuring that selected personnel possess requisite relational skills (in addition to technical skills), parents can promote the attainment of IJV goals and objectives.

Consideration must also be given in the planning process to the pre-venture training of selected managers. Environmental briefing, alone, is not sufficient. More comprehensive training programs need to be developed to encompass the cross-cultural and other issues identified above. Tung (1981) found that only 32% of the firms offered formal training programs to prepare people to live and work overseas. Most did not offer in-depth cross-cultural training as a part of their relocation program, with firms citing the lack of time between selection and relocation as a major reason for the same. The problem of time can certainly be alleviated if these issues are considered early in the planning phase.

The importance of selecting the right personnel for an IJV can never be overemphasized. A venture is very unlikely to succeed if parents are hesitant to assign their most qualified people or, worse still, if they view the IJV as a "dumping ground" for sidetracked or poorly performing managers. Personnel selection for an IJV requires serious planning–involving both qualitative and quantitative forecasting of the critical HR requirements for managing the venture and an assessment of the availability of such resources. HR strategies should then be developed to close the gap between what is required and what is available (see Figure 11.2). Such strategies should also include the training and development of those selected.

5. Career and family issues. In addition to the problems mentioned above, there are other difficulties associated with finding good managers for an IJV. Managers are often reluctant to take up an IJV assignment because they fear that such an assignment will disrupt their career progression and not contribute adequately toward furthering their career goals. Another important factor dissuading good managers from taking up IJV assignments is the stress experienced by them and their families in adjusting to the culture and living conditions in a foreign country (Carter, 1989). Moving an employee overseas for a prolonged assignment may interrupt the spouse's career and the children's education (Dowling and Schuler, 1990). Problems arising from dual careers can be even more serious, especially when it is the wife who is offered the assignment abroad. Planning is therefore important in attracting good managers to an IJV, allaying their fears, and winning their commitment. Only in this way can the firm reduce costly and disruptive turnover in overseas IJV assignments.

In the last decade, the concept of providing "realistic job previews" in recruitment and selection has attracted considerable attention (Dungani and Ilgen, 1981). Such previews are likely to be particularly beneficial in the context of IJVs and should include, among other things, information on the goals and mission of the proposed venture, the performance evaluation criteria along with benefits, and compensation plans. Also, it is important that a reasonably accurate picture be provided of how the joint-venture assignment might impact career development and fit in with the individual's career path. Realistic job previews also help in the assessment of the fit of individuals' goals with the requirements of the IJV operations and should, therefore, result in the selection of personnel who are more satisfied with their assignments, perform better, and

FIGURE 11.2. Developing IJV HR Strategies

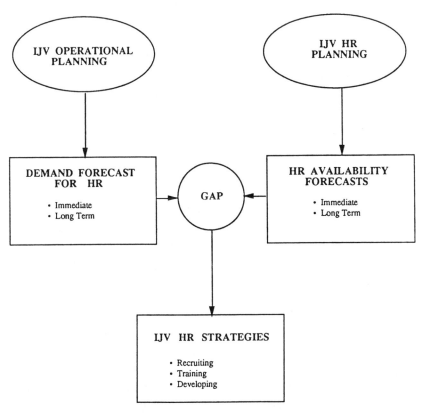

Adapted from Manzini & Gridley (1986)

are less likely to leave prematurely. The issue of turnover is particularly important because, in addition to the substantial costs associated with relocation, frequent changes in managerial personnel disrupts continuity, thus increasing the odds of failure.

Administrative Factors

In addition to the cultural and personal factors discussed above, the planning process must also deal with several potential administrative problems in the management of the venture. These include:

(1) managerial autonomy, (2) differences in organizational policies, and (3) reporting relationships and control systems. Addressing these problems requires an accommodation between the apparently conflicting administrative requirements of unified, and unambiguous direction and control on the one hand, and the effective participation of partners on the other.

1. Managerial autonomy. As a part of the planning and negotiations process, partners in an IJV need to consider the degree of autonomy they wish to give to the venture. Differences of opinion may arise when significant interdependencies exist between the IJV and the operations of one of the partners. Conflicts also arise when parent firms wish to maintain close operating control of an IJV. Such problems are further aggravated if one of the partners attempts to integrate the joint venture's operations with its own against the wishes of the other partner. Differences of opinion on the appropriate level of autonomy can be minimized, if not avoided, when the matter is discussed and agreed upon by the partners before the venture gets under way. The question of how much autonomy is to be given is also critical because autonomy is an important factor in attracting and retaining good managers (Killing, 1982). Without adequate autonomy, joint-venture managers can become frustrated, especially if they find themselves caught in the middle of a power struggle between parent firms.

2. Differences in organizational policies. Incompatible organizational policies must also be addressed during IJV planning. For example, firms may have very different opinions on the nature of markets being exploited, the right distribution channels, the correct level of advertising, the desirable quality-control standards, or the appropriate personnel and human resource policies. Differences in HR policies might exist among the partners in a number of areas, such as in the selection of personnel, the nature of reporting relationships, rules regarding nepotism, attitudes toward labor and unions, and policies governing the hiring and firing of employees. To prevent such differences from becoming major stumbling blocks in the future, they should be addressed and minimized as early as possible, preferably in the planning stage. Also, given that all differences cannot possibly be foreseen, equitable mechanisms should be developed during the planning process to resolve future conflicts and decision-making deadlocks.

3. Reporting relationships and control systems. Successful management of a joint venture requires that well-defined reporting relationships and control systems be established in the early stages of the venture. Since control systems involve a great number of factors, developing an effective control system can be a difficult proposition. Moreover, there is neither "one best way" to organize nor the one "best" control system. Therefore, most successful ventures use a mix of organizational and managerial control mechanisms. A study by Janger (1980) of 168 joint ventures identified a wide variety of control mechanisms. The more common mechanisms are management and financial audits, staff performance reviews, and evaluation and reward mechanisms.

An appropriate evaluation and reward system can be a very effective control system and can be used to influence IJV performance. However, choosing one can be an especially challenging task. The selection of reward systems is further complicated by the fact that the compensation levels of expatriate and local managers may be significantly different, particularly if the IJV is in a developing country. Such differences can generate feelings of deprivation and contribute to low morale among employees. It is also difficult to establish uniform performance review criteria, given potential differences in the objectives and policies of the partners. However, it is critical that acceptable performance criteria be developed, through a process of negotiations if necessary. Without a suitable personnel evaluation and reward system, it will be difficult to take the necessary corrective action when required.

The above points raise an important question: Should parent firms seek to transfer their HRM practices to the IJV? It should be noted that HR practices are deeply grounded in the national culture of a firm. This makes such policies difficult to apply in other countries, even in situations where consistent HR policies between an IJV and parent may be very desirable. Difficulties experienced in transferring American HR policies to Chinese JVs have been documented by Von Glinow and Teagarden (1988). It may therefore be far more effective to tolerate diversity in HR practices and accept host-country cultural requirements than to impose the alien practices of the home country.

CONCLUSIONS

While international joint ventures have been plagued by high failure rates, it is also generally recognized that systematic pre-venture planning can help improve the chances of success. Much of the current disenchantment with IJVs can be attributed to inadequate planning, along with a failure to consider the critical human resource issues as a part of the planning process. This chapter has stressed the importance of HR issues in planning IJVs. These issues dominate implementation and management considerations and also play an important role in other stages of the planning process. By systematically examining and evaluating HR issues in the planning stage, managers can identify and address many problems before they jeopardize the success of the joint venture. In Table 11.1, we have summarized the key HRM questions that can form the basis for such an assessment.

The importance of human resources as a strategic resource is being increasingly recognized in the literature (Nkomo, 1988; Tung, 1984). As with any other strategic resource, HR needs to be managed proactively. Nowhere is this task as important, and perhaps as complex, as in an IJV, where it can make the difference between success and failure. This chapter also highlighted the importance of having HR personnel involved in the planning and implementation of IJVs. Unfortunately, the HR dimension of planning is usually treated as a short-term implementation issue rather than as a critical factor influencing strategic choices. If international joint ventures are to be successful, it is essential that top management make a strong commitment to the consideration of human resource issues in the planning of such ventures. By identifying and discussing the key HRM issues associated with the planning of IJVs, this chapter seeks to fulfill two objectives. First, it provides guidance to managers involved in the making of IJV decisions and emphasizes the need to consider HR issues in the planning of such ventures. Second, it provides direction to researchers who are interested in examining the influence and impact of human resource issues in the planning and implementation of international joint ventures. We believe that such research is important, because it is only through empirical investigations that meaningful prescriptions can be provided to managers who are involved in the making of key decisions pertaining to international joint ventures.

TABLE 11.1. Summary of Key HRM Questions in the Planning of International Joint Ventures

---

Evaluation of Environmental Forces
    Are required skills available at proposed IJV locations?
    Is cost of labor low enough to provide cost parity, if not cost advantage over competitors?
    Is there adequate supply of labor?
    Does the dominant culture and work ethic in the country help or hinder productivity?
    Are local customs and business practices compatible with the IJV?
    How will existing labor laws affect the operations of the IJV?

Assessing Objectives
    What is the strategic importance of the proposed IJV to the partners?
    Are both partners willing to commit requisite human resources to the IJV?
    Are the partners' objectives compatible?
    What are the host government's objectives and policies in terms of local employment?
    Are there significant differences in human resource policies of the partners?

Partner Capabilities
    What competencies and skills will each partner bring to the IJV?
    What is the competence of managerial personnel who are likely to be involved in the IJV?
    Will the capabilities of personnel in the local partner help overcome one's own knowledge deficiencies?

Selection of the IJV Form
    What is the extent of likely resentment towards "expatriate" managers?
    Are qualified and willing managers available within the company to staff the venture?
    How different are the organizational cultures of the parents?
    How different are the HR policies of the parent firms?

Management and Implementation Considerations
    To what extent will cultural differences inhibit communication between parents?
    How different are the parents' management styles?

Are loyalty conflicts likely and what mechanisms will be required to resolve them?

Is there adequate agreement and understanding among partners about staffing?

Do managers assigned to the IJV have a realistic understanding of the likely impact on their career progression?

Are mechanisms in place to help expatriate managers and family cope with the stress associated with living overseas?

Is there clear understanding between the partners about the extent of autonomy to be given to the IJV?

How different are the HR policies of the partners?

Can parents' HRM practices be reasonably transferred to the IJV?

What reward and evaluation system will be perceived as being equitable by both expatriate and local employees?

REFERENCES

Business Week (1989, July 24). When U.S. joint ventures with Japan go sour. 30-31.

Christelow, D. B. (1987). International joint ventures: How important are they? *Columbia Journal of World Business,* 22(2), 7-13.

Conway, M. A. (1986). Mergers and acquisitions: Ten pitfalls of joint ventures. *Personnel,* 63(9), 50-51.

Carter, N. J. (1989). Moving managers internationally: The need for flexibility. *Human Resource Planning,* 12(1), 43-47.

Datta, D. K. (1988). International joint ventures: A framework for analysis. *Journal of General Management,* 14(2), 78-91.

Desatnick, R. L., & Bennett, M. L. (1978). *Human resource management in the multinational company.* New York: Nichols.

Dowling, P. J., & Schuler, R. S. (1990). *International dimensions of human resource management.* Boston, MA: PWS-Kent Publishing Co.

Devlin, G., & Bleackley, M. (1988). Strategic alliances–guidelines for success. *Long Range Planning,* 21(5), 18-23.

Dungani, B. L., & Ilgen, D. R. (1981). Realistic job previews and the adjustment of new employees. *Academy of Management Journal,* 24, 579-591.

Geringer, J. M. (1988). Selection of partners for international joint ventures. *Business Quarterly,* 53(2), 31-36.

Harvey, M. G. (1983). The multinational corporation's expatriate problem: An application of Murphy's law. *Business Horizons,* 26(1), 71-78.

Janger, A. R. (1980). *Organization of international joint ventures.* New York: The Conference Board.

Killing, J. P. (1982). How to make a global joint venture work. *Harvard Business Review,* 61(1), 120-127.

Kogut, B. (1988). Joint ventures: Theoretical and empirical perspectives. *Strategic Management Journal*, 9, 319-332.

Lasserre, P. (1984). Selecting a foreign partner for technology transfer. *Long Range Planning*, 17(6), 43-49.

Lorange, P. (1986). Human resource management in multinational cooperative ventures. *Human Resource Management*, 25(1), 133-148.

Menderhall, M. E., Dunbar, E., & Oddou, G. R. (1987). Expatriate selection, training, and career pathing: A review and critique. *Human Resource Management*, 26, 331-345.

Nkomo, S. M. (1988). Strategic planning for human resources–let's get started. *Long Range Planning*, 21(1), 66-72.

Ohmae, K. (1989). The global logic of strategic alliances. *Harvard Business Review*, 68(2), 143-154.

Peterson, R. B., & Schwind, H. F. (1977). A comparative study of personnel problems in international companies and joint ventures in Japan. *Journal of International Business Studies*, 8(1), 45-55.

Revesz, T. R., & de la Sierra, M. C. (1987). Competitive alliances: Forging ties abroad. *Management Review*, 76(3), 57-59.

Reynolds, L. J. (1984). The pinched shoe effect of international joint ventures. *Columbia Journal of World Business*, 19(2), 23-29.

Scanlon, P. (1986). Collaborative ventures. *Journal of Business Strategy*, 6, 81-83.

Shenkar, O., & Zeira, Y. (1990). International joint ventures: A tough test for HR. *Personnel*, 67(1), 26-31.

Tappan Jr., D. S. (1986). Joint venture in China: Economic marriage of convenience. *Financier*, 10(6), 61-64.

Tung, R. L. (1981). Selection and training of personnel for overseas assignments. *Columbia Journal of World Business*, 16(1), 68-78.

Tung, R. L. (1982). Selection and training procedures of U.S., European and Japanese multinationals. *California Management Review*, 25(1), 57-71.

Tung, R. L. (1984). Strategic management of human resources in multinational enterprises. *Human Resource Management*, 23, 129-143.

Von Glinow, M. A., & Teagarden, M. B. (1988). The transfer of human resource technology in Sino-U.S. cooperative ventures: Problems and solutions. *Human Resource Management*, 27, 201-229.

Wright, W. W., & Russell, S. S. (1975). Joint ventures in developing countries: Realities and responses. *Columbia Journal of World Business*, 10(2), 74-80.

Wysocki, Jr., B. (1990). Cross-border alliances become favorite way to crack new markets. *The Wall Street Journal*, March 26, 1 & 5.

Chapter 12

Ethnocentrism and Group Cohesiveness: Implications for International Joint Ventures

Hoon Park
Pamela S. Lewis
Patricia M. Fandt

International joint ventures have become a popular form of cross-national strategic alliance. As international business activity continues to escalate, organizations across the globe are establishing partnerships with firms from other nations. The benefits of such ventures have been espoused by many in recent years, and in fact both practitioners and academics have suggested that the development of effective strategic alliances across national boundaries may be the key to success in the global marketplace.

International joint ventures are not, however, without disadvantages. In fact, while the benefits of these partnerships have been highly publicized in recent years, statistics indicate that many such ventures fall short of expectations and/or are disbanded prematurely (Harrigan, 1984). Although organizations are less willing to discuss their failed ventures than they are their successful ventures, the data suggest that unsuccessful international partnerships may be quite common.

Given the increasing popularity of international joint ventures in recent years, coupled with the dismal success experienced by many firms, researchers have begun to scrutinize such arrangements more closely. In general, most of the research on joint-venture management has focused on examining the macro-level structural and contractual dimensions of the venture (Beamish, 1985, 1987; Connolly,

1984; Contractor and Lorange, 1988; Friedman and Beguin, 1971; Gomes-Casseres, 1987; Harrigan, 1984, 1985, 1987; Janger, 1980; Killing, 1983; Kogut, 1988). A significant body of literature also exists that examines control structure and its impact on the performance of joint ventures (Anderson, 1990; Dang, 1977; Geringer, 1988; Geringer and Herbert, 1989; Killing, 1983; Schaan, 1983, Tomlinson, 1970). Many of these studies provide prescriptive guidelines for the initial development of the enterprise.

Far less research attention, however, has been directed toward considering the micro-level behavioral dimensions of joint-venture management–despite evidence that implies that idiosyncratic behavioral problems can cause considerable instability in many international joint ventures (Killing, 1982; Park, 1988; Peterson and Schimada, 1978; Pucik, 1988; Reynolds, 1984; Schaan and Beamish, 1988; Simiar, 1983; Sullivan and Peterson, 1982). Clearly, while most would argue that macro-level structural and contractual issues are of critical importance in the establishment and development of international joint ventures, favorable conditions in these areas do not ensure venture stability in the long-term. In fact, long-term success may be a function of more fundamental behavioral dynamics.

Many of the dysfunctional behaviors that occur in the management of an international joint venture are attributable to deeply rooted ethnocentric attitudes on the part of venture managers. Since managers from dissimilar cultural backgrounds may have very different perceptions of effective and appropriate management practices, ethnocentric attitudes may prevent the achievement of common group goals and the development of group cohesiveness. This situation can be extremely detrimental to the long-run performance of the firm, since the success of a multi-cultural firm may depend largely on its ability to organize a cohesive management group (Toyne, 1976).

The purpose of this chapter is to examine the impact of ethnocentric attitudes on the development of managerial group cohesiveness in international joint ventures. A model of the organizational elements that influence group cohesiveness is presented and the effect of ethnocentrism on each of these organizational elements is discussed. Suggestions for overcoming ethnocentrism in a multi-cultural work environment are offered and mechanisms for developing an environment that fosters group cohesiveness are discussed.

BACKGROUND

Ethnocentrism

Central to the concept of ethnocentrism is the attitude or view that one's own group is the standard by which all other groups must be measured. Each group nourishes its pride and vanity, boasts of superiority, exalts its own divinities, and looks with contempt upon those who do not conform to their standards. Each group remains convinced that its ways are superior to the ways of others. Sumner (1979) pointed out that ethnocentrism is a universal phenomenon, exhibited by virtually all groups throughout the world. The ethnocentric syndrome is functionally related to in-group/out-group polarization and intergroup hostility.

The concept of ethnocentrism has been of interest to social scientists for many years. Freud (1951) interpreted ethnocentrism as a form of group narcissism. He suggested that hostility toward the out-group satisfies tendencies toward aggression and, thus, facilitates the development of cohesion within the group. In a similar vein, Guetzkow (1955) discussed ethnocentrism as a phenomena that increases the negative attitudes toward the out-group by encouraging the use of in-group norms to judge the behaviors of others. There often exists powerful internal conformity mechanisms that encourage in-group members to limit their behavior to certain ranges, devalue certain behaviors, and prize others.

Ethnocentric behaviors often serve to weaken the viability of joint ventures. Although ethnocentrism may strengthen the cohesiveness of ethnic subgroups, such attitudes often aggravate differences caused by cultural dissimilarity and thereby weaken the link between ethnic subgroups. Since the management team of an international joint venture is typically comprised of at least two ethnic subgroups, the cohesiveness within the total group is adversely affected. In fact, as Laurent (1983) suggested, the cultural differences of managers working for multicultural organizations are often exaggerated and, in turn, the managers may become more ethno-centric than managers working for companies in their native coun-tries. In other words, the multi-cultural work environment inherent in international joint ventures actually serves to amplify ethnocen-tric attitudes in many cases. Consequently, the joint-venture man-agement team may find it more difficult to work together effectively toward the achievement of organizational goals and objectives.

Group Cohesiveness

Cohesion is an important theoretical construct that must be con-sidered in the study of group phenomena. Consequently, the con-cept of cohesion has received substantial research attention. Cohe-siveness is a group property that is inferred from the number and strength of mutual positive attitudes or forces among the members of a group (e.g., Lott and Lott, 1965). These forces act to keep members in the group and include the degree of attractiveness; the level of interpersonal liking; the closeness and commonality of attitudes; behavior; and performance expectations of group mem-bers. Individuals who belong to highly cohesive groups, in contrast to groups with a low level of cohesiveness, are more strongly moti-vated to contribute to the group's welfare, to advance its objective, and to participate in its activities (Shaw, 1981).

Cohesiveness also characterizes the degree to which members value their group membership. In highly cohesive groups, there is a sense of goodwill and team spirit. Members enjoy one another's company and consider the chance to work with co-workers to be an important source of personal satisfaction. This attraction is missing in less cohesive groups. In extreme cases, individuals lack respect for their co-workers and may even be outwardly hostile toward them. Low cohesive groups are typically comprised of persons who are outwardly indifferent, whereas the absence of cohesion may result in actual hostility between group members.

Much of the classical cohesion research was conducted and pub-lished in the 1950s (e.g., Berkowitz, 1956; Homan, 1950; Seashore, 1954). More recently, there appears to be a renewed interest in explor-ing task-group cohesion and behavior in relation to work organizations and performance (Adler and Adler, 1988; Narayanan and Fahey, 1982; Summers, Coffelt, and Horton, 1989; Whitney and Smith, 1983). Existing research generally supports a positive relationship between group cohesion and job satisfaction, productivity, and success. That is, facilitating group cohesion in an organization will positively influence both the satisfaction and the productivity of employees.

A MODEL OF THE DETERMINANTS
OF GROUP COHESIVENESS

While many organizational factors influence cohesiveness, the model presented below identifies those factors that are most affected by ethnocentric attitudes. The model proposes that group cohesiveness is predicated on the agreement on–and success in–achieving goals, the development of an organizational system in which group cohesiveness is fostered, and the presence of effective group leadership. Given these three antecedents of group cohesiveness, it is appropriate to examine how each might be affected by the ethnocentric management attitudes often found in multi-cultural work environments (Figure 12.1).

Goals

Goal Congruence. The first element upon which group cohesion is dependent is goal congruence. Goal congruence requires an alignment of the goals of individual group members with those of other group members and the organization as a whole (Schnake and Cochran, 1985). When this occurs, group members attempt to cooperate and strive collectively for mutually agreeable ends. Without such goal congruence, the relationship between members can disintegrate into competition and conflict.

The importance of goal orientation to the organization is evident. When members of the organization subjugate their actions to the collective, and jointly align their actions toward group goals, they achieve cooperation, harmony, loyalty, and success (Adler and Adler, 1988). When individual actions became misaligned, the atmosphere created is one of jealousy, mistrust, competitiveness, and conflict. Such an atmosphere impedes the development of cohesion and camaraderie, as well as the achievement of collective goals.

Unfortunately, a lack of goal congruence among partners of international joint ventures is quite common. In fact, goal incongru-

FIGURE 12.1. Group Cohesiveness Determinants Affected by Ethnocentrism

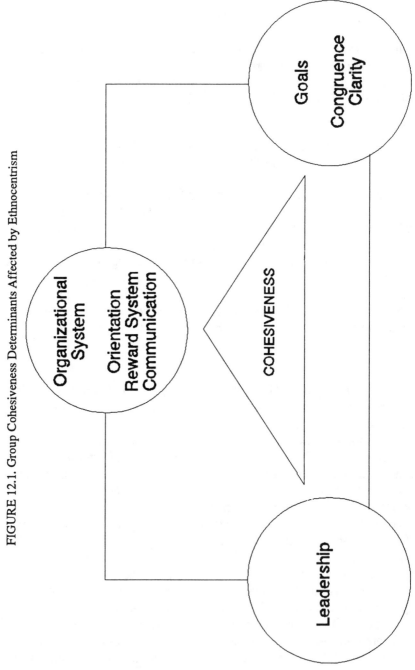

ence is often a significant source of friction between the partners (Reynolds, 1984; Simiar, 1983). Efforts to arrive at mutually agreeable goals may be thwarted by each group's suspicion of covert intentions on the part of its partner.

While there are several potential causes of goal incongruence in multi-cultural partnerships, one of the most significant factors is the "multiple loyalty dilemma" faced by many international joint-venture managers. Originally conceptualized by Guetzkow (1955), multiple loyalty dilemma refers to a feeling of loyalty to one party that results in a feeling of disloyalty to another party. Typically, joint-venture managers must reconcile their loyalties to at least two parties–the joint-venture management team and their home-country parent company. In an international joint venture, where in-group/out-group distinctions based on ethnic origin tend to develop more readily, the concept of multiple loyalties is of more significance and has greater implications for managerial behaviors. This is particularly true in situations where one of the parent companies has covert goals in mind for the venture and the representative management must work behind the scenes to accomplish such goals.

Triandis (1984) argued that in situations where in-group/out-group distinctions are strong, both groups tend to prescribe to the theory of "limited goods." In other words, each group perceives a situation whereby the out-group receiving some "good" means there is less "good" left for the in-group. Perceiving a zero-sum game, both parties act to maximize their part of the pie rather than attempt to expand the pie. Clearly, goal congruence is impossible in a situation where the interests of one party can only be achieved to the detriment of the other party.

Although one would presume that there exists some level of goal congruence between the partners at the outset of the venture, divergent goals can develop as the venture matures. For example, as Wright (1979) pointed out, if one partner's primary objective becomes to maximize profits, while the other partner feels that growth is more important, significant operational problems will result. Earnings allocation and transfer pricing policies are also common areas where goal divergence may occur. Where divergent goals do exist, joint-venture managers may be forced to make decisions that will appear disloyal to either the venture group and/or their parent firm.

Goal incongruence can seriously damage the cohesiveness of a joint venture management team. Dysfunctional behaviors on the part of both parties will result when managers are forced to subordinate the goals of the out-group to those of their own group. While the managers may realize the importance of goal congruence at a fundamental level, the pressures inherent in their multi-cultural organizational environment creates greater ethnocentrism and less cooperativeness on the part of both partners.

Goal-Path Clarity. Developing effective goal orientation within a management team requires not only goal congruence but also goal-path clarity. To the extent that clear, well-defined, and feasible group goals exist, group cohesiveness is enhanced. In an experimental study by Raven and Rietsema (1957), subjects who were clearly informed as to their goal–and the means to achieve that goal–were more satisfied with the task, felt closer to their group, and showed greater concern for their group's performance, as well as their own. Anderson (1975) also found that where goals and the paths to goal achievement were clear, feelings of group belongingness and sympathy for group emotion were greater. In contrast, where goals and paths to goal achievement were ambiguous, there was greater disinterest and hostility among group members. Further, when group members do not agree on problems that prevent goal achievement, cohesiveness is more difficult to achieve (French, 1941). Research suggests that goal-path clarity is greatest when group members agree upon problem identification and develop a clear path to resolve the problem and achieve group goals.

Joint-venture managers often exhibit fundamentally different cultural "frames of reference" that impede the development goal-path clarity. Since the managers come from different cultural backgrounds, their perceptions of what constitutes a problem may be dramatically different. For example, Anglophone and Francophone managers may have very different perceptions of the appropriate length and purpose of lunch hours. In one Canadian organization, Anglophone managers complained that Francophone managers consistently took extended lunch hours. The Francophone managers did not see this as a problem, however, because they viewed lunch as an opportunity to improve relations with business associates–an activity they considered crucial for the long-term prosperity of the firm. So while the Francophone managers perceived the lunch break to be nothing more than an extension of work, the Anglophone managers felt that their extended lunch breaks were a significant organizational problem.

Another example of dissimilar cultural frames of reference can be seen by examining Asian and Western perceptions of subordinate control. While Western expatriate managers do not mind subordinates leaving the office before they do (given it is after regulated hours), Oriental managers view this action as highly disrespectful. To the Oriental manager, such actions provide a clear sign that the manager is losing control over his/her subordinates.

As both of the above examples illustrate, differing frames of reference can lead to very different views of organizational and/or operational problems. Yet even when there is consensus on the nature of the problem, agreement on a viable resolution of the problem may be difficult to achieve. For example, while a management team may agree that morale is a problem in their organization, they may prescribe very different methods for resolving such problems. Western managers are likely to prefer individual, pecuniary rewards as a mechanism for improving morale, whereas their Oriental counterparts would prescribe honorary, group rewards as a resolution for the same problem.

While the situations described above might also occur in purely domestic organizations, they tend to be more pronounced in multi-cultural firms. The ethnocentric attitudes of both venture partners serve to intensify the in-group/out-group distinction, thereby polarizing management views even further. The managers become increasingly convinced their methods of problem identification and resolution are "correct" and the out-group's methods are "incorrect." Ethnocentrism fuels managerial dissension and hinders management's ability to envision a clear path to problem resolution and goal attainment. Thus, goal-path clarity is lessened significantly by epistomelogical differences that are magnified by management's ethnocentric beliefs.

Organizational System

The most general category of factors contributing to cohesiveness is the venture's organizational system. While there are a number of components to the organization's system of operation that affect group cohesiveness, the most salient components for issues of ethnocentrism include the organization's communication structure, reward system, and corporate culture.

Communication Structure. Studies of organizational behavior have clearly illustrated the importance of effective communication structures to group cohesiveness. Restrictions on information flow between group members can severely disrupt a group's ability to develop cohesiveness and work toward the achievement of group goals. In fact, studies have shown that individuals in groups with restrictive communication structures experience significant frustration and antagonism. Group members who are at disadvantaged, peripheral positions in the communication network tend to be relatively dissatisfied with their jobs, while members who are more central to the communication network are more satisfied (Bravelas, 1950).

Bonner (1959) suggested that communication structures that fail to support effective interaction between the members of the group lead individual members to form stereotypical attitudes about other group members–attitudes that are based on inadequate and, perhaps, inaccurate information. Such perceptual distortions breeds what Newcomb (1947) originally termed "autistic hostility." Autistic hostility results from communication barriers that prohibit the development of a clear understanding of other group members. It is typically manifested as animosity and can lead to withdrawal and self-isolation.

Communication problems are a frequent occurrence in international joint ventures. Since managers are typically not proficient in their partner's language, they may have a limited capacity to understand their foreign colleagues. As a consequence of such language deficiencies, certain managers are forced to assume peripheral positions in the communication network. These managers often experience significant frustration as a result of their limited access to information. As their communication frustrations intensify, they may eventually begin to exhibit autistic hostility towards the out-group members. In fact, language-deficient managers may mask their inability to command the foreign language by showing excessive hostility toward their partners and/or demonstrating an unwillingness to communicate with their foreign colleagues in any capacity.

The hostility that results from communication frustrations may be directed not only toward members of the out-group but may also be directed toward in-group members who are better prepared to communicate with members of the out-group. Some managers may even criticize in-group members who are more fluent in the language of the out-group as being "turncoats," in an effort to build their own credibility among in-group members.

Another potential in-group behavioral problem that often results from communication barriers is "selective transmission" of information. This occurs when individuals tell other in-group members only that information that supports existing ethnocentric beliefs. As a consequence, ethnocentric attitudes are strengthened and effective communication between subgroups is further hindered.

In summary, ethnocentric attitudes reduce group cohesiveness by obstructing the development of effective communication structures within the venture. This is true of communication networks both between and within ethnic subgroups. While language differences are inherent in the joint-venture structure, ethnocentric attitudes exacerbate the situation further by discouraging both partners from making the concessions necessary to overcome this critical communication barrier.

Reward System. One of the important functions of a group is to ensure "distributive justice" among group members and the ability of a group to do so is a key element in group cohesiveness. Groups induce members to conform to group behavioral norms by providing an equitable distribution of rewards to group members. Kleine and Ritti (1984) argue that the equitable allocation of group rewards and/or perquisites that are obtained through collective efforts to achieve group goals enhances internal group cohesion. Phillips and D'Amico (1956) reported that where rewards were not evenly distributed, group cohesion was negatively affected. Homan (1950) concluded that continued inequity in distributive justice endangered the relationship among group members and significantly reduced their attraction to the group.

There are a number of factors that restrict the development of a sense of reward equity among international joint-venture managers. Ethnocentric attitudes on the part of both ethnic subgroups may cause each group to see the out-group as inferior. As a result, each subgroup views the in-group's contribution to the venture to be significantly greater than that of the out-group. Further, each group often perceives the hardship they must endure, as a result of having to work and cooperate with the out-group, to be much greater than that of their partner. Consequently, they believe that they should receive greater compensation than their foreign colleagues.

In addition, it is common for expatriate managers to receive additional funds/benefits to compensate for their relocation over-seas–earnings that their local counterparts do not receive. Local managers, particularly those who have never been expatriated, may find it difficult to understand why this additional compensation is being provided to the foreign managers. Local managers tend to believe that since all the venture managers work for the same company, equitable reward distribution requires no consideration of nationality.

Similarly, many expatriate managers do not fully understand the unique circumstances faced by the local managers. Burdened with many tasks that require host-country knowledge and expertise (i.e., internal and external document generation, public relations, govern-ment relations, etc.), local managers may feel as though they assume a disproportionately large share of organizational responsibilities. While expatriate managers may take such activities for granted, local managers tend to believe that their unique contributions are particularly important. Further, while most joint-venture reward structures clearly recognize the expatriate manager's hardship by providing for additional compensation, local managers are rarely given additional compensation for assuming sole responsibility for many important functions.

Finally, foreign-language differences further hinder the development of a sense of reward equity in international joint ventures. Each ethnic subgroup may truly understand only that performance that is expressed in their language and may have a much lesser appreciation for productivity expressed in the language of their partner. The performance of managers who are relatively proficient in the out-group's language may be overvalued, whereas the performance of managers with limited foreign-language skills may be systematically underrated by the members of the out-group. In fact, foreign-language-proficient managers have been known to take advantage of in-group peers by accepting undue credit for their colleague's accomplishments. Even if their fellow managers recognize what has happened, they are unlikely to attempt to try to rectify such a delicate situation, given their limited communication skills.

Regardless of whether reward inequities are imaginary or genuine, perceptions of an inequitable reward distribution system will result in fundamental problems that undermine the cohesiveness of the joint-venture management group. Ethnocentric attitudes contribute to feelings of reward allocation inequities since the venture managers are unlikely to receive rewards that are consistent with their inflated view of their relative contribution to the venture's success.

Organizational Orientation. Organizational orientation, also termed "organizational culture," is the third organizational system component that affects cohesiveness. This concept represents the: basic philosophy of the organization; values that underlie organizational norms; status accorded to certain individuals; formal and informal rules; and type of language used in the organization (Schein, 1985).

Firms that operate beyond their national boundaries often attempt to develop a strong corporate culture to facilitate control of their geographically dispersed operating units (Baliga and Jaeger, 1984). Cultural control is a means of ensuring unanimity of purpose without imposing strict bureaucratic controls (i.e., explicit and detailed rules and procedures). This typically requires extensive training of home-country managers, who are then expatriated to overseas facilities to occupy key managerial posts. Their job is to disseminate the corporate culture of their home-country unit in an effort to develop cohesiveness and unanimity of purpose in the offshore facility.

While this may work effectively for wholly owned subsidiaries located beyond home-country boundaries, it is far more difficult to achieve in international joint ventures. This is unfortunate, since the development of a strong corporate culture may be particularly important for multi-cultural ventures. Hopes for bridging national cultural gaps often hinge on the management team's ability to develop a synergistic corporate culture that capitalizes on the best part of each culture involved. International joint-venture managers face significant challenges in attempting to achieve cultural synergy. They often find that their epistemological differences are profound and very deeply rooted. Such differences impede the development of shared corporate values and philosophies. Ethnocentric attitudes exacerbate this situation, because each party believes that their own corporate culture is most suitable for the venture. Overcoming cultural differences to achieve corporate cultural synergy is unlikely in the face of strong ethnocentrism.

Leadership

Research suggests that effective leadership provides a strong base for the development of group cohesiveness. Berkowitz (1958) and White and Lippit (1960) found a positive correlation between leadership effectiveness and group cohesion. While this relationship is moderated by several variables (e.g., the nature/structure of the task and the characteristics of group members), strong leadership is undoubtedly an important prerequisite for the development of management cohesion in a multi-cultural work environment.

Effective leadership is difficult to develop in most international joint ventures. One reason for this problem is that leadership ability is not typically a criteria for the selection of expatriated managers. Instead, most expatriates are selected as a result of some specific technical skill or set of skills that can be of particular value to the venture. Relational skills, which are essential for a leader in a multi-cultural work environment, are rarely considered in the decision-making process of selecting personnel.

Further, one of the most salient ethnocentric symptoms is a refusal to accept members of the out-group as authority figures–regardless of a particular manager's technical and/or relational skills. Thus, since both ethnic subgroups are out-groups (depending on one's perspective), it is difficult to find effective leaders from either partner's management group. To accept an out-group member as a leader without approval from in-group authority figures could provoke reprisals and admonishments from in-group members. In fact, in situations where joint-venture stability has deteriorated significantly, in-group managers may look for the endorsement of in-group leaders before carrying out orders from an out-group boss– even though the in-group leader may have no functional authority over the action. By doing so, the employee protects him/herself from potential reprisals should the in-group not approve of the action.

In some cases, venture managers assume a condition of "intended inertia"–a defensive mechanism by which the manager avoids inciting the disapproval of the in-group and/or out-group leaders by simply choosing to do nothing (Park, 1988). While there may be repercussions from such inaction, the penalties associated with a failure to act may be less severe than provoking the disapproval of either party's leader for doing something "disloyal." This behavior is highly dysfunctional and can severely disrupt the operation of the venture.

The in-group/out-group distinction that results from the joint-venture managers' ethnocentric attitudes creates a situation in which it may be impossible for an effective leader to emerge and/or survive. Because each ethnic subgroup refuses to accept a member of the out-group as an authority figure, the venture is without a viable candidate to encourage group cohesiveness and lead the group toward the accomplishment of the goals of the venture.

MANAGERIAL IMPLICATIONS

As has been illustrated, ethnocentric attitudes and behaviors on the part of joint-venture managers impede the development of group cohesiveness within the venture management team. The resultant behavioral difficulties often lead to instability in the venture and, in some cases, to the venture's demise.

Ethnocentrism is not a unique phenomenon–it is a universal syndrome evidenced in virtually all ethnic groups. Ethnocentrism is particularly relevant for the study of international joint-ventures because the collision of at least two distinct cultures is unavoidable in such organizations. Further, ethnocentric attitudes and behaviors appear to be amplified in multi-cultural environments. The managerial behaviors that result are often dysfunctional and disruptive to the effective operation of the venture. The instability that results may eventually render the venture incapable of responding effectively to environmental change and, in turn, will undermine the ability of the venture to compete successfully with other firms.

Cross-cultural training programs provide a mechanism for coping with the forces that undermine the development of a cohesive management team in multi-cultural organizations. Cohesiveness in international joint ventures can be cultivated and nurtured, but only through education and training that both reduce the individuals' ethnocentric attitudes and expand their ability to adapt to cultural differences. A comprehensive review of studies that examined the efficacy of cross-cultural training programs suggests that such training reduces ethnocentrism and fosters the development of cross-cultural skills (Earley, 1987). Cross-cultural training has been recommended to improve an individual's relationships with host nationals, to allow that person to adjust more rapidly to a new culture and to improve his or her work performance. This, in turn, leads to better cooperation among employees and greater organizational success (Black and Mendenhall, 1990).

There are a variety of training techniques available that attempt to prepare individuals for joint-venture relationships by reducing their tendencies toward ethnocentrism. Most of these programs can be classified as either cognitive or experiential approaches to training. Cognitive approaches are documentary programs that expose employees to a new culture through written materials on the country's sociopolitical history, geography, economics, and cultural institutions. In contrast, experiential approaches provide more intense interpersonal experiences by engaging individuals in role-playing exercises, simulated social settings, and similar experiences so that they can "feel" the differences associated with the new culture. Many experts advocate programs combining cognitive and experiential training approaches, which tend to be more effective than programs that use either approach in isolation (Harrison, 1990).

Clearly, a better understanding of the impact of ethnocentrism on group cohesiveness is needed by those who develop and manage international joint ventures. Academics can assist practitioners by identifying characteristics of successful and unsuccessful joint ventures—not only from a macro-organizational perspective, but also from a micro-organizational/behavioral perspective. Further, behavioral modification tools that assist in developing management styles that resist traditional ethnocentric attitudes and actions will be increasingly important as international joint ventures continue to emerge across the globe.

REFERENCES

Adler, P., & Adler, P. (1988). Intense loyalty in organizations: A case study of college athletics. *Administrative Science Quarterly*, 33, 401-417.

Anderson, A. (1975). Combined effects of interpersonal attraction and goal-path clarity on the cohesiveness of task-oriented groups. *Journal of Personality and Social Psychology*, 31(1), 69-75.

Anderson, E. (1990). Two firms, one frontier: On assessing joint venture performance. *Sloan Management Review*, 31(2), 19-30.

Baliga, B. & Jaeger, A. (1984). Multinational corporations: Control systems and delegation issues. *Journal of International Business Studies*, 15(1), 26-28.

Beamish, P. (1985). The characteristics of joint ventures in developed and developing countries. *Columbia Journal of World Business*, 20(1), 1-15.

Beamish, P. (1987). Joint ventures in LDCs: Partner selection and performance. *Management International Review*, 27(1), 23-33.

Berkowitz, L. (1956). Group norms among bomber crews: Perceived crew attitudes, actual crew attitudes, and crew liking related to air crew effectiveness in far eastern combat. *Sociometry*, 19(1), 141-153.

Berkowitz, L. (1958). *An experimental study of the relations between group size and social organization.* Ph.D. Dissertation. (Yale University).

Black, J. & Mendenhall, D. (1990). Cross-cultural training effectiveness: Review and a theoretical framework for future research. *Academy of Management Review*, 15(1), 113-136.

Bonner, H. (1959). *Group dynamics: Principles and Applications.* New York, NY: The Ronald Press Company.

Bravelas, A. (1950). Communication patterns in task oriented groups. *Journal of Acoustical Society of America*, 22, 725-730.

Connolly, S. (1984). Joint venture with third world multinationals: A new form of entry to international markets. *Columbia Journal of World Business*, 19(1), 18-22.

Contractor, F. & Lorange, P. (Eds.). (1988). *Cooperative strategies in international business.* Lexington, MA: Lexington Books.

Dang, T. (1977). *Ownership, control and performance of the multinational corporation: A study of U.S. wholly-owned subsidiaries and joint ventures in the Philippines and Taiwan.* Unpublished doctoral dissertation. University of California, Los Angeles.

Earley, P. (1987). Intercultural training for managers: A comparison of documentary and interpersonal methods. *Academy of Management Journal*, 30(4), 685-698.

Friedman, W. & Beguin, J. (1971). *Joint international business ventures in developing countries.* New York, NY: Columbia University Press.

French, J., Jr. (1941). The disruption and cohesion of groups. *Journal of Abnormal Behavior*, 3, 361-377.

Freud, S. (1951). *Civilization and its discontents.* London: Hogarth.

Geringer, J. (1988). *Joint venture partner selection; strategies for developed countries.* Westport, CT: Quorum Books.

Geringer, J. & Herbert, L. (1989). Control and performance of international joint ventures. *Journal of International Business Studies*, 20(2), 235-54.

Gomes-Casseres, B. (1987). Joint venture instability: Is it a problem? *Columbia Journal of World Business*, 22(2), 97-107.

Guetzkow, H. (1955). *Multiple loyalties: A theoretical approach to a problem in international organizations*. Princeton, NJ: Princeton University Press.

Harrigan, K. (1984). Joint ventures and global strategies. *Columbia Journal of World Business*, 19(2), 7-16.

Harrigan, K. (1985). *Strategies for joint ventures*. Lexington, MA: Lexington Books.

Harrigan, K. (1987). Strategic alliances: Their new role in global competition. *Columbia Journal of World Business*, 22(2), 67-69.

Harrison, J. (1990). *The combined effect of behavior modeling and the cultural assimilator in cross-cultural management training*. Paper presented at the annual meeting of Southern Management Association.

Homan, G. (1950). *The human group*. San Diego, CA: Harcourt Brace.

Janger, A. (1980). *Organization of international joint ventures*. New York, Conference Board, Report No. 787.

Killing, J. (1982). How to make global joint venture work. *Harvard Business Review*, May-June, 120-127.

Killing, J. (1983). *Strategies for joint venture success*. New York, NY: Praeger Publishers, Inc.

Kleine, S. & Ritti, R. (1984). *Understanding organizational behavior*. Boston, MA: Kent Publishing Company.

Kogut, B. (1988). A study of the life cycle of joint venture. In F. J. Contractor & P. Lorange (Eds.), *Cooperative Strategies in International Business* (pp. 169-85). Lexington, MA: Lexington Books.

Laurent, A. (1983). The cultural diversity of Western conception of management. *International Studies of Management and Organization*, 13(1), 75-96.

Lott, A. & Lott, B. (1965). Group cohesiveness as interpersonal attraction: A review of relationships with antecedent and consequent variables. *Psychological Bulletin*, 64(4), 259-309.

Narayanan, V. & Fahey, L. (1982). The micropolitics of strategy formulation. *Academy of Management Review*, 7(1), 99-102.

Newcomb, T. (1947). Autistic hostility and social reality. *Human Relations*, 1, 69-75.

Park, H. (1988). *Comparative analysis of the cohesiveness of joint ventures and domestic firms in Korea*. An unpublished doctoral dissertation, Georgia State University, Atlanta, GA.

Peterson, R. & Shimada, J. (1978). Sources of management problems in Japanese-American joint ventures. *Academy of Management Review*, October, 796-804.

Phillips, B. & D'Amico, L. (1956). Effects of cooperation and competition on the cohesiveness of small face-to-face groups. *Journal of Educational Psychology*, 47(1), 65-70.

Pucik, V. (1988). Strategic alliances with the Japanese: Implications for human resource management. In F. Contractor & P. Lorange (Eds.), *Cooperative Strategies in International Business* (pp. 487-98). Toronto: Lexington.

Raven, B. & Rietsema, J. (1957). The effects of varied clarity of group goal and path: The individual and his relation to his group. *Human Relations*, 10(1), 29-45.

Reynolds, J. (1984). The pinched shoe effect of international joint ventures. *Columbia Journal of World Business*, 19(1), 23-29.

Schaan, J. (1983). Parent control and joint venture success: The case of Mexico. Unpublished doctoral dissertation. University of Western Ontario.

Schaan, J. & Beamish, P. (1988). Joint venture general managers in LDC's. In F. Contractor & P. Lorange (Eds.), *Cooperative Strategies in International Business* (pp. 279-99). Toronto: Lexington.

Schein, E. (1985). *Organizational culture and leadership*. San Francisco, CA: Josey-Bass.

Schnake, M. & Cochran, D. (1985). Effect of two goal-setting dimensions on perceived intraorganizational conflict. *Group & Organization Studies*, 10(2), 168-183.

Seashore, S. (1954). *Group cohesiveness in the industrial work group*. Ann Arbor, MI: The University of Michigan Press.

Shaw, M. (1981). *Group Dynamics*. New York, NY: McGraw-Hill.

Simiar, F. (1983). Major cause of joint venture failures in the Middle East: The case of Iran. *Management International Review*, 23(1), 59-68.

Sullivan, J. & Peterson, R. (1982). Factors associated with trust in Japanese-American joint ventures. *Management International Review*, 22(2),30-40.

Summers, I., Coffelt, T., & Horton, R. (1989). Work-group cohesion. *Psychological Reports*, 63(2), 627-636.

Sumner, G. (1979). *Folkways and Mores*. Needham Heights, MA: Ginn Press.

Tomlinson, J. (1970). *The joint venture process in international business: India and Pakistan*. Cambridge, MA: MIT Press.

Toyne, B. (1976). Host country managers of multinational firms: An evaluation of variables affecting their managerial thinking patterns. *Journal of International Business Studies*, 7(1), 39-45.

Triandis, H. (1984). Dimensions of cultural variation as parameters of organizational theories. *International Studies of Management and Organization*, 13(1), 139-169.

White R. & Lippit, R. (1960). Leader behavior and members reaction in three social climates. *Group Dynamics: Research and Theory*, 2nd edition, D. Cartwright and A. Sander (Eds.), Evanston, IL: Row Peterson, 527-553.

Whitney, J. & Smith, R. (1983). Effects of group cohesiveness on attitude polarization and the acquisition of knowledge in strategic planning context. *Journal of Marketing Research*, 20(May), 167-176.

Wright, W. (1979). Joint venture problems in Japan. *Columbia Journal of World Business*, 14(1), 25-31.

Chapter 13

Self-Management Training for General Managers of International Joint Ventures

Colette A. Frayne
J. Michael Geringer

Joint ventures have become an important element of many firms' international strategies. These ventures involve two or more legally distinct organizations (the parents), each of which actively participates in the decision-making activities of the jointly owned entity. It is considered to be an international joint venture (IJV) when at least one parent organization is headquartered outside the venture's country of operation, or if the venture has a significant level of operations in more than one country (Geringer and Hebert, 1989).

One of a range of possible interorganizational structures, IJVs represent an attractive option for coping effectively with the competitive and technological challenges of firms' operating environments (Perlmutter and Heenan, 1986; Geringer, 1991). Through the use of such ventures, firms may reduce risk, attain economies of scale or scope, overcome government-mandated investment barriers, and pool or exchange complementary technologies or other resources (Moxon and Geringer, 1985; Porter and Fuller, 1986; Contractor and Lorange, 1988). Recent data suggest that the frequency of IJVs is increasing and that most of the ventures established since 1975 have been formed between existing or potential competitors and have involved products or markets that constitute the primary, or "core," activities of the parent firms (Harrigan, 1988; Hergert and Morris, 1988; Geringer and Woodcock, 1989).

The authors would like to thank Dick Peterson and Yoram Zeira for their useful comments on an earlier draft of this paper.

Despite their increased frequency and strategic importance, many IJVs have encountered performance problems (Franko, 1971; Holton, 1981; Harrigan, 1987; Shenkar and Zeira, 1987; Pucik, 1988; Geringer and Hebert, 1991). These performance problems have often been linked to the unique managerial requirements of IJVs. The complexity associated with the presence of two or more parent organizations, who may be competitors as well as collaborators, often causes IJVs to be difficult to manage (Young and Bradford, 1977; Janger, 1980; Killing, 1983). The complexity is further exacerbated by the tendency to use IJVs in risky, uncertain settings (Anderson, 1990). This can result in a substantial level of transaction costs associated with coordination of, and communication between, parent organizations (Geringer and Hebert, 1989; Brown, Rugman, and Verbeke, 1989), as well as between the parents and the IJV. As noted by Drucker (1974), IJVs represent one of the most demanding and difficult but least understood of all organizational forms. Thus, performance problems of IJVs constitute a major concern for the parent firms, and effective management of these ventures poses a formidable challenge.

There is extensive literature on the important role played by the general manager (GM) in the operation of organizations (Barnard, 1938; Chandler, 1977; Kotter, 1982; Aguilar, 1988). The GM position is particularly critical to the effective management of IJVs. In addition to running the IJV itself, the venture's GM must also manage relationships with *each* of the parent organizations, which often have conflicting motivations, operating policies, and cultures (Janger, 1980; Sullivan and Peterson, 1982; Killing, 1983; Schaan and Beamish, 1988; Brown, Rugman, and Verbeke, 1989; Geringer and Frayne, 1990). Yet, despite the unique managerial challenges associated with this job, the role of the IJVGM and its relationship to the performance of IJVs have largely been overlooked in the academic and practitioner literatures. For example, there has been essentially no discussion of variables associated with successful or unsuccessful IJVGM performance, or of training programs that might enable IJVGMs to function better within the complex environment of the IJV. The absence of such programs may inhibit efforts to form IJVs that can successfully achieve the strategic objectives for which the ventures were formed.

Prior literature in clinical psychology and organizational behavior suggests that self-management techniques, which have exhibited significant improvements with performance of individuals in other challenging contexts, might also be useful for enhancing performance of IJVGMs. The potential usefulness of self-management techniques was further reinforced by results of a pilot study examining IJVGMs (the details of which are contained in this chapter's Appendix). Therefore, the objective of this chapter is to propose a program for training IJVGMs to become more effective self-managers, and thus to improve the performance of IJVGMs. First, a discussion of the characteristics of the IJVGM's role is presented, including factors that make IJVs difficult to manage and variables that are associated with performance of IJVGMs and their ventures. Next, the concept of self-management is discussed, and the techniques required for a comprehensive self-management training program for IJVGMs are presented. After outlining research hypotheses and addressing issues associated with the measurement of IJVGM training effectiveness, the chapter concludes with a discussion of the implications of self-management training for IJVGM performance and offers suggestions for future research on this topic.

THE ROLE OF THE IJVGM

Frequently, the job of the GM has been equated with that of an organization's chief executive. Yet the IJVGM position, by its very nature, is subordinate to the chief executive and represents more of a middle-management type of position. As defined by Uyterhoeven (1972: p. 75), a middle-level GM is "a general manager who is responsible for a particular business unit at the intermediate level of the corporate hierarchy." The job of a middle-level GM differs significantly from top-level GM positions, and in many respects it is more difficult.

The role of the IJVGM typically differs from that of a GM in a wholly owned subsidiary, and a strong argument can be made that the role of the IJVGM tends to be much more difficult than similar intracorporate positions. Role conflict, ambiguity, and overload are inherent to the practice of management. However, for general managers of IJVs, these factors are typically magnified. The problems confronting the IJVGM include: the presence of two or more parent organizations; geographic as well as cultural distance; divergent sets of expectations, goals, and desired performance outcomes; multiple and often conflicting objectives of stakeholders; and increased susceptibility to, and greater complexity of, corporate politics. All of these problems have been well documented in several studies on IJVs (e.g., Janger, 1980; Killing, 1983; Schaan and Beamish, 1988; Frayne and Geringer, 1990; Anderson, 1990). Similarly, results of the pilot study indicated that 86 percent of IJVGMs and 82 percent of parent company executives responded that the skills required to be an effective IJVGM differed from the skills required to be an effective GM in the firms' non-joint venture-businesses. Furthermore, 74 percent of IJVGMs and 58 percent of parent company executives indicated that the requirements of the IJVGM position were more challenging than those of similar general-management positions in the parent firms' non-joint-venture businesses. None of the IJVGMs and only 6 percent of parent executives indicated that the IJVGM position was less challenging than similar non-joint venture GM positions.

Among the challenges of the IJVGM role is the fact that the IJVGM often simultaneously confronts conflicting demands of superiors within the parent firms (who may disagree not only on how to achieve particular results but even on defining exactly what results are wanted). Second, the IJVGM may get caught between peers within one or another of the parent firms (who may have more direct relationships with the parent firm's senior managers and so, have less incentive to cooperate on issues of pooled sales forces, corporate staff assistance, research and development (R&D) or manufacturing assistance, etc.). Third, the IJVGM may face difficulty in managing subordinates in the IJV (who may have primary allegiances to one or another of the parent firms, rather than to the IJV). In fact, for the pilot study, 76 percent of the IJVGMs indicated that the existence of more than one parent firm had proven to be a problem to the effective management of the venture. Further, 60 percent of the IJVGMs indicated that they had encountered managerial or non-managerial employees of the venture who exhibited stronger loyalty to one of the parent firms than to the IJV itself.

The IJVGM must address these conflicts within a complex and

dynamic milieu of external factors, including those of an economic, political, marketing, technological, and competitive nature. Success often requires balancing and tradeoffs; in the process of attempting to satisfy the demands of one set of relationships, the IJVGM's effectiveness in managing another may be reduced. The challenges of being an effective manager in such an environment may be further exacerbated by the manner in which IJVGM performance is evaluated. Only 11 percent of the IJVGMs reported that their performance was evaluated by parent firms exclusively using specific performance criteria. In contrast, for 39 percent of the IJVs, the parents reportedly did not employ *any* specific performance criteria for such evaluations. These results were consistent with Janger's (1980) finding that only 22 percent of his sample ventures used formal performance reviews to evaluate IJV staff. The existence of challenges such as these requires IJVGMs to not only be able to manage others effectively but to manage themselves as well.

Yet, newly appointed IJVGMs typically have little in the way of guidelines or support systems to help them in their new jobs, and they often encounter greater difficulty in being effective. For instance, Kotter (1982: p. 127) found that effective GMs "relied on more continuous, more informal, and more subtle methods to cope with their large and complex job demands." Thus, outsiders were often a risky choice for GM, regardless of their talent and track record. He argued that an outsider rarely has detailed knowledge of the business and organization or good, solid relationships with the large number of people upon whom the GM is dependent. Yet by the job's very nature, the IJVGM is an outsider to at least one of the parent firms.

In addition to being an outsider, factors such as geographic distance, time-zone differences, staffing limitations, and communication problems often make it more difficult for the IJVGM to obtain assistance. For an intracorporate position, the new GM may receive training to prepare him or her for the specific job—including lines of communication, plans and policies for the business unit, and the competitive and politico-legal environment. However, such training is seldom available for IJVGMs, particularly in the start-up phase of a venture involving two or more parent firms that embody disparate objectives, resources, and policies. Since the parent firms themselves are often unsure of the exact form the IJV will assume, providing appropriate training and other support to the new GM is often not possible. In addition, several studies have noted that a major impetus for IJV formation is rapid market entry and exploitation of products or technologies during the early stages of their life cycles (Young and Bradford, 1977; Janger, 1980; Geringer, 1988). In confronting such a situation, the new IJVGM must take quick and decisive action within an environment characterized by complexity, inadequate information, and nonexisting relationships. As a result, the new IJVGM is forced to be more self-reliant than in a corresponding intrafirm job.

The above line of reasoning was supported by results of our pilot study. Only 8 percent of the IJVGMs had any prior experience managing in a joint venture. Yet, while over 92 percent of the IJVGMs felt that specialized training might have been beneficial in helping to prepare them for managing the unique challenges of an IJV, such training was provided to the IJVGMs of only 6 percent of the sample ventures. Therefore, there appears to be great potential for developing appropriate training programs to assist IJVGMs in effectively managing within a complex and challenging IJV environment.

Training programs designed to improve relational skills that are crucial to effective performance in expatriate job assignments have focused upon different kinds of learning and have varied in terms of mode of instruction, information content, and resource requirements (Tung, 1981). These programs have consisted of area studies, culture assimilators, language training, sensitivity training, and field experiences. Depending upon the type of job and country of foreign assignment, it has been possible to use these programs individually or in conjunction with one another.

In actuality, many of the problems faced by IJVGMs are quite similar to those faced by expatriates in overseas assignments. Thus, the aforementioned training programs could be useful in the management of IJVs as well. However, the principal difference resulting from the management of IJVs is attributable to the additional complexity associated with the "two boss" (multiple parent company) situation. Because of this additional complexity, it is apparent that the IJVGM needs a varied skill set. This should include such skills as effective leadership skills; networking and interpersonal skills; a vision of where the venture is going; an ability to manage both parent company needs as well as those of the venture; and a high degree of perceived self-efficacy and task accomplishment. In addition, the IJVGM must be able to set realistic goals, monitor performance of the venture, and respond to changes in the market or preferences by the board of directors through goal readjustment and evaluation. These attributes are consistent with the concept of self-management. Anecdotal evidence gathered from case studies, managerial literature, and interviews with parent company executives and IJVGMs suggested that IJVGMs who have performed best have been those who were effective self-managers, while those with little or no self-management skills were more prone to performance problems.

The relationship between self-management skills and performance of IJVGMs was empirically examined using data from this project's pilot study (Frayne and Geringer, 1990). Based on prior research, an 18-item scale assessing the use of self-management practices by the IJVGM was constructed (Kolenko and Aldag, 1984). The IJVGMs used five-point Likert-type scales to indicate how often they engaged in each of the specific self-management behaviors. Each parent company used a similar five-point scale to evaluate the performance of the IJVGM. Parent companies' overall satisfaction with IJVGM performance was found to be significantly related ($p \leq 0.05$) with the IJVGM's use of self-management practices (Pearson $r = 0.46$). Due to the critical role of the IJVGM and its relationship to the venture's operations, performance of the overall venture also represents an important proxy of IJVGM performance. Therefore, to assess the reliability of these results, the performance of the IJV itself was also measured, using parent company assessments of their satisfaction with the IJV's overall performance, as well as the IJV's performance versus initial projections at the time it was formed. Analysis revealed that the IJVGM's use of self-management practices was significantly related ($p \leq 0.05$) with both of these performance measures (Pearson $r = 0.36$ and 0.47, respectively).

These findings, though based solely on correlational data, suggest that there is a strong relationship between the use of self-management practices and the performance of IJVGMs and their ventures. This raises the prospect that many of the performance problems afflicting IJVGMs and their ventures may be mitigated through the development and implementation of appropriate training programs. Furthermore, one technique that has proven effective in other organizational settings, and that seems applicable and appropriate for managing this additional complexity as well, is training specifically targeted toward assisting IJVGMs to be more effective self-managers.

THE SELF-MANAGEMENT APPROACH

The self-management approach is based on social learning theory (Bandura, 1977, 1986). Social learning theory represents a unified theoretical framework for analyzing and explaining human behavior in that it states that a person's cognitions, behavior, and environment are reciprocal determinants of one another. Thus, people respond both proactively and reactively to external influences, and the external influences themselves can be altered as a result of an individual's responses.

Self-management (Mills, 1983) is an effort by an individual to exert control over certain aspects of his or her decision making and behavior. Training in self-management teaches an individual to assess what the problem is, establish a specific goal(s), monitor the ways in which the environment is hindering the attainment of an individual's goal(s), determine whether the plan is successful, and refine or change one's tactics when necessary (Kanfer, 1980; Karoly and Kanfer, 1982). For self-management to be effective, an individual must first set and commit to specific goals (Kanfer, 1975). Otherwise, self-monitoring, which is a pre-condition for self-evaluation, will have no effect on behavior (Simon, 1979). Written contractual agreements are used to increase goal commitment by specifying the reinforcing conditions for acceptance of the self-set goal (Erez and Kanfer, 1983). Obviously, while many individuals may practice self-management, not every individual is an *effective* self-manager.

Karoly and Kanfer (1982) developed a model of self-control that was based on a negative feedback loop. Their model showed that self-controlling behaviors are initiated when a choice point is reached. These points occur when: one's attention is directed toward a specific behavior (e.g., a parent company executive tells the IJVGM that continued inability to achieve performance objectives is likely to result in the loss of his or her job); there are changes in reinforcement contingencies (e.g., the IJVGM's written memos to the parent companies were formerly ignored, now they are reinforced); expected outcomes are no longer forthcoming (e.g., informal sessions with the venture's board of directors cease to be enjoyable). When these activities are interrupted or fail to produce the effects that the person anticipated, the self-regulation process begins (Karoly and Kanfer, 1982).

Self-regulation involves three distinct stages. First, self-observation, or self-assessment, provides the individual with a baseline against which change can be evaluated. On the basis of the individual's past experience and his or her expectations regarding what should happen in a given situation, specific performance goals are set. Second, the person compares the information obtained from self-observation and the goals for the given behavior. It is at this stage that the individual engages in self-monitoring. If the discrepancy shows that one's behaviors exceed the goal, higher goals are usually set (Bandura, 1977). The third stage involves the self-administration of reinforcers or punishers that are contingent upon the degree to which the behavior diverges from the performance goals. Support for this model has been obtained in both laboratory (e.g., Kanfer, 1970; Mahoney, Moura, and Wade, 1973) and clinical settings (e.g., Kanfer, Cox, Greiner, and Karoly, 1974; Kanfer, 1975; Karoly and Kanfer, 1982).

The organizational behavior and human resource management literature has only recently focused attention on self-management training for increasing employee effectiveness (Luthans and Davis, 1979; Manz and Sims, 1980; Frayne and Latham, 1987; Latham and Frayne, 1989), thus providing a valuable addition to traditional organizational efforts used to influence behavior (Tannebaum, 1962; Lawler and Rhode, 1976). Most of the advocates have used Bandura's (1977) social learning theory as their conceptual foundation.

Luthans and Davis (1979), for example, demonstrated the effectiveness of self-management techniques with managers in advertising, retailing, and manufacturing. The managers' self-monitoring and self-rewarding procedures for overcoming such problems as spending too much time on the phone, leaving one's own work to assist others, and failing to get to work on time were effective in changing their behavior. Manz and Sims (1980) described self-management as a "substitute for leadership" (Kerr and Jermier, 1977), in that it teaches a subordinate to exercise control over the same contingencies of reinforcement available to the subordinate's supervisor. Manz and Sims' research on self-management suggested that self-leadership can be a critical component for achieving high performance on the job (1980). Implicit in this latter view is the notion that employee self-management can be instrumental in furthering organizational goals by freeing supervisors to perform other important tasks (e.g., strategic planning). Frayne and Latham (1987) applied Bandura's concepts and Kanfer's (1980) self-management by training employees in goal setting, self-monitoring, and self-reinforcement. Training significantly improved employee attendance by increasing self-efficacy among experimental subjects. These results were replicated in a follow-up study one year later with the control subjects.

While various case studies (Luthans and Davis, 1979), conceptual frameworks (Manz and Sims, 1980), and empirical studies (Frayne and Latham, 1987; Latham and Frayne, 1989) of self-management training have been presented in the management literature, there have been no efforts to apply these techniques to management training within international settings. Yet, 70 percent of the IJVGMs in our pilot study responded that their parent firms failed to provide definite performance standards to assist them in their jobs. In addition, 73 percent responded that, in their role as the venture's GM, they were largely required to manage themselves. As a result, the effective application of self-management techniques appears to be an appropriate objective for addressing many of the difficulties confronting IJVGMs. Therefore, and consistent with studies of managers in other challenging contexts, self-management training is also expected to be effective in improving IJVGM performance.

APPLICATION OF SELF-MANAGEMENT TO IJVGMs

As previously stated, the work life of an IJVGM is hectic, time-consuming, and often torn between the wants and needs produced by the existence of multiple parents. The manager is expected to plan, set priorities, direct others, mediate between parents, and, most importantly, execute his or her responsibilities in a way that produces desired results. When all goes according to plan, when interruptions are minimal, and when the work is rewarding and stimulating, managers may have little or no need for self-management. In this context, the environment is operating to encourage and reward productivity. However, few if any IJV operating environments function in this manner, at least for extended time periods.

The IJVGM may find that the resources necessary to accomplish the task are not at his or her disposal; insufficient information is available to complete critical projects; telexes or telephone calls are constantly being received from one of the parent companies; and just as it appears that progress is possible, notification arrives from a parent or the IJV's board of directors concerning a shift in priorities. The IJVGM attempting to resolve the emerging crises abandons all hope of conforming to initial work plans or maintaining a long-term perspective on the IJV's operations.

In the face of competing demands on their time, it is essential that IJVGMs have clearly stated objectives agreed upon by each parent company. However, even if they exist, objectives alone seldom provide sufficient guidelines within the often unpredictable IJV environment. The relatively isolated, complex, and highly ambiguous position occupied by IJVGMs requires that they be adept at self-management if they are to be effective in managing the venture. Self-management enables them to assess what is and is not being accomplished; monitor the ways in which the environment is subverting their plans; restructure their environment to support identified goals or objectives; determine whether or not the plan was successful; and refine or change the self-management program, if necessary. Through skill development, self-management aids IJVGMs in effectively implementing their strategies. A self-management approach can be invaluable for helping IJVGMs to manage their efforts more effectively and to ensure that they are spending sufficient time on the most important management responsibilities.

Recognizing the need for effective self-management behavior and putting it into practice, however, are two different matters. The specific techniques comprising a self-management training program provide a means for managers to direct their behavior toward the most critical management activities and thus free them to use creative management judgment in establishing a direction for the IJV operations. The net result should be the development and implementation of effective strategies for management of the venture. The six essential components in the sequence required for a comprehensive IJVGM self-management training program are discussed below.

1. Self-Assessment

Self-assessment provides the foundation for self-management. This technique involves systematic data gathering about one's own behavior, thus establishing a basis for self-evaluation, which in turn provides information on where to base self-reinforcement. The aim is to identify when, why, and under what conditions a person behaves in certain ways and achieves certain levels of performance. For example, the IJVGM who desires to reduce the frequency of non-productive communications with parent company managers might record the number of such interactions in each day and the conditions that existed at the time. In this way, a base is established for self-evaluation and reinforcement as well as possible insight regarding the causes of one's behavior. The manager should record these instances over a period of time to obtain a specific baseline of behavior. Self-assessment can help managers to better understand their past behavior and provide insight into how they can better manage themselves in the future.

2. Goal-Setting

Goal-setting is another essential component of effective self-management programs. After determining which behaviors need to be changed, as identified during the self-assessment session, the

IJVGM can develop self-established goals. Goals provide direction for a manager's efforts that might otherwise be characterized by sporadic, and reactionary activity that has no consistent or purposeful basis. This technique also allows the individual to set both proximal (short-term) and distal (long-term) goals for improving his or her performance. For example, many IJVs encounter difficulties in technology transfer and product development due to an "us-them" environment between employees originating from the individual parent companies. An IJVGM may establish goals regarding the type and frequency of interactions he or she will promote between the employee groups (e.g., weekly meetings, monthly review reports). The IJVGM will also plan out his or her participation in these interactions, in order to enhance effective technology transfer and, ultimately, promote employee identification with the IJV rather than the parent firm. Similarly, an IJVGM who is unfamiliar with the operations and resources of one of the parent firms may establish goals regarding the number and frequency of contacts to cultivate within that firm, particularly during the IJV's start-up phase.

Goal-setting theory states that given that a goal is accepted, a specific, difficult goal leads to higher levels of performance than nonspecific, do-your-best, or easy goals (Locke, 1968; Locke and Latham, 1984). Furthermore, goals mediate the effects of variables such as feedback, praise, participative decision making, and monetary incentives.

3. Self-Monitoring

Self-monitoring can be described as the process by which the individual records his or her behavior consisting of when, where, or for how long the behavior occurs or does not occur. The behavior(s) to be monitored or identified during the goal-setting session (e.g., interactions with IJV engineers involved in the technology transfer process, or contacts with parent company managers regarding progress in effecting technology transfer) would be used by the manager to determine what self-monitoring system would be employed. Critical to the effectiveness of this technique is training the manager on both the selection of a measurement instrument (e.g., wall graphs, charts, diaries, performance reports) and the need to record behavior in a timely, accurate manner (i.e., daily, weekly, as close in time to the occurrence of the behavior as is practical). Although it may appear to be time-consuming to a busy manager, this activity is critical, since research has shown that self-monitoring in the absence of goal-setting had no effect on behavior. In fact, when used alone, the effects of self-monitoring are at best short-lived (Watson and Tharp, 1984).

4. Self-Evaluation

Self-evaluation, which leads to either self-reinforcement and/or self-punishment strategies being enacted, is a powerful method for enhancing self-management effectiveness. Self-reinforcement involves the self-delivery of pleasant consequence after the occurrence of desirable behavior. By providing oneself with rewards for desirable behavior, a positive influence on future actions can be exerted (Mahoney and Arnkoff, 1978). These self-administered consequences may, but need not, be tangible (e.g., they may consist of simply a "pat on the back" or giving oneself a half-day off for goal accomplishment).

Self-punishment, which attempts to reduce undesired actions or behavior by self-administering aversive consequences, does not seem to exhibit the same high level of effectiveness as self-reinforcement. Successful use of self-punishment requires the consequence to be sufficiently aversive to suppress undesired behavior, yet not so aversive that it will not be used (Mahoney and Arnkoff, 1978). So, for the IJVGM who has not achieved a monthly objective regarding the frequency or quality of interactions with the parent or IJV employees, requiring that a set proportion of the next month's lunches or dinners will be devoted solely to business purposes might be a more effective self-punishment than requiring himself or herself to relinquish a weekend recreational trip. The importance of the self-reinforcement and punishment strategies is that it gives the managers the opportunity to reinforce or punish their own behavior with reinforcers that are important and motivating to them, thus eliminating the need for organizations to constantly seek reinforcers of motivating importance. Although the IJVGM can learn the required management skills for success, he or she must also be motivated to spend time applying these skills to the appropriate management tasks.

5. Written Contracts

Written contracts are another integral part of self-management training. A written contract is an agreement with oneself that specifies expectations, plans, and contingencies for the behavior to be changed (Epstein & Wing, 1979; Kanfer, 1980; O'Banion and Whaley, 1981). The purpose of the contract is to specify, in writing: (1) the goal(s) that are set, (2) the actions that the person will take to attain the goal(s), and (3) the contingencies for self-administering the rewards or punishers (Kanfer, 1975). The contract is an antecedent to implementing the self-management program; it will prompt the IJVGM to follow through on the planned course of action, as well as serving as another form of goal commitment. Contracts for self-management programs are basically contracts with one's self, although the participation of another person (e.g., a parent company manager or a member of the IJV board) may improve the contract's effectiveness.

6. Maintenance

Maintenance is one test of the usefulness of self-management training (Hall, 1976). The behavior change is likely to remain in effect if the IJVGM has been allowed to practice the desired skills during the training program (Goldstein and Kanfer, 1979), has been encouraged to practice these skills in different situations (on the job), and has been continually self-monitoring his or her performance of these new behaviors (Watson and Tharp, 1984).

Maintenance strategies include training the IJVGM to recognize common problems and pitfalls in applying self-management techniques as well as developing strategies for overcoming them (Andrasik and Heimberg, 1982). The objective of this technique is to prevent relapse by having the IJVGM trainees identify high-risk situations, plan ahead for such situations, and utilize coping strategies to deal with these potentially problematic situations when they occur (Andrasik and Heimberg, 1982; Marx, 1982). For the IJVGM, this skill is imperative. For example, an IJVGM may anticipate that product developments may be delayed due to complications in effective transfer of technology from a parent firm to the IJV. By anticipating the possibility of such an outcome, the IJVGM can focus his or her efforts on identifying and managing variables critically influencing the extent of such complications (e.g., clashes of national or corporate culture among the IJV and/or parent firm employees). The IJVGM can also work on developing contingency plans (e.g., identifying other sources for transfer of technology, or arranging for importation of the product until IJV production begins) for effectively responding to problems if and when they might occur.

TRAINING BENEFITS

Training in self-management can lead to positive outcomes through enhancement of expectations of personal efficacy (Bandura, 1986). Self-efficacy is a cognitive variable. It is a measure of an individual's conviction that he or she can successfully execute the behavior or behaviors required in a given situation. Such expectations are assumed to influence both the acquisition of coping behavior and the effort that a person will expend to maintain coping behavior in the face of real or perceived obstacles. People who judge themselves as inefficacious in coping with environmental demands perceive their difficulties (e.g., existence of multiple parents, barriers to parent-IJV resource allocation) to be more formidable than they actually are. In contrast, people who have a strong sense of self-efficacy focus their attention and effort on the demands of the situation (e.g., maintaining high performance in the IJV) and are spurred to an increase in effort by perceived obstacles.

The implicit theory of IJVGM performance in this chapter is that GMs who are managing an IJV successfully may be individuals who are able to effectively use self-management skills to overcome the personal obstacles, as well as the situational demands, that influence one's ability to perform effectively. IJVGMs who are unable to manage the IJV successfully may be those who perceive that they are unable to overcome problems that interfere with IJV performance. That is, they have low self-efficacy. This relationship received support from our pilot study's results, as discussed earlier. Indirect support for this argument can also be found in the work done by Killing (1983). This author found that a common pattern of decline in IJVs, labelled the "failure cycle," often causes an IJVGM to be monitored more closely by the parent companies and eventually destroys the IJVGM's ability, or perceived ability, to manage the operations effectively. In addition, Anderson (1990) noted that this tendency to increase the frequency and scope of performance evaluations can actually reduce an IJV's prospects for success. Furthermore, recent studies have prescribed that one way to manage IJVs successfully is to hire an independent-minded, strong-willed individual to run the IJV from the outset (Deloitte, Haskins, and Sells International, 1989; Killing, 1989).

Bandura (1977) has argued the need to differentiate between self-efficacy and outcome expectancies. Whereas self-efficacy refers to beliefs regarding one's ability to overcome obstacles, outcome expectancies refer to beliefs concerning the extent to which one's responses will produce favorable or unfavorable outcomes. Behavior is less likely to be affected when people believe that they can overcome obstacles preventing them from managing the IJV, but that the environment (e.g., parent companies, or the IJV board of directors) will be unresponsive to their behavior. Therefore, outcome expectancies should also be examined as an intervening variable in terms of their effect on IJVGM performance.

The benefits to be obtained from implementing the proposed training program in self-management are therefore hypothesized to be as follows:

1. The IJVGMs will perceive the self-management training to be effective (reaction criteria).
2. The self-management training program will enable the IJVGMs to acquire knowledge or skills that will help overcome obstacles preventing them from effectively managing the IJV (learning criteria).
3. The self-management training program will increase the IJVGMs' self-efficacy and outcome expectancies (cognitive mastery).
4. The self-management training program will improve the IJVGMs' management of the IJV (results criteria).

MEASURING THE EFFECTIVENESS OF IJVGM TRAINING PROGRAMS

Training in self-management is offered as one approach to improving the effectiveness of the IJVGM by providing the manager with techniques designed to help manage his or her own behavior. While self-management training programs do vary in length and content, recent research has shown that performance (measured by employee attendance) may be significantly increased based on a straightforward, 12-hour training program consisting of group and individualized sessions (Frayne and Latham, 1987; Latham and Frayne, 1989). The content of this latter study's training program consisted of lectures, group discussions, case studies, and individualized sessions. Thus, with proper design and a skilled trainer, effective self-management training programs can be simple, flexible, and not time-intensive. This is critical given the chaotic nature of the IJVGM position and the frequent demands for quick performance after assignment to the venture. Nevertheless, simply designing and implementing the training sessions is not enough. Measurement of training effectiveness is critical if we are to rigorously evaluate the program and advance our understanding of the field of international human resource management.

The effectiveness of the training of IJVGMs in self-management techniques can be evaluated using four criteria: reaction, learning, cognitive self-reports, and behavioral criteria (Kirkpatrick, 1967). The *reaction* criteria measure how well an IJVGM trainee likes the program with respect to its content, the techniques used, and the perceived relevance of the training to his or her needs. Measures of an individual's reactions to the training would be assessed by a multiple-item questionnaire that would be administered to trainees during different time intervals subsequent to the training sessions. This would permit an assessment of the stability (test-retest reliability) of the trainee reactions. *Learning* criteria assess the knowledge and skills that were acquired by the trainee (Wexley and Latham, 1981). For example, did the IJVGM learn new ways of responding to performance-related issues? Did the IJVGM acquire problem-solving principles to deal with problems preventing his or her job from being accomplished effectively and efficiently? The trainees would complete a multiple-item situational test. The methodology is similar to that used in a situational interview (Latham, Saari, Pursell, and Campion, 1980). Each item would be a description of an IJV problem that the person wished to manage more effectively. *Cognitive self-reports* are concerned with why the training is effective from a psychological standpoint. Did training in self-management affect one's perceived self-efficacy and outcome expectancies? Do these variables predict IJVGM performance? Perceived self-efficacy would be measured with a multiple-item scale regarding obstacles affecting a person's ability to manage the IJV. For each of the items, the trainees would indicate whether they felt that they would be able to manage the situation described (efficacy level). If they answered yes, they were asked to rate their confidence separately on a scale from 0 to 100 (efficacy strength). Outcome expectancies would be measured using a multiple-item questionnaire that contained both positive and negative consequences for self-managing the IJV (as perceived by the IJVGM). *Behavioral criteria* are concerned with the performance of the trainee in the IJV work setting, and they can help explain why the training was or was not effective in improving IJVGM performance. Each of these types of measures would be used to examine different aspects regarding the value for the IJVGM of the self-management training program.

CONCLUSIONS

With increasing reliance on international joint ventures and other forms of alliances, and the subsequent demands on IJVGM performance, an increasing need for effective self-management techniques seems to prevail. In response, this chapter represents one of the few attempts to apply training theory to international settings. The concepts we have presented are particularly valuable since, in contrast to many human resource training proposals, self-management appears to have the potential for application across an array of industrial and cultural environments. The range of strategies available for practicing effective self-management should further increase the attractiveness of these techniques to IJVGMs, who must largely manage their own behavior rather than relying extensively on outside sources for direction and motivation.

Overall, we have taken the position that training IJVGMs in effective self-management techniques would enhance IJV performance. Nevertheless, it is naive to assume that self-management and external forms of control are mutually exclusive (Mills, 1983). External control by parent organizations will always play an important role in IJV operations. Managers must always exercise some degree of self-management, even in the most intensive external control situations. However, even when self-management is deliberately encouraged, some external control by the parent companies—whether focused primarily on output measures, resource allocation, or the task boundary—will commonly be found and will typically be encouraged by the IJVGMs. The essential tasks of each of the parent companies is to provide the IJVGM with clear task boundaries within which discretion and knowledge can be exercised. What is being suggested is that the IJVGM should be loosely supervised in terms of specific task activities but more closely in terms of clarification of task boundaries and support for the discretionary activities undertaken (Mills, 1983). In addition, external reinforcement of self-management training by the parent companies is necessary to enable the training to be successful and for performance of the behaviors to be maintained. By proposing training paradigms that include self-management skills and organizational support, the effectiveness of the training may be enhanced.

Self-management research efforts hold potential for improving understanding of how IJVGMs can increase their effectiveness on the job. Based on research findings of self-management practices in particular organizations, training programs could be developed and targeted to increase skill levels of participating general managers. Evidence relating specific self-management practices to personal outcomes for the manager (e.g., bonus levels, subordinate satisfaction with the IJVGM) would provide added incentive for adoption of those practices. Furthermore, comparison of effective and ineffective IJVGMs across self-management dimensions could pinpoint those areas needing improvement. Job-specific self-management skill profiles could be identified to ensure that managers considered for promotion into IJVGM positions did in fact possess the requisite skills.

Past research in academic and practitioner journals has failed to address the complex role the IJVGM has in managing venture operations. Conflict caused by the existence of multiple parents, geographic and cultural distance, and multiplicity of goals and objectives are problems well known to IJVGMs. What is less understood is how the IJVGM should manage these situations while also managing as well as himself or herself. What is required is a comprehensive approach to training the IJVGMs to: monitor their own behavior; provide themselves with ongoing feedback of their performance; and take control of the environment wherever possible to regulate and anticipate difficult situations, the emotional responses that they engender, and the consequences of the behavior. Self-management training for IJVGMs, by focusing primarily on managing and improving job performance, appears to be one such approach.

APPENDIX 13.1: DETAILS OF PILOT STUDY EXAMINING IJVGMs AND THEIR ROLES

To identify and develop appropriate training programs for IJVGMs, despite the limited existing literature on these topics, a pilot study was undertaken to examine IJVGMs and their roles. From a Statistics Canada database listing the population of two- and three-parent IJVs in manufacturing industries that were formed in Canada since 1981 and were still in existence at the end of 1988, a sample of 48 ventures was randomly selected. The Canadian headquarters of each parent company, both domestic and foreign in origin, as well as the IJVGM were contacted. Participation was obtained from 101 managers involved with 42 IJVs, including 41 current or prior IJVGMs and 60 parent company executives. Each parent company respondent had direct-line responsibility for the IJV's operations, and virtually all had been intimately involved with the venture since its formation. Data on the IJVGM and his or her role were collected via a brief questionnaire, followed by in-person interviews to confirm and further probe responses. Questions addressed IJVGMs' managerial backgrounds, IJV responsibilities, and job performance. Respondents were also queried regarding the skills required for effective performance in IJVs, as well as potential IJVGM training needs.

REFERENCES

Aguilar, F.J. (1988). *General managers in action*. New York: Oxford University Press.

Anderson, E. (1990). Two firms, one frontier: On assessing joint venture performance. *Sloan Management Review*, Winter: 19-30.

Andrasik, F. & Heimberg, J. (1982). Self-management procedures. In L.W. Frederiksen (Ed.), *Handbook of organizational behavior management*: 219-248. New York: Wiley.

Bandura, A. (1977). *Social learning theory*. Englewood Cliffs, NJ: Prentice-Hall.

Bandura, A. (1986). *Social foundations of thought and action: A social cognitive theory*. Englewood Cliffs, NJ: Prentice-Hall.

Barnard, C.I. (1938). *The functions of the executive*. Cambridge, MA: Harvard University Press.

Brown, L.T., Rugman, A.M. & Verbeke, A. (1989). Japanese joint ventures with Western multinationals: Synthesizing the economic and cultural explanations of failure. *Asia-Pacific Journal of Management*, 6 (2): 225-242.

Chandler, A.D., Jr. (1977). *The visible hand*. Cambridge, MA: Harvard University Press.

Contractor, F.J. & Lorange, P. (1988). Why should firms cooperate? The strategy and economics basis for cooperative ventures. In F.J. Contractor & P. Lorange (Eds.), *Cooperative strategies in international business*: 3-28. Lexington, MA: Lexington.

Deloitte, Haskins, & Sells International (1989). *Teaming up for the Nineties–Can you survive without a partner?* New York: Deloitte, Haskins, & Sells.

Drucker, P. (1974). *Management: Tasks, responsibilities, promise*. New York: Harper & Row.

Epstein, L.H. & Wing, R.R. (1979). Behavioral contracting: Health behaviors. *Clinical Behavior Therapy Review*, 1: 2-21.

Erez, M. & Kanfer, F. (1983). The role of goal acceptance in goal setting and task performance. *Academy of Management Review*, 8: 454-463.

Franko, L.G. (1971). *Joint venture survival in multinational corporations*. New York: Praeger.

Frayne, C.A. & Geringer, J.M. (1990). The relationship between self-management practices and performance of international joint venture general managers. *Proceedings of the Administrative Sciences Association of Canada*, 11 (9): 70-79.

Frayne, C.A. & Latham, G.P. (1987). The application of social learning theory to employee self-management of attendance. *Journal of Applied Psychology*, 72: 387-92.

Geringer, J.M. (1988). *Joint venture partner selection: Strategies for developed countries*. Westport, CT: Quorum Books.

Geringer, J.M. (1991). Strategic determinants of partner selection criteria in international joint ventures. *Journal of International Business Studies*, 22 (1): 41-62.

Geringer, J.M. & Frayne, C.A. (1990). Human resource management and international joint venture control: A parent company perspective. *Management International Review*, 30: 103-120.

Geringer, J.M. & Hebert, L. (1989). Control and performance of international joint ventures. *Journal of International Business Studies*, 51: 235-254.

Geringer, J.M. & Hebert, L. (1991). Measuring performance of international joint ventures. *Journal of International Business Studies*, 22 (2): 249-263.

Geringer, J.M. & Woodcock, C.P. (1989). Ownership and control of Canadian joint ventures. *Business Quarterly*, Summer, 97-101.

Goldstein, A.P. & Kanfer, F.H. (1979). *Maximizing treatment gains*. New York: American Press.

Hall, S.M. (1976). Self-management and therapeutic maintenance: Theory and research. In P. Karoly & J.J. Steffen (Eds.), *Improving the long-term effects of psychotherapy: Models of durable outcome*: 263-293. New York: Garden-Press.

Harrigan, K.R. (1988). Joint ventures and competitive strategy. *Strategic Management Journal*, 9 (2): 141-158.

Harrigan, K.R. (1987). Strategic alliances: Their new role in global competition. *Columbia Journal of World Business*, 22 (2): 67-70.

Hergert, M. & Morris, D. (1988). Trends in international collaborative agreements. In F. Contractor & P. Lorange (eds.), *Cooperative strategies in international business*, 99-109, Lexington, MA: Lexington Books.

Holton, R.H. (1981). Making international joint ventures work. In L. Otterbeck (Ed.), *The management of headquarters-subsidiary relations in multinational corporations*: 255-267. London: Gower.

Janger, A.R. (1980). *Organization of international joint ventures*. New York: Conference Board.

Kanfer, F.H. (1975). Self-management methods. In F.H. Kanfer & A.P. Goldstein (eds.), *Helping people change*, 309-355. New York: Pergamon.

Kanfer, F.H. (1980). Self-management methods. In F.H. Kanfer & A.P. Goldstein (eds.), *Helping people change: A textbook of methods* (2nd ed.), 178-220. New York: Pergamon.

Kanfer, F.H. (1970). Self-regulation: Research, issues and speculations. In C. Neuringer & J.L. Michael (eds.), *Behavior Modification in Clinical Psychology*, 178-220. New York: Appleton-Century-Crofts.

Kanfer, F.H., Cox, L.E., Greiner, J.M. & Karoly, P. (1974). Contracts, demand characteristics, and self-control. *Journal of Personality and Social Psychology*, 30: 605-619.

Karoly, P. & Kanfer, F.H. (1982). *Self-management and behavior change: From theory to practice*. New York: Pergamon.

Kerr, S. & Jermier, J. (1977). Substitutes for leadership: Their meaning and measurement. *Organizational Behavior and Human Performance*, 22: 375-403.

Killing, J.P. (1983). *Strategies for joint venture success*. New York: Praeger.

Killing, J.P. (1989). Managing international joint ventures: After the deal is signed. Working paper, University of Western Ontario.

Kirkpatrick, D.L. (1967). Evaluation of training. In R.L. Craig (Ed.), *Training and development handbook: A guide to human resource development*: 230-233. New York: McGraw-Hill.

Kolenko, T.A. & Aldag, R.J. (1984). Self-management practices, self-reinforcement perceptions, and employee responses. *Proceedings*, American Institute for Decision Sciences.

Kotter, J.P. (1982). *The general managers*. New York: Free Press.

Latham, G.P. & Frayne, C.A. (1989). Self-management training for increasing job attendance: A follow-up and replication. *Journal of Applied Psychology*, 72: 411-416.

Latham, G.P., Saari, L.M., Pursell, E.D. & Campion, M.A. (1980). The situational interview. *Journal of Applied Psychology*, 65: 422-427.

Lawler, E.E. & Rhode, J.G. (1976). *Information and control in organizations*. Pacific Palisades, CA: Goodyear Publishing.

Locke, E. (1968). Toward a theory of task motivation and incentives. *Organizational Behavior and Human Performance*, 3: 157-189.

Locke, E. & Latham, G.P. (1984). *Goal setting: A motivational technique that works!*, Englewood Cliffs, NJ: Prentice-Hall.

Luthans, F. & Davis, T. (1979). Behavioral self-management: The missing link in managerial effectiveness. *Organizational Dynamics*, 8: 42-60.

Mahoney, M.J., Moura, N.G. & Wade, T.C. (1973). The relative efficacy of self-reward, self-punishment, and self-monitoring techniques for weight loss. *Journal of Consulting and Clinical Psychology*, 40: 404-407.

Mahoney, M.J. & Arnkoff, D.B. (1978). Self-management: Theory, research, and application. In J.P. Brady & D. Pomerleau (Eds.), *Behavioral medicine: Theory and practice*: 75-96. Baltimore: Williams and Williams, 1979.

Manz, C. & Sims, H., Jr. (1980). Self-management as a substitute for leadership. *Academy of Management Review*, 5: 361-367.

Marx, R. (1982). Relapse prevention for managerial training: A model for maintenance of behavior change. *Academy of Management Review*, 8: 445-453.

Mills, P. (1983). Self-management: Its control and relationship to other organizational properties. *Academy of Management Review*, 8: 445-453.

Moxon, R.W. & Geringer, J.M. (1985). Multinational ventures in the commercial aircraft industry. *Columbia Journal of World Business*, 20 (2): 55-62.

O'Banion, D. & Whaley, D. (1981). *Behavioral contracting: Arranging contingencies of reinforcement*. New York: Springer Publishing.

Perlmutter, H.V. & Heenan, D.A. (1986). Cooperate to compete globally. *Harvard Business Review*, 64 (2): 136+.

Porter, M.E. & Fuller, M.B. (1986). Coalitions and global strategy. In M.E. Porter (Ed.), *Competition in global industries*: 315-344. Boston: Harvard Business School Press.

Pucik, V. (1988). Strategic alliances with the Japanese: Implications for human resource management. In F.J. Contractor & P. Lorange (Eds.), *Cooperative strategies in international business*: 487-498. Lexington, MA: Lexington.

Schaan, J.L. & Beamish, P.W. (1988). Joint venture general managers in LDCs. In F. Contractor & P. Lorange, (eds.), *Cooperative strategies in international business*, 279-299. Lexington, MA: Lexington Books.

Shenkar, O. & Zeira, Y. (1987). Human resources management in international joint ventures: Directions for research. *Academy of Management Review*, 12: 546-557.

Simon, K.N. (1979). Self-evaluative reactions: The role of personal valuation of the activity. *Cognitive Therapy and Research*, 3: 111-116.

Sullivan, J. & Peterson, R.B. (1982). Factors associated with trust in Japanese-American joint ventures. *Management International Review*, 30-40.

Tannebaum, A. (1962). Control in organizations: Individual adjustment and organizational performance. *Administrative Science Quarterly*, 7: 236-257.

Tung, R.L. (1981). Selection and training of personnel for overseas assignments. *Columbia Journal of World Business*, 16 (1): 68-78.

Uyterhoeven, H.E.R. (1972). General managers in the middle. *Harvard Business Review*, 50 (2): 75-85.

Watson, D.L. & Tharp, R.G. (1984). *Self-directed behavior: Self-modification for personal adjustment* (3rd ed.). Monterey, CA: Brooks/Cole.

Wexley, K. & Latham, G.P. (1981). *Developing and training human resources in organizations*. Glenview, IL: Scott Foresman.

Young, G.R. & Bradford, S., Jr. (1977). *Joint ventures: Planning and action*. New York: Financial Executives Research Foundation.

IV. THE FUTURE OF GLOBAL
BUSINESS ALLIANCES

Chapter 14

Global Dependence
and Corporate Linkages

Refik Culpan

The ecological view of organizations suggests that to understand the behavior of an organization one must understand the context of that behavior. Moving from this premise, Pfeffer and Salancik (1978) argue that "[o]rganizations are embedded in an environment comprised of other organizations. They depend on those other organizations for the many resources they themselves require. . . . Organizations must transact with other elements in their environment to acquire needed resources" (p. 2). In this respect, business firms are linked to their environments by a series of interactions, including customer-supplier and competitive relationships (Lewis, 1990). Based on this resource dependency view, this chapter turns to the dynamics of the global market and projects corporate linkages as a response to these market changes.

The striking developments in the areas of political establishments, market economy, and values and expectations of people around the world have already occurred and, most likely, will continue to occur. All these sweeping changes will shape interfirm relationships and business strategies. In the midst of all these changes, the most distinguishing characteristic of the next century probably will be global dependence. No country or international firm will succeed without heavily relying on its trading or business partners. As Culpan and Kostelac (Chapter 5 of this volume) report, cooperative arrangements between firms have proliferated across national borders.

The author wishes to thank J. Michael Geringer for his constructive criticism of an earlier draft of this chapter.

This chapter elaborates on recent changes and prospects in the global market, explores possible international corporate linkages, and discusses the merits of these linkages. Furthermore, it incorporates the fundamentals of strategic alliances presented in previous chapters to introduce an integrated view for the entire volume.

CHANGES IN GLOBAL MARKET AND FUTURE TRENDS

Three major trends will most likely shape world trade and business in the next two decades. They are the emergence of regional trading blocks, the evolution of new markets, and the dispersion of technological advances. Each of these trends is discussed in turn.

The Emergence of Regional Trading Blocks

Three major trading blocks–the so-called Triad–comprise Western Europe, North America, and Japan. The underlying characteristics of each block can be summarized as follows.

Single Market of Europe

Of course, the most vivid example of regional cooperation is an attempt by the European Community (EC) to create an integrated market:

> By December 31, 1992, the European Community (EC) will remove numerous trade barriers in order to free the flow of goods, services, and people across national boundaries. The result of this historic undertaking will be the creation of a substantially unified market of 323 million consumers–50 percent larger than the U.S. market–with an estimated gross national product of $4.5 billion. (Goette, 1990, p. 10)

In Europe, Germany (after recovering from the shock of reunification) will emerge as an economic power and a major player in world trade. Although some observers have reservations regarding the unification and emerging of a single powerful Germany, it will most likely be a team player because of its existing commitments to a democratic system of government and to a market economy–both of which produced a vested interest for Germany in the Western world. Germany will be the locomotive of European economic revitalization. Such a political and economic choice by Germany will encourage its firms to undertake cooperative ventures, especially with other European firms and, to a lesser degree, with American and Japanese firms.

Ball (1989) asserts that "[i]n analyzing the effect of European integration, a great deal of emphasis has been placed in part on economies of scale, with regard to production and research and development, which would lead to re-allocation of resources and act as a spur to innovation" (p. 18). Yet he argues that strategic decisions of firms must be based on a clear understanding of the competitive character of their market structure. Thus, the future market structure in Europe will entail further cooperative arrangement between firms, because of its integrated nature and the pressure from multinational competition. The nature of competitive advantage for a firm may turn out to be related to its relationships with suppliers, its chain masters, and even with its competitors (Culpan, Chapter 1).

A widespread perception exists outside Europe that the Single Market will create a "fortress Europe." Although a degree of protectionism against non-European firms, especially against the Japanese and East Asian firms, is inevitable, such a protectionism will stimulate non-European firms either to invest directly in the Single Market or to engage in cooperative arrangements with European firms. Larger markets create greater risks and awards for traditional manufacturers faced with an influx of new participants. Therefore, manufacturing firms will adopt cooperative strategies more frequently than they had previously. Among other strategic options, for example, Goette (1990) suggests that American firms seek out joint-venture opportunities with European companies in their field and consider acquiring or merging with European companies. Similarly, Lynch (1990) asserts that "long constrained by governmental restrictions, new, more powerful, and highly innovative companies–strategic alliances, joint ventures, acquisitions, and mergers–are being established in Europe to gain competitive position" (p. 5). However, in favor of joint ventures, Lynch contends that "[f]or the same amount of time and money to make one acquisition, several joint ventures could be consummated in multiple markets, as AT&T has done with Philips, Olivetti, and Italatel" (p. 6).

As outsiders try to assure their presence in the Single Market, European firms will develop new competitive strategies. For example, it is interesting to note the outcome of a survey conducted on the perception of European business people with reference to European integration. In this regard, Emerson et al. (1988) writes that

> two main responses emerge: measures to improve productivity, and increases in the number of international co-operative agreements. It should be noted that the intentions to increase the number of agreements is by far the dominant one, with partners located in non-member countries. Firms of all sizes display a similar desire for co-operation. (p. 113)

As a result of these developments, many European companies will build strategic linkages and gain experience in dealing with a broad, geographically diversified market. As they gain this experience, they will be more likely to consider cooperative strategies to enter into the U.S. and Japanese markets.

The North American Trading Block

In 1991, the U.S.-Canada Free Trade Agreement entered its third year of operation. While merchandise trade between the U.S. and Canada–the world's largest bilateral trading relationship–exceeded $175 billion in 1990, bilateral foreign direct investment (FDI), totaling $104 billion, continues at an increasing pace (Bucher, 1991). The U.S. now accounts for nearly 70% (or $71 billion) of FDI in Canada, while Canada remains the fourth-largest foreign investor in the U.S., with 8% (or $33 billion) of total FDI. The North American trading block, by the turn of the century, will be the second largest in the world, perhaps twice the size of the U.S.-Canada market today. Of course, the U.S.-Canada Free Trade Agreement has had consequences well beyond the scope of commerce.

At the same time, Mexico is seeking a free-trade pact and more business arrangements with the U.S. and Canada, while many American producers–from job-shop pipemakers to such global giants as Ford, General Electric, and Kodak–have built plants across the U.S.-Mexico border. Such plants are called *Maquiladoras*, meaning built to take advantage of the cheaper costs of labor. General Electric, for example, has invested $200 million in a joint venture to make gas ranges south of the border. IBM, Hewlett-Packard, Wang, and others are making computers there for domestic and for export markets (*Business Week*, 1990, November 12). Suppliers are following these manufacturers. For example, SCI, a computer-parts maker, set up a $6 million plant to supply IBM. Besides U.S. companies, Canadian firms are interested in investing in Mexico.

Mexico is also talking with the U.S., France, and Japan about arrangements in which firms from those countries would make advance payments in return for guaranteed access to Mexican oil. For example, Pemex, the state oil monopoly in Mexico, is seeking the technology needed for deep-water drilling, which U.S. or other foreign investment can help provide. Pemex and firms from the U.S. and Canada can work together to expand the exploration of oil and natural gas.

Vitro, a Mexican glass maker, has acquired 49% of Corning's (U.S.) consumer products and business. This new venture will produce and distribute major Corning-brand products, along with Vitro's glassware and crystal, in the U.S. and in Mexico. It will have sales of over $800 million, with neither side producing consumer housewares outside of the venture.

According to *Business Week:* "The nearly $6 trillion manufacturing and consuming block of Mexico, the U.S., and Canada . . . is fully the equivalent of the New Europe of 1992 and Japan's domain in East Asia." (Nov. 12, 1990, p. 104). A free-trade accord will create a new wave of investment and will also open up the Mexican market and encourage further cooperative ventures. While it will stimulate the Mexican economy by providing investments, jobs, and production, it will boost Mexican demand for U.S. and Canadian machinery and transportation equipment.

Japan

In comparison to the two blocks already cited, Japan seems to be a lone player in the game of global business competition. Nonetheless, the role of Japan in the world economy has changed from being merely one among several industrialized countries to being one of the world's economic powers. As a result, Japanese companies have built strategic ties with many American and European companies to assure their sales in those two blocks; they have also been trying to build linkages with the East Asian countries. For example, on the Western side, Japan and the U.S.–old rivals in steel–have become new partners, each looking to profit as they breathe life into an industry that suffered throughout most of the last decade. The Japanese are helping to rebuild the U.S. steel industry, mostly through joint ventures (see Table 14.1).

On the Eastern side, Japan has established alliances with Asian companies. Intra-Asian investments are gradually leading to a horizontal division of labor within the region. Wu and Eng (1991) describe Japan's strategic linkage to Asian countries as follows:

> Countries now produce only part of a whole product according to their comparative advantages, and import the rest of the parts from other markets for final assembly. As an example, Matsuhita's audio equipment plant in Singapore sources its input requirements from at least four different regional markets including Singapore, Japan, Taiwan, and Malaysia, and exports 35 percent of the final products back to the ASEAN markets. (p. 11)

Japan is seriously considering the idea of establishing an Asian economic group in which it would take the leading role. East Asian economic integration reflects a growing cohesiveness in the region and anticipates a shrinking demand for goods by the U.S. Nevertheless, because of its established dominant economic linkages with East Asian countries, Japan has been playing a vital role in the region.

Evolution of New Markets

Eastern Europe and the former U.S.S.R.

The changes occurring through Eastern Europe and the continuing transformation in the former Soviet Union have started a new era for global business: "The dismantling of the centrally-planned economies of East Europe and the desire of the [former] Soviet Union to transform its economy to market-based system both have

TABLE 14.1. U.S.-Japanese Joint Ventures in the U.S. Steel Industry

Year	U.S. Company	Japanese Company	Equity %
1984	National Steel	NKK	30-70
1986	Wheeling-Pittsburgh	Nisshin Steel	33-67
1987	Inland Steel	Nippon Steel	60-40
1987	USX	Kobe Steel	50-50
1987	LTV Steel	Sumitomo Metal	60-40
1991	Armco	Kawasaki Steel	50-50

the potential to create new and very desirable markets over the long term" (Peapples, 1990, p. 80). Quelch et al. (1990) share this view and make this prediction:

> Eastern Europe represents both a marketing and low-cost manufacturing opportunity. In the short term, the East European countries need to obtain industrial technology and know-how to upgrade their manufacturing facilities. In turn, Western companies will be further encouraged to invest in low-cost manufacturing in the East. Later with economic development, the product being made in Eastern Europe for export will also become affordable in the countries that make them, and the market for consumer products in particular will boom. (p. 376)

In analyzing East-West partnerships in the automobile industry, Wells (1991) suggests that strategies of Western firms are likely to entail:

> A commitment to longer term partnership which goes beyond simple license arrangements. . . . The integration of Eastern European plants within the Western firms' overall European production structures and marketing systems. The production and development of an independent supplier base in the Eastern Europe. The promotion and development of market infrastructures in Eastern Europe, for example, dealerships, parts distribution, and finance companies. (p. 80)

In this transformation, such strategic alliances as licensing, joint ventures, and countertrade will play a vital role. For example, the recent 650 international business partnerships in Hungary alone illustrate this point. Geringer's (Chapter 9) thoughts on the issues of ownership and control in East-West joint ventures and his suggestion for better management of these ventures merit attention. While caution is in order, seizing of opportunity in this emerging market will require creative thinking and some extra effort, but especially sound corporate linkages.

It must be noted, however, that given the current political restructuring in the former U.S.S.R, Western firms should take caution in their investments in this region until democratic and economic reforms become well established, which, we believe, will eventually happen.

Newly Industrialized Countries

The four tigers of Asia–Hong Kong, the Republic of Korea, Taiwan, and Singapore–as well as Brazil are considered Newly Industrialized Countries (NICs) because of their ever-increasing manufacturing- and export-oriented economies. They are capturing a growing share of global markets for products ranging from semi-conductors to automobiles. Although the growing market power of NIC companies stirred protectionist movements by the trading blocks, especially the EC, the economic affluence of the NICs has offered an opportunity for some Western firms. Two significant implications are worth attention. First, firms from the Triad are seeking cooperative ventures in NICs, to source their cheap and relatively educated labor as well as their technology. For example, in Southeast Asia, U.S. and EC firms have experienced some successful business links. Second, NIC firms are preparing to overcome the barriers imposed (or will be imposed) by European integration and by other trading blocks that develop their own cooperative ventures.

Firms from NICs are capable of helping or hindering firms from industrialized nations in their effort to achieve globalization. The industrialized countries' recognition of interdependence with the Third World will be the essential factor behind successful global manufacturing and marketing.

The Dispersion of Technology

In explaining the global logic of strategic alliances, Ohmae (1989) deems that the worldwide dispersion of technology is one major determinant. He argues that

Today's products rely heavily on so many different critical technologies that most companies can no longer maintain cutting-edge sophistication in all of them. . . . The inevitable result is the rapid dispersion of technology. No one company can do it all, simultaneously. No one company can keep all the relevant technologies in-house, as General Motors did during the 1930s and 1940s. And that means no one can truly keep all critical technologies out of the hands of competitors around the globe. (p. 145)

Another factor accountable for dispersion of technologies is the advent of the trading blocks described above. Especially within the same block, government and research organizations and business firms are encouraged to cooperate. For example, Nueno and Quelch (1990) make this observation about the situation in Europe:

Technological alliances had become more prevalent since 1984, when several EC organizations were established to review and fund project proposals. The most important of these frameworks were: ESPRIT (European Strategic Program for Research and Development in Information Technology), BRITE (Basic Research in Industrial Technologies for Europe), and RACE (Research and Development in Advanced Communication Technology for Europe). All these funded alliances only to develop technology, generally between partners from different EC states. More than 1,000 companies participated in these programs since 1987. (p. 182)

In addition to the inadequacy of individual firms to develop sophisticated and complex technologies alone, the pace of technological change and short product life cycles have led to firms sharing technologies (Gugler and Dunning, Chapter 6). Overall, operating globally basically requires working with partners, which in turn results in a further spread of technology. Matsushita's support for Philips' Digital Compact Cassette (DCC) technology illustrates this point in the consumer electronics industry. In space technology, Hitachi (Japan) and TRW (U.S.) formed a strategic alliance to pursue opportunities, while McDonnell Douglas (U.S.) and Shimuzu

(Japan) worked together to develop space-exploration technologies for the proposed U.S. lunar/Mars initiative.

Diken (1988) calls this worldwide dependency "global shift," and he describes it as follows:

> The interrelationship between firms of different sizes and types increasingly span national boundaries to create a set of *geographically nested relationships* from local to global scales. These interfirm relationships are the threads from which the fabric of the global economy is woven. It is through such links that changes are transmitted between organizations and, therefore, between different parts of the global economy. (p. 184)

As a result of global forces and this "shift," companies have sought strategic linkages to overcome their manufacturing and marketing difficulties, or to sustain their effective operations; they will most likely continue to pursue such courses of action. Hence, it will be appropriate to conclude that success will come by embracing the global market through alliances–not by trying to avoid it.

FUTURE CORPORATE LINKAGES

Justification for Strategic Linkages

Strategic alliance is, of course, only one choice from among two other conventional choices: go-it-alone and arm's-length trade (usually market transactions between buyers and sellers). Firms tend to pursue go-it-alone or arm's-length transactions instead of building a strategic alliance. Indeed, they traditionally prefer a go-it-alone strategy as much as possible, thereby trying to internalize (i.e., integrate through internal expansions or acquisitions) various business activities for their own gains. Then the central question is: Why and when should firms prefer strategic alliance over other options? Principal arguments for strategic linkages are as follows.

First, as the advocates of transaction cost theory attest, a strategic alliance can–compared with arm's–length trade-reduce transaction costs of firms by reducing uncertainties and forbearance and by increasing cooperation, commitment, and trust between partners

(Buckley and Casson, 1988). Internalization may not produce the same benefits when a firm reaches such a size that the coordination of, and control over, activities cannot be conducted efficiently. When the production cost to be achieved through internalization is significantly higher than a cooperative arrangement, a firm should seriously consider a strategic linkage.

Second, strategic linkages often provide competitive advantages by gaining market power, by developing new technology and new products, or by entering new markets. Moreover, interfirm partnerships enable a participating firm to build a competitive edge by deterring entry or by eroding their competitors' position (Kogut, 1988). By engaging in alliances, firms can often obtain scale economies and they can also overcome either investment or trade barriers (Contractor & Lorange, 1988). Integrating vertically in the value chain with a partner enhances the competitive position of a firm.

Third, firms acquire "tacit knowledge" (Polanyi, 1967) through alliance that cannot be acquired otherwise. It is argued that mere technology transfer often cannot guarantee success. Corporate subtleties play a significant role in managing production and marketing operations effectively. But inherent knowledge cannot be transferred to another firm easily unless the company with such knowledge mutually participates in some shared business activity in particular. Organizational learning is linked with the degree of closeness between firms in association. It enables the building of internal structures and systems for information sharing, planning, and control. Through interfirm linkages, firms learn to adopt improved techniques, search the market, and identify solutions for their problems. The NUMMI case (the very successful joint venture between General Motors and Toyota) illustrates this point. As Badaracco (1991) claims, a knowledge link presents a great opportunity to enhance organizational learning.

Fourth, strategic alliances as an interorganizational network are formed to transfer, exchange, and develop or produce technology, raw materials, products, or information (Auster, 1990). Such multifaced relationships help a firm to screen the environment and to acquire needed resources. Technological collaborations in industrial networks especially are of strategic importance to companies (Gugler and Dunning, Chapter 6; Hakansson, 1991). Networking facilitates synergistic benefits beyond the advantages of dyad and triad relationships.

Having presented a review of the literature of strategic alliances and also having identified the major factors pertinent to them, let us now compare these factors with go-it-alone and arm's-length strategies. Table 14.2 displays the strategic choices of firms, along with their strategic advantages, and shows that alliance offers substantial benefits for a firm. It must be noted, however, that the advantages provided by interfirm linkages may vary, depending on the form of alliance. While the changing global and industry conditions described above may foster disregard for go-it-alone and arm's-length strategies, they may also encourage firms to establish close ties with other actors involved in market transactions.

Prospective Linkages

While most interorganizational links are of the conventional arm's-length variety, a major feature of today's global economy is the proliferation of corporate alliances (Kanter 1990; Lewis, 1990). Among very large firms, for example, it is not uncommon to find market-sharing arrangements whereby they collude (often covertly for fear of legal action) on the sharing out of geographical markets (Pickering, 1974). However, future corporate linkages will go beyond such arrangements and will involve product and technology developments (Gugler and Dunning, Chapter 6).

While the Big Three U.S. automobile manufacturers are forming alliances with their Japanese counterparts, they hasten the era of cooperation among themselves. For example, they are launching several joint research efforts and cooperating on lobbying the U.S. government. Table 14.3 demonstrates an increase in corporate accords among the Big Three and other companies in recent years. Such alliances will stimulate further cooperation in the automobile industry and also in industries related to it.

While interorganizational cooperations with rivals and other actors in the value chain warrant further inquiries (Culpan, Chapter 1), we also need to know more about prospective forms of alliances. Thus, let us turn next to a discussion of recently established (and probable future) cooperative ventures that will shape global business competition in the upcoming decade. Although the cooperative

TABLE 14.2. Comparison of Strategic Choices

Strategic Factors	Strategic Choices		
	Go-it-alone	Arm's-length	Alliance
Ownership[a]	F		P/none[b]
Control[a]	F	I	P/none[b]
Transaction cost minimization	I	P	F
Economies of scale	F	I	F
Profit maximization	F	P	P
Preempting/blocking competition	F	I	F
Risk sharing		I	F
Resource pooling			F
New market development	F	P	F
New technology dev./acquisition	F	I	F
Overcoming investment/trade barriers	P		F
Vertical integration	F		F
Minimize forbearance	F	I	F
Partner's commitment and firm's trust	P	P	F
Organizational learning	P	I	F
Flexibility (reversing the choice)	I	F	F/P

[a]Some consider these are not significant factors (e.g., Ohmae, 1989).
[b]Varies depending upon the forms of alliance.

    F Full advantage
    P Partial advantage
    I Insufficient

TABLE 14.3. Forging Closer Ties in the U.S. Automobile Industry

August 1988	GM, Ford, and Chrysler create consortium to develop more practical composite materials for cars and trucks.
October 1989	Chrysler and GM form New Venture Gear—first parts-making joint venture between U.S. automakers.
October 1989	The Big Three and 14 oil companies launch joint research effort to reduce tailpipe emissions and develop alternative fuels.
January 1991	GM, Ford, and Chrysler form battery venture, with help from the U.S. Department of Energy and utility companies, to improve the range and performance of electric vehicles.
March 1991	The Big Three and Navistar International Transportation Corp. pool their research on environmental issues such as emissions research.
May 1991	GM, Ford, Chrysler agree to work together on "high-speed multiplexing," which boosts performance of a vehicle's electronic controls.
June 1991	The Big Three file formal charges that Japanese automakers are "dumping" their minivans in the U.S.

Source: *The Wall Street Journal*, 6.28.1991, p. B4.

arrangements described below may overlap, it is useful to present them separately to better understand their individual characteristics and functions.

Equity Participation

As explained in previous sections (Osborn and Baughn, Chapter 3; Osland and Yaprak, Chapter 4), a firm's equity participation in a partner's venture (either with minority or majority ownership) is an increasingly way of establishing linkages. For example, Ford holds a 25% interest in Mazda in addition to its numerous vehicle and component supply arrangements with Mazda. Ford also holds a

10% interest in Kia (South Korea), which produces the Festiva mini-car for Ford. In the electric industry, GE has acquired a part of the Thorn EMI lighting business in Europe in an effort to expand its share in this highly-competitive market. This acquisition makes GE Lighting the third largest electric lighting manufacturer in Europe, where GE has been trying to expand partly in response to expansion moves in the U.S. by European companies. Separately, GE bought a majority stake in Tunsgram, Hungary's state-owned electric-lighting manufacturing monopoly.

Although an acquisition provides greater control for the investing firm, the majority ownership and control are not the only avenue to building lasting cooperative relationships. Firms may establish sound relationship through joint ventures or non-equity partnerships as well.

International Joint Ventures

International joint ventures (IJVs) have been the most common form of strategic alliance for many years. Thus, they have received the most attention in the literature (Beamish, 1985; Franko, 1971; Geringer, 1988; Geringer and Frayne, 1990; Harrigan, 1986, 1985; Killing, 1983). (In this volume, special attention is paid to IJVs in Chapter 9.) In recent years, for example, the U.S.-Japanese steel firms have established many joint ventures. After suffering great losses, Inland Steel Industries decided to form a joint venture with Nippon Steel of Japan. Inland has 60% of the partnership; Nippon has 40%. I-N Tek, the joint-venture, has produced premium quality steel for cars, appliances, and office furniture. These same two companies are also 50-50 partners in I-N Kote, two lines of galvanizing used to coat steel to prevent corrosion.

Moreover, the 1980s have witnessed an accelerated liberalization in the economic policies of nations with reference to foreign-investment (Contractor, 1990). This relaxation of foreign investment restrictions will stimulate the formation of new joint ventures, despite their earlier high rates of failures. Two important aspects of joint-venture formations are: the motives to cooperate and the selection of partners. (Chapters 6, 7, 8, and 9 of this volume exhibit examples of the kinds of conducive environments in which joint-venture relationships develop and the importance of knowing the IJV partner.)

To expand and diversify a company, acquisitions are considered a major alternative to IJVs. Of course, acquisitions vis-à-vis IJVs provide the advantages of full ownership and control over operations. They can also offer such benefits as being much quicker and cheaper for a company in developing a new product and a new technology, or for entering into a new market. Nevertheless, full ownership and control does not necessarily constitute effective management or produce satisfactory results. Moreover, the acquiring companies usually do not have strategic flexibility in getting rid of the acquired company if the acquisition fails to meet their expectations. In addition, most business acquisitions of an unrelated nature to their parent often result in failures, essentially because managers in the acquiring company know little or nothing about managing the unrelated business.

IJVs, however, pose a host of managerial issues. Culpan and Kostelac list disadvantages of IJVs in Chapter 5. Selecting an appropriate partner is a major challenge (Geringer, 1988). Managing and controlling the operations of IJVs present special problems, due to multiple ownership. In particular, Geringer (Chapter 9) demonstrates the ownership-control dilemma in East-West joint ventures. Measuring performance of IJVs has been complex and difficult because of disagreements on the comparability and reliability of alternative performance measures and methods (Geringer and Hebert, 1991). While Ross (Chapter 8) identifies special issues for U.S. companies involved in forming IJVs with *keiretsu*, the Japanese corporate groups, Daniels and Magill (Chapter 7) note the concerns of IJVs formed between U.S. high-technology firms and Asia-Pacific companies.

Managers should be aware of these issues, and so the present volume addresses them.

International Subcontracting

The emergence of international subcontracting as a strategic partnership marks one of the most significant developments of the last two decades. The success of many Japanese firms has been attributed to their effective use of subcontracting (Ouchi, 1981). Diken (1988) argues that many multinational companies (MNCs) increasingly "engage in global, rather than merely domestic, production, whether directly or through the establishment of overseas branch plants or indirectly through international sourcing and subcontracting" (p. 399). It is clear that such companies as Boeing, McDonnell Douglas, and Short Brothers took the long view in the 1970s and early 1980s by placing subcontracting work in China. As a result, they are being rewarded by having their products sold in China.

As Ross shows in Chapter 8, a single company in Japan can have a large number of subcontractors in its industrial group. It is not unusual for a Japanese firm to assist its suppliers and subcontractors in cutting costs and improving product quality. Overall, companies will seek not only domestic but international subcontracting arrangements for efficient production in the foreseeable future.

Supplier and Channel Agreements

Increasingly, the success of a company is becoming a function of how well the company links with its suppliers and channels. For example, frequent and timely deliveries by suppliers–known as Just-In-Time (JIT) inventory management–reduces a firm's handling costs and the required level of inventory, providing an opportunity for savings. JIT aims to supply each manufacturing process with what is needed, when it is needed, and the quantity needed (Lu, 1986). Many American companies such as Exxon, General Motors, General Electric, Black & Decker, Xerox, Hewlett-Packard, and Steelcase have adopted some form of JIT (Hall, 1989). Of course, a harmonious supplier-buyer relationship must exist for such a system to be productive. In this regard, Borys and Jemison (Chapter 2) emphasize supplier arrangements in terms of ensuring product quality, manufacturing capability, and delivery reliability.

Other Linkages

In other kinds of international corporate linkages, different patterns seem to prevail.

R&D Partnership

Technoglobalization will continue to be used as a metaphor for the various new ways in which enterprises formulate strategies for collectively developing, acquiring, and embodying technology. Technology is globalized in various ways, including subcontracting and research and development (R&D) cooperations. The highly complex nature, and enormous costs, of recent technological advances have forced companies to pool resources (Culpan, Chapter 1). Gugler and Dunning (Chapter 6) provide a comprehensive review and analysis of R&D agreements across national borders. The authors point out that high-technology firms operate through a large web of cooperative agreements. For example, General Electric and United Technologies, once archrival jet-engine makers, agreed to jointly study the possible development of a new commercial supersonic engine. This partnership would probably lead to the joint production of engines that would power planes faster and bigger than the French-British Concorde, the only current supersonic civilian aircraft (*The Wall Street Journal*, 1990, November 10).

Interfirm R&D cooperations are very common, especially in high-technology industries. For example, European biotechnology firms used alliances to pursue research links with Japanese and American firms: "Fison (United Kingdom) and Novo (Denmark) had been particularly active in Japan and in the United States, respectively. L'Oreal (France) had established joint ventures with U.S. and Japanese firms" (Nueno and Quelch, 1990, p. 182). In the aircraft industry, while Daimler-Benz broke an agreement with GE Aircraft to develop a new generation of high-thrust engines, it linked up with Pratt & Whitney of United Technologies on a similar project.

Joint Marketing

Firms with different marketing superiorities or with advantages in different geographic regions will cooperate to distribute and promote their products and/or services across borders. For example, Daimler-Benz and the Mitsubishi group reached an agreement that will expand the role of Mitsubishi Motors in distributing Daimler's Mercedes-Benz luxury sedans in Japan. Under this arrangement, Daimler-Benz seeks to promote sales by distributing cars through Mitsubishi dealerships.

In the area of Computer-Aided Design and Manufacturing (CAD/CAM), Fujitsu of Japan and McDonnell Douglas of the U.S. agreed on a wide-ranging factory-automation alliance that could include joint development and worldwide marketing. Under the agreement, Fujitsu markets a McDonnell Douglas design and manufacturing system that improves the degree of precision in making dyes and molds. Fujitsu will also get the license to a McDonnell Douglas software product used for advanced three-dimensional design. In the automobile industry, Ford has entered into a joint venture with Nissan to build a minivan for the U.S. market. In this joint venture, Nissan did the design and engineering work and Ford will manufacture the minivan at its plant.

All the cases cited above illustrate that firms will use each other's production and marketing competence in an alliance. To penetrate or to expand a foreign market, international firms will continue to benefit from a local partner.

Production Sharing

This phenomenon (dealt with in Chapter 1), also called co-production, presents another form of promising partnership. Production sharing has become a common practice in international manufacturing industries. In fact, Culpan and Kostelac (Chapter 5) report that the greatest number of alliances were designed to engage in joint manufacturing and other production activities. For example, South Korea has a co-production accord with McDonnell Douglas, through which some F/A18 fighter aircraft are to be built and assembled in Korea. Separately, the creation of the U.S.-Mexico co-production zone will encourage further production sharing among firms in both countries.

In the electronics industry, Kim (1986) observed that the most obvious manifestation of global production sharing is the growth of intermediate product trade in the Pacific region. Japan's production sharing in this geographical region enables it to export to the U.S. through Asian NICs. Japan supplies the Asian NICs with intermediate products, which are then incorporated into finished products destined for the U.S. (Kim, 1986).

Certainly, multinational manufacturers will utilize production sharing as a means to compete effectively, based on low-cost manufacturing and indirect exporting devised to overcome protectionism. As these case examples suggest, this kind of cooperative arrangement often occurs between a Western multinational and firms from NICs or developing countries.

Service Accords

Strategic alliances are not limited to one industry in particular, but apply to a wide range of industries (including those in the service sector). As Culpan and Kostelac reported in Chapter 5, the increase is apparent in service alliances, primarily in the banking, the hotel, and the advertising industries. Brooks et al. (Chapter 10) demonstrate that such ties are commonly established in the global container transport industry. Also, such practices are frequently seen in the airline industry as well as in the telecommunications industry. Some companies selectively subcontract information-technology services to effect a fundamental shift in business practices. Others build alliances to penetrate new markets.

CONCLUSIONS

A close examination of the global market conditions and the present developments in interfirm cooperations suggests that in the future companies will engage in a host of equity or non-equity forms of strategic alliances. Strategic alliances will particularly grow in industries undergoing structural change or escalating competition. Increasingly, they will also extend beyond a single business function to encompass multiple value-chain activities. Inquiry into strategic alliances in relationship to research propositions is formulated by Borys and Jemison (Chapter 2). Osborn and Baughn (Chapter 3) examine interorganizational governance forms. In addition, managerial dimensions are investigated to recommend guidelines for the practitioners. To succeed with these ventures, managers should pay attention to the features of, and the prospects for, strategic alliances.

Establishing a business cooperation between two firms may lead to a broader strategic alliance between partners (even in multiple industries). For example, Daimler-Benz and Mitsubishi are seeking to forge a broader range of cooperative ventures, covering everything from microelectronics to jet engines. Ford's Autolatina partnership with Volkswagen has paved the way to a possible joint venture between the two companies to produce a new multi-purpose vehicle in Portugal for sale in Europe. Yet these kinds of extended alignments will usually take years to bring to full fruition, without producing concrete results in the short run. Managers, therefore, should be patient with stalled negotiations and keep their expectations realistic.

A trust between partners, another essential component of strategic alliances, builds over years and only then does it smooth the relations. Osland and Yaprak (Chapter 4) view trust as a foundation for strategic alliances. As proven by Japanese practices, a harmonious relationship between supplier and buyer is the key to the success of JIT management. However, traditional adversarial supplier relations in the U.S., it is claimed that, have made transition to the JIT system more painful for American firms. Kanter (1990) emphasizes the transition from adversarial mode to cooperative mode for use by U.S. companies in strategic alliances. After partners know each other closely enough to eliminate suspicions about each other, they can then develop better relations and, therefore, probably enter into further joint business ventures.

Firms interested in alliances should value forming an enduring relationship and commit their resources to this end. Success in partnership follows the commitment leading to the long struggle. Additionally, they should be tolerant of the unfamiliar practices and also the demands made by their partners. As Lewis (1991) claims, "[firms] must appreciate and adjust to their partner's views, learning to rely on each other's information, and respecting each other's need to maintain its own internal culture. These are all ingredients of a successful alliance" (p. A10). Like marriage, an alliance will have its ups and downs. But once the bond of unity is established, alliances will create a solid base for success. Kanter (1990) asserts even further that "[w]hen an alliance existed for a long time, the bonds between representatives of the two cooperating organizations can sometimes be even closer than those within their own organizations" (p. 120).

Managing human resources effectively (as demonstrated in Part III of this volume) will be another determinant of the success of

IJVs and other cooperative ventures. By examining and evaluating human resource issues–as suggested by Datta and Rasheed (Chapter 11), Park et al. (Chapter 12), and Frayne and Geringer (Chapter 13)–managers can solve many problems before they erode the success of alliances. In fact, cultural, personal, and administrative problems present major issues for managers of IJVs. Most frequently, however, ethnocentric attitudes of managers prevent them from taking viable actions. To overcome ethnocentric biases, it would be helpful to develop cultural empathy and group cohesiveness (Park et al.). Self-management training methods (Frayne and Geringer) offer a practical alternative, especially when other kinds of assistance are unavailable for IJV general managers who want to adapt to their situation and to enhance their managerial skills.

Greater employee involvement in decision making and in management have been increasingly recognized in the literature (Lawler, 1986) and will be a decisive factor for the success of alliances. For example, NUMMI achieved huge increases in labor productivity only after employee involvement in management. This was largely brought about by changing how work was organized. Partners in an alliance may have no shortage of scientists and inventions; however, they can stumble in getting innovations from the lab to the factory floor quickly and efficiently–a task dependent on a highly skilled cadre of cooperative personnel.

An emphasis should be placed on the creation of long-term joint values instead of on majority ownership and control of operations that seek quick financial returns. Many of the U.S. steel companies have improved their prospects through alliances with Japanese only after they have given up majority ownership and control. In this regard, Ohmae (1989) argues that "having control does not necessarily mean a better managed company. You cannot manage a global company through control. In fact, control is the last resort. . . . Good partnerships, like good marriages, don't work on the basis of ownership or control. It takes efforts and commitment and enthusiasm from both sides if either is to realize the hoped-for benefits" (p. 148).

Although alliances are no panacea, they are a response to uncertainty, and they enable firms to cope with market forces. Cooperative strategies differ, but their underlying philosophy is remarkably similar, echoing themes introduced in the earlier chapters. A commitment to the cooperative venture and trusting the partner set true alliances apart from others. Building alliances could make it easier to sense and respond to possibilities for upgrading competitive advantage. The movement toward strategic alliance might be far-reaching, yet managers in nearly every industry must consider strategic alliance a possibility, if not already a reality.

REFERENCES

Auster, E.R. (1990). The international environment: Network theory, tools, and applications. In F. Williams and D. Gibson (Eds.), *Technological Transfer* (pp. 63-89). Sage Publications.

Badaracco, Jr., J.L. (1991). *The knowledge link.* Boston: Harvard Business School Press.

Ball, J. (1989). The Progress of the European Community: After Albert and Ball. *European Business Journal*, 1 (1), 8-19.

Beamish, P. (1985). The characteristics of joint ventures in developed and developing countries. *Columbia Journal of World Business*, 20 (Fall), 13-20.

Bucher, P. (1991). U.S. Canada Free Trade Agreement encourages bilateral business. *Business America*, 112 (7), 14-15.

Buckley, P.J. and Casson, M. (1988). A theory of cooperation in international business. In F.J. Contractor & P. Lorange, (Eds.), *Cooperative Strategies in International Business*. (pp. 3-30). Lexington, MA: Lexington Books.

Business Week. (1990, November 12), pp. 103-104.

Contractor, F.J. (1990). Ownership patterns of U.S. joint ventures abroad and the liberalization of foreign government regulations in the 1980s: Evidence from a benchmark survey, *Journal of International Business Studies*, 21(1), 55-74.

Contractor, F.J. and Lorange, P. (1988). Why should firms cooperate? The Strategy and economic basis for cooperative ventures. In F.J. Contractor & P. Lorange, (Eds.), *Cooperative Strategies in International Business*. (pp. 31-54). Lexington, MA: Lexington Books.

Diken, P. (1988). *Global Shift: Industrial Change in a Turbulent World*. London: Paul Chapman Publication Ltd.

Emerson et al. (1988). The Economics of 1992. *Commission of the EC*, European Economy No. 35, March.

Franko, L.G. (1971). *Joint venture survival in multinational corporations*. New York: Praeger.

Geringer, J.M. (1988). *Joint venture partner selection: Strategies for developed countries*. Westport, CT: Quorum Books.

Geringer, J.M. & Frayne, C.A. (1990). Human resource management and international joint venture control: A parent perspective. *Management International Review*, 30, 103-120.

Geringer, J.M. & Hebert, L. (1991). Measuring performance of international joint ventures. *Journal of International Business Studies*, 22(2), 249-263.

Goette, E.E. 1990. Europe in 1992: Update for Business Planners. *Journal of Business Strategy*, Mar-Apr., 10-13.

Hakansson, H. (1991). Technological collaboration in industrial networks. *European Management Journal*, 8(3), 371-379.

Hall, E.H. (1989). Just-In-Time management: A critical assessment. *The Academy of Management Executive*, 3(4), 315-317.

Harrigan, K.R. (1985). *Strategies for joint ventures*. Lexington, MA: Lexington Books.

_____. (1986). *Managing for joint venture success*. Lexington, MA: Lexington Books.

Kanter, R.M. (1990). *When giants learn to dance: Mastering the strategy, management, and careers in 1990s*. New York: Simon and Schuster.

Killing, J.P. (1983). *Strategies for joint venture success*. New York: Praeger.

Kim, W.C. (1986). Global production sharing: An empirical investigation of the Pacific electronic industry. *Management International Review*, 26(2), pp. 62-70.

Kogut, B. (1988). Joint ventures: Theoretical and empirical perspectives. *Strategic Management Journal*, 9, 319-332.

Lawler, E.E. (1986). *High-involvement management, participative strategies for improving organizational performance*. San Francisco: Jossey-Boss.

Lewis, J.D. (1991, July 29). IBM and Apple will they break the mold? *The Wall Street Journal*, p. A10.

_____. J.D. (1990). *Partnership for profit, structuring and managing strategic alliances*. New York: Free Press.

Lu, D.J. (Translator) (1986). *Kanban Just-In-Time at Toyota*. Edited by Japanese Management Association. Cambridge, MA: Productivity Press.

Lynch, R.P. (1990). Building Strategic Alliances to Penetrate European Market. *Journal of Business Strategy*, March-April, pp. 4-8.

Nueno, J.L. & Quelch, J.A. (1990). Biokit S.A. In J.A. Quelch, R.D. Buzzell, & E.R. Salama (Eds.). *The marketing challenge of Europe 1992*, (pp. 160-184). Reading, MA: Addison-Wesley.

Ohmae, K. (1989). The global logic of strategic alliances. *Harvard Business Review*, March-April, 143-154.

Ouchi, W.G. (1981). *Theory Z: How American business can meet the Japanese challenge*. Reading, MA: Addison-Wesley.

Peapples, G.A. 1990. Competing in the Global Market. *Business Quarterly*, 55 (2), 80-84.

Pfeffer, J. & Salancik, G.R. (1978). *The external control of organizations*. New York: Harper & Row.

Pickering, J.F. (1974). *Industrial Structure and Market Conduct*, London: Martin Robertson.

Polanyi, M. (1967). *The Tacit Dimension*. New York: Doubleday.

Quelch, J.A., Buzzell, R.D. & Salama, E.R. (Eds.) (1990). *The marketing challenge of Europe 1992.* Reading, MA: Addison-Wesley.

The Wall Street Journal. (1990, November 10), p. B1.

Wells, P.E. (1991). East-West partnership in automobiles. *Long Range Planning,* 24 (2), 75-81.

Wu, F. & Eng, N. B. (1991). Singapore's strategy for the 1990s. *Long Range Planning,* 24 (2), 9-15.

Index

Accords, service, 340
Acquisitions, 35
Administrative factors, 265
Agreements (arrangements)
  channel, 337
  contractual, 59,62
  equipment/chassis-sharing, 223
  informal, 82,84
  license, 35,43,53,181
  R&D, 128,145
  supplier, 54,337
  switching, 26
  U.S.-Canada Free Trade, 324
Alliance, *see also* cooperation
  control, 143
  formation, 109
  forms (patterns, types),
      104,106,145
  efficiency of R&D, 154
  intra-, 188
  minority equity, 83
  planning, 144
  purpose, 113
  responsibilities, 143
  scale, 89
  trends, 104
Airbus Industrie, 20
America, North, 324
Apple, Inc., 25
Appropriability, low partner, 179
Assessment, self-, 304
Asia North Eastbound Rate
      Agreement (ANERA), 245
Asia-Pacific firms, 169
Atlantic Container Line (ACL), 244
AT&T, 137,146
Authority relations, 197
Auster, E.R., 82,168,331

Badaracco, Joseph L., 90,117
Bargaining strength, 173
BASF, 88
Berg, S.V., 105,106
Boundary, 43
  permeability, 44
Buckley, Peter, 132
Bull, 91
Buzzell, R.D., 327

Canada, 230
Career issues, 264
Charters, slot, 223
Ciba-Geigy, 83,123
Clauses
  exclusivity, 142
  restrictive, 142
Cohesiveness, group, 276
Coalitions, 14,18
Collaborations, contractual, 83
Collaborative strategies, 1,13. *See*
      strategic alliances
Communication, 92
  structure, 282
Compagnie Generale Maritime, 243
Competencies, 86,89
Competitive advantage, 331
Conferences, 222
Contextual analysis, 183,194
Contracts, written, 307
Contractor, Farok J., 13,14,87,106,
      130,133,183,226
Control
  extent, 213
  fit, 216
  focus, 210
  mechanism, 175,214
  systems, 267
Consortium, 26,244

Consortia, 224
Cooperation, 94
  equity forms, 106
  modes of, 24
  non-equity forms, 106
  process, 195
Cooperative ventures, 1,13
Corporate
  culture, 28
  grouping, 185. *See also*
    keiretsu
  philosophy, 28
Countertrade, 23
Culpan, Refik, 23
Cultural differences, 260

Daewoo, 83
Daimler-Benz, 17,340
Diken, P., 330
Duncan, J., 105,106
Dunning, John H., 133

Echelon, lower, 190
EDISHIP, 232
Effectiveness, measuring, 310
Efficiency, 88
Electronic Data Interchange (EDI),
    223,227,232
Eli Lilly, 83
Environmental forces, 20,255
Ethnocentrism, 275
Europe (single market), 103,322
  Eastern, 204,326
European Community (EC), 230,322
Evaluation, self-, 306
Evaluation criteria
  behavioral, 310
  cognitive self-report, 310
  learning, 310
  reaction, 310

Ford, 341
Foreign direct investment (FDI), 133

Friedman, P., 105,106
Friedmann, W.G., 167
Fuller, M.B., 17

General Electric (GE), 140,335
Geringer, Michael, J., 205,293,336
Germany, 323
G-form, 186,194
Ghemawat, P., 104,105
Global
  markets, 231
  production, 231
  shift, 330
Globalization, 20,138
Goal
  congruence, 277
  path clarity, 280
  setting, 304
Gomez-Casseres, B., 105
Governance forms, 60,63,64

Hapag-Lloyd, 242
Harrigan, Kathryne, R., 62,69,91,
    105,116,119,184
Hawkins, Robert, 154
Hebert, J.M., 205,293
Heenan, D.A., 14,65,140
Hergert, M., 22,107
Hierarchies, quasi-, 61
Hladik, K.J., 107
Honeywell, 91
Horaguchi, H., 15
Human resource management, 253
Hybrids
  arrangements, 33
  purpose, 41
  stability, 42,47
  theory, 39
Hyundai, 23

IBM, 25,137,153,325
Industry setting, 110
Inland Steel, 335
Innovation process, 196

Interdependence,
 build, 180
 pooled, 45
 reciprocally, 46
 sequential, 46
Internalization, 63
International,
 competition, 20
 joint ventures (IJVs), 25,26,253,
  273,293,335,336
 IJV general managers, 294
 marketing and purchasing (IMP),
  84

Japan, 22,185,325
Joint marketing, 26,338
Joint ventures, 35,43,50,61,83,
  167,169
 control, 177,206
 form, 258
 East-West, 203
 independent, 259
Jones, G., 62,67
Just-In-Time (JIT), 341

Kalmanoff, G., 167
Kanfer, F.H., 300
Kanter, Rosabeth M., 115,116,341
Karoly, P., 300
Keiretsu, 7,185,186. *See also*
  corporate groupings
Killing, Peter K., 64,118,119,197,258
Kogut, Bruce, 15,16,87,90,128
Knowledge, tacit, 331

Leadership, 286
Lewis, J.D., 321
Licensing, 26
 cross, 26
Linked, industrially, 189
Lorange, Peter, 13,87,106,130,183,226
Loyalty, 262

Maersk Line, 240
Management
 autonomy, 266
 considerations, 260
 self-, 300,303
 shared, 259
 styles, 261
Managers,
 general, 294
Mankin, E.D., 141
Maquiladoras, 325
Market
 expansion, 22
 power, 87
Markets,
 quasi-, 61
Matsushita, 17,24
Mazda, 23
McDonald's, 214,215
McDonnell Douglas, 339
Mergers and acquisitions, 42,50
Mexico, 325
Mitsubishi, 17,23,340
Monitoring, self-, 305
Morris, M., 22,107
Motives of parties, 21
Multinational corporations (MNCs),
  2,3,13,20,27

NEC, 25,26,91
Neilsen, 14
Network
 dynamics, 147,150
 organizational, 36,331
 relationship, 196
Newly Industrialized Countries
  (NICs), 328,339
Nippon Steel, 335
Nowak, 16
Nueno, J.L., 329
NUMMI, 83,193,331,342

OECD, 124,189
Ohmae, K., 13,88,139,168,342

OLI paradigm, 133,135
Olivetti, 22
Organizational
    competencies, 89
    learning, 89,331
    orientation, 285
    pattern, 29
    policies, 266
    system, 281
Ownership, 207
    sharing, 174

Parent, dominant, 259
Participation, equity, 334
Partner,
    capabilities, 258
    country of origin, 107,114
    fit, 196
    objectives, 256
Partnership (joint),
    interfirm, 2
    Japanese, 194
    R&D, 5,20,22,65,74,337
Pepsi Co., 23
Performance sentiment, 95
Perlmutter, H.V., 14,140
Philips, 21,24
Pfeffer, Jeffrey, 15,16,37,39,86,
    321
Porter, Michael E., 14,17,105,115
Pratt & Whitney, 16
Production sharing, 23,339
Purpose, breadth, 40,41

Quasi
    heirarchies, 61
    markets, 61
Quelch, J.A., 327,329

Reich, Robert, 163
Resource
    dependency, 16,321
    pooling, 21

Reward system, 283
Risk/cost sharing, 21

Salancik, 16,86,321
Sea-Land Services, Inc., 238
Siemens, 18,20
Singh, H., 16
Size, parent, 66
Staffing, 262
Strategic
    alliances, 1,13,184,340
    forms, 82
    gap, 86
    responses, 233
Strategy,
    competitive, 17
    cooperative, 195
Sturmey, S.G., 222
Subcontracting, international, 336
Sun Microsystems, 17

Technologies, convergence of, 137
Technology
    conversion, 137
    dispersion, 328
    high, 169
    protection, 178
    transfer, 196
Technological
    advancement, 20
    alliances, 329
    developments, 232
    innovation, 136,150
    intensity, 60
    positioning, 64
Teece, D.J., 37,172
Theory
    agency, 40
    cooperative games, 130
    organization, 16,67
    transaction cost, 15,39,44,61,131,
        171,330
Thompson, J.D., 45,75
Thorelli, H.B., 36,61,115
Toshiba, 18,20,21,192

Toyne, B., 15
Trading blocks, 322,324
Training, 262,308
Transnational corporations (TNCs),
        123
Transpacific Westbound Rate
        Agreement (TWRA), 245
Transportation
    container, 221
    ocean, 222
Triad, the, 322

Trust, 92,179,341
Tung, R., 263

U.S.S.R., former, 117,208,326

Value creation, 41,45
Volkswagen, 22,341

Wells, P.E., 327
Williamson, O.E., 15,47,60,75,172